Health Communication in the 21st Century

Health Communication in the 21st Century

Kevin B. Wright, Lisa Sparks, and H. Dan O'Hair

Blackwell
Publishing

BLACKWELL PUBLISHING

350 Main Street, Malden, MA 02148-5020, USA
9600 Garsington Road, Oxford OX4 2DQ, UK
550 Swanston Street, Carlton, Victoria 3053, Australia

First published 2008 by Blackwell Publishing Ltd

1 2008

Library of Congress Cataloging-in-Publication Data
Wright, Kevin B.
    Health communication in the 21st century/Kevin B. Wright, Lisa Sparks, H. Dan O'Hair.
        p. ; cm.
    Includes bibliographical references and index.
    ISBN 978-1-4051-5593-9 (hardcover : alk. paper) – ISBN 978-1-4051-5594-6 (pbk. : alk. paper) 1. Communication in medicine. 2. Communication in medicine–Forecasting.
I. Sparks, Lisa. II. O'Hair, H. Dan. III. Title. IV. Title: Health communication in the twenty-first century.
    [DNLM: 1. Communication. 2. Delivery of Health Care. 3. Communications Media. 4. Health Promotion. 5. Professional–Patient Relations. W 84.1 W951h 2008]
    R118.H4386 2008
    610.69′6–dc22

                                2007009671

A catalogue record for this title is available from the British Library.

Set in 11/13.5pt Bembo
by SNP Best-set Typesetter Ltd, Hong Kong
Printed and bound in Singapore
by Markono Print Media Pte Ltd

The publisher's policy is to use permanent paper from mills that operate a sustainable forestry policy, and which has been manufactured from pulp processed using acid-free and elementary chlorine-free practices. Furthermore, the publisher ensures that the text paper and cover board used have met acceptable environmental accreditation standards.

For further information on
Blackwell Publishing, visit our website:
www.blackwellpublishing.com

Contents

Part I

Introduction

Chapter 1

Overview of Communication and Health

This book provides an in-depth look at one of the fastest growing and pragmatic areas of research in the communication discipline: health communication. Most people would agree that our health and our ability to communicate are two central and very important aspects of human life. Yet, at some point in your study of communication, you may be asked the same thing that family members and friends frequently ask us: *What exactly is health communication?* Many people do not understand how the concept of health is related in any way to the term communication. For most people, the term *health* conjures up images that seem to have little or nothing to do with communication, including doctors, laboratory tests, waiting rooms, dieting, and exercise regimes. Moreover, the term *communication* is usually associated with things like interpersonal relationships, the Internet, and radio and television.

However, as we will see throughout this book, many different aspects of health and a variety of communication processes are intertwined in complex and interesting ways. We will examine many contexts of communication and communication-oriented topics, including communication and perceptions of health, provider–patient relationships, everyday relationships and physical health, communication networks within health organizations, intercultural communication and health beliefs, health risk messages, health campaign message design and dissemination, health information and images in the mass media, and the use of new communication technologies in healthcare. We hope that as you read this book you will be excited and intrigued by the rich perspective the study of health communication can bring to our everyday understanding of health and healthcare.

Arguments for the Need to Study Health Communication

Despite vast improvements in public health and healthcare in the US and worldwide over the last century, we still have a long way to go in terms of making our society and the world a healthier place. Within the United States, we currently spend over one trillion dollars a year on healthcare services, making it the leading sector of the US economy (US Census Bureau, 2005). However, a wide variety of problems still exist in terms of our nation's ability to provide adequate care for everyone and in terms of maximizing efforts to prevent and control diseases and other health problems. It appears that the severity of many of these problems could potentially be lessened by improving communication among providers, between providers and patients, between health researchers, and between public health leaders and the public.

One-half of all deaths in the US can be attributed to preventable behavioral and social factors, such as unhealthy diets, smoking, alcohol use, and inadequate exercise (Neuhauser & Kreps, 2003). Over 60 percent of Americans are over-weight and only 24 percent engage in moderate physical exercise on a regular basis (Neuhauser & Kreps, 2003). Current disease screening is inadequate. Cancer mortality rates alone could be reduced by 60 percent if people were to follow early detection recommendations (Willett, Colditz, & Mueller, 1996). Cancer is still one of the most significant health challenges facing society, and the second leading cause of death in the United States (American Cancer Society, 2006). A lack of health maintenance behaviors among people who are currently living with a disease has been found to be significantly related to mortality rate. For example, one study found that only 30 percent of hyper-tensive men act to control their high blood pressure (USDHHS, 1999). In addition, there have been relatively few studies of how to improve the quality of life among people living with disease, such as cancer and HIV survivors, especially the ways in which communication processes and practices may help people to cope with living with disease (Kreps, 2003a).

In terms of health promotion, a large portion of health campaigns have not led to substantial health behavior change among members of the US population (Snyder & Hamilton, 2002). For example, health campaign designers spent mil-lions of dollars on California's 5-a-day campaign, which was designed to raise people's awareness of the benefits of eating more fruits and vegetables. While the campaign was successful at raising people's awareness of the issue, researchers found that relatively few people actually increased their consumption of fruits and vegetables following the campaign (Foerster & Hudes, 1994).

Worldwide, we see a number of health issues that are directly and indirectly related to communication. Global issues such as lack of access to adequate

healthcare, war, poverty, hunger, environmental injustice, and lack of education about health issues continue to pose problems for people around the
world. Unfortunately, many of these issues have had the greatest impact in
underdeveloped countries and among the underserved populations. In Africa,
for example, over nearly 25 million people are living with HIV/AIDS, and
over 6 million are living in Asian countries (Joint United Nations Program on
HIV/AIDS, 2004). More recent issues, such as avian flu and terrorism, present
health communication researchers with numerous challenges in terms of finding
ways to best communicate information about health risks and in terms of
coordinating efforts to cope with these types of crises after they occur.

Health communication researchers are currently working to better understand these issues so that they can offer suggestions for improvement. While
communication issues may not account for all of the problems mentioned
above, it is clear that communication is an important underlying factor for most
of them. A better understanding of how communication is related to these and
other health problems may ultimately help to reduce incidents of disease, human
suffering, and mortality rates while increasing physical and psychological well-
being and satisfaction with healthcare among members of society. The chapters
in this book examine multiple ways in which a better understanding of health
communication in a variety of contexts, including relationships, organizations,
and the mass media, can improve health outcomes.

Defining Health Communication

Despite the fact that we all have ideas about what it means to be healthy or
ill, the term health is a complicated concept to define, due to multiple interpretations based on individual experience and culture. The World Health
Organization (WHO) defines health as a "state of complete physical, mental
and social well-being" (cited in Costello, 1977, p. 558). Moreover, the WHO
definition conceptualizes health and disease as dynamic processes as opposed to
stable entities. In other words, both health and disease are seen as being in a
constant state of change. This definition also recognizes that health goes beyond
physical and psychological health to include aspects such as a person's quality
of life. As we will see in this book, a variety of communication problems can
occur in healthcare settings due to different conceptions of health and disease.

Defining communication presents similar challenges. Most definitions of
communication view it as a process that involves a sender, a receiver, a
message, and a channel. However, a variety of issues, such as the ability of
multiple messages to be communicated simultaneously through both verbal and
nonverbal channels, the transactional nature of communication (when sender

and receiver mutually influence one another), physical and psychological noise in the channel, channel limitations on multiple senders and receivers, and many other facets of the communication process, make it difficult to define.

If you are a communication major, then you may have noticed that communication courses typically focus on one context of communication (e.g., interpersonal or mass communication). Health communication researcher encompasses many different contexts of communication. For example, researchers who study health communication from an intrapersonal communication perspective tend to focus on people's attitudes, beliefs, values, and feelings about health-related concepts and messages. Interpersonal health communication scholars tend to focus on relationships, such as those between providers and patients, or they study how everyday relationships (i.e., family members, co-workers, and friends) impact our health.

Other health communication scholars examine health from an organizational standpoint, and they tend to focus on features of the health organizations such as hierarchies, information flow in organizations, and employee–management relationships. Intercultural health communication scholars tend to focus on the unique role that culture plays in terms of how people understand health and illness as well as how intercultural differences affect healthcare relationships. A large number of health communication scholars focus on social influence and they devote their efforts to understanding how health messages and campaigns can be improved in terms of leading to health behavior changes for large groups of people. Many health communication researchers are interested in the role of the mass media in helping to shape our understanding of specific health-related issues and our more general conceptions of health and illness. Finally, a growing number of health communication researchers are interested in the role that new technologies play in disseminating health information, facilitating relationships among people who share similar health conditions, and improving communication between providers and patients and within health organizations.

A Brief History of Health Communication Research

Although the term health communication has only been around since the mid-1970s (Atkin & Marshall, 1996; Rogers, 1996), communication scholars have taken a scientific approach to studying communication within health contexts for decades. Prior to the formation of the communication discipline in the twentieth century, the United States has had a rich history of communication campaigns addressing a variety of health issues, such as alcohol abuse, smallpox, improper handling and storage of food, and inadequate healthcare for underserved populations (Paisley, 2001). According to Thompson, Robinson, Anderson, and Federowicz (in press), research in the area of health communication has grown exponentially over the last 30 years. This growth has not only occurred in the United States, but can also be seen in the work of scholars from around the world, including researchers from the eastern European/Scandinavian countries, Australia/New Zealand, Asia, and the United Kingdom. Organizations such as the European Association for Communication and Healthcare now publish the journal *Patient Education and Counseling*, and it sponsors a conference every two years that attracts interdisciplinary health communication researchers from all over the world.

Scholars in the social sciences who were interested in the study of communication began to examine the healthcare system in the late 1960s, which encouraged communication scholars to follow. Korsch and Negrete's (1972) "Doctor–Patient Communication," published in *Scientific American*, is still regarded as a foundation of the field (Thompson et al., in press). Much other work came from medical researchers, influencing the study of provider–patient interaction in particular. In 1972 a group of scholars with backgrounds in communication formed the Therapeutic Communication interest group of the International Communication Association (ICA), which was renamed the Health Communication Division in 1975 (Thompson et al., in press).

The formation of this area provided the earliest forum for the presentation of research on health communication. When ICA began publishing annual reviews in *Communication Yearbook*, there were many chapters on health communication that began defining and showcasing the field. The Commission on Health Communication of the Speech Communication Association (later renamed the National Communication Association) was formed in 1985, further indicating the growth of work in this area. These developments were followed by numerous conferences and mini-conferences focusing on health communication, including those at the University of Kentucky.

This widespread interest in health communication led to the creation of two important publication outlets for health communication researchers. The first issue of the journal *Health Communication* appeared in early 1989. This was followed in 1996 by the *Journal of Health Communication*. These publications played an instrumental role in helping to spur the growth of health communication as an area by disseminating health communication research to a wider audience within and outside of the communication discipline.

At the same time that these developments were taking place, important curricular growth was being observed in health communication courses at universities around the world. Many universities now offer programs focusing primarily on health communication and others have strengthened and expanded their health communication offerings. Funding opportunities have increased. Health communication scholars have moved into important policy and administrative positions within the Centers for Disease Control, the National Cancer Institute, and the National Institute for Drug Abuse.

The area of health communication is now widely recognized as vibrant, theoretically driven, pragmatic, and a key contributor in shaping national health policies (Kreps, 2003b). The research in health communication has always focused on real-world, significant problems, not "ivory tower" concerns that are sometimes seen in academia, and this is still the case today. According to Atkin and Marshall (1996),

> This specialization has grown rapidly in response to growing pragmatic policy interests, particularly in the public health agencies of the federal government and among private sector healthcare providers. Pressing needs to address alarming problems such as smoking, substance abuse, poor nutritional habits, and AIDS have given a strong impetus (and expanded funding) to the systematic study of communication processes and effects. (p. 479)

The many opportunities for researchers to address real-world health concerns make health communication an exciting area to study. Health communication scholars have had a rich history of conducting research outside of the academic setting. In fact, many of the health communication research studies you will read about in this book were interventions designed to improve physical and mental health outcomes in a number of contexts, such as health campaigns, provider–patient relationships, organizations, and the use of new technologies in healthcare.

The area of health communication continues to grow and diversify. New areas of research have expanded health communication into health domains that many people in the communication discipline probably did not consider 30 years ago, such as hospice and palliative care, spirituality and health, on-line support groups, and telemedicine. However, a number of health communication topics have remained as prominent themes in the health communication literature over the past 30 years. According to Thompson et al. (in press), in an analysis of the topics that appeared in the journal *Health Communication* between 1989 and 2003, over 20 percent of the articles have dealt with provider–patient interaction, followed by health campaigns (13.4%), risk communication (11.8%), health and aging (8.4%), language and health (7%), media (5.9%), and social support and health (4.3%).

Many of the prominent theories that are still used in the area of health communication have their origins in communication, social psychology, and anthropology (Atkin & Marshall, 1996). This reflects the ways in which theory has developed in the various contexts of health communication research. For example, several theories of provider–patient interaction have their roots in interpersonal communication research, a number of the theories used to understand intercultural health issues have their origins in anthropology, and many of the theories of social influence that are associated with health campaigns have been borrowed from social psychology. As we will see, communication scholars are continuing to refine these earlier theories as well as developing new health communication theories.

Current Challenges to the Healthcare System and the Role of Health Communication Research

There are a number of other current issues that may challenge the US healthcare system in the future. This section presents a brief overview of some of the most prominent issues affecting healthcare within the United States, and some of the ways in which health communication research can make a difference.

Aging population

The next several decades will witness a substantial increase in older adults within the United States. As we will see, while age by itself is not necessarily predictive of illness, health problems do tend to occur more frequently as we age. Unfortunately, our healthcare system still suffers from a number of communication-related problems when it comes to providing care to older patients. In terms of physician training, geriatrics is still a subspeciality of family medicine, and other issues, such as negative stereotypes of older patients, misunderstandings about the aging process, and health insurance needs of older people, will likely present numerous challenges to the healthcare system. There is a substantial need for health communication researchers to gain a better understanding of health issues associated with our aging population and for the development of interventions that can make a positive impact on this situation.

Cultural diversity and healthcare

Cultural diversity will continue to have a major influence on our healthcare system as people from cultures that have very different perceptions of illness, health, and healthcare immigrate to the United States. As we will see, some cultural belief systems regarding health can be at odds with more mainstream conceptions of health, causing problems for both patients and providers. In addition, within the United States, there are many different co-cultures based on ethnicity, region, and socioeconomic status. Culture is often related to health disparities, access to healthcare services, and health literacy, which puts many groups within the United States at greater risk for health problems. Health communication scholars are attempting to gain a better understanding of how intercultural differences impact health and healthcare. In addition, many health communication scholars are researching ways that health communication problems based on intercultural differences can be improved as well as ways in which health disparities can be reduced.

Tension between traditional and new approaches to healthcare

Healthcare providers have followed a number of traditional approaches to healthcare that have been challenged in recent years, and the tension between advocates of these approaches and people who favor new ways of thinking about healthcare will likely continue in the future. For example, physicians and other healthcare providers have traditionally been trained to follow the *biomedical model of medicine*. This is an evidence-based (and largely physical health–oriented) approach to medicine that relies on scientific methods and procedures for verifying disease, such as laboratory tests. While the strength of this approach lies in its ability to accurately pinpoint causes of symptoms (which also aids in selecting the appropriate treatment), it is not without its limitations. By focusing primarily on physical causes of illness, the biomedical approach does not always take into account *psychosocial* aspects of illness, such as cultural norms, coping abilities, and life events that may interact with physical health problems. Allegiance to this approach may result in a number of problems, including failure to recognize how features of a patient's day-to-day world (such as cultural beliefs, support networks, and financial status) may lead to their inability to comply with recommended treatments. In addition, conditions that do not necessarily have a clear biological cause (e.g., Gulf War Syndrome) may be dismissed by providers who follow this approach.

Other traditional approaches to healthcare include a *curative* approach to fighting disease. While most people would agree that using available medications and procedures that can save a person from suffering or death are beneficial, the nature of illness makes this a more complicated issue. With many diseases, such as cancer, chemotherapy and other curative treatments may only temporarily fight the disease. Moreover, these approaches have negative implications for a patient's quality of life (e.g., sickness from chemotherapy, loss of hair from radiation treatment, time spent in the hospital while recovering from surgery). In many cases, a person who does not have long to live due to a terminal illness may spend his or her days in the hospital, sick, embarrassed, or in pain rather than spending quality time with family and friends. As a result, in recent years, we have seen a greater interest in homeopathic and other alternative treatments to fighting disease that have fewer side effects than traditional medications. In addition, there has been a rising interest in *palliative care*, or an approach to medicine that emphasizes reducing pain and suffering among terminally ill patients as opposed to prolonging life at the expense of sickness, pain, embarrassment, and time away from loved ones. As you can imagine, there are many differences of opinion on what is best for the patient when dealing with these issues, and these debates are likely to continue in the future. Health communication researchers will continue to play an important role in examining how people often view illness and treatment differently, in providing evidence for the benefits of alternative approaches to medicine, and as advocates for alternative ways of understanding illness and treatment.

Funding for health research

Since September 11, 2001 and the continued threat of terrorist attacks, funding for a variety of healthcare initiatives has been reallocated to the War on Terror. While curtailing terrorist threats is certainly related to our physical and psychological health, the costs of fighting terrorism are substantial. As a result, money that was once allocated to government agencies such as the Department of Health and Human Services, which provides money for research to such organizations as the National Institutes of Health and the Centers for Disease Control and Prevention, has been diverted to the Department of Homeland Security. This funding is important in order to gain a better understanding of health problems and develop healthcare interventions for important underserved populations within the United States. The threat of terrorism will likely continue to impact funding for healthcare research in the future. Health communication scholars play an important role as advocates for health research funding and in providing scientific evidence for the key role of communication in improving health outcomes. Such efforts are needed to insure that government funding of research in this area continues.

Changes to health insurance and managed care

The rising cost of health insurance and health services will likely continue to have a substantial impact on consumers in the coming years. Healthcare organizations are always trying to find innovative ways to reduce the cost of healthcare services (which ultimately influences the cost of healthcare insurance). Health communication researchers have discovered that many costly problems, such as high provider turnover rates, are often related to communication problems. As a result, health communication researchers have developed interventions designed to ameliorate these problems and reduce costs that are ultimately passed along to consumers. However, much more research is needed to discover how communication interventions can be used to make healthcare organizations more efficient, helpful, and satisfying for patients.

The impact of new technologies on healthcare

In recent years, the widespread adoption of computers, new software programs, the Internet, and other new technologies (e.g., cellular technology, global satellite positioning chips) has led to a variety of changes in communication within the healthcare system, the ways in which people obtain health information, and the ways in which they communicate about health in daily life. Communication technologies will likely continue to develop and significantly impact the ways in which we communicate about health. At no other time has health information been more accessible to people due to the advent of the Internet. However, not all people have access to this technology, the skills to use it, or the ability to interpret the available health information. The Internet has also become an important channel for providers to communicate with other providers, as a source of social support for patients, and as a means for health campaign designers to reach large numbers of individuals with unique health-oriented messages due to the features of this new medium (e.g., interactivity, multimedia, and the ability to use the computer to tailor health messages). Health communication researchers will continue to play a crucial role in examining the benefits and limitations of these technologies.

Overview of the Book

Chapter 2 examines key issues and theories related to provider–patient interaction, including patient information and affective needs, communication skills training for providers, patient/provider differences in perspective of health, barriers to effective provider–patient communication, communication issues related to medical malpractice and dissatisfaction, and privacy issues in provider–patient communication.

Chapter 3 explores a number of communication issues and theories related to caregiving, including communication needs of patients and caregivers, hospice and palliative care, and communication issues related to end-of-life decision-making, death, and dying.

Chapter 4 provides an in-depth look at social support theories and processes as they relate to health. It examines dilemmas of social support and the relationship between support and health outcomes, and it takes an in-depth look at research on support groups for people coping with various types of health issues. Chapter 5 examines cultural differences in beliefs about health and healthcare and different cultural healthcare practices within the United States, integrating intercultural communication theories and intergroup theories. The chapter also examines topics such as homeopathic approaches to healthcare and spirituality and health. Chapter 6 explores health organizations from the standpoint of organizational communication theory. The chapter focuses on issues such as the flow of information in organizations, the history and influence of managed care, the interrelationships of multiple organizations in the allied health professions, and current issues facing healthcare organizations.

Chapter 7 looks at the growth and application of new communication technologies in healthcare settings. It examines a variety of topics, such as telemedicine, provider and patient use of the Internet for health information, electronic records, computer-mediated support groups, and the use of new technologies to tailor and disseminate health campaign messages. Chapter 8 focuses on the role of the mass media in influencing our health beliefs, attitudes, and behaviors. It discusses theories about the influence and uses of mass media. It explores topics such as the relationship between mass media messages and lifestyle choices, the mass media and health policy, and direct-to-consumer advertising.

Chapter 9 provides an introduction to theory/research in the area of risk communication. In addition, the chapter discusses current issues such as responding to terrorism and natural disasters, and various approaches to campaigns designed to target at-risk populations. Chapter 10 examines health communication campaigns. It introduces a number of social influence theories related to the design and implementation of health campaigns. In addition, it focuses on mediated and interpersonal approaches to health campaigns, message design issues, and campaign evaluation.

Chapter 11 looks at theories of teamwork and group communication as they relate to healthcare teams. In addition, it focuses on interdisciplinary healthcare teams, leadership, and problems that can occur in healthcare group decision-making.

Chapter 12 focuses on three important and growing areas of health communication research: health literacy, breaking bad news to patients, and older adult healthcare issues. It focuses on such topics as the relationships among health literacy, medical decision-making, and health outcomes, the complexities of delivering bad news in an appropriate manner, and issues associated with aging that can lead to problems for older adults in receiving quality healthcare.

Summary

Health communication is a vibrant and growing area of the communication discipline. In addition, researchers from other disciplines, such as medicine, public health, psychology, and business, are making significant contributions to our knowledge of this area. While health communication has been a defined area of academic research for only about 30 years, the United States has had a rich history of addressing public health issues. However, statistics dealing with disease incident rates, patient dissatisfaction with healthcare, and the failure of many health campaigns to significantly impact health outcomes point to the need for health communication research in the future. People who are interested in a variety of contexts of communication are attracted to the area of health communication, particularly because of the ability to address significant real-world problems. Despite advances in health communication over the last three decades, there are a number of current issues that will likely pose problems for the healthcare system in the future. Health communication researchers are in a unique position to find ways to confront these issues and ultimately make improvements to the healthcare system and health outcomes.

References

American Cancer Society. (2006). *Cancer statistics*. Retrieved January 23, 2006, from www.cancer.ogr/cancerinfo/.

Atkin, C., & Marshall, A. (1996). Health communication. In M. B. Salwen & D. W. Stacks (Eds.), *An integrated approach to communication theory and research* (pp. 93–110). Mahwah, NJ: Lawrence Erlbaum.

Costello, D. E. (1977). Health communication theory and research: An overview. In B. D. Ruben (Ed.), *Communication yearbook I* (pp. 557–568). New Brunswick, NJ: Transaction Books.

Foerster, S. B., & Hudes, M. (1994). *California dietary practices survey: Focus on fruits and vegetables, trends among adults, 1989–1993, topline report*. Sacramento, CA: California Department of Health Services and California Public Health Foundation.

Joint United Nations Program on HIV/AIDS. (July, 2004). 2004 report on the global AIDS epidemic. Retrieved August 28, 2004, from www.unaids.org/.

Korsch, B., & Negrete, F. (1972). Doctor–patient communication. *Scientific American, 227*, 66–74.

Kreps, G. L. (2003a). The impact of communication on cancer risk, incidence, morbidity, mortality, and quality of life. *Health Communication, 15*, 161–169.

Kreps, G. L. (2003b). Opportunities for health communication scholarship to shape public health policy and practice: Examples from the National Cancer Institute. In

T. L. Thompson, A. M. Dorsey, K. I. Miller, & R. Parrott (Eds.), *Handbook of health communication* (pp. 609–624). Mahwah, NJ: Lawrence Erlbaum.

Neuhauser, L., & Kreps, G. L. (2003). Rethinking communication in the e-health era. *Journal of Health Psychology, 8,* 7–23.

Paisley, W. J. (2001). Public communication campaigns: The American experience. In R. E. Rice & C. K. Atkin (Eds.), *Public communication campaigns* (3rd ed., pp. 3–21). Thousand Oaks, CA: Sage.

Rogers, E. M. (1996). The field of health communication today: An up-to-date report. *Journal of Health Communication, 1,* 15–23.

Snyder, L. B., & Hamilton, M. A. (2002). A meta-analysis of US health campaign effects on behavior: Emphasize enforcement, exposure, and new information, and beware the secular trend. In R. C. Hornik (Ed.), *Public health communication: Evidence for behavior change* (pp. 357–383). Mahwah, NJ: Lawrence Erlbaum.

Thompson, T. L., Robinson, J. D., Anderson, D. J., & Federowicz, M. (in press). Where have we been and where can we go? In K. B. Wright & S. C. Moore (Eds.), *Applied health communication: A sourcebook.* Cresskill, NJ: Hampton Press.

US Census Bureau. (2005). Healthcare and social assistance industry data. Retrieved October 24, 2006, from www.census.gov/econ/www/servmenu.html.

US Department of Health and Human Services (USDHHS). (1999). *Health people 2000, progress review: Heart disease and stroke.* Bethesda, MD: Department of Health and Human Services.

Willett, W., Colditz, G., & Mueller, N. (1996). Strategies for minimizing cancer risk. *Scientific American, 275,* 325–333.

Part II

Interpersonal Perspectives

Chapter 2

Provider–Patient Communication

Chances are you have had an experience similar to the following when visiting the doctor. You arrive 15 minutes early for your appointment for a sinus congestion, a persistent cough, and fatigue, and find that you have to wait 30 minutes in the waiting area for a nurse to bring you into an examination room where you have to wait another 10 minutes for the doctor to arrive. Finally, the doctor arrives, briefly listens to your lungs, and asks you only a few questions before calling in the nurse to give you a prescription for some antibiotics. You might feel that the doctor did not spend as much time as you would have liked him or her to spend with you, or perhaps you had questions about whether or not you were contagious, questions about the prescription, or how long your symptoms might last. Maybe you did not get the opportunity to voice your concerns about how frequently you have been sick lately, or you never got an opportunity to ask the doctor for a note for your boss verifying that you are sick. You may have left the doctor's office feeling unsatisfied with the visit because you were still uncertain about what caused you to be sick, what to expect in terms of getting better, or because he or she did not meet your other needs.

Negative experiences such as these that you may have had with your doctor or other healthcare providers are often due to a variety of communication problems that commonly occur within healthcare settings. While it might be easy to blame providers in these cases, it is important to remember that communication problems are rarely one-sided, and there may have been a variety of reasons for them. Communication between providers and patients can potentially lead to successful health outcomes and improved quality of life, or it can create major problems for both providers and patients depending upon how it is handled. Many patients feel that their doctors do not listen to them, they are controlling, or they are not sensitive to many of their concerns. However, people often do not recognize that they play an important role as patients in the provider–patient relationship, and the way they communicate with their physician and other providers is important in terms of receiving the care they need in a satisfying manner. Providers also want their patients to be satisfied with the care they receive. Health communication does not just influence whether or not we are satisfied with our healthcare providers. Scholars within the fields of medicine, nursing, and communication have extensively studied provider–patient communication over the last few decades, and they have found that how providers and patients communicate in healthcare settings can potentially impact physical and psychological health outcomes, and problems such as medical errors and malpractice suits.

This chapter explores many aspects of provider–patient relationships. Specifically, it examines how providers and patients often differ in their perceptions of healthcare and healthcare needs, characteristics of communication between provider and patient, and successful and unsuccessful outcomes of provider–patient interaction.

Provider and Patient Views of Health and Healthcare

As you probably already know, providers and patients typically view health and the healthcare system in very different ways. The perspective of providers is heavily influenced by the specialized training and education they receive when training to be providers and through the day-to-day practices associated with working in healthcare settings. Most patients typically do not have specialized training in healthcare or related subjects such as biology and anatomy. Instead, everyday people learn about health and the healthcare system largely through the media, interpersonal channels, and their own subjective everyday experiences of health (such as living with a cold or feeling energetic after eating right and exercising). The following sections explore the different perspectives providers and patients have of health and the healthcare system, and how these perceptions can influence provider–patient communication as well as health and quality of life outcomes.

Provider Perspective

Provider training

In many ways, providers learn about many aspects of health in ways that are similar to patients (at least prior to their training). For example, providers learn about a variety of health issues and lifestyle behaviors that affect health from the media, in the same way that patients do. In addition, providers have typically been patients themselves at some point in their lives. Yet, the specialized training most providers receive socializes them in ways that can lead to a much different perspective of health and healthcare than the average patient. The amount, length, and complexity of training, of course, depend upon the type of provider we are talking about. Physicians, physician assistants, nurses, and technicians differ from each other in their education and training, but all of these providers share some commonalities in terms of their socialization into medical and health occupations.

Being a medical doctor is one of the most difficult professions an individual can prepare for in terms of education and skills training, and this is one of the reasons why physicians have such a high status among healthcare professionals. Most physicians begin their college education as pre-medicine majors, and they take an extensive amount of coursework in the physical and biological sciences. Similar to other standardized tests, potential medical students have to take the MCAT exam and obtain a high enough score to get into a medical school. Medical school is an arduous process for most medical students, who in addition to hundreds of hours of study and clinical training have to cope with rites of passage such as hazing and often intense criticism from medical faculty and peers.

Medical school is also a socialization process where physicians learn formal medical terminology and informal jargon. In addition, medical students often earn a privileged status due partially to the power and status that society attributes to physicians and the reinforcement of these perceptions during day-to-day activities in medical school (du Pre', 2004), such as when medical students interact with patients and lower-status providers (e.g., technicians) during clinical rounds. While many medical schools now teach students about the importance of communication in healthcare settings, and there are classes that emphasize communication skills, the majority of physician training is focused on aspects of physical health and the development of clinical skills. Following medical school (which typically requires four years of study), most states require an internship period followed by a residency period (time varies depending upon state licensure requirements and specialty) prior to obtaining a license to practice medicine.

Physicians, of course, are among many healthcare professionals who comprise the provider segment of the healthcare system. Physician assistants, nurse practitioners, technicians, pharmacists, occupational therapists, and dieticians are some of the many types of providers that are typically seen in most hospitals and clinics. Like physicians, these occupations vary in terms of amount of education, training, and status. In terms of communication, these providers often interact with patients as frequently (or more often than) physicians and are important contributors to successful patient outcomes.

Other health fields, such as dentistry, also have similar diversity and status differences among providers. Dental school can be similar to medical school in terms of education, training, and stress. Dentists parallel medical doctors in the world of dentistry as regards professional status. Other dental occupations, such as dental hygienists and dental assistants, vary as to level of education and training. In most states, a bachelor of science degree is needed to become a dental hygienist whereas only a two-year degree or certificate is required to be a dental assistant. Health organizations also typically have a number of staff positions, such as receptionists, office managers, and individuals who handle insurance claims. While the focus of this chapter is primarily on physician–patient communication, it is important to recognize that patients interact with many other providers when seeking healthcare, and a number of the provider–patient communication issues that are examined in this chapter can be applied to other providers as well. However, given the education and social status of physicians, and their important role in medical decision-making when diagnosing and treating health problems, it is not surprising that most communication research has focused on physician–patient interaction.

Provider communication skills training

As you probably have already observed, healthcare providers spend a great deal of their time communicating with patients. However, it may surprise you to know that until relatively recently most providers have received relatively little training about how to effectively communicate with patients. Over the last several decades, researchers have found that communication skills training may improve provider–patient communication, and effective provider communication skills have been linked to positive health outcomes for patients, such as improved compliance, satisfaction with care, and benefits to physical and psychological health (Greene, Adelman, Friedmann, & Charon, 1994; Kaplan, Greenfield, & Ware, 1989; Stewart, 1995).

Most likely because of the rigorous training dealing with physical aspects of health in medical schools, nursing schools, and other health-related occupational training, communication skills training is a relatively underdeveloped part of the medical/healthcare curriculum at most universities and colleges in the United States. While efforts by medical school and health science faculty in recent years have succeeded in adding more content dealing with psychosocial concerns in medical and health-related courses (including communication issues), communication skills training is still typically only a small part of medical and health education. However, the growing evidence from research that suggests communication skills, such as the ability to competently break bad news to patients (Eggly & Tzelepis, 2001; Wakefield, Cooke, & Boggis, 2003), have important health implications for patients has gained the attention of influential organizations such as the American Medical Association (AMA)

(Association of American Medical Colleges, 1999). The AMA has recently required all medical schools to test medical students on their knowledge of communication skills as part of the medical licensing process.

Despite the belief among professional medical organizations, such as the AMA, that communication skills are an important part of quality healthcare, people studying to be healthcare providers often have negative attitudes towards communication skills training (Batenburg & Smal, 1997; Rees, Sheard, & McPherson, 2002) and towards taking communication skills training courses. Medical students often feel that these courses are basically common sense or too easy, or they feel that they already have sufficient communication skills for practicing medicine. Compared to courses in medicine, biology, and other physical sciences, medical students and other future providers often view communication as a "soft science," or as having less scientific rigor and/or practical value, and this can lead to the perception that communication skills are relatively unimportant. However, given the number of communication problems that often occur between provider and patients and negative health outcomes related to communication, it appears that physicians and other providers would benefit from communication skills training.

When communication skills are taught in medical education, "many courses do not introduce teaching of communication skills until midway into the medical curriculum, to coincide with the traditional starting point of the clinical component of training" (Humphris & Kaney, 2001, p. 225). Third- and fourth-year medical student training is much more focused on actual clinical work than the training of first- and second-year students, who primarily deal with classroom lectures about communication or simulated training with standardized patients (people who pretend to be patients). It appears that actual experience with patients is important for learning and practicing medical communication skills. Kaufman, Laidlaw, and Macleod (2000) found that medical students who had performed basic communication skills with patients in a clinical setting had more confidence in their ability to communicate with patients than medical students who lacked this experience. Female medical students also tend to have more positive attitudes towards communication skills learning than male students, and researchers have found that male medical students are slower at learning communication skills than females (Marteau et al., 1991; Wright et al., in press).

Challenges providers face in healthcare delivery

Rising costs of healthcare and competition

Americans spend over 1 trillion dollars on healthcare each year, and this figure is projected to increase substantially over the next decade (US Census Bureau,

2005). Given these costs, providers face a number of challenges in communicating with patients and providing quality care in today's healthcare system. The pressure from health organizations to provide services to a large number of patients while simultaneously cutting costs in order to remain financially viable has influenced provider behaviors in many ways. Increased competition in terms of the number of hospitals and health facilities providing healthcare in most US markets has given consumers many different choices of where to obtain healthcare, and health organizations have become increasingly concerned about losing market share to competitors. In many urban areas, specialized health organizations such as cancer centers, acute care service facilities, and women's health centers are competitors to larger hospitals. While these specialized services give consumers more choices in terms of obtaining services, the increased competition from their presence has augmented economic pressures in these markets, and they have led many organizations to raise provider workloads while also limiting many types of services that providers are allowed to offer patients in an effort to stay competitive financially.

Impact of managed care on provider–patient communication

Since the mid-1980s, the rise of managed care has been an important response to rising costs and increased competition. Managed care refers to "a financial and organizational arrangement for the provision of health care services" (Lammers, Barbour, & Duggan, 2003). The term managed care is often perceived negatively because it has become synonymous with the idea of control by big business, loss of autonomy, and limited choices over services. However, most providers would have a difficult time surviving financially without managed care, and most patients would not be able to afford healthcare services if these organizations did not exist. We will examine managed care in greater depth in chapter 6.

Most managed care plans place financial restrictions on the types of procedures, medications, diagnostic tests, and other treatment recommendations physicians can make to any given patient as a means of controlling costs. This practice is known as *capitation*. Capitation helps to keep the overall costs of managed care plans relatively low for consumers by eliminating costly procedures and service in cases when lower-cost alternatives can be found. However, in cases where the patient would benefit from a more expensive procedure or medication, providers and patients often feel frustrated if the plan will not pay for these services (or only a small portion) and the patient has to cover these costs. The first author's wife recently had to have her physician write to her managed care organization to request increased coverage for a $600 a month medication that is normally not covered by her plan because her physician thought the medication would be helpful for her condition.

Working within a managed care system is often a source of stress for providers who often feel that their ability to provide patients with the best care possible is compromised by the restrictions of the managed care health plan. Providers often feel too constrained by the limitations of plans, and some may resent having plan administrators dictate the course of patient treatment. Physicians often feel pressure to see patients for shorter periods of time, and this may lead to communication behaviors that negatively affect the provider–patient relationship. In addition, because the provider–patient relationship under managed care plans is subject to the conditions of the plan, this relationship can be disrupted when a patient's plan is bought by another managed care organization or if the organization decides to drop a provider from the patient's list of eligible providers.

Provider perceptions of patients and communication

While physicians are trained in medical school to conduct medical interviews, communicating with patients effectively can be an extremely complex process. In a relatively short amount of time, physicians must be able to make one or more diagnoses from hundreds of possible diseases and medical conditions, and patients' self-disclosures about their medical history and their ability to articulate their chief complaint play a crucial role in helping physicians narrow down a wide array of competing possibilities for the causes of their condition or source of concern (Mentzer & Snyder, 1982). Many diseases and conditions can have similar symptoms. For example, chest pain can be associated with something as benign as indigestion or as serious as a myocardial infarction (heart attack).

Because identifying the causes of patient problems is largely a process of elimination, physicians and other providers need specific information from patients to help rule out factors that are not influencing the patient's condition. Gathering this information from a patient is often a difficult task for providers. They will typically ask a number of questions they feel are useful for narrowing down probable causes of the patients' condition while simultaneously steering away from information that they perceive to be irrelevant. Providers rarely rely solely on patient self-disclosures about problems, and the information that a patient provides is corroborated with information from physical exams, diagnostic tests, consultations with peers, and information from medical books and databases. Physicians who adhere to a more biomedical approach to medicine tend to focus specifically on the physical dimension of health, and their communication with patients tends to be very focused and specific, such as gathering information about physical symptoms (Roter et al., 1997).

Problems can occur when information that a provider thinks is irrelevant is perceived by the patient to be relevant, and a patient might feel a provider is being insensitive if one or more of his or her comments is ignored. Complicating the situation further, providers are not always correct when it comes to assessing the causes of a patient's condition initially, and in these cases further information from the patient is often crucial to help establish the right diagnosis. Patients may also withhold sensitive information about their lifestyles about body parts or functions they feel uncomfortable talking about, and patients often vary in their ability to accurately disclose information about their health. For example, some patients do not want to disclose information about drinking, eating, and smoking habits because they feel their provider will negatively judge them or because they are afraid that this information might raise their medical insurance premium. It is also difficult for many patients to talk about their sex organs, bowel movements, or other topics they don't perceive to be appropriate or relevant. Talking about these types of issues also violates many ethnic and cultural norms, and this can be problematic in health settings where there is a diverse patient population.

Other factors, such as the age of the patient, are associated with problematic provider–patient communication. Young children often lack the developmental skills to give a provider accurate information about their health history or symptoms, and older adults with cognitive impairment may have a difficult time recalling or communicating health information that might be useful to providers in making a correct diagnosis (Nussbaum, Ragan, & Whaley, 2003). This can create additional challenges for providers when communicating with pediatric or older adult patients.

As you can see, providers must walk a fine line between attempting to obtain the information they need from a patient in order to make a correct diagnosis, assessing what might be irrelevant information and discouraging it, and encouraging the patient to provide information he or she may be reluctant to discuss with the provider but may be relevant to the case.

Assessing patient cues

Physicians and other providers are trained to rely on both verbal and nonverbal cues from patients when assessing their health problems. However, preexisting beliefs and attitudes towards patients can influence the ways in which providers communicate with them. Physicians' interpretations of patient cues not only affect their interaction with patients but can also influence their medical decisions when treating patients (Geist & Hardesty, 1990). For example, social cues, such as race, gender, and age, and physical cues, such as if a patient is overweight, have been found to influence the type of information a physician provides to the patient and the type of treatment options he or she discusses.

Providers also assess patient attitude cues, such as whether a patient has a "good" attitude or if he or she is seen as a "bad patient" (typically a complainer/arguer, or someone who challenges the doctor's authority). Doctors often try to get rid of "bad patients" more quickly. A problem is that providers' perceptions of patients are often based upon socialization and prior experiences with patients. Providers, like all human beings, may engage in _selective perception_, or the tendency to perceive information in ways that are consistent with past experiences. In other words, providers may see patients the way they have learned to see them based on training and past experiences, and this may lead them to misjudge patient cues or ignore cues that contradict their assumptions.

Patient Perspective

Patient socialization

Most people learn about the healthcare system from a variety of sources, including the mass media, family members and friends, and through their experiences interacting with providers when seeking healthcare (Brashers, Goldsmith, & Hsieh, 2002; Johnson, 1997). All of us have been patients at one time or another, but few people critically examine how they learn the role of being a patient or their own communication behaviors when interacting with providers. Much of what we know about being a patient comes from what we see and hear in the mass media. Television shows, such as _Grey's Anatomy_ and _ER_, give us insight into the world of medicine, and through these types of shows we see examples of how patients interact with providers. We will examine the relationship between health in the mass media and individual perceptions in chapter 8.

Most people learn perceptions of health and the healthcare system through everyday language (Cline, 2003). In other words, our perceptions of reality about health and health situations are shaped by our day-to-day interactions. This perspective is known as the social construction of reality (Berger & Luckman, 1966). Our families and friends play an important role in socializing us when it comes to learning about providers and how to behave as a patient, and over our lifetime the language we encounter involving health each day influences our perceptions over a long period of time. Even our first-hand experiences with providers and healthcare settings are mediated through language, and common perceptions of illness, providers, the healthcare system, and many other aspects of health are shaped by the way in which language about health is used by the people in our social networks.

Language is rarely neutral, and common uses of language, such as metaphors like "doctors are mechanics," convey meanings and understandings about doctors and drug use that imply certain behaviors. For example, if a woman thinks her doctor is essentially a mechanic, then this understanding of a doctor might influence her to think about doctors in very specific ways. Most individuals have relatively little interaction with mechanics other than telling them what needs to be fixed and obtaining an estimate, and mechanics feel little need to convey warmth or empathy to a car when fixing a radiator. Thus, referring the term "doctor" to the term "mechanic" conveys certain expectations for a doctor's behavior, such as the doctor being somewhat impersonal and perfunctory when "repairing" a broken arm.

Other factors, such as health history, gender, socioeconomic status, culture, and age, play an important role in socializing patients. Individuals who have an ongoing health problem are more likely to see providers more frequently than people with fewer health problems and they often develop different perceptions of providers and health settings due to their relational history with providers and their more extensive experience with the healthcare system. Women are more likely to seek healthcare than men in general in the US, they are more likely to make regular visits to providers such as gynecologists for female-specific health concerns, and they often experience more problems with healthcare than men (Beck, 1997). Cultural differences, including ethnic differences, sexual orientation, and religious beliefs, are important factors in patient socialization (see chapter 5). For example, some immigrants mistrust the US healthcare system or do not follow mainstream cultural conceptions of health. Finally, older adults in our society often have very different views of providers and the healthcare system than younger adults. Many older adults lived the majority of their life in a time when few people questioned a physician's authority and before the advent of managed care, and these experiences often impact perceptions older adults have of healthcare and the way they communicate with providers. Not only do these factors influence patient perceptions of healthcare, but also providers often communicate with patients much differently based upon age, gender, status, and ethnicity.

Patient perceptions and expectations

Think about how you think about health and healthcare. It is likely that the way you see them has been influenced by a variety of sources, such as television and other mass media, our everyday interactions with others, our first-hand experiences with being ill and going to the doctor, or a combination of all of these things. Each of these experiences influences our current perceptions of health and health providers. Over time, these experiences are stored in memory as *schema*, which are mental structures or templates that help guide our behaviors (Reed, 1988; Schank & Abelson, 1977). Schema are useful to us since they help to reduce the amount of thinking, or cognitive effort, we exert when performing daily activities. For example, if we had to process all of the information available to us each time we went to the doctor, such as understanding the role of receptionists, nurses, or the process of the medical interview, as if we had never experienced them in the past, we would probably suffer from what is called cognitive overload, or too much information for our brain to process.

Fortunately, schema give us a mental blueprint that helps to guide our expectations and behaviors in medical settings. However, because schema are based upon previous experiences, they can influence our expectations and communication behaviors during provider–patient interaction (O'Hair, Allman, & Moore, 1996). People may react positively or negatively when their initial expectations for a social situation are violated, and this appears to be true in health settings. For example, if a patient expects her new doctor to be warm and empathetic based upon her previous experiences with other physicians, and the new doctor violates this expectation by communicating in a cold and distant manner, then the patient will probably be unsatisfied with the interaction. However, another patient, such as an elderly male, might expect his doctor to be controlling, and he may be uncomfortable about the interaction if the physician violates this expectation by encouraging him to be more involved in selecting treatment options.

It is important to recognize that patients differ considerably in terms of their perceptions of providers and their expectations for provider–patient interaction. Some patients may not expect their doctor to talk about their lifestyles, feelings, or to have time to answer their questions, while other patients may have high expectations for these behaviors. However, many patients desire both technical and interpersonal competence in providers, although in the case of physicians, technical competence is often one of the most important expectations for patients (Anderson, 2001).

Patient expectations can be influenced by broader perceptions of the provider–patient relationship. For example, patients who have a *paternalistic* view of provider–patient relationships tend to feel that their role as patients is to obey and cooperate, that the provider should take a dominant role during provider–patient interaction, that the provider is more knowledgeable than the patient, and that the provider has their best interest in mind (Beisecker & Beisecker, 1993). Patients who have a paternalistic view of the provider–patient relationship tend to expect and be satisfied with a provider who communicates in ways that are consistent with this view.

Other patients hold a *consumeristic* view of the provider–patient relationship and are more likely to take an active role when communicating with a doctor (e.g., ask questions, communicate concerns), expect the provider to be less dominant during interaction, and place less emphasis on the provider's authority or status (Beisecker & Beisecker, 1993). Patients with a consumeristic view tend to have much different expectations about provider–patient interactions than patients with a paternalistic view. They see the relationship more as an exchange of information between the two parties, similar to a business transaction that would take place among providers and consumers of other types of services. In other words, patients with this view of the provider–patient relationship often feel: "I am paying a lot of money for this visit . . . I should get what I want!" This need may override perceptions of a physician's social status. For example, think about how much money you pay for college tuition. College students often do not care about how prestigious a professor is if they do not feel they are getting their money's worth from a class (e.g., if they are not learning much or the professor is boring).

Yet, the consumeristic view of medicine is not without its problems. Sometimes we do not know what is best for us as patients. Similarly, college students often do not have the expertise in a class to know what is important to learn about a given subject, and they may object to having to read certain books or participate in some assignments. In much the same way, patients often object to some tests or procedures and may perceive them as unimportant or excessive, while their doctor may view them as a crucial part of treating a patient's health problem.

Patient uncertainty

Think about how worried you might be if you were to suddenly develop a rash that rapidly spreads across your body. Is it poison oak, food poisoning, or something worse? The experience of uncertainty is directly linked to the communication processes of gathering and interpreting information about an illness (Babrow, 2001; Brashers, 2001; Parrott, Stuart, & Cairns, 2000), and it can affect provider–patient communication in a variety of ways. Patients often experience considerable uncertainty in provider–patient interactions because their knowledge level of medicine is typically much less than their physician (Sheer & Cline, 1995). In addition, contradictory information about diseases from the media, family, and friends and uncertainty about the healthcare system are among the many reasons patients feel uncomfortable when talking to healthcare professionals (Shore, 2003).

Sources of uncertainty during times of illness and when visiting the doctor can stem from many sources, such as the technical language and discourse used by physicians, the known potential for mistakes by the healthcare provider, and the stress of gathering accurate information while attempting to stay positive when coping with an illness (Babrow, Kasch, & Ford, 1998). Reducing uncertainty about illness may help patients cope with their health problems better, but this is not always the case (Czaja, Manfredi, & Price, 2003). Sometimes, a diagnosis of a life-threatening illness, such as cancer or HIV, may increase uncertainty rather than reduce it. While the patient may learn that the symptoms he or she is experiencing are due to cancer, the diagnosis may raise a host of uncertainties, such as uncertainty about their prognosis, treatment options, and how the disease will affect his or her relationships.

Austin Babrow (2001) developed *problematic integration theory* in an effort to investigate the communicative processes people facing illness use to manage health information in order to deal with uncertainty. Babrow (2001) argued that the meaning of uncertainty is largely dependent on the values of the individual who is experiencing an illness, with those values guiding the ways that information is used to manage uncertainty. For example, a person with cancer may decide to gather certain types of information about the most aggressive forms of chemotherapy if he or she primarily values stopping the progression of cancer, regardless of the side effects of the treatment, whereas another person might be more concerned with acquiring information that enhances the quality of his or her life.

Patient needs and goals

Have you ever seen a doctor even when you were feeling relatively well so that you could get a note from him or her to help document an absence from work or school? Or perhaps there have been times when you were not really suffering from symptoms, such as a rash or a pain in your stomach, when visiting the doctor, but you were concerned that the symptoms might be a sign of a larger health problem. Patients often have multiple needs and goals when they communicate with physicians and other providers. While many patients go to their doctor to obtain relief from physical symptoms, they also have other needs that they want their providers to meet. These include the need for the provider to validate or legitimize their health concern. For example, after several visits to the emergency room for abdominal pain several years ago, the first author of this book was told on each visit that it was "most likely indigestion," and he was told to take an antacid. At the time, he was working on his doctoral dissertation, and several physicians told him that the indigestion was probably related to stress. However, he felt that the pain might be related to a more serious problem despite the fact that his doctors had dismissed the problem as "nothing serious." He felt angry that nobody seemed to take the problem seriously. Finally, after going to the emergency room one night at

3:00 a.m. with severe pain, a doctor decided to run a blood test and a sonogram, and it turned out that he needed emergency gallbladder surgery. As in this case, patients often want physicians to validate their perceived health problem as a legitimate problem.

Even when a patient is experiencing physical symptoms, the need to manage the symptoms is secondary to the patient's need to reduce his or her fear over possible causes of the symptoms. For example, a patient may have an ongoing skin rash that is causing him some discomfort, but due to his past history of unprotected sex with multiple partners, coupled with information from a pamphlet he read about symptoms of HIV that include skin rashes, this patient may be more concerned about whether or not he has HIV than obtaining relief for the rash. Other patients might have a need to confess their medical fears to a provider. Some people suffer from health problems in silence and they are afraid to see a doctor because of the fear that the symptoms might be caused by a serious disease (such as cancer). In this scenario, the physician might be the first person a patient has told about the symptoms after living with the fear of them for weeks, months, or years, and the patient's need to alleviate or understand the symptoms might be secondary to getting the issue out into the open. In addition, patients also have a need for providers to convey concern, emotional support, reassurance, and interpersonal warmth during medical interviews. Having these needs fulfilled by the provider may be just as important as or more important to the patient than the need for medical treatment.

Provider–Patient Interaction

Provider–patient communication has seen many changes in recent years. Until relatively recently, providers and patients were both accustomed to a paternalistic approach towards healthcare where the doctor "knows best" and should not be questioned. Today, healthcare providers are encouraged to focus more on their patients and their needs, while patients are taking more responsibility for their care. Communication scholars and medical researchers have become increasingly interested in provider–patient communication in the past decade, and even the *Journal of the American Medical Association* (*JAMA*) now devotes a regular section to provider–patient communication issues. The following section explores characteristics of provider–patient communication and their relationship with various outcomes. It begins by exploring *communication accommodation theory* as a conceptual framework for studying provider–patient communication.

Communication accommodation theory as a framework for understanding provider–patient interaction

Communication accommodation theory (CAT) proposes that when speakers from different social groups interact, they adjust or modify their verbal and nonverbal communication in order to accommodate each other (Giles, Coupland, & Coupland, 1991; Giles, Mulac, Bradac, & Johnson, 1987). Although each person is individually unique, we are all members of multiple social groups based on variables such as age, race, ethnicity, socioeconomic background, beliefs, attitudes, values, and interests, and we are constantly in the process of making judgments about other people in terms of whether they are members of in-groups (groups to which we feel we belong) or out-groups (groups to which we feel we don't belong). Providers and patients can be seen as members of different social groups based upon education, training, status (in the case of physicians), and perceptions of health and healthcare. Not only do provider and patients speak different languages, but also these differences often reflect very different perceptions of health and medicine.

Communication accommodation theory predicts that our perceptions of members of out-groups will influence our communication behaviors in a variety of ways. When we adapt our verbal and nonverbal communication in a way in which we emphasize similarities (in terms of speech, gestures, topics, etc.) between ourselves and another person, this is known as *convergence*. Although physicians and patients come from different social groups, a physician can engage in convergence with a patient by explaining his or her problem or the recommended treatment using language that the patient can understand (as opposed to using medical jargon).

Conversely, if we emphasize differences between ourselves and another individual based upon perceived social group differences when communicating, this is known as *divergence*. Providers may engage in divergence when communicating with patients by emphasizing their medical expertise or social status. Providers may use medical jargon or communicate their medical expertise in other ways when attempting to persuade a patient to try a certain treatment option or to get them to comply with a treatment. Providers can engage in *overaccommodation* when communicating with patients if they emphasize expertise or status differences too much. In these cases, patients may feel that their doctor is patronizing them or communicating with them in other condescending ways (e.g., talking to the patient as if he or she is a child, chastising the patient for an unhealthy lifestyle or not adhering to a treatment).

As we discuss examples of both good and bad provider–patient communication below, think of how communication accommodation theory can be used to explain how perceptions of providers and patients from the standpoint of in-group and out-group differences may influence the ways providers and patients interact with each other.

Characteristics of problematic provider–patient communication

Unfortunately, many providers do not thoroughly listen to what a patient has to say, or they interrupt patients, causing them to miss diagnoses or pertinent information. As we saw earlier in this chapter, physicians and other providers spend a great deal of their time with patients attempting to isolate specific causes of their symptoms or complaints. Given the heavy workloads of most physicians and other pressures that limit their time with individual patients (such as managed care pressures), doctors try to assess possible causes of the patient's problems in a time-efficient manner. In an attempt to help the patient in an opportune manner and to systematically rule out factors that are unrelated to the patient's condition, providers often engage in specific communication behaviors that allow them to control the direction of the conversation.

Physicians may attempt to control conversations with patients by using close-ended questions or by providing the patient with directive statements (e.g., "lie down on your side and breathe normally"). Physicians sometimes have an agenda for their conversations with patients based upon information about the patient they view in his or her chart prior to the interaction. In these cases, the chart can give the physician information about the patient's complaint and medical history, and this information may provide the physician with some insight into possible causes of the problem. And while this agenda may help the physician save time, it can cause problems if the patient feels that he or she is not being allowed to give adequate input into the conversation.

Nonverbal communication often plays a problematic role in provider–patient communication. Communication occurs at the *content level*, or what is said verbally, and the *relational level*, which relies heavily on nonverbal cues. Power, status, and control are often communicated at the relational level. We tend to give people with higher status (such as doctors) more physical space, and we often yield the conversation to them. The tone of voice that is used when communicating often reveals more about the relationship between two people than what is actually said. Patients may sound assertive or passive when communicating information to their providers, and this can affect the relationship in a variety of ways. Physicians are allowed to touch patients, but it would be considered inappropriate for a patient to touch his or her doctor. Patients wait for their physicians to see them and not the other way around.

According to O'Hair (1989), physicians and patients attempt to negotiate relational control in medical encounters. Physicians may try to assert control by questioning patients, making assertions, talking over patient responses, or interrupting patients. Patients also attempt to control conversations with their physician by questioning their doctor, asking for certain medications or treatments, or by changing the topic. O'Hair (1989) found that physicians were twice as likely as patients to assume control of the conversation when the patient did not attempt to gain control or responded to the doctor with a neutral message. However, patients were unlikely to attempt to gain control after their physician responded to them with a neutral message. In other words, patients, while attempting to control the conversation at times, often concede control to their physicians.

If patients concede control to the physician (or another provider), then they run the risk of not being able to provide information that could be helpful to the diagnosis or of not having their needs met during the interaction. While asserting control over a conversation may be necessary at times, physician–patient communication can become problematic if a physician uses control strategies to dominate the conversation and does not allow for patient input (Eggly & Tzelepis, 2001). In these cases, the physician runs the risk of not obtaining useful information from the patient or not meeting his or her needs. Moreover, patients who feel their doctor dominated the conversation may feel less satisfied with the encounter, but this depends upon their expectations for the interaction (e.g., whether they have a more paternalistic or consumeristic view of the physician–patient relationship).

Improving Provider–Patient Communication

Although the different backgrounds, perceptions, needs, and expectations of provider and patients make it challenging for successful and satisfying communication to take place in medical encounters, understanding these issues and how they may impact health outcomes is a first step towards improving provider–patient communication. This section explores several ways that communication between providers and patients can be improved so that it is beneficial to both parties.

Addressing patient concerns

Providers can often address psychosocial concerns when communicating with patients without significantly increasing the amount of interaction time, although it can be more time consuming depending upon the specific circumstances (Brown, Stewart, & Ryan, 2003). Addressing patient concerns is important to patient satisfaction and improved health outcomes (see discussion below), so providers and managed care organizations have become increasingly more interested in *patient-centered communication*. Patient-centered communication focuses on the patient as a "whole person" in the context of his or her psychological and social circumstances (Hirsch et al., 2005; Mast, Kindlimann, & Langiwitz, 2005). In other words, a patient-centered perspective promotes healthcare based on individual patients' unique characteristics, conditions, and circumstances (Smith, 2002). Patient-centered communication has been associated with higher levels of general satisfaction and improved biomedical and functional outcomes (Smith, 2002; Wanzer, Booth-Butterfield, & Gruber, 2004).

As a result, a growing number of healthcare centers offer relatively "holistic" approaches to better meet the physical and psychosocial needs of individual patients (Lefkowitz, 2006). This includes environmental restructuring of traditional healthcare environments, such as designing them so that they more closely resemble a living room in a private home than an institutional setting (Frey, Adelman, Flint, & Query, 2000; Richardson, Sanders, Palmer, Greisinger, & Singeltary, 2000). Moreover, an increasing number of healthcare centers are offering patients alternative services to traditional healthcare in an effort to meet psychosocial needs, such as relaxation therapies, massage, counseling, and support groups (see Wright & Frey, in press).

Lambert et al. (1996) argue that patient-centered care "requires that patient needs, preferences, and beliefs be respected at all times" (p. 27). Vanderford, Jenks, and Sharf (1997) argue that patients are active interpreters, managers, and creators of the meaning of their health or illness, rather than passive receivers of or reactors to messages. These researchers advocate a patient-centered approach to healthcare that has three assumptions: (1) patients' experiences matter; (2) patient identity is a central issue in patients' experience of illness; and (3) patients' experiences must be understood in context. Providers also need to take into account how a patient's age, gender, education, needs, expectations, cultural conceptions, and many other perceptions and experiences of health may influence his or her viewpoint during medical encounters.

Providers can encourage talk about psychosocial concerns by asking more open-ended questions about patients' feelings and needs. Providers should avoid interrupting patients, and they should encourage patient input whenever possible. By being aware of relational communication and their specific communication patterns, providers can alter their communication to be more accommodating to patients. Providers should not assume that patients understand everything that is discussed during medical interviews, and whenever possible the provider should attempt to tailor his or her language to the patient's level of education and background. In addition, providers should try to communicate with patients in ways that do not patronize them, that express respect for their feelings and perspective about health, and that communicate concern for the patient.

Recognizing provider perspectives and needs

Successful provider–patient communication is not only the responsibility of providers; patients need to recognize the constraints that providers face and they should take a more active role during medical encounters. Patients need to realize that their providers cannot do everything, and they should be aware of the many pressures providers must cope with in attempting to diagnose and treat illness among multiple patients in today's complex healthcare system. While patients have a right to expect providers to be respectful and provide quality care, they should also realize that providers are only human, and as in any business situation, the occupational pressures providers face can have a negative impact on communication. Patients can also improve provider–patient communication by becoming more knowledgeable about health and being more assertive when talking to providers. Of course, this is no easy task given the diversity of patients' education level, cultural conceptions of health, needs, and perceptions of healthcare. However, health education and patient communication skills training have been found to improve provider–patient communication in terms of increased involvement on the part of the patient (Cegala, McClure, Marinelli, & Post, 2000; Cegala, Post, & McClure, 2001).

Outcomes of Provider–Patient Communication

A number of successful and unsuccessful outcomes have been linked to provider–patient communication. While communication is rarely the only influence on outcomes in health settings, it has been shown to have a significant impact on whether or not people feel their encounters with providers were satisfactory and whether or not their needs have been met. This section explores various outcomes of provider–patient interaction for both patients and providers.

Satisfaction with healthcare

Patient satisfaction appears to be one of the key outcomes associated with provider–patient communication. Satisfaction with one's providers may affect other outcomes such as adherence to treatment, and ultimately better physical health outcomes. Patients who are more satisfied with their provider are more likely to continue seeing him or her, and they may also refer friends and family members. This, of course, is a potentially positive financial outcome of patient satisfaction for providers.

Patient satisfaction with providers is largely associated with a provider's interpersonal communication skills. Studies have found that satisfaction is often linked to a provider's ability to communicate warmth, emotional support, availability, understanding, and caring to the patient (Brown et al., 2003), and a provider's success at achieving a balance between addressing biomedical and psychosocial concerns when communicating with patients (Roter et al., 1997). Patients are also more satisfied with their providers when they are encouraged to express concerns, raise topics for discussion, and ask questions (Linn, Linn, & Stein, 1982). In addition, patient satisfaction has been linked to factors such as perceptions of technical competence, although this does not appear to be as important as perceptions of a provider's interpersonal skills (Tarrant, Windridge, Boulton, Baker, & Freeman, 2003). Conversely, patient dissatisfaction has been found to be associated with lack of interpersonal warmth or friendliness on the part of a provider, waiting room time, provider failure to acknowledge patient concerns, unclear explanations of medical condition, diagnosis, and treatment, and inappropriate use of medical jargon (Brown et al., 2003).

Adherence to treatment

Successful provider–patient communication is also related to increased patient compliance to treatments and health condition management strategies suggested by their providers (Golin, DiMatteo, & Gelberg, 1996; Kjellgren, Ahlner, & Saljo, 1995; McLane, Zyzanski, & Flocke, 1995). In fact, researchers consider provider–patient communication to be the most important variable in terms of predicting patient adherence (Brown et al., 2003). Good provider–patient communication often leads to more knowledgeable patients, and when patients know more about their condition, symptoms, and treatment options, they are more likely to follow their doctor's suggestions. Communication plays an important role in terms of influencing patient perceptions of provider credibility, which has been found to influence patient adherence to recommended treatments (Avtgis, Brann, & Staggers, 2006; Wrench & Booth-Butterfield, 2003).

Physicians play an important role in educating patients and explaining complex medical information to them in ways that increase understanding. Physicians and other providers who try to communicate too much information to patients, who use too much medical jargon or do not attempt to explain what it means, or who assume the patient understands his or her medical situation run the risk of not having their patients adhere to their proposed treatment suggestions.

In addition, providers who do not take the time to understand aspects of the patient's life that can inhibit adherence limit the likelihood that patients will successfully adhere to treatment of their condition. For example, suppose a physician prescribes several different medications and a physical therapy regime for an elderly patient who has just had a hip replacement, and the physician fails to ask pertinent questions about the patient's daily life, such as the availability of family members for support, or the patient's understanding of the medications. The patient may not make it to physical therapy sessions if he or she lacks adequate family support or transportation. In terms of medications, the patient may not understand that taking two or three medications at the same time can lead to drug interaction effects such as making the patient drowsy or nauseous, and this might keep the patient from using some or all of the medications.

Physical and psychological health outcomes

Successful provider–patient communication has also been linked to a variety of physical and psychological health outcomes, including reduced patient anxiety, psychological distress, reduced reports of pain and symptoms, and increased ability to function normally (Greenfield, Kaplan, Ware, Yano, & Frank, 1988; Roter et al., 1995).

Communication and Medical Malpractice Lawsuits

Most people do not necessarily think of communication playing a role in medical malpractice suits. As you may be aware, medical malpractice litigation is a serious problem facing the United States healthcare system, and many of these lawsuits have been linked to provider–patient communication problems (Hickson et al., 2002). Medical malpractice suits are costly to the healthcare system, and that cost is passed on to you in the form of higher health insurance premiums and charges for visiting the doctor. Between 1995 and 2000, medical malpractice awards rose 70 percent to approximately 3.5 million dollars per claim (Freedman, 2002). While most patients do not sue their providers, the amount of money that is awarded to those patients who do win malpractice suits often ranges from hundreds of thousands to millions of dollars. The increase of medical malpractice claims has led to the need among physicians to purchase malpractice insurance, and physicians often cannot afford the insurance or their practices suffer financially due to the additional cost of the insurance.

In order to cover the cost of malpractice insurance and lawsuit awards, managed care organizations have substantially raised patient premiums in recent years. Money for new equipment or other services that could benefit patients is often used to pay for malpractice insurance. Even tax-supported government healthcare agencies such as Medicaid and Medicare have begun to request more federal funding (resulting in the need for higher taxes) as a result of malpractice litigation. Recently, many states have pushed to pass laws that limit the amount of money a person can receive from malpractice lawsuits, but this issue will likely continue to be a problem for the healthcare system in the future.

Provider–patient communication problems may increase the risk of malpractice litigation (Hickson et al., 2002; Vincent, Young, & Philips, 1994). Hickson et al. (2002) found that when patients feel that they have not been treated well by their physician or another member of the medical organization during a medical visit, or if their complaints are not adequately addressed, this can increase the likelihood of the patient suing the provider or the organization. Most patients who are prone to making malpractice claims report communication problems such as their feelings being ignored by their physician, inadequate explanation of the diagnosis or treatment, or feeling hurried by the physician (Hickson et al., 1994). Moreover, patients who feel that their doctor is not empathetic to their situation or needs, if they feel he or she lacks interpersonal warmth, or if they feel he or she is dismissive of their problems or deceptive may be more likely to pursue legal action. Conversely, good provider–patient communication has been linked to fewer malpractice suits (Beckman, Markakis, Suchman, & Frankel, 1994).

Summary

Communication between providers and patients can be complex due to the different perceptions of health and healthcare that result from each party's level of education, training, and life experience. Despite the differences between provider and patients, it is possible for competent and satisfying communication to occur in the provider–patient relationship. To achieve this goal, it is important for both providers and patients to recognize important differences between them in terms of perceptions about health and healthcare, needs, goals, and interaction styles. Successful communication between healthcare providers and patients can lead to a number of important outcomes, including greater patient satisfaction, improved health outcomes, and lower healthcare costs.

References

Anderson, C. M. (2001). Communication in the medical interview team: An analysis of patients' stories in the United States and Hong Kong. *Howard Journal of Communications, 12*, 61–72.

Association of American Medical Colleges (AAMC). (1999, October). Contemporary issues in medicine: Communication in medicine (Report III). Washington, DC.

Avtgis, T. A., Brann, M., & Staggers, S. M. (2006). Perceived information exchange and health control expectancies as influenced by a patient's medical interview situation. *Communication Research Reports, 23*, 231–237.

Babrow, A. S. (2001). Uncertainty, value, communication, and problematic integration. *Journal of Communication, 51*, 553–573.

Babrow, A. S., Kasch, C. R., & Ford, L. A. (1998). The many meanings of uncertainty in illness: Toward a systematic accounting. *Health Communication, 10*, 1–23.

Batenburg, V., & Smal, J. A. (1997). Does a communication skills course influence medical students' attitudes? *Medical Teacher, 19*, 263–269.

Beck, C. S. (1997). *Partnership for health: Building relationships between women and health caregivers.* Mahwah, NJ: Lawrence Erlbaum.

Beckman, H. B., Markakis, K. M., Suchman, A. L., & Frankel, R. M. (1994). The doctor–patient relationship and malpractice: Lessons from plaintiff depositions. *Archives of Internal Medicine, 154*, 1365–1370.

Beisecker, A. E., & Beisecker, T. D. (1993). Using metaphors to characterize doctor–patient relationships: Paternalism versus consumerism. *Health Communication, 5*, 41–58.

Berger, P. L., & Luckman, T. (1966). *The social construction of reality.* New York: Anchor Books.

Brashers, D. E. (2001). Communication and uncertainty management. *Journal of Communication, 51*, 477–497.

Brashers, D. E., Goldsmith, D. J., & Hsieh, E. (2002). Information seeking and avoiding in health contexts. *Human Communication Research, 28*, 258–271.

Brown, J. B., Stewart, M. A., & Ryan, B. L. (2003). Outcomes of patient–provider interaction. In T. L. Thompson, A. M. Dorsey, K. I. Miller, & R. Parrot (Eds.), *Handbook of health communication* (pp. 141–161). Mahwah, NJ: Lawrence Erlbaum.

Cegala, D. J., McClure, L., Marinelli, T. M., & Post, D. M. (2000). The effects of communication skills training on patients' participation during medical interviews. *Patient Education and Counseling, 41*, 209–222.

Cegala, D. J., Post, D., & McClure, L. (2001). The effects of patient communication skills training on the discourse of elderly patients during a primary care interview. *Journal of the American Geriatrics Society, 49*, 1505–1511.

Cline, R. J. (2003). Everyday interpersonal communication and health. In T. L. Thompson, A. M. Dorsey, K. I. Miller, & R. Parrott (Eds.), *Handbook of health communication* (pp. 285–313). Mahwah, NJ: Lawrence Erlbaum.

Czaja, R., Manfredi, C., & Price, J. (2003). The determinants and consequences of information seeking among cancer patients. *Journal of Health Communication, 8*, 529–562.

du Pre', A. (2004). *Communicating about health: Current issues and perspectives* (2nd ed.). Boston: McGraw-Hill.

Eggly, S., & Tzelepis, A. (2001). Relational control in difficult physician–patient encounters: Negotiating treatment for pain. *Journal of Health Communication, 6*, 323–347.

Freedman, M. (2002, June). The tort mess. *Forbes*. Retrieved September 29, 2002, from www.forbes.com.

Frey, L. R., Adelman, M. B., Flint, L. J., & Query, J. L., Jr. (2000). Weaving meanings together in an AIDS residence: Communicative practices, perceived health outcomes, and the symbolic construction of community. *Journal of Health Communication, 5*, 53–72.

Geist, P., & Hardesty, M. (1990). Reliable, silent, hysterical, or assured: Physicians assess patient cues in their medical decision making. *Health Communication, 2*, 69–90.

Giles, H., Coupland, J., & Coupland, N. (Eds.). (1991). *Contexts of accommodation: Developments in applied sociolinguistics*. Cambridge: Cambridge University Press.

Giles, H., Mulac, A., Bradac, J. J., & Johnson, P. (1987). Speech accommodation theory: The next decade and beyond. *Communication Yearbook, 10*, 13–48.

Golin, C. E., DiMatteo, M. R., & Gelberg, L. (1996). The role of patient participation in the doctor visit: Implications for adherence to diabetes care. *Diabetes Care, 19*, 1153–1164.

Greene, M. G., Adelman, R. D., Friedmann, E., & Charon, R. (1994). Older patient satisfaction with communication during an initial medical encounter. *Social Science and Medicine, 38*, 1279–1288.

Greenfield, S., Kaplan, S. H., Ware, J. E., Jr., Yano, E. M., & Frank, H. J. (1988). Patients' participation in medical care: Effects on blood sugar control and quality of life in diabetes. *Journal of General Internal Medicine, 3*, 448–457.

Hickson, G. B., et al. (1994). Obstetricians' prior malpractice experience and patients' satisfaction with care. *Journal of the American Medical Association, 272*, 1583–1587.

Hickson, G. B., et al. (2002). Patient complaints and malpractice risk. *Journal of the American Medical Association, 287*, 2951–2957.

Hirsch, A. T., Atchison, J. W., Berger, J. J., Waxenberg, L. B., Lafayette-Lucey, A., Bulcourf, B. B., & Robinson, M. (2005). Patient satisfaction with treatment for chronic pain: Predictors and relationship to compliance. *Clinical Journal of Pain, 21*, 302–310.

Humphris, G. M., & Kaney, S. (2001). Assessing the development of communication skills in undergraduate medical students. *Medical Education, 35*, 225–231.

Johnson, J. D. (1997). *Cancer-related information seeking*. Cresskill, NJ: Hampton Press.

Kaplan, S. H., Greenfield, S., & Ware, J. E., Jr. (1989). Assessing the effects of physician–patient interactions on the outcomes of chronic disease. *Medical Care, 275,* S110–S127.

Kaufman, D. M., Laidlaw, T. A., & Macleod, H. (2000). Communication skills in medical school: Exposure, confidence, and performance. *Academic Medicine, 75,* S90–S92.

Kjellgren, K. L., Ahlner, J., & Saljo, R. (1995). Taking antihypertensive medication: Controlling or co-operating with patients? *International Journal of Cardiology, 47,* 257–268.

Lambert, B. L., Street, R. L., Cegala, D. J., Smith, D. H., Kurtz, S., & Schofield, T. (1996). Provider–patient communication, patient-centered care, and the mangle of practice. *Health Communication, 9,* 27–43.

Lammers, J. C., Barbour, J. B., & Duggan, A. P. (2003). Organizational forms of the provision of health care: An institutional perspective. In T. L. Thompson, A. M. Dorsey, K. I. Miller, & R. Parrott (Eds.), *Handbook of health communication* (pp. 319–345). Mahwah, NJ: Lawrence Erlbaum.

Lefkowitz, B. (2006). *Community health centers: A movement and the people who made it happen.* New Brunswick, NJ: Rutgers University Press.

Linn, M. W., Linn, B. S., & Stein, S. R. (1982). Satisfaction with ambulatory care and compliance in older patients. *Medical Care, 6,* 606–614.

McLane, C. G., Zyzanski, S. J., & Flocke, S. A. (1995). Factors associated with medication noncompliance in rural elderly hypertensive patients. *American Journal of Hypertension, 8,* 206–209.

Marteau, T. M., Humphrey, C., Matoon, G., Kidd, J., Lloyd, M., & Horder, J. (1991). Factors influencing the communication skills of first-year clinical medical students. *Medical Education, 36,* 127–134.

Mast, M. S., Kindlimann, A., & Langiwitz, W. (2005). Recipients' perspective on breaking bad news: How you put it really makes a difference. *Patient Education and Counseling, 58,* 244–251.

Mentzer, S. J., & Snyder, M. L. (1982). The doctor and the patient: A psychological perspective. In G. S. Sanders & J. Suls (Eds.), *Social psychology of health and illness* (pp. 161–181). Hillsdale, NJ: Lawrence Erlbaum.

Nussbaum, J. F., Ragan, S., & Whaley, B. (2003). Children, older adults, and women: Impact on provider–patient interaction. In T. L. Thompson, A. M. Dorsey, K. I. Miller, & R. Parrott (Eds.), *Handbook of health communication* (pp. 183–204). Mahwah, NJ: Lawrence Erlbaum.

O'Hair, H. D. (1989). Dimensions of relational communication and control during physician–patient interactions. *Health Communication, 1,* 97–115.

O'Hair, H. D., Allman, J., & Moore, S. D. (1996). A cognitive-affective model of relational expectations in the provider–patient context. *Journal of Health Psychology, 1,* 307–322.

Parrott, R., Stuart, T., & Cairns, A. B. (2000). The reduction of uncertainty through communication during adjustment to spinal cord injury. In D. O. Braithwaite & T. L. Thompson (Eds.), *Handbook of communication and people with disabilities: Research and application* (pp. 339–352). Hillsdale, NJ: Lawrence Erlbaum.

Reed, S. K. (1988). *Cognition: Theory and applications* (2nd ed.). Pacific Grove, CA: Brooks/Cole.

Rees, C., Sheard, C., & McPherson, A. C. (2002). A qualitative study to explore undergraduate medical students' attitudes towards communication skills learning. *Medical Teacher, 24*, 289–293.

Richardson, M. A., Sanders, T., Palmer, L. J., Greisinger, A., & Singeltary, S. E. (2000). Complementary/alternative medicine in a comprehensive cancer center and the implications for oncology. *Journal of Clinical Oncology, 18*, 2505–2514.

Roter, D. L., Hall, J. A., Kern, D. E., Barker, L. R., Cole, K. A., & Roca, R. P. (1995). Improving physicians' interviewing skills and reducing patients' emotional distress: A randomized clinical trial. *Archives of Internal Medicine, 155*, 1877–1884.

Roter, D. L., Stewart, M., Putnam, S. M., Lipkin, M. J., Stiles, W., & Inui, T. S. (1997). Communication patterns of primary care physicians. *Journal of the American Medical Association, 277*(4), 350–356.

Schank, R., & Abelson, R. (1977). *Scripts, goals, and understanding*. Hillsdale, NJ: Lawrence Erlbaum.

Sheer, V. C., & Cline, R. J. (1995). Testing a model of perceived information adequacy and uncertainty reduction in physician–patient interactions. *Journal of Applied Communication Research, 23*, 44–59.

Shore, D. A. (2003). Communicating in times of uncertainty: The need for trust. *Journal of Health Communication, 8*, 13–14.

Smith, R. C. (2002). *Patient-centered interviewing: An evidence-based method* (2nd ed.). Philadelphia: Lippencott Williams & Wilkins.

Stewart, M. A. (1995). Effective physician–patient communication and health outcomes: A review. *Canadian Medical Association Journal, 152*, 1423–1433.

Tarrant, C., Windridge, K., Boulton, M., Baker, R., & Freeman, G. (2003). Qualitative study of the meaning of personal care in general practice. *British Medical Journal, 326*, 1310–1315.

US Census Bureau. (2005). 2005 service sector annual survey: Health care and social assistance services. Retrieved February 10, 2007, from: www.census.gov/svsd/www/services/sas/sas_data/sas62.htm.

Vanderford, M. L., Jenks, E. B., & Sharf, B. F. (1997). Exploring patients' experiences as a primary source of meaning. *Health Communication, 9*, 13–26.

Vincent, C., Young, M., & Philips, A. (1994). Why do people sue doctors? A study of patients and relatives taking legal action. *Lancet, 343*, 1609–1613.

Wakefield, A., Cooke, S., & Boggis, C. (2003). Learning together: Use of simulated patients with nursing and medical students for breaking bad news. *International Journal of Palliative Nursing, 9*, 32–40.

Wanzer, M. B., Booth-Butterfield, M., & Gruber, K. (2004). Perceptions of health care providers' communication: Relationships between patient-centered communication and satisfaction. *Health Communication, 16*, 363–384.

Wrench, J. S., & Booth-Butterfield, M. (2003). Increasing patient satisfaction and compliance: An examination of physician humor orientation, compliance-gaining strategies, and perceived credibility. *Communication Quarterly, 51*, 482–503.

Wright, K. B., & Frey, L. R. (in press). Communication and care in an acute cancer center: The effects of patients' willingness to communicate about health, healthcare environment perceptions, and health status on information seeking, participation in care practices, and satisfaction. *Health Communication.*

Wright, K. B., Bylund, C., Ware, J., Parker, P., Query, J. L., Jr., & Baile, W. (in press). Medical student attitudes toward communication skills training and knowledge of appropriate provider–patient communication: A comparison of first-year and fourth-year medical students. *Medical Education Online.*

Chapter 3

Caregiving and Communication

While you may never have had to care for a loved one who is living with an illness, chances are that you will be a caregiver at some point in the future. Most young people do not think about the possibility of becoming a caregiver for someone who is ill. Caregiving is one of the most difficult yet rewarding processes one may experience during one's lifetime. However, when faced with such a daunting prospect, most of us are not prepared for the relatively unknown caregiving challenges that lie ahead. According to the National Family Caregivers Association (2005), there are more than 50 million caregivers in the United States. These individuals are family members and friends who do not receive payment for the assistance they provide their loved ones. The number of lay caregivers in the US is expected to increase within the next several decades due to factors such as an average increased life span, a growing segment of older adults, and advances in medical technology that can prolong the lives of people with a long-term illness (Stoltz, Uden, & Willman, 2004).

Mark Twain once said, "The difference between the right word and the almost right word is the difference between the lightning and the lightning bug." Communication is a central component to a successful and effective caregiving experience for the patient, who will encounter many formal and informal caregivers and medical professionals at any given time from the onset of illness to either recovery or, for many, the process of dying. Unfortunately, most people in our culture do not feel comfortable talking about caregiving and the dying process. As a result, many find themselves unprepared to deal with these issues when they are faced with caring for someone or coping with the death of a loved one. Caring for a loved one who is facing a long-term illness and coping with the process of dying are difficult aspects of life, and the discussion of death and dying is a taboo topic in our culture. Younger individuals often feel that caring for a loved one is something that they will not have to deal with for many years to come. Unfortunately, researchers have found that lay caregivers are often unprepared to deal with the many challenges of caregiving, and they often find it difficult to cope with the demands of providing care for family members and other loved ones (Andrews, 2001; Sarna & McCorkle, 1996).

Researchers have found that the US healthcare system often provides inadequate care for the dying (Field & Cassel, 1997; Foley & Gelband, 2001), and dying individuals frequently experience underdiagnosis and undertreatment for pain and psychosocial concerns (Bernabei et al., 1998; Martin, Emanuel, & Singer, 2000; Reb, 2003). In addition, dying individuals are not always treated with respect, they experience communication problems with providers, and their family members often do not receive adequate social support during the dying process (Lawton, 2000). In the United States and other countries, end-of-life care is typically provided by doctors and nurses who have limited training in caring for the dying (Barclay et al., 2003; Rhymes, 1990). Researchers have suggested that we need to learn how to communicate more effectively about these issues and take measures as a society to reform this important aspect of health (e.g., Sparks, 2003; Travis, Sparks-Bethea, & Winn, 2000). This chapter explores communication issues surrounding the caregiving process, end-of-life care, and the dying process.

Caregiving

Characteristics of people requiring long-term care and caregivers

As we mentioned earlier, a growing number of people are becoming caregivers in our society (Sparks, Travis, & Thompson, 2005; Travis & Sparks-Bethea, 2001; Travis et al., 2000). Many of these individuals, such as middle-age adults, find themselves simultaneously supporting both their children and parents, a phenomenon known as the "sandwich generation" (Richards, Bengston, & Miller, 1989; Williams & Nussbaum, 2001). As the length of the human life span increases individuals are living longer, and with advances in medicine it is now possible for people with a variety of long-term illnesses to live with their condition for many years. However, despite the ability of medical advances to prolong life, terminally ill people often experience pain and discomfort from the symptoms of their illness, psychological distress from living with their illness and coping with their own mortality, and conditions that may limit their mobility or make them incapable of living on their own.

Getting older does not necessarily mean being unhealthy or requiring care from loved ones. Only about 5 percent of older Americans currently experience institutional long-term care, but this number is projected to grow in the next several decades with the aging of the baby boomer age cohort (Blevins & Deason-Howell, 2002). Most older individuals are healthy, although people over the age of 65 represent the majority of deaths in the United States (Blevins & Deason-Howell, 2002). The majority of dependent older adults in the United States who require long-term assistance currently receive care from family members (Sparks-Bethea, 2002), and the number of couples in their middle years who will have to care for their parents is expected to increase over the next decade (Moody, 1994).

While most people tend to equate long-term illness with older adults, it is important to remember that a person requiring long-term care may be of any age. Diseases, such as certain types of cancer, affect people of all ages (although older adults tend to be at higher risk for most types of cancer), and other diseases that can create the need for long-term care, such as HIV and AIDS, are more likely to affect younger individuals. The majority of individuals who are dying of long-term illnesses today have conditions such as cardiovascular disease, cancer, and cerebrovascular disease (Centers for Disease Control and Prevention, 2004).

Relatively few people in our society have the financial means to afford a professional caregiver for their loved ones, so they take on the responsibility themselves. As caregivers, marital partners and family members may have to spend an enormous amount of time meeting the physical needs of a parent, and most people do not have the experience, skills, or training that are necessary to handle the immense responsibility of caregiving. Women are much more likely than men to become caregivers in our society because of factors such as women having a longer life span than men and the tendency for men to marry younger women. In addition, women are often stereotyped as more nurturing than men, and these perceptions shape societal expectations that women are better suited as caregivers than men. Unfortunately, these conditions and expectations have led to a situation where women have had to bear the brunt of caregiver responsibilities in our society. Many of these female caregivers are older women living on fixed incomes and who may have limited financial and social resources (Williams & Nussbaum, 2001).

Caregiver roles

Caregivers play a vital role in meeting patient needs (Andrews, 2001; Meyers & Gray, 2001; Siegel, Raveis, Houts, & More, 1991; Weitzner, McMillan, & Jacobson, 1999), and they often deal with a variety of communication-related issues that have important implications for the physical and psychological well-being of patients and for the caregivers themselves. According to Allen, Haley, Small, and McMillan (2002), "prior research suggests that the quality of communication among terminally ill individuals, their caregivers, and hospice staff influences patient and caregiver outcomes" (p. 508). Although researchers have identified communication as an important part of the process of providing care (Bakas, Lewis, & Parsons, 2001; Martinez, 1996; Zamborsky, 1996), few studies have actually examined how specific communication variables are related to health outcomes of people with long-term illnesses.

Some of the many responsibilities caregivers must contend with include: (1) providing physical assistance and emotional support to the patient; (2) being a liaison between the patient and an interdisciplinary team of providers; (3) handling financial and social affairs for the patient; and (4) monitoring symptoms and communicating them to providers. These tasks present numerous communicative challenges for caregivers of people with cancer enrolled in hospice programs, and we will examine these in greater detail below.

As we have seen, most primary caregivers for people facing illnesses are family members who are ill-equipped to deal with the physical and emotional stress of caregiving duties (Andrews, 2001; Rusinak & Murphy, 1995; Sarna & McCorkle, 1996). While trained health workers (such as hospice workers, which we will discuss later) provide support in terms of administering medical care and attending to a variety of the patient's physical needs, family caregivers must handle a variety of tasks, including providing emotional support, providing transportation, managing finances, monitoring symptoms, coordinating schedules, coping with increased housework, and running errands, and caregiver burden has been found to increase as patients enter into later stages of the disease (Andrews, 2001; Laizner, Yost, Barg, & McCorkle, 1993). These activities, coupled with the stress of coming to terms with the imminent death of a loved one, can lead to physical and emotional exhaustion for the caregiver.

Caregivers' communication with their social network and providers can have a positive impact on their stress levels, particularly when they are able to use their communication skills to obtain assistance and emotional support. In addition, many caregivers have found the use of humor to be an effective way of coping with the complexities of caregiving as it often provides relief from the stresses involved in the caregiving process (Harzold & Sparks, 2007; Sparks et al., 2005; Sparks-Bethea, Travis, & Pecchioni, 2000). Unfortunately, caregivers often lack the diverse communication skills necessary to effectively meet the needs of the patient and their own needs (Andrews, 2001; Bakas et al., 2001). One variable that may influence a caregiver's ability to use communication to mobilize support from his or her social network is *communication competence*. Communication competence refers to the ability to construct and use appropriate and effective messages to meet goals/needs and to successfully create and maintain satisfying relationships (Wiemann, 1977). Query and Wright (2003) found that both older adults with cancer and their caregivers with higher communication competence had lower perceived stress levels and higher satisfaction with their support networks than individuals with lower communication competence.

Caregiving and changes in relationships

Communication between family members may exhibit a number of changes when they take on caregiver roles (Sparks–Bethea, 2002; Williams & Nussbaum, 2001). Marital satisfaction can be damaged by the financial cost of providing for children and parents, as well as the emotional costs associated with the caregiving relationship. Married couples caring for a parent who report lower marital satisfaction state that the presence of a parent in the home reduces the amount of overall communication time within the marital dyad, the amount of private time between the couple, and increases certain types of communication between the couple, such as decision-making. These changes in communication appear to affect even long-term marriages, since partners have been found to experience declines in marital satisfaction when they are caring for an aging parent (Sparks–Bethea, 2002).

It is also important for caregivers to understand that patients often experience dramatic shifts in their identities as they move through the stages of being healthy and well to being sick. Identification as someone who was previously healthy shifting to someone who is sick, identification as a patient, and identification as a survivor are all important aspects to consider. Whether we experience a difficult health issue such as cancer through a friend, family member, or personal experience, it is our various relationships and/or conversations about the health experience across the continuum of care from prevention, diagnosis, treatment, survivorship to end of life that continually reinforce, renegotiate, and bring about shifts in our social identities across the life span (Sparks & Harwood, in press). Another issue here is that particular conceptualizations of self within the health condition(s) have the capacity to change psychological orientation and behaviors related to one's health, and hence to influence concrete outcomes (see, e.g., Harwood & Sparks, 2003; Sparks & Harwood, in press). For example, cancer patients concerned about the stigma associated with a cancer diagnosis may pursue numerous strategies to avoid such stigma while they are fighting the disease. Such shifts in a patient's social identity may greatly impact the way the patient and the various caregivers involved relate to the patient.

As Harwood and Sparks (2003) further point out, family identity may be crucial among those who have family histories of particular health issues (e.g., cancer or heart disease). Women in a family with a history of breast cancer, for instance, are in a situation where information and awareness about the disease should be heightened, preventive measures should be relatively automatic, and knowledge about treatment options in the case of illness should be readily available (Harwood & Sparks, 2003; Pecchioni & Sparks, in press). However, the extent to which those women identify with the family may be crucial. People who are less involved and identified with their family may dissociate from the medical history and perhaps perceive themselves as less vulnerable (Harwood & Sparks, 2003; Sparks & Harwood, in press).

Shifts in one's social identity(ies) from one who is healthy (belonging to group memberships reinforcing this) to one who is not healthy (introduced to new group memberships not previously experienced) is an important component for formal and informal caregivers to consider when communicating with patients. By understanding the complexities involved in patients who were previously vital and energetic, full of life, and so on but who now exhibit characteristics not demonstrating these strong dimensions, caregivers can use more appropriate, effective, and understanding communication strategies in relating to patients and their strong identity orientations and subsequent shifts in identity.

Communication issues surrounding symptom management

Researchers have found that caregivers and people with a long-term illness mutually influence one another during interactions in ways that can affect both parties psychologically and physically. For example, several researchers have found a relationship between patient symptom distress and caregiver depression and/or perceptions of caregiver burden (Andrews, 2001; Given, Given, Helms, Stommel, & DeVoss, 1997; Sarna & Brecht, 1997). Increased patient symptom distress can increase the number of tasks in a caregiver's daily schedule as well as add to his or her stress level. People with cancer may experience a number of symptoms associated with the disease and its treatment, including pain (Allen et al., 2002; Donnelly, Walsh, & Rybicki, 1994), fatigue, and dyspnea (Nail, 2002). According to Bakas et al. (2001), "family caregivers must be able to not only recognize these symptoms, but also assist patients in managing them" (p. 849).

The need to alleviate pain is a common aspect of caring for individuals with a terminal illness (Brescia, Portenoy, Ryan, Krasnoff, & Gray, 1992). Adequate pain relief among terminally ill patients has been found to be a significant problem across studies (Foley & Gelband, 2001; MacMillan & Small, 2002), and many of the problems related to pain control are associated with communication problems experienced by the patient or between the patient and caregiver (Panke, 2002). Pain is a multifaceted concept and it is experienced differently by different people. For example, people vary in terms of their tolerance of pain and they may react to pain in a variety of ways. Different experiences and perceptions of pain make it difficult for people with cancer and caregivers to assess the degree to which people are in pain and how pain should be treated. Most studies have concluded that self-reports of pain are the most reliable indicator of the pain a terminally ill patient is experiencing, but according to Allen et al. (2002), "the presence of cognitive and sensory deficits, however, may hamper an individual's ability to communicate painful experiences" (p. 508).

In situations where a patient cannot communicate the amount of pain they are experiencing due to their illness, caregivers run the risk of under-medicating or over-medicating their loved ones. According to Panke (2002), "patients who aren't able to communicate verbally are at risk for underassessment and inadequate pain relief, those at highest risk being patients with cognitive impairment, intubated patients, infants, and patients older than 85" (p. 28). Family caregivers are important sources of information about patient behaviors, and they are often crucial in communicating information about pain to providers (Pecchioni & Sparks, in press). Family caregivers commonly typically act as liaisons between patients and providers in terms of reporting pain, but family caregivers may have difficulty accurately assessing the actual amount of pain their loved one is experiencing (Allen et al., 2002; Elliot, Elliot, Murray, Braun, & Johnson, 1997), and this can lead to a situation where a patient remains in pain due to under-medication but cannot do anything about it.

In cases where people with an illness cannot verbally communicate with their caregivers, a caregiver must rely on nonverbal signs of pain, such as facial expressions and body movements. Nonverbal and behavioral cues indicating pain are often used by caregivers as a sign of whether to increase pain medications. However, it can be difficult for caregivers to "recognize that a particular behavior indicates pain, especially if they are unfamiliar with how the patient usually behaves" (Panke, 2002, p. 28). Effective assessment of pain is important in order to control it, and information about pain needs to be effectively communicated to providers in order to achieve a balance between adequate pain control and over- or under-medication (Panke, 2002; Travis & Sparks-Bethea, 2001; Travis et al., 2000). Over-medicating a patient can lead to numerous problems, such as the accumulation of toxins associated with pain medications, renal dysfunction, decreased cognitive functioning, and organ failure. Under-medication can lead to inadequate pain control and unnecessary suffering for the patient.

Communication challenges associated with caregiving

Willingness to communicate concerns

Many family caregivers are reluctant to communicate problems they encounter during the caregiving process to the people they are caring for or to others within their social network because they do not want to burden them with the added stress of thinking about these concerns (Bakas et al., 2001; Laizner et al., 1993). This is consistent with other research that has found that family member caregivers often avoid communicating about their problems with others because they do not want to overstep interpersonal boundaries or add stress to the lives of others by raising concerns about caregiving (Chesler & Barbarin, 1984).

However, by not communicating their concerns to others, caregivers do not give themselves the opportunity to vent their frustrations or to receive advice or other offers of assistance from their social network. Caregivers may experience added stress when they do not have the opportunity to express their concerns, and this can lead to depression, burnout, anxiety, social withdrawal, and reduced quality of life (Bakas et al., 2001; Given et al., 1993). In addition, the reluctance of caregivers to communicate their needs and concerns may also affect their ability to provide care (Bakas et al., 2001).

Communication of emotional support

Researchers have found that the provision of emotional support is one of the most time-consuming and challenging aspects of caregiving, often requiring more of a caregiver's time and effort than other daily caregiving tasks (Bakas et al., 2001; Egbert & Parrott, 2003; Toseland, Blanchard, & McCallion, 1995). This has been found to be true for both lay and professional caregivers (Travis & Sparks-Bethea, 2001; Travis et al., 2000). According to Andrews (2001), "because the caregiver is the center of support for the needs of the patient with cancer, if the caregiver fails, the patient suffers" (p. 1469). Given the uncertainty and fear associated with coming to terms with one's own mortality among people with diseases like cancer, it is not surprising that emotional support is a common need among terminally ill patients and other patients requiring long-term care. Listening to patient concerns and providing empathetic responses to patients is an important aspect of providing holistic hospice care. However, it can be very time consuming for caregivers (professional and lay), especially when faced with accomplishing multiple tasks when providing daily care to patients. Patient irritability, confusion, and aggressive behaviors during late-stage cancer may make it even more difficult and exhausting for caregivers to provide emotional support. Moreover, both professional

and lay caregivers often have little training regarding the provision of emotional support, and there is a need for education and training about how
to deal with these issues and effectively provide emotional support (Bakas
et al., 2001).

Hospice and Palliative Care

Over the past two decades, hospice and palliative care have become popular
options for people facing terminal illness and their loved ones. It is the desire
of most patients with serious, incurable diseases to die at home. Dying at home
is associated with greater satisfaction by bereaved family members (Ratner,
Norlander, & McSteen, 2001). Lynn (2001) described the importance of dying
with dignity: "most people want more than just longer life; they want the end
of life to be meaningful, comfortable, and supportive to loved ones" (p. 926).
This section will explore the growth and impact of hospice and palliative care
and a variety of communication issues associated with them.

History of hospice and palliative care

The term hospice refers to programs that provide support and care for people
in the last phases of an incurable disease, with a focus on maintaining the
quality of their remaining life by providing services that both aid physical
comfort and address psychological and spiritual needs (National Hospice and
Palliative Care Organization, 2004). While hospice began as an alternative
health movement, the goals of hospice care – to provide a dignified, comfortable death for the terminally ill and to care for the patient and family together
– are being given increasing recognition in mainstream medical care (Query,
Wright, & Gilchrist, 2006).

The hospice movement originated in England and was largely influenced
by the work of Dame Cicely Saunders, an English nurse who promoted the
idea that a patient's care should be managed by an interdisciplinary team, that
pain and symptom management should be a primary goal of hospice nursing,
and that death education and bereavement counseling for family members
should be included in hospice care (National Hospice and Palliative Care
Organization, 2004). Saunders, who originally studied to be a nurse, was
motivated by the pain and loneliness of the dying to become a physician. In
1957, she began her first job as a physician investigating terminal pain and its
relief. As a result of her ideas, in 1967 St. Christopher's Hospice was opened
in Sydenham, London (Howarth & Leaman, 2001). Saunders continued to

work full-time as St. Christopher's chair well into the 1980s (Moore, 1998). In addition, hospice programs were influenced by the work of Elizabeth Kubler-Ross, a psychiatrist who brought attention to the taboo topic of death in our culture, and who promoted the idea that the focus of medicine for people facing incurable diseases should be to control pain and symptoms, and to promote quality of remaining life (Query et al., 2006).

In 1974, hospice arrived in the United States with the opening of *Hospice Inc.* in Connecticut. Since that time, we have witnessed the rapid growth of hospice organizations in the US. In 1983, Medicare began offering a hospice option to Medicare Part A insurance to reimburse terminally ill patients who meet certain criteria, and the number of US hospices grew from 516 in 1983 to over a thousand today (Medicare Payment Advisory Commission report to Congress, 2002). More than 90 percent of hospice care is provided in patients' homes and 78 percent of hospice care is for cancer patients (Moore, 1998).

Hospice services and care

When a candidate for a hospice program is identified, hospice staff members generally hold an initial meeting with the patient's primary physician(s) and a hospice physician to discuss the patient's history, physical symptoms, and life expectancy. Following this initial meeting, hospice staff members meet with both the patient and his or her family to discuss the hospice philosophy, available services, and expectations. In addition, staff and patients discuss pain and comfort levels, support systems, financial and insurance resources, medications, and equipment needs. A plan of care is then developed for the patient, and this plan is regularly reviewed and revised according to the patient's condition.

Most hospice care takes place in the patient's home, although more and more in-patient hospice facilities are becoming available. In-patient hospice facilities are helpful for patients who do not have family members or other loved ones to care for them. In home settings, hospice staff members do not usually serve as primary caregivers for a patient enrolled in a hospice program. A family member is typically the primary caregiver and he or she often helps make decisions for the terminally ill individual (Sparks et al., 2005; Sparks, Villagran, & Wittenberg-Lyles, 2008, forthcoming). Members of the hospice staff support the family caregiver by making regular visits to assess the patient and provide additional care or other services. Hospice staff are usually on-call 24 hours a day, seven days a week.

The hospice physician and/or nurses are usually responsible for making decisions about increases and decreases in pain medication and the treatment of other physical symptoms, although pain and symptoms are usually monitored on a daily basis by the family caregiver (Travis & Sparks-Bethea, 2001; Travis et al., 2000). Hospice staff members provide family caregivers with training in pain and symptom monitoring as well as a host of other caregiver tasks, and the hospice program provides all medications and supplies needed to care for the patient (National Hospice and Palliative Care Organization, 2004). Home care hospice programs sometimes make short-term in-patient care available (usually through an affiliated hospital) when pain or symptoms become too difficult for the family caregiver to manage at home, or the caregiver needs respite time (time to cope with the physical and emotional strain of caregiving). The hospice team also assists the patient with the emotional, psychosocial, and spiritual aspects of dying. Following the death of a hospice patient, bereavement services and counseling are typically available to loved ones for a year (Hospice Foundation of America, n.d.).

Barriers to hospice care

Despite the increased number of hospice organizations in the past 15 years, there are many barriers that may inhibit their growth. In the late 1990s, fewer than 50 percent of patients with terminal illness received the benefit of hospice care (Emanuel & Emanuel, 1998), and the situation has not improved much in recent years. Even among individuals who are admitted to hospice programs, many problems exist that may hinder the quality of care patients receive, such as the lack of continuity of care between hospice team members, the inability of hospice staff to meet the emotional and spiritual needs of patients, and the lack of adequate training among healthcare professionals in taking care of those who are dying (Egbert & Parrott, 2003; Gloth, 1998; Ragan & Goldsmith, in press). There is currently no mandatory nationwide accreditation for hospice organizations. Many programs are accredited by the Joint Commission on Accreditation of Healthcare Organizations (JCAHO) or by the Community Health Accreditation Program (CHAP).

One reason for the relatively low number of people entering into hospices is the hospice eligibility requirements for Medicare patients (which reimburses older patients and their families for hospice services) that require physicians to certify potential hospice patients have six months or less to live (Foley & Gelband, 2001; Reb, 2003). According to Reb (2003), many hospices are reluctant to accept patients whose conditions might improve over time. Doctors are often reluctant to certify that a person only has six months or less to live because it can be extremely difficult to estimate how long a person will live when he or she has certain types of diseases, such as heart disease or dementia (Zerzan, Stearns, & Hanson, 2000). Complicating this matter are the continuous advances that are being made in medicine that can prolong the lives of individuals with a "terminal" illness. For example, a diagnosis of HIV was once thought to be 100 percent fatal to a patient, but new HIV medications have made it possible for HIV-positive individuals to live for many years. Similar advances (although not always as promising) are being made with Alzheimer's disease and a variety of other diseases and conditions.

In addition, providers may be reluctant to refer individuals to hospice programs because current healthcare insurance options do not provide many financial incentives for doing so (Reb, 2003). Also, according to Walsh and Gordon (2001), physicians are also hesitant to refer people to hospice programs because they fear punitive damages from insurance company oversight committees and organizations such as the Centers for Medicare and Medicaid. In recent years, these organizations have targeted physicians who referred patients to hospice programs who ended up living longer than six months in an effort to investigate insurance fraud. Walsh and Gordon (2001) contend that because of these investigations, physicians may be more conservative when estimating the survival times of patients and cautious about referring people to hospice programs.

Most insurance plans to not adequately cover services needed for quality end-of-life care (Raphael, Ahrens, & Fowler, 2001). Outside of hospice organizations, there are few ways that people can be reimbursed for these types of services. One of the reasons that insurance plans are reluctant to cover end-of-life care is the fact that some diseases, such as cancer, progress to late stages where people experience multiple physical symptoms that can be expensive to treat. Most insurance plans currently do not recognize or provide only limited reimbursement for services that meet the psychosocial needs of patients, such as patient counseling, counseling for family members, or other services that do not deal with physical health (Reb, 2003).

The result of these factors is that most individuals who are referred to hospice programs often do not live long enough to reap the benefits that these programs provide. Thirty percent of hospice patients on Medicare die within one week of admission, and hospice care providers often label this "brink of death" care, as compared to genuine end-of-life care (Nicoll, 2002). Such services are also described as "drive-by hospice care" as hospice team members often move from one patient to the next, rushing to complete visits, documentation, and follow-up only to learn of the death of the patient the next morning before "care" could be provided (see Nicoll, 2002). One week or less of hospice care does not give hospice staff sufficient time to meet the various physical, psychological, spiritual, and social needs of patients and their families.

There are other barriers to the hospice movement as well. Many physicians and nurses have not been trained in caring for the terminally ill and most feel uncomfortable doing so (Block & Sullivan, 1998; Rhymes, 1990). Also, hospice staff members often have difficulty communicating with other members of the hospice team because hospice teams tend to be interdisciplinary, and members often have limited knowledge of each member's area of expertise (Coopman, 2001; Street & Blackford, 2001). In addition, studies have found that individuals with lower socioeconomic status are less likely to be referred to hospice programs (Grande, McKerral, & Todd, 2002), and Karim, Bailey, and Tunna (2000) found that black/minority ethnic populations are referred to hospice less often than white populations. There are cultural barriers to hospice as well, and despite the inclusion of psychosocial concerns, most hospice organizations have largely adopted a mainstream western perspective of healthcare. Poulson (1998) identified several salient cultural issues to be considered during end-of-life care, including the possible need for translators, varying religious traditions, differing communication patterns, diverse social customs, familial hierarchies, and death rituals.

Additionally, although one of the goals of the hospice movement is to provide end-of-life care to patients at home rather than in hospitals, the majority of individuals in the United States still die in hospitals and nursing homes (von Gunten, 2002). Each of these barriers seriously undermines the original goals and ideals of the hospice movement, and they will need to be reexamined in order for the hospice movement to thrive in the future.

Palliative care

Palliative care refers to the comprehensive care of terminally ill individuals and their family members using an interdisciplinary approach. The term *palliation* refers to any treatment, care, or support that relieves symptoms and suffering (Query et al., 2006). This is in contrast to *curative* care, which has the primary goal of curing disease and prolonging life. In terms of comprehensive care, palliative care includes pain and symptom relief, attention to psychological and spiritual aspects of dying, and involving a patient's family and other support network members in the process of dying. Palliative care accepts death as a normal process and focuses on improving the quality of life for terminally ill patients and their families by compassionately helping them to make the transitions that precede the final stages of life (Winker & Flanagin, 1999). As you can see, dealing with all of these facets of health requires an interdisciplinary team of health professionals (see chapter 11 for a discussion of interdisciplinary teams), and palliative care organizations often include the services of physicians, nurses, counselors, and clergy.

Palliative care is closely associated with the hospice movement. Hospice organizations attempt to provide clients with palliative care. However, while palliative care may include services provided by hospices, palliative care can be offered at any point during an illness while hospice services are usually only provided during the last six months of life due to medical insurance reimbursement requirements (Reb, 2003; Zerzan et al., 2000). Ragan, Wittenberg, and Hall (2003) noted a further distinction between hospice and palliative care: "In contrast to hospice care, which precludes the use of any curative treatment at life's end stages, PC [palliative care] seeks primarily to comfort patients and to keep them pain free, yet it does not necessarily preclude medical treatment" (p. 219).

Barriers to palliative care

Much like the barriers to hospice care, quality palliative care in the United States has been limited by insurance reimbursement requirements as well as by a shortage of well-trained healthcare providers who are knowledgeable about end-of-life issues. Even among cancer centers and other sites that offer palliative care to patients, few organizations have the resources or the trained staff to address the various needs of dying individuals. Among those organizations that do provide palliative care, services are severely limited by insurance reimbursement restrictions. Ragan et al. (2003) conclude from their review of palliative care literature:

> The practice of and the research in palliative care in particular need to focus more on patients' psychological, emotional, and spiritual needs rather than on their physical needs alone – this entails the adoption of a holistic perspective that recognizes the inextricable blending of physical, mental, and spiritual health for patients' overall quality of life. (p. 225)

Healthcare professionals who provide palliative care often have limited training in pain control. Physicians and nurses often lack information about the appropriate dosages of narcotics used in pain control, and many providers fear that increased dosages of pain medication will cause addiction or a heightened tolerance for the medication among patients receiving palliative care (Rhymes, 1990). As a result, patients often receive insufficient doses of pain medication and may suffer needlessly. Providers are even less educated in most cases about addressing the psychosocial needs of patients receiving palliative care. This, coupled with few resources within the healthcare system to address psychosocial concerns (due to insurance reimbursement restrictions), is a significant barrier to quality palliative care. More education is needed among providers about end-of-life care, and insurance organizations will need to create new policies for the reimbursement of services in order for palliative care to flourish in the United States.

Attitudes Towards Death and Dying

Death and dying are taboo topics that most people avoid talking about in the United States and other western cultures. According to Martin et al. (2000), while death has historically been a central focus of social and religious life, modern society has privatized and secularized death, keeping it hidden behind institutional walls. Most Americans know relatively little about the day-to-day activities of medical examiners or the embalming process, and even fewer individuals feel comfortable discussing these things. The mass media, our families, religious groups with whom we affiliate, and the larger culture and co-culture to which we belong influence our attitudes, beliefs, and values about death and dying. In general, serious discussion of death is largely avoided in our culture, and when it is talked about, people tend to joke about death or talk about it in indirect ways.

Most people spend little time thinking about their own inevitable death or the death of those who are close to them, and this can cause problems when death needs to be discussed with friends, family members, and healthcare providers. People facing life-threatening illnesses often find it frustrating when loved ones or healthcare providers avoid talking about death and dying, especially at a time when they desire validation, empathy, and other types of support from these individuals. Studies have found that people will even distance themselves from individuals who have lost a loved one or negatively view a bereaved person who talks about their loss beyond a certain (and often limited) amount of time (Cluck & Cline, 1989).

At some point in the life span, most individuals realize that they are not going to live forever, and they must decide how they will cope with the idea of their mortality and their eventual death. Keith (1979) developed a typology of attitudes that people commonly have towards death and dying. According to Keith, individuals who feel that they have largely achieved the goals they have set for themselves in life and who reflect positively upon their present life are known as *positivists*. *Negativists* are people who reflect negatively upon their lives, especially those individuals who did not have the opportunity to fulfill dreams or who have regrets about their behaviors, and these people may look on death with despair. People who view death as an end to future opportunities for achievement and self-fulfillment but who are largely satisfied with their past are known as *activists*, and those people who see death as an end to life's problems and suffering are called *pacifists*. A person's attitude towards death and dying may influence the way he or she communicates about these topics, or whether or not he or she talks about them at all.

In terms of talking about death with providers, there is a bias among physicians and providers in our culture towards being optimistic when talking to patients about life-threatening illnesses. Many doctors feel that they will be perceived as "giving up" on the patient if they talk about dying, and that this will eliminate the patient's sense of hope and lead to depression. Although physicians are trained to deliver bad news to patients in medical school, studies have found that medical students feel anxious communicating with dying patients and that they have inadequate training in communicating and caring for dying patients (Fields & Howells, 1985; Sykes, 1989).

Communicating with others about death and dying

While coming to terms with death and dying is largely a process that occurs on the individual level, it is also important to consider the ways in which we communicate with others about death and dying. Most people tend not to think about their own end-of-life care, and healthcare professionals and researchers have paid relatively little attention to this subject until recently. Given the increase in technological innovations that allow healthcare providers to prolong life, more and more people have become aware that the preservation of life does not necessarily mean quality of life. Many people die in severe pain or with uncontrolled symptoms, and family members and others often shoulder the psychological and financial burden of making and living with decisions about end-of-life care for a loved one (Ramsay, 1999). For example, a person may not want his family to deal with the stress of keeping him alive on a life support machine for months or years after he loses consciousness, so he might include a "do not resuscitate" or DNR order within an *advance care directive*. Advance care directives are legal documents that instruct family members and other loved ones about the wishes of an individual after he or she dies. While these are not easy topics to discuss, individuals may need to express their wishes to family members over what should be done if they should face a terminal illness or impending death.

Advanced care directives give individuals much more control over how they will be treated by healthcare professionals if they should lose their ability to communicate with others. Advanced care planning helps people to determine settings for healthcare and limits for life-sustaining treatments that may lengthen the dying process. Advanced care directives allow people the reassurance that they will be treated in ways that are consistent with their values in situations where others are making decisions about their life and death. For example, some people value life at all costs, and they may specify in an advanced care directive that providers should do anything they can to keep them alive even if they are in a long-term coma. Other individuals are more concerned with quality of life or the needs of their loved ones, and may consider death to be a better alternative to being kept alive by a machine. These kinds of personal and emotional choices are often very difficult to make and certainly involve complexities that vary greatly for each individual as well as family members who may or may not be involved in the decision-making.

Physicians play an important role in discussing the implications of advanced care directives with patients (Martin et al., 2000). There are many types of advanced care directives that people can choose from, and they can be confusing to laypersons due to the legal language and specific goals of different types of advanced care directive documents. For example, one type of advance care directive is an instruction directive, or living will, which describes what type of care a person wants to receive in various situations (does the person want to be resuscitated by providers or should surgery be performed if there is little hope for recovery?). Proxy directives (also known as durable powers of attorney for healthcare) indicate whom a person would want to make treatment decisions on his or her behalf (usually a spouse or family member). Advanced care directives also vary in terms of detail. Non-detailed directives provide basic information about a person's wishes if he or she were to become incapacitated due to a wide range of scenarios, such as ending up in a coma as the result of an automobile accident or facing some other chronic disability. More detailed directives, such as disease-specific directives, can be drafted for individuals who know they are likely to die from a long-term illness, such as HIV or cancer. In these more detailed directives, patients can indicate preferences for treatment options and other important decisions that are directly related to the disease they are facing.

For example, a person with cancer might opt to stop chemotherapy treatment once the cancer has progressed to an advanced stage in order to avoid side effects from chemotherapy (such as nausea, reduced energy, and hair loss) during the last part of his or her life. Less detailed directives may be helpful for individuals who want to be sure their basic end-of-life wishes (such as a "do not resuscitate" order) are taken care of for a variety of unforeseen circumstances (e.g., an accident), while more detailed directives may be more helpful for individuals who have been diagnosed with a life-threatening illness and might have greater ability to predict the course of the disease.

Despite the importance of provider–patient communication in clarifying the details of advanced care directives, both patients and providers often find it difficult to communicate about them. According to Martin et al. (2000):

> Unfortunately, many patients consider their physician to be too busy for lengthy discussions about end-of-life issues; other patients consider these issues as private. Physician-identified barriers to communication also exist, including discomfort talking about death and dying, lack of knowledge, difficulty determining appropriateness, and time constraints. (p. 1675)

Physicians often introduce patients to advanced care directives, but they often don't discuss a patient's values concerning life and death. Discussion of these values is important in order to insure that a patient's wishes will ultimately be carried out if they are unable to communicate in a life-threatening situation. According to Martin et al. (2000), providers should consider patient goals and values when advising patients about advanced care directives, tailor advanced care directives to a patient's needs (and the needs of his or her family), translate difficult information and terminology contained in advanced care directives in terms that the patient can understand, and approach the topic of advanced care directives in an open, warm, and caring manner. Furthermore, patients should think critically about their values and goals when it comes to end-of-life care and talk to their providers and family members about advanced care directives. As we have seen, this is not an easy subject for most people to talk about given societal norms surrounding the discussion of death and dying. However, given advances in medicine and technology, people are more likely to be faced with end-of-life decision-making than in the past, and these decisions can help insure that people will die in a way that is consistent with their values and thus minimize stressful decisions for family members and other loved ones.

Coping with the death of a loved one

Coping with the death of a loved one is a very difficult process whether the death is the result of a long-term illness or an unexpected event. This section examines the grieving process and discusses ways in which family members and friends can help each other following the loss of a loved one.

Grief can be defined as the normal process of reacting both internally and externally to the perception of loss (Corr, Nabe, & Corr, 1997). *Bereavement* refers to the period of time in which an individual experiences grief and mourns the death of a loved one. When a person is dying from a long-term illness, his or her loved ones often experience *anticipatory grief*. This is the normal mourning that occurs when a patient or family is expecting a death, and it may have many of the same symptoms as those experienced after a death has occurred. However, anticipatory grief does not always occur while a loved one is dying, and the grief experienced before a death does not make the grief after the death last a shorter amount of time.

Family members and friends must contend with many issues following the death of a loved one, including making funeral arrangements, writing obituaries, and other important decisions such as whether or not to perform an autopsy or donate organs (discussed below). All of these activities can become overwhelming for individuals coping with grief, and family and friends play an important role in helping the bereaved individual adjust.

Reactions to grief

Individuals often experience and express grief in different ways, and the way in which a person will grieve depends on the personality of the grieving individual and his or her relationship with the person who died. People who have unresolved issues with a loved one may experience grief differently than those individuals who do not, and some people may be troubled by unfulfilled wishes or goals they had for the deceased. Some people feel shock, disorientation, disappointment, and separation anxiety following the death of a loved one. Physical reactions can include sleep difficulties, appetite changes, somatic complaints, or illness. In time, people learn to cope with their loss in their own unique ways, but bereaved individuals may vary considerably in terms of the amount of time it takes them to adjust. Members of a bereaved person's social network do not always understand grief or do not know how to communicate appropriately with someone who has experienced the death of a loved one.

For example, Cluck and Cline (1989) found that members of a bereaved person's social network often distance themselves from him or her. In addition, social network members sometimes have unrealistic expectations about the appropriate period of time for grief to take place. In Cluck and Cline's (1989) study, bereaved individuals reported that family members and friends often wanted them to stop grieving after a relatively short period of time, and the bereaved person was seen as not adjusting well if he or she grieved for more than a few weeks or months. It is important to remember that it can take a great deal of time for some people to grieve, and there is no appropriate amount of time for someone to work through the difficulties of experiencing death. In addition, and perhaps most importantly, our relationships with those who have passed away are not gone forever. Instead, our relationship changes form. In other words, we still carry on a different type of relationship when those we are close to die. We continue to think about the times shared together. When a person sees something that reminds him or her of the loved one, aspects of the relationship resurface in their own way, often bringing joy, sometimes bringing sadness, but the relationship continues, changing from the way it was to take on a different form (e.g., through memories).

It is also possible for people to experience grief in unhealthy ways. Some individuals may experience prolonged periods of depression, survivor's guilt, substance abuse, or have suicidal thoughts during the bereavement process. For these people, grief counseling and/or joining a grief support group may be helpful. If you have a friend or family member who is having a difficult time adjusting to loss, be sure to talk with that person when possible so you can be there to help show him or her how to get appropriate help if needed.

Organ donation

At present, over 88,000 Americans are awaiting a life-saving organ donation (OPTN, 2005). Unfortunately, many of these people will not receive a life-saving organ because individuals may be unwilling to sign an organ donation card and because family members are reluctant to donate organs from their deceased loved ones. The discussion of questions such as autopsies and organ donation with providers is often emotionally charged and difficult for bereaved individuals (Marchand & Kushner, 2004; Morgan & Miller, 2002), and these issues, along with a generally negative perception of organ donation in the United States, have led to a severe shortage of available organs for transplant patients.

Individuals can become designated organ donors during life, but they need to remember to carry their organ donor card and discuss their wishes with family members so that their families are aware of their desire to donate organs and feel more comfortable with the idea. It is important to remember that there are different age limits on the donation of some organs and tissue, and a person's age and medical history are taken into consideration when an organ donation is made. However, at least some organs from the majority of individuals who die can be used to prolong or enhance the quality of life of another person. In many ways, knowing that a deceased family member is helping another human being through the donation of an organ can be a comforting thought for bereaved individuals. However, more education and awareness about organ donation are necessary in order to help people who need organ transplants, and more research needs to be done into communication issues surrounding this topic.

Summary

A greater number of individuals are finding themselves in the role of caregiver due to factors such as an increased life span and life-prolonging medical and technological advances. Caring for a loved one with a long-term illness is a challenging experience for most people, and communication plays an important role in the caregiving process. Hospice and palliative care can help people who are dying and their lay caregivers by providing important holistic services, including pain monitoring and control, symptom management, education about the dying process, and psychological and spiritual counseling. However, barriers to hospice and palliative care, such as undertrained providers and insurance eligibility requirements, have limited the use of these services in the United States.

Coping with the dying process and death are difficult for most individuals to think and talk about, but communication is important in creating advanced care directives, comforting dying individuals and their family members, and in getting through the grieving process following the death of a loved one.

References

Allen, R. S., Haley, W. E., Small, B. J., & McMillan, S. C. (2002). Pain reports by older hospice cancer patients and family caregivers: The role of cognitive functioning. *Gerontologist, 42*, 507–514.

Andrews, S. C. (2001). Caregiver burden and symptom distress in people with cancer receiving hospice care. *Oncology Nursing Forum, 28*, 1469–1474.

Bakas, T., Lewis, R. R., & Parsons, J. (2001). Caregiving tasks among family caregivers of patients with lung cancer. *Oncology Nursing Forum, 28*, 847–854.

Barclay, S., Wyatt, P., Shore, S., Finlay, I., Grande, G., & Todd, C. (2003). Care for the dying: How well prepared are general practitioners? A questionnaire study in Wales. *Palliative Medicine, 17*, 27–39.

Bernabei, R., Gambassi, G., Lapane, K., Landi, F., Gatsonis, C., Dunlop, R., et al. (1998). Management of pain in elderly patients with cancer. *Journal of the American Medical Association, 279*, 1877–1882.

Blevins, D., & Deason-Howell, L. M. (2002). End-of-life care in nursing homes: The interface of policy, research, and practice. *Behavioral Sciences and the Law, 20*, 271–286.

Block, S. D., & Sullivan, A. M. (1998). Attitudes about end-of-life care: A national cross-sectional study. *Journal of Palliative Medicine, 1*, 347–355.

Brescia, F. J., Portenoy, R. K., Ryan, M., Krasnoff, L., & Gray, G. (1992). Pain, opioid use, and survival in hospitalized patients with advanced cancer. *Journal of Clinical Oncology, 10*, 149–155.

Centers for Disease Control and Prevention. (2004). Vital and health statistics. Available at: www.cdc.gov/.

Chesler, M. A., & Barbarin, O. A. (1984). Difficulties of providing help in a crisis: Relationships between parents of children with cancer and their friends. *Journal of Social Issues, 40*, 113–134.

Cluck, G. G., & Cline, R. W. (1989). The circle of others: Self-help groups for the bereaved. *Communication Quarterly, 34*, 306–325.

Coopman, S. J. (2001). Democracy, performance, and outcomes in interdisciplinary health care teams. *Journal of Business Communication, 38*, 261–284.

Corr, C. A., Nabe, C. M., & Corr, D. M. (1997). *Death and dying, life and living* (2nd ed.). Pacific Grove, CA: Brooks/Cole.

Donnelly, S., Walsh, D., & Rybicki, L. (1994). The symptoms of advanced cancer in 1,000 patients. *Journal of Palliative Care, 10*, 57.

Egbert, N., & Parrott, R. (2003). Empathy and social support for the terminally ill: Implications for recruiting and retaining hospice and hospital volunteers. *Communication Studies, 54*, 18–34.

Elliot, B. A., Elliot, T. E., Murray, D. M., Braun, B. L., & Johnson, K. M. (1997). Patients and family members: The role of knowledge and attitudes in cancer pain. *Journal of Pain and Symptom Management, 12,* 209–220.

Emanuel, D. J., & Emanuel, L. L. (1998). The promise of a good death. *Lancet, 351,* 21–29.

Field, M. J., & Cassel, C. K. (Eds.). (1997). *Approaching death: Improving care at the end of life.* Washington, DC: National Academy Press.

Fields, D., & Howells, K. (1985). Medical students' self-reported worries about aspects of death and dying. *Death Studies, 10,* 147–154.

Foley, K. M., & Gelband, H. (Eds.). (2001). *Improving palliative care for cancer.* Washington, DC: National Academy Press.

Geist-Martin, P., Ray, E. B., & Sharf, B. F. (2003). *Communicating health: Personal, cultural, and political complexities.* Belmont, CA: Wadsworth.

Given, B. A., Given, C. W., Helms, E., Stommel, M., & DeVoss, D. N. (1997). Determinants of family caregiver reaction. New and recurrent cancer. *Cancer Practice, 5,* 17–24.

Given, C. W., Stommel, M., Given, B. A., Osuch, J., Kurtz, M. E., & Kurtz, J. C. (1993). The influence of cancer patients' symptoms and functional states on patients' depression and family caregivers' reaction and depression. *Health Psychology, 12,* 277–285.

Gloth, F. M. (1998). Foreword. *Hospice care: A physician's guide.* Alexandria, VA: National Hospice Organization.

Grande, G. E., McKerral, A., & Todd, C. J. (2002). Which cancer patients are referred to hospital at home for palliative care? *Palliative Medicine, 16,* 115–123.

Harwood, J., & Sparks, L. (2003). Social identity and health: An intergroup communication approach to cancer. *Health Communication, 15,* 145–170.

Harzold, E., & Sparks, L. (2007). Adult child perceptions of communication and humor when the parent is diagnosed with cancer: A suggestive perspective from communication theory. *Qualitative Research Reports in Communication, 7,* 1–13.

Hospice Foundation of America. (n.d.). Available at www.hospicefoundation.org/.

Howarth, G., & Leaman, O. (Eds.). (2001). *Encyclopedia of death and dying.* London: Routledge.

Karim, K., Bailey, M., & Tunna, K. (2000). Nonwhite ethnicity and the provision of specialist palliative care services: Factors affecting doctors' referral patterns. *Palliative Medicine, 14,* 471–478.

Keith, D. M. (1979). Life changes and perceptions of life and death among older men and women. *Journal of Gerontology, 34,* 870–878.

Laizner, A. M., Yost, L. M., Barg, F. K., & McCorkle, R. (1993). Needs of family caregivers of persons with cancer: A review. *Seminars in Oncology Nursing, 9,* 114–120.

Lawton, J. (2000). *The dying process: Patients' experiences of palliative care.* London: Routledge.

Lynn, J. (2001). Serving patients who may die soon and their families: The role of hospice and other services. *Journal of the American Medical Association, 285*(7), 925–932.

MacMillan, S. C., & Small, B. J. (2002). Symptom distress and quality of life in patients with cancer newly admitted to hospice home care. *Oncology Nursing Forum, 29,* 1421–1428.

Marchand, L., & Kushner, K. (2004). Death pronouncements: Using the teachable moment in end-of-life care residency training. *Journal of Palliative Medicine, 7,* 80–84.

Martin, D. K., Emanuel, L. L., & Singer, P. A. (2000). Planning for the end of life. *Lancet, 356,* 1672–1676.

Martinez, J. M. (1996). The interdisciplinary team. In D. C. Sheehan & W. B. Forman (Eds.), *Hospice and palliative care: Concepts and practices* (pp. 21–29). Sudbury, MA: Jones and Bartlett.

Meyers, J. L., & Gray, L. N. (2001). The relationships between family primary caregiver characteristics and satisfaction with hospice care, quality of life, and burden. *Oncology Nursing Forum, 28,* 73–82.

Moody, H. R. (1994). *Aging: Concepts and controversies.* Thousand Oaks, CA: Pine Forge.

Moore, A. (1998). Hospice care hijacked? *Christianity Today, 42,* 38–41.

Morgan, S. E., & Miller, J. K. (2002). Beyond the organ donor card: The effect of knowledge, attitudes, and values on willingness to communicate about organ donation to family members. *Health Communication, 14,* 121–134.

Nail, L. M. (2002). Fatigue in patients with cancer. *Oncology Nursing Forum, 29,* 537–546.

National Family Caregivers Association. (2005). Who are family caregivers? Retrieved August 27, 2005, from www.thefamilycaregiver.org/who/.

National Hospice and Palliative Care Organization. (2004). Accessed April 18, 2004. Available at www.nhpco.org/.

Nicoll, L. H. (2002). When there's little time left. *Journal of Hospice and Palliative Nursing, 4,* 4–5.

O'Hair, H. D., Kreps, G. L., & Sparks, L. (in press). Conceptualizing cancer care and communication. In H. D. O'Hair, G. L. Kreps, & L. Sparks (Eds.), *Handbook of communication and cancer care.* Cresskill, NJ: Hampton Press.

O'Hair, H. D., Thompson, S., & Sparks, L. (2005). Negotiating cancer care through agency. In E. B. Ray (Ed.), *Health communication in practice: A case study approach.* Mahwah, NJ: Lawrence Erlbaum.

OPTN. (2005). The organ procurement and transplantation network: Waiting list removal reasons by year. Retrieved April 30, 2005, from www.optn.org/latestData/rptData.asp.

Panke, J. T. (2002). Difficulties in managing pain at the end of life. *American Journal of Nursing, 102,* 26–33.

Pecchioni, L., & Sparks, L. (in press). Health information sources of individuals with cancer and their family members. *Health Communication.*

Pecchioni, L., Ota, H., & Sparks, L. (2004). Cultural issues in communication and aging. In J. F. Nussbaum & J. Coupland (Eds.), *Handbook of communication and aging research* (pp. 167–207). Mahwah, NJ: Lawrence Erlbaum.

Poulson, J. (1998). Impact of cultural differences in care of the terminally ill. In N. MacDonald (Ed.), *Palliative medicine: A case-based manual* (pp. 244–252). New York: Oxford University Press.

Query, J. L., Jr., & Wright, K. B. (2003). Assessing communication competence in an on-line study: Toward informing subsequent interventions among older adults with cancer, their lay caregivers, and peers. *Health Communication, 15*, 205–219.

Query, J. L., Jr., Wright, K. B., & Gilchrist, E. S. (2006). Communication and cancer hospice care: Towards negotiating attitudinal and research obstacles. In H. D. O'Hair, L. Sparks, & G. L. Kreps (Eds.), *Health communication and cancer* (pp. 301–319). Cresskill, NJ: Hampton Press.

Ragan, S. L., & Goldsmith, J. (in press). End-of-life communication: The drama of pretense in the talk of dying patients and their MDs. In K. B. Wright & S. C. Moore (Eds.), *Applied health communication: A sourcebook*. Boston: Allyn & Bacon.

Ragan, S. L., Wittenberg, E., & Hall, H. T. (2003). The communication of palliative care for the elderly cancer patient. *Health Communication, 15*, 219–226.

Ramsay, S. (1999). International research agenda set for end-of-life care. *Lancet, 354*, 1361.

Raphael, C., Ahrens, J., & Fowler, N. (2001). Financing end-of-life care in the USA. *Journal of the Royal Society of Medicine, 94*, 458–461.

Ratner, E., Norlander, L., & McSteen, K. (2001). Death at home following a targeted advanced-care planning process at home: The kitchen table discussion. *Journal of the American Geriatrics Society, 49*, 778–781.

Reb, A. M. (2003). Palliative and end-of-life care: Policy analysis. *Oncology Nursing Forum, 30*, 35–50.

Rhymes, J. (1990). Hospice care in America. *Journal of the American Medical Association, 264*, 369.

Richards, L., Bengston, V., & Miller, R. (1989). The "generation in the middle": Perceptions of changes in adult intergenerational relationships. In K. Kreppner & R. Lerner (Eds.), *Family systems and life span development* (pp. 341–366). Hillsdale, NJ: Lawrence Erlbaum.

Rusinak, R. L., & Murphy, J. F. (1995). Elderly spousal caregivers: Knowledge of cancer care, perceptions of preparedness, and coping strategies. *Journal of Gerontological Nursing, 21*, 33–41.

Sarna, L., & Brecht, M. (1997). Dimensions of symptom distress in women with advanced lung cancer: A factor analysis. *Heart and Lung, 26*, 23–30.

Sarna, L., & McCorkle, R. (1996). Burden of care and lung cancer. *Cancer Practice, 4*, 245–251.

Siegel, K., Raveis, V. H., Houts, P., & More, V. (1991). Caregiver burden and unmet patient needs. *Cancer, 68*, 1131–1140.

Sparks, L. (Ed.). (2003). Cancer communication and aging [Special issue]. *Health Communication, 15*(2).

Sparks, L. (in press). The SMILE health care communication model (SMILE-HCCM): An interpersonal theory-based approach to message framing in health care interventions. In S. S. Travis & R. Talley (Eds.), *Caregiving across the professions*. New York:

Oxford University Press. Project supported by a grant from Johnson and Johnson and the Rosalynn Carter Institute for Human Development.

Sparks, L., & Harwood, J. (in press). Cancer, aging, and social identity: Development of an integrated model of social identity theory and health communication. In L. Sparks, H. D. O'Hair, & G. L. Kreps, (Eds.), *Cancer communication and aging*. Cresskill, NJ: Hampton Press.

Sparks, L., & McPherson, J. (2007). Cross-cultural differences in choices of health information by older cancer patients and their family caregivers. In K. Wright & S. D. Moore (Eds.), *Applications in health communication* (pp. 179–205). Cresskill, NJ: Hampton Press.

Sparks, L., Travis, S., & Thompson, S. (2005). Listening for the communicative signals of humor, narratives, and self-disclosure in the family caregiving interview. *Health and Social Work, 30*, 340–343.

Sparks, L., Villagran, M. M., & Wittenberg-Lyles (2008, forthcoming). Family decision-making across the continuum of healthcare. In W. Donsbach, J. Bryant, & R. Craig (Eds.), *International encyclopedia of communication*. Oxford: Blackwell.

Sparks-Bethea, L. (2002). The impact of an older adult parent on communicative satisfaction and dyadic adjustment in the long-term marital relationship: Adult children and spouses' retrospective accounts. *Journal of Applied Communication Research, 30*, 107–125.

Sparks-Bethea, L., & Balazs, A. (1997). Improving intergenerational healthcare communication. *Journal of Health Communication, 2*, 129–137.

Sparks-Bethea, L., Travis, S. S., & Pecchioni, L. L. (2000). Family caregivers' use of humor in conveying information about caring for dependent older adults. *Health Communication, 12*, 361–376. Project supported by a grant from the Nursing Research Program, Clinical Applications Research, Glaxo-Wellcome, Inc.

Stoltz, P., Uden, G., & Willman, A. (2004). Support for family carers who care for an elderly person at home: A systematic literature review. *Scandinavian Journal of Caring Sciences, 18*, 111–119.

Street, A., & Blackford, J. (2001). Communication issues for the interdisciplinary community palliative care team. *Journal of Clinical Nursing, 10*, 643–650.

Sykes, N. (1989). Medical students' fears about breaking bad news. *Lancet, 2*, 564.

Toseland, R. W., Blanchard, C. G., & McCallion, P. (1995). A problem solving intervention for caregivers of cancer patients. *Social Science in Medicine, 40*, 517–528.

Travis, S. S., & Sparks-Bethea, L. (2001). Medication administration by family members of dependent elders in shared care arrangements. *Journal of Clinical Geropsychology, 7*(3), 231–243. Project supported by a grant from the Nursing Research Program, Clinical Applications Research, Glaxo-Wellcome, Inc.

Travis, S. S., Sparks-Bethea, L., & Winn, P. (2000). Medication hassles reported by family caregivers of dependent elders. *Journals of Gerontology: Medical Sciences, 55A*, 7, M412–M417. Project supported by a grant from the Nursing Research Program, Clinical Applications Research, Glaxo-Wellcome, Inc.

von Gunten, C. F. (2002). Secondary and tertiary palliative care in US hospitals. *Journal of the American Medical Association, 286*(7), 875–881.

Walsh, D., & Gordon, S. (2001). The terminally ill: Dying for palliative medicine? *American Journal of Hospice and Palliative Care, 18,* 203–205.

Wanzer, M., Sparks, L., & Frymier, A. B. (2007). The function of communication within the lives of older adults: An exploration of the relationships among humor, coping efficacy, age, and life satisfaction. Unpublished manuscript.

Weitzner, M. A., McMillan, S. C., & Jacobson, P. B. (1999). Family caregiver quality of life: Differences between curative and palliative cancer treatment settings. *Journal of Pain and Symptom Management, 17,* 418–428.

Wiemann, J. M. (1977). Explication and test of a model of communicative competence. *Human Communication Research, 3,* 195–213.

Williams, A., & Nussbaum, J. F. (2001). *Intergenerational communication across the lifespan.* Mahwah, NJ: Lawrence Erlbaum.

Winker, M. A., & Flanagin, A. (1999). Caring for patients at the end of life. *JAMA, 282,* 1965.

Zamborsky, L. J. (1996). Support groups for hospice staff. In D. C. Sheehan & W. B. Forman (Eds.), *Hospice and palliative care: Concepts and practices* (pp. 131–137). Sudbury, MA: Jones and Bartlett.

Zerzan, J., Stearns, S., & Hanson, L. (2000). Access to palliative care and hospice in nursing homes. *Journal of the American Medical Association, 284,* 2489–2494.

Part III

Social, Cultural, and Organizational Contexts

Chapter 4

Social Support and Health

You may have noticed that when you are experiencing problems at school, work, or in relationships, you often feel better when you have friends or family members to talk with. Sometimes these individuals give us good advice or they help us to forget our problems for a while by involving us in activities, such as playing golf or going to the movies. At other times you may feel that your friends and family members will not understand the problem you are facing, or they give you bad advice, so you may turn to other sources of information to help you cope with the problem, such as looking up information on the Internet.

Our relationships with family, friends, and even acquaintances can have a positive effect on our physical and mental health throughout our lives through the various types of social support they offer us. We, in turn, can influence the health of our social network members through the support we provide them. This is true not only during times when we face a health crisis, but also when we are coping with everyday stressful events. Moreover, research suggests that our social network members can be beneficial in helping us to avoid stressful situations that could adversely affect our health, and the companionship of significant others can help us to be more resistant to certain types of illness. However, the relationship between social support and health outcomes is extremely complicated, and some types of support (or sources of support) can actually negatively affect health. This chapter will examine the concept of social support, the various ways in which support networks can impact health, and benefits and problems with supportive messages. In addition, it discusses characteristics of support networks and support groups for people with health concerns.

Types and Functions of Social Support

Types of support

Our social networks, such as friends, family members, and co-workers, provide us with many different types of social support (Goldsmith, 2004). *Instrumental support* refers to tangible types of assistance, such as when parents give children money so they can go to the movies with friends, or when a friend helps another friend with a household project. *Emotional support* refers to such diverse activities as listening to a person's troubles, validating his or her problems, offering encouraging words when someone is not feeling well, and simply "being there" during a time of need. *Esteem or appraisal support* deals with efforts to make a person who is facing a stressful situation feel validated, or that their problems are legitimate. *Informational support* can take many forms, such as when you receive good advice about a relationship problem from a close friend or if a person with pancreatic cancer receives information about medications in an Internet support group.

Social support can also be proactive or reactive (Sarason, Sarason, & Pierce, 1990). *Proactive support* is any type of assistance that helps an individual to circumvent problems, such as if a doctor recommends a diet that helps a patient lower his or her risk of hypertension. *Reactive support* is usually assistance that is provided in response to some crisis a person is facing or a disruption of normal life events. For example, a diagnosis of cancer is a major crisis event, and members of the social network of a person with cancer typically provide emotional support or some other type of assistance to help him or her cope with the disease.

Positive and negative functions of support

Each type of support mentioned above has been linked to positive psychological and physical health outcomes as well as improved quality of life (Cobb, 1976; Goldsmith, 2004; Hughes, 2005). However, people often differ as to the types of support they find useful due to factors such as the context of the stressful situation they are facing, their perceived coping skills, and their relationship with the support provider (La Gaipa, 1990). Depending upon the situation, a recipient of support may perceive some types of support negatively, and this may negate the positive effects of the supportive attempt or it may actually have a negative impact on health or quality of life.

Instrumental support is a common type of support that people provide individuals with health problems, and it is crucial for people who require long-term care due to an illness. In these situations, individuals who are sick often rely heavily on others to take care of physical needs, such as preparing meals, transportation, and basic daily tasks such as going to the bathroom, bathing, and providing medications. While individuals typically appreciate the support they receive in these situations, inappropriate instrumental support can be perceived negatively.

For example, when people feel that they can successfully perform physical tasks, they may perceive tangible assistance negatively, especially if it is viewed as patronizing or if it undermines their sense of competence. People with disabilities often resent others who go out of their way to open doors or who engage in other types of instrumental support when they feel that they could accomplish these tasks themselves. In some cases, such as within nursing homes, older residents may initially resent some types of instrumental support, but they may eventually accept it if they feel they have little control over their situation. Older nursing home residents have been found to acquire a "learned helplessness" when it comes to many physical tasks as a result of workers engaging in over-accommodating behaviors when they provide tangible assistance (Grainger, 1995).

When informational support is perceived as useful, people with health problems may feel they have more control over their situation (Roter & Hall, 1992). However, too much information about a disease or condition from a physician or other healthcare provider can be perceived negatively if the information overwhelms the patient or causes him or her to worry (Brashers, Neidig, & Goldsmith, 2004). For example, if a physician gives a patient a large amount of information about treatment options, side effects, and the progression of symptoms after an HIV-positive diagnosis, all of this information is likely to be perceived as overwhelming to the patient, particularly if he or she has not had a chance to think about all of the implications of the diagnosis. In this type of case, patients are often unable to cognitively process the information they receive from their doctor.

Informational support from family members and friends during times of stress can also be seen as inappropriate, especially when it takes the form of unwanted advice (Goldsmith & Fitch, 1997) or if it is perceived as patronizing or intrusive. For example, a caregiver who reminds a sick spouse that he needs to eat something prior to taking his medication might think that she is being helpful, while the spouse may see it as "butting in." As you can see, the provision of informational support can be quite complicated, depending upon how it is perceived. Albrecht and Goldsmith (2003) point out other complications when providing informational support:

One may receive information and advice about how to cope with a health problem and yet find that the advice is uninformed and therefore of little use.

Worse yet, the advice others give might lead an individual to feel that others are critical of his or her own coping efforts or that others are condescending by providing information that the individual already knows. (p. 270)

Emotional support is often perceived as more beneficial than informational support among people with health concerns, particularly in helping them to cope with the emotional distress of illness (Cwikel & Isreal, 1987; Magen & Glajchen, 1999). However, emotional support can also be perceived negatively, especially when the support provider denies or draws attention away from the feelings that the support recipient is experiencing or if the type of emotional support offered is perceived as inappropriate in other ways (Burleson, 1994). For example, a woman with breast cancer may want her partner to simply listen to and accept her fear about an upcoming mastectomy, but rather than acknowledging this fear the partner might say "try not to worry so much – these operations are usually very successful." In this case the partner, while most likely having the best of intentions, is attempting to minimize the woman with cancer's fear by implying that she is perhaps worrying too much.

Esteem support is an important type of support in helping distressed individuals who feel socially stigmatized as a result of their health condition (e.g., people with HIV or people with visible disabilities) to feel valued at times when their self-esteem is low as a result of struggles dealing with their daily lives (Wills, 1985). As we will discuss in greater depth in chapter 5, stigma refers to negative feelings attached to a health condition or a group of people who are living with it. Disabilities, HIV, cancer, and eating disorders are a few of the many health conditions that carry a social stigma, and the individuals who are living with them often experience communication problems with people who do not share their condition. Both the negative societal perceptions of these diseases and the communication problems associated with these perceptions may lead a person with one of these conditions to feel socially isolated or depressed. Esteem support or validation may help individuals increase their sense of self-worth when it is provided by an understanding loved one or others facing similar circumstances.

However, support providers do not always view a person's situation as a legitimate problem, and they may not be able to adequately provide esteem support. For example, a father might see his daughter's struggle with anorexia as something that is within her control rather than as a psychological disorder. While wanting to be supportive, his perception of his daughter's condition may lead him to say things that reflect an inaccurate understanding of anorexia or that do not legitimize her condition or her feelings. When people have a better understanding of a health condition and see it as a legitimate concern, they are often better able to provide esteem support. This is one of the reasons why members of peer support groups are often able to provide a person with esteem support. Because members of peer support groups are facing a health condition themselves, it is often easier for them to validate the feelings of other members of the group. (See the discussion of support groups later in this chapter.)

Models of Social Support and Health

Stress and health

In order to understand the relationship between stress and psychological/physical health, it is important to have a basic understanding of the physiology of stress. While the general association between stress and physical health is easy to understand, researchers have actually found this relationship to be extremely complex. Similar to many species of animals, the physiological responses to stress have evolved in human beings to promote survival during times of crisis. Essentially, the body's response to a stressor prepares it for rapid physical action (fight or flight). In others words, the brain helps to insure that there is sufficient oxygen and energy to the brain and muscles so that a person can survive a crisis situation by either fighting or running. Unlike the stressors that many animals face in the wild, such as encountering predators, few aspects of modern life are immediately life-threatening to human beings. However, exposure to everyday stressors, such as threats to our sense of financial security, a heavy workload at the office, relationship problems, and minor hassles such as traffic jams, taxes, and household chores, all trigger physiological responses from the body.

At the psychological level, people appraise stressful events in terms of their severity and duration (i.e., short-term problems and long-term problems) as well as their available resources and abilities to cope with or manage the stressor. The central nervous system plays an important role when people encounter stressful situations. The central nervous system consists of millions of specialized cells known as neurons. Sensory neurons sense changes to the body due to environmental stimuli such as stressors and relay information to the brain. The brain makes sense of this information, and if a situation is perceived as threatening, emotional responses to the stressor trigger physiological reactions from the body's limbic system. The limbic system can activate an area of the brain known as the hypothalamus. The hypothalamus regulates the body's stress response systems, which include the sympathetic adrenal medullary (SAM) response system and the hypothalamic-pituitary-adrenal (HPA) system (Clow, 2001). Neurons associated with both systems regulate cardiovascular activity, such as heart rate and blood pressure, and the immune system by releasing chemicals into the bloodstream known as neurotransmitters. These neurotransmitters stimulate the release of other chemicals into the bloodstream. For example, they activate the release of adrenaline from our adrenal glands (located above the kidney), known as the sympathetic adrenal medullary response system. Adrenaline provides the needed energy to the brain and muscles to make quick decisions in the face of threatening situations. It is likely that you have experienced an "adrenaline rush" after a stressful episode such as nearly hitting another vehicle while driving, being startled by someone, or after engaging in a conflict with a friend or family member.

Over time, when our body's stress response system is repeatedly activated, this can lead to wear and tear on the body's cardiovascular system (Clow, 2001). For instance, the increase in blood pressure and the release of cortisol associated with stress response (both of which are associated with the release of adrenaline) can damage certain blood vessels. When these blood vessels are damaged, it allows for the build-up of fatty nutrients within the damaged walls of the vessels, a condition known as atherosclerosis. When this process occurs within blood vessels located in the arteries supplying the heart, it can lead to heart disease (such as heart attacks). Moreover, the frequent release of cortisol into the bloodstream can disturb the balance of the body's immune system and make us more susceptible to disease. The release of cortisol (over an extended period of time) has also been linked to negative psychological states, such as depression (Clow, 2001). In short, our body's physiological response to stressful situations can lead to a variety of physical and mental health problems.

Stress and social support

Researchers have focused on the relationship between social support and health outcomes for several decades, and study findings indicate benefits to both mental and physical health (Aneshensel & Stone, 1982; Berkman & Syme, 1979; Cohen, 1988; Krause, 1990; Wills, 1985). In terms of specific health outcomes, a variety of studies have found a relationship between social support and stress (Aneshensel & Stone, 1982; Ballieux & Heijen, 1989; Berkman & Syme, 1979; Billings & Moos, 1981; Dean & Lin, 1977).

Two models explaining this relationship have emerged from the social support literature: (1) the buffering model and (2) the main effects model. The *buffering model* suggests that social support shields individuals from the negative effects of stress, such as weakened immunity and depression, over time (Cohen & Wills, 1985; Dean & Lin, 1977; La Rocca, House, & French, 1980). The *main effects model* asserts that there is a direct rather than buffering relationship between social support and physical and psychological outcomes (Aneshensel & Stone, 1982; Thoits, 1982).

Researchers have linked both models to positive effects in terms of morbidity and mortality (Berkman & Syme, 1979; Cohen, 1988; Uchino, Cacioppo, & Kiecolt-Glaser, 1996). The reduction of stress associated with supportive behaviors appears to affect physical health in a variety of ways. As we have seen, prolonged exposure to stress has been found to impair immune system response (Ballieux & Heijen, 1989), and it can create damage to internal organ systems through the production and maintenance of chemicals such as cortisol. Elevated levels of other chemicals, such as adrenaline, have been found to be associated with colds and flu, tension and nervousness, and elevated systolic blood pressure (Kohn, 1996). In addition, physiological responses to stress may exacerbate other physical problems that a person is currently experiencing.

However, there are a number of variables that make the relationship between social support and health more complicated. These include differences in individual coping styles and adaptation to stressful situations (Kohn, 1996; Pierce, Sarason, & Sarason, 1996), and perceptions of support providers and recipients within the context in which support takes place (Barbee, 1990; Edwards & Noller, 1998).

Coping strategies and health outcomes

People cope with stressful situations in a variety of ways, and these individual differences in coping styles have been linked to health outcomes. For example, suppose a young man suspects there is a possibility that he has HIV given his sexual history. He may decide to avoid getting tested for HIV or obtaining information about the disease as a way of coping with this particular stressful situation. However, his partner might have similar suspicions regarding her HIV status, and she might obtain as much information about the disease as she can from her physician or she might get tested to resolve the uncertainty over her HIV status. This example shows two radically different ways of coping with a health-related stressful situation. The man chose to avoid the situation as a coping strategy whereas his partner chose a more active set of actions for coping with it.

Kohn (1996) identifies three general types of coping strategies that individuals use when confronted with a stressful situation. *Problem-focused coping* is a strategy that is "directed at remedying a threatening or harmful situation" (Kohn, 1996, p. 186). When people engage in active behaviors they think will reduce a threatening situation or at least help them to deal with it better, they are using problem-focused coping. For example, if a person gets tested for HIV, learns that she has the disease, and attempts to find as much information about it as possible, she might find ways to reduce the threat of the disease. In recent years, early diagnosis of HIV and advances in HIV medication have made it possible for HIV-positive individuals to live without HIV-related medical problems (or with minimal problems) for many years. By choosing a problem-focused coping strategy such as early diagnosis and treatment, a person with HIV might actually prolong his or her life. Problem-focused coping has been linked to positive adaptation to stressful situations in a variety of studies, and it is thought to reduce psychological and physical stress (Endler & Parker, 1990; Heady & Wearing, 1990).

Emotional-focused coping refers to behaviors such as venting frustrations about a stressful situation or expressing some type of emotional response to it rather than making an attempt to remedy or improve the situation (Kohn, 1996). For instance, a person who discovers that he has hypertension might complain about having the disease or his doctor's request to make changes to his diet (e.g., avoiding salt and foods with high fat content) rather than taking active steps to manage it. Not surprisingly, emotional-focused coping has been linked to negative adaptation to stressful situations (Edwards & Trimble, 1992; Turner, King, & Tremblay, 1992), although some of the research has produced mixed findings.

Finally, *avoidance-focused coping* refers to an "attempt to disengage mentally or even physically from threatening or damaging situations" (Kohn, 1996, p. 186). Many people choose to avoid threatening situations, particularly when dealing with health issues. Our mortality and susceptibility to illness are difficult concepts for most people to deal with, and many people use avoidance-focused coping when confronted with stressful health-related situations. Rather than actively obtaining information about diseases such as diabetes or breast cancer, some people would rather avoid talking about them or engage in some type of diversion as opposed to dealing with the threat of illness. Researchers have found mixed results for avoidance-focused coping strategies in terms of adaptation to stressful situations. For some people, avoiding stressful situations actually helps them to cope with them, while others find that avoidance leads to negative adaptation. In other situations, people may feel that they have no control over their health status, and this might lead to an avoidance-focused strategy.

For example, an individual who is facing a terminal illness might find that spending more time with family and friends serves as a diversion to thinking about the illness, and this actually helps to reduce stress. Sometimes dwelling upon problems that are out of our control leads to additional stress, and we find it less stressful when we divert our attention from the problem. However, some individuals who choose avoidance strategies when dealing with a stressful health situation might better adapt to it if they were to choose a more problem-focused coping strategy, such as seeking information about treatment options for a disease that might help their prognosis over time.

Problematic integration theory helps to explain both how people engage in information-seeking behaviors and manage uncertainty when coping with an illness and why people may or may not choose information and other types of support. Babrow (2001) argued that the meaning of uncertainty is largely dependent on the values of the individual who is experiencing an illness, and those values guide the ways that information is used to manage uncertainty. For example, a person with cancer may decide to gather certain types of information about the most aggressive forms of chemotherapy if he or she primarily values stopping the progression of cancer, regardless of the side effects of the treatment, whereas another person might be more concerned with acquiring information that enhances the quality of his or her life.

Perceptions of Support Providers

In addition to individual differences in coping with stressful situations, our perceptions of our social support network members during times of stress influence whether or not we find helpful a person's attempts to be supportive. *Support appraisals*, or the perceptions of the appropriateness of social support behaviors (such as the degree to which an individual is satisfied with the support he or she receives), influence how people adjust to stressful situations (Albrecht, Burleson, & Goldsmith, 1994). In this section, we will examine perceptions of support providers and situations where supportive attempts can be perceived negatively and have negative effects on our stress levels.

Social comparison theory and social support

Our social networks provide many opportunities to give and receive social support, and while expanding our social networks is thought to increase opportunities for social support, our perceptions of others within these networks influence our evaluations of supportive behaviors. *Social comparison theory* (Festinger, 1954) is a useful framework for examining perceptions of people within our support networks and for understanding why support from these individuals may not always lead to positive outcomes. According to social comparison theory, individuals make assessments about their own health and coping mechanisms by comparing them to others in their social network (Helgeson & Gottlieb, 2000).

Helgeson and Gottlieb (2000) mention that *lateral comparisons*, comparisons to similar others, may normalize people's experiences and reduce uncertainty and stress for those dealing with health concerns. However, when individuals compare themselves to others, their self-assessment could be either positive or negative. For example, if a person with cancer feels that he is coping with problems less effectively than others in his network (such as a friend or relative who has or had cancer or a similar life-threatening illness), this may create *upward comparisons*, which could produce feelings of frustration or serve as a source of inspiration to the person to cope more effectively by emulating the successful behaviors of those other members. Conversely, *downward comparisons* to others in the social network, such as when an individual feels that he or she is coping better than other members, can lead to positive self-assessments and/or to negative feelings about people if interaction with the other members is perceived as being unhelpful.

Reciprocity and social support

Perceptions of *reciprocity* within supportive relationships are another important aspect of the social support process. According to equity theory (Deutsch, 1985), we tend to feel troubled in a relationship when we feel that we are *underbenefited*, that is, when we perceive that we are incurring too many costs in a relationship while simultaneously receiving too few rewards. For example, if you devoted many hours of time taking care of a friend when she was ill or providing emotional support when she was facing a health crisis, such as a miscarriage, but she never seems to have time to call you or listen to your problems when you are facing a similar stressful situation, you would probably feel underbenefited, or that the relationship was inequitable. A similar problem can occur when a person in a relationship feels *overbenefited*. In this case, you may have received help from a friend during a stressful time without having the opportunity to reciprocate. Most people feel uncomfortable in situations where they perceive themselves as overbenefited in a relationship, particularly when they feel unable to reciprocate support they have received.

Reciprocity issues are common in caregiving relationships (see chapter 3), especially in cases when a healthy relational partner is caring for a loved one. For example, a woman who is caring for her husband with prostate cancer may spend a considerable amount of time offering tangible assistance and managing a large number of caregiver duties, such as monitoring symptoms, giving medication, and managing daily household chores. The husband in this scenario would likely feel overbenefited while the wife might feel underbenefited, although in marital relationships role obligations often lead people to accept these types of inequities. Receiving support without having the opportunity to reciprocate, which is common in caregiver–patient relationships, often leads individuals to feel overbenefited, and this can lead to feelings of inadequacy, helplessness, and demoralization (Bakas, Lewis, & Parsons, 2001). However, research suggests that caregivers often feel overwhelmed and frustrated by the inequitable nature of caregiver–patient relationships (Andrews,

2001; Sarna & McCorkle, 1996), yet they are often unable to express their frustrations about their situation to members of their social network because they do not want to burden friends and family with the added stress of thinking about these concerns or because they may fear being judged negatively by these individuals for expressing negative feelings about caring for a loved one (Bakas et al., 2001; Laizner, Yost, Barg, & McCorkle, 1993).

Strong Tie Versus Weak Tie Support Networks

Most support takes place between close ties, such as family members and friends. Family members and friends are likely to be support providers during times of illness due to the role obligations that exist in these relationships. Family members are typically in the best position to provide us with tangible support during illness, such as taking care of our physical needs. Our relational histories with our family members and close friends also make them good candidates for being able to understand us and provide us with emotional support. While the role obligations and relational history associated with close tie networks are typically beneficial, they can also cause problems for people who are seeking support when facing a health problem. As we have seen, role obligations can lead to problems with reciprocity.

In addition, our intimate knowledge of close tie network members and our relational history with them can create problems in times when support is needed. While close ties know us intimately, they can also know us too well, and it is sometimes difficult to disclose certain topics to these individuals, particularly when we feel embarrassed by them or if they have a social stigma attached to them. Unfortunately, in the case of many health problems, there are a number of topics, such as symptoms and bodily functions, which can be difficult to talk about with people who are close to us. An alternative to close ties for support is weak tie support networks.

Weak tie relationships (Granovetter, 1973) occur between individuals who communicate on a relatively frequent basis but who do not consider one another to be members of their close personal network (e.g., close friends, family). Weak tie networks for most individuals typically consist of neighbors, service providers, people within Internet groups, and other individuals a person could turn to during times of stress when closer ties were unavailable. Individuals facing stressful situations, such as a life-threatening disease or other health problems, often find that weak tie networks offer them certain advantages over strong tie networks in terms of social support.

One reason why some individuals may decide to seek support through weak tie networks instead of within their strong tie network is that weak tie networks often provide access to diverse points of view and information that may not be available within more intimate relationships (Adelman, Parks, & Albrecht, 1987). Typically, many individuals form close relationships with others who are similar to them in terms of demographics, attitudes, and backgrounds. This homogeneous preference can limit the diversity of information and viewpoints obtained about topics, including health concerns. Access to more diverse viewpoints about health problems can provide individuals with more varied informational support about health issues, and interacting with varied types of people increases the number of social comparisons a person can make about his or her health condition vis-à-vis others (Adelman et al., 1987).

For example, a person who has been recently diagnosed with cancer will probably not find many people within his or her traditional support network who also have cancer, and these network members may only have a limited perspective about how to cope with the disease. By moving outside of one's traditional support network and using weak tie networks, such as support groups for people who have cancer, a person with cancer can obtain more information about the disease from someone who also has it and who is likely to share similar feelings about it. By interacting with multiple individuals with cancer in a support group, assessments about how one is coping with the disease compared to others can be made, and this process can help reduce uncertainty. For instance, individuals who are in earlier stages of cancer can interact with others who are in the later stages and learn about possible trajectories of the disease, and/or glean first-hand information about the efficacy of treatment options. Other aspects of support groups for people facing health concerns are discussed later in this chapter.

Communicating about illness in weak tie vs. close tie networks

Close tie support networks are sometimes perceived to be inadequate in providing satisfactory support for a variety of reasons, and this notion may influence a person's decision to use weak tie support networks as an alternative. Life-threatening illnesses are difficult topics for most people to discuss, especially when they affect a close relative or friend. In terms of talking about cancer, researchers have found that family members and friends often minimize the concerns of people with cancer, avoid interacting with them, and/or steer conversational topics away from emotional talk about the disease or refrain from any discussion of cancer (Dakof & Taylor, 1990; Helgeson, Cohen, Shultz, & Yasko, 2000; Wortman & Dunkel-Schetter, 1979).

By comparison, certain members of weak tie networks may be more willing to talk about illness since these individuals tend to be less emotionally attached to a person (Adelman et al., 1987). Weak tie network members are often able to provide more objective feedback about a problem since they are less emotionally attached to a person with cancer than family and friends. According to La Gaipa (1990), "confidants are not likely to provide an accurate reflection of what a person is worth. Rather, one must turn to less intimate friends for more accurate feedback" (p. 126). People with whom we have close relationships, in an effort to spare our feelings when talking about a health problem, may be more likely to "sugar coat" the advice they give us or not be completely honest when discussing how they feel about our illness.

In addition, studies have found that role obligations in close ties and reciprocity issues can lead to problems with the provision of social support. Support for a loved one who is ill in close ties can lead to increased conflict or negative feelings towards the person due to role obligations (Albrecht & Goldsmith, 2003; Chesler & Barbarin, 1984; La Gaipa, 1990; Pitula & Daugherty, 1995), despite the fact that people may care deeply for the person. According to La Gaipa (1990), "social obligations may override the positive effect of companionship and social support. Such constraints can have a negative effect on mental well-being that may not make up for the beneficial aspects of personal relationships" (p. 126).

The Role of Communication in the Social Support Process

Communication has been identified as a key component of social support (Albrecht & Goldsmith, 2003; Albrecht et al., 1994), and it has been found to be important in helping individuals manage psychosocial stressors associated with a variety of illnesses and other health conditions (Walsh-Burke, 1992). Communication researchers have focused much of their attention on characteristics of supportive messages, perceptions of support providers and recipients, and appraisals of supportive behaviors (Adelman et al., 1987; Albrecht & Goldsmith, 2003; Barnes & Duck, 1994).

Brant Burleson is a communication researcher who has extensively studied supportive communication, specifically characteristics of supportive messages that are exchanged between people during times of stress. Burleson (1990, 1994) argues that individuals vary in their ability to effectively communicate comforting messages to people experiencing stressful situations. In terms of providing support, Burleson (1990) contends that "since the helpee is already in a distressed state, failure of a relational partner to provide support (or the right kind of support) may exacerbate the stressful situation" (p. 67).

Comforting messages, or those messages that are intended to alleviate or lessen the emotional distress experienced by others (Burleson, 1990), require a certain degree of cognitive complexity and skill to accomplish. Burleson contends that individuals often differ in the *cognitive complexity* required to produce appropriate comforting messages. Cognitive complexity refers to a person's ability to differentiate between different aspects of a concept or situation and to use information in complicated and intricate ways (Crockett, 1965). For example, individuals with low cognitive complexity may see a person or a situation as either good or bad, whereas someone with higher cognitive complexity may be able to see both good and bad aspects.

Cognitive complexity is influenced by a number of factors, including intelligence and life experience. During the process of communication, cognitive complexity is linked to a person's ability to construct messages. In general, people with lower levels of cognitive complexity tend to construct relatively simplistic messages, while people with higher levels of cognitive complexity are able to construct more complex messages. For example, in terms of comforting messages, individuals with higher levels of cognitive complexity are often more sensitive to the self-esteem needs of others and are often able to produce supportive messages that are perceived as more helpful by the support recipient (Burleson, 1990).

Comforting messages generally tend to be viewed as more effective when they exhibit concern for the support recipient and legitimize his or her feelings, perspective, and situation. In addition, Burleson (1990) argues that sophisticated comforting messages, "compared to less sophisticated messages, project a greater degree of involvement with the distressed other, are more neutral evaluatively, are more feeling centered, are more accepting of the other, and contain more cognitively oriented explanations of feelings experienced by the other" (p. 70). In other words, producing satisfying comforting messages when attempting to support a person in his or her time of need is a relatively complex behavior, and many individuals may not possess the necessary skills to comfort others adequately. Studies have shown that more sophisticated comforting messages tend to be evaluated more positively and are perceived as more helpful by distressed individuals (see review by Goldsmith, 2004). Moreover, the physical and psychological experience of many health conditions is not easy for people who have not experienced them to understand or identify with. This may make it difficult for a support provider who has little or no experience of the health condition to identify effectively with the person facing the condition, and it could affect his or her ability to produce satisfying comforting messages. As you can see, although supporting others seems to be a relatively straightforward process and a common part of life, the ability to do so effectively can be a complex process and can be challenging for many people.

Interactive nature of support provision

Helping individuals to effectively cope with the many stresses of illness is also complicated by the perception the support provider has of the support recipient and his or her situation. The provision of support is transactional in nature, which means that both the support provider and recipient mutually influence each other's behaviors through communication. Barbee (1990) argues that support providers' perceptions of the person in need of support can influence the type of support they provide. For example, according to Barbee (1990), a support provider may attempt to (1) *solve the person's problem*, such as offering some type of assistance or resource; (2) *support the person emotionally*, by listening empathetically or affirming his or her abilities to cope; (3) *dismiss the person's problem*, such as telling the person not to worry so much; or (4) *escape from dealing with the issue*, which would include behaviors such as changing the subject, ignoring the person, or leaving.

If a support provider perceives that she has the skills to help the individual with a problem, then she may attempt to solve it. In other cases, a provider may feel that she can only support the person emotionally. When the provider feels that the distressed person is worrying too much about a problem or if the problem is seen as controllable, then the provider may dismiss it. Finally, in situations where the problem or the distressed person's reaction to it are seen as too overwhelming or complex for the support provider, she may choose an escape strategy.

Support Groups for People with Health Concerns

Do you know someone who is a member of Alcoholics Anonymous or a similar type of 12-Step group? If not, it is likely that you have at least seen slogans from 12-Step groups, such as "One Day at a Time" or "Easy Does It." Support groups for people coping with a variety of illnesses have become a popular source of health information and comfort for over 25 million US Americans (Kessler, Mickelson, & Zhao, 1997), and they are the most common way that individuals in the United States attempt to change health behaviors (Davison, Pennebaker, & Dickerson, 2000). Support groups have a long history in the United States, arising from a variety of grassroots efforts in which people bypass professional healthcare institutions and structures to form communities based on their collective experience of facing similar illnesses and medical conditions (Katz, 1993; Katz & Bender, 1976; Yalom, 1995). These and other healthcare practices (e.g., residential care facilities) have added an important alternative voice to the traditional authorities (e.g., hospitals) that have defined healthcare (see Adelman & Frey, 1997).

Currently, there are support groups for almost every conceivable physical or mental health condition. Most support groups follow the structure of early types of support groups, such as Alcoholics Anonymous, but they often differ in terms of their affiliation, structure, and focus. Some support groups are affiliated with hospitals and other healthcare facilities. Other support groups, such as those found on the Internet, operate independently of any healthcare organization. Support groups are also distinguished by whether they are facilitated by health professionals (typically, a counselor or an oncology nurse) or are self-led (often with informal or no leadership) (Cline, 1999). In addition, such groups differ in the type of support they offer members, with some groups focusing primarily on providing information about cancer (e.g., educating people about the nature of the disease, helping them to cope with lifestyle changes, and suggesting treatment options), some groups primarily providing peer-based emotional support, and some offering both informational and emotional support.

Reasons why people join support groups

Although many people who have been diagnosed with an illness or who are dealing with other health concerns never feel the need to join a support group, many other individuals experience difficulties with the social implications of having a health condition or illness and in communicating with others about it. In particular, some individuals with an illness appear to be drawn to support groups because of problems they experience with traditional support providers (e.g., physicians, family members, and close friends) in their existing social network who do not always behave in supportive ways when dealing with the issue of illness.

Inadequate support is not just a social problem for people facing illness; it has been linked to negative health outcomes, such as suppressed immune systems, prolonged recovery time, disease vulnerability, and increased stress (Cohen & Wills, 1985; DiMatteo & Hays, 1981). Conversely, satisfaction with one's support network has been found to be associated with positive health outcomes, including reduced stress and better adjustment to living with a disease (Lepore, Allen, & Evans, 1993; Wills, 1985). Such effects are important because successful adjustment to an illness has been associated with longer survival times (Jones & Reznikoff, 1989), improved psychological well-being and sense of control (Fritz, Williams, & Amylon, 1988; Sullivan & Reardon, 1985), and improved ability to cope with the experience of pain (Spiegel & Bloom, 1983).

Difficulties communicating about illness within traditional social networks

As we have seen, many diseases and medical conditions have been found to carry a social stigma in the United States, as they do in many other cultures (Goffman, 1963; Mathieson, Logan-Smith, Phillips, MacPhee, & Attia, 1996; Sullivan & Reardon, 1985), and this may negatively affect the provision of social support (MacDonald & Anderson, 1984). The stigma associated with various health conditions and the social implications of being diagnosed with them can lead people to struggle with their identity. This identity crisis is exacerbated because illness may limit people's ability to perform various taken-for-granted roles they engage in on a daily basis (e.g., work and family roles), and the strain of these changes in roles contributes to feelings of being socially and emotionally isolated (Bloom & Spiegel, 1984). For example, Spiegel (1992) found that discussion of cancer often arouses relational partners' fears, which may lead to avoidance of the person with cancer or a lack of discussion of cancer-related topics when interacting with him or her. Such responses can contribute to the person with cancer feeling alienated and isolated, feelings that can create even greater psychological stress, which in turn can exacerbate the person's physical health problems (Cohen & Wills, 1985; DiMatteo & Hays, 1981).

People may feel socially isolated due to embarrassing aspects of disease symptoms and treatment. Weber, Roberts, and McDougall (2000) argued that "the diagnosis and treatment for prostate cancer may cause incontinence and sexual dysfunction, [and] men often feel embarrassment and shame" (p. 251). As another example, Bloom (1982) contended that mastectomy as a treatment for breast cancer often undermines a woman's sense of her attractiveness and that this can lead to both embarrassment and mutual withdrawal from relationships with significant others. A woman who has had a mastectomy may be hesitant to engage in intimate communication with her spouse; in turn, he "perceives her withdrawal as rejection and responds by further withdrawal" (Bloom, 1982, p. 1330). This mutual withdrawal can lead a woman with breast cancer to feel isolated and disconnected from a vitally important potential source of social support.

In addition, the difficulties of caring for a person with an illness can also damage relationships within an individual's primary support network due to factors such as stress and burnout (Chesler & Barbarin, 1984; Helgeson & Gottlieb, 2000), and this may foster a greater sense of isolation for the individual facing the illness. Researchers have suggested that simply expressing their needs can be problematic for people facing illness because this may lead to a secondary stigma of feeling inadequate, nonactive, and/or weak (Chesler & Barbarin, 1984; DiMatteo & Hays, 1981). Such isolation and alienation from traditional sources of support may help to make peer support groups attractive for people with health problems. According to Davison et al. (2000), "Alienation from one's usual support network may be precisely the kind of social anxiety that in turn increases the value of the mutual support context" (p. 213). These researchers found that the amount of support that health–related support group participants sought was highly associated with their feelings of embarrassment due to the social stigma assigned to their disease or condition.

Illness can be a difficult topic to discuss because it may make people think about their mortality, lead to the expression of strong, often uncontrollable, emotional feelings (e.g., crying), and create general discomfort because people may not have the skills to communicate about sensitive topics such as illness. Because of these and other difficulties, members of the traditional support network of a person with an illness may not encourage him or her to express negative emotions about the illness, either because they feel that it is unhealthy or because it makes them feel uncomfortable. They may minimize the concerns of the person, avoid interacting with him or her, and/or steer conversational topics away from emotional talk about the disease or from discussion of it altogether (Dakof & Taylor, 1990; Helgeson et al., 2000; Sullivan & Reardon, 1985; Wortman & Dunkel-Schetter, 1979).

Other factors influencing support group participation

All of these issues may increase a person's decision to join a support group when facing a health problem. Of course, other variables, such as people's perceptions of these groups in general, whether or not they perceive them as helpful, and the availability of these groups, may influence whether or not they join them. Other factors, such as gender, race, and social status, are also important in determining whether or not people join support groups in our culture. Support group members tend to be white, middle class, well educated (compared to the national average), and female (Kessler et al., 1997). However, given that most support groups try to protect the anonymity of their members, it has been difficult for researchers to obtain data about the demographics of individuals who use them.

Communication Processes within Support Groups

Support researchers have identified a number of communicative features of support groups that appear to influence health outcomes. This section examines a variety of communication processes that occur in support groups and their possible health benefits to members.

Use of narrative

Support groups encourage participation among members through group norms of "telling one's story" to the group on a voluntary basis (Arntson & Droge, 1987; Cline, 1999; Yalom, 1995). This process usually begins with a member providing a brief history of his experience with the disease or illness and then discussing current issues and feelings with which he is dealing (Helgeson & Gottlieb, 2000). Rappaport (1993) contends that members of self-help groups use narratives like this as a means of forming a social identity. People with a variety of diseases and conditions often experience feelings of isolation, and support groups provide an environment where these individuals feel they share a common identity with the other members. Support group members learn to identify with other members' experiences and feelings about the illness through the sharing of narratives, and this appears both to validate their own experiences and feelings and to lessen their sense of isolation (Mok & Martinson, 2000; Wright & Bell, 2003). According to Davison et al. (2000), "The stories told and heard in this context carry the weight of shared experience, the emotional potency of common suffering, and an avenue for social learning" (p. 206).

In addition to identifying with other members' experiences and feelings, newer members of support groups often find experienced members' stories particularly credible (Wright, 1997). Moreover, the experiences of other health-related support group members is often perceived as more credible than information obtained from other people, even healthcare professionals, especially information about the psychosocial aspects of their disease, due to the fact that other support group members are actually living with the disease on a daily basis.

Arntson and Droge (1987) point to some specific functions served by the sharing of narratives within support groups that may benefit both the narrator and those who listen to his or her story. For example, because narratives typically place events within a sequence, they "organize the relevant symbols in one's environment, making it possible to gain meaning from the past, give meaning to the present, and reduce uncertainty about the future" (p. 161).

Such meaning may help people coping with illness to perceive health-related events as less unpredictable, which may strengthen their sense of control over their situation. Moreover, listening to stories told in support groups is a way to receive advice nondidactically, and individuals are free to follow or disregard it (Arntson & Droge, 1987; Wright, 2000). For example, a narrator might disclose through a story that a certain type of medication was helpful in alleviating nausea during chemotherapy, without actually telling others that they should take the medication themselves.

Being helped by helping

Helping others is usually part of a support group's ideology that is reinforced during group interaction (Antze, 1976; Frank & Frank, 1991; Wright, 1997). Support groups typically consist of individuals who vary in terms of the amount of time they have been members of the group, and members who have participated for longer periods of time are in a better position to proactively help others. They can be especially influential in providing new members with opportunities to learn vicariously about the illness, helping them to understand how to cope with physical, psychological, and social issues associated with the disease, offering them emotional support, and sharing information with them about treatment options (Wright, 2002).

Although newer members certainly receive a great deal of support from more experienced members, support groups are not a one-way street as regards helping behaviors: the act of helping others appears to have psychological benefits as well. Support groups thus encourage members who have been with the group for a longer period of time to share their experiences with newer members through the idea that helping others is important to one's own recovery. Helping others has been found to increase helpers' sense of self-worth and value and, simultaneously, to reduce their feelings of powerlessness (Spiegel, Bloom, & Yalom, 1981; Yalom, 1995). According to Spiegel et al. (1981), "Patients who feel helpless and demoralized learn that they can be enormously useful to others" (p. 528). Moreover, Rosenberg (1984) states: "members feel that by improving their own competence in handling the situation they are also improving the competence of other group members and perhaps the social conditions of the group as a whole" (p. 175).

Support group members often reap benefits by helping others within the support group. This phenomenon has been named "the helper principle" (Riessman, 1965). According to Cline (1999), the helper principle "encompasses a complex process of cognitive reframing during which rookie helpers become veterans" (p. 524). New support group members go through a socialization process in which they learn that helping others is an important part of the process of coping with the disease. Cline (1999) contends that "as members make the transition from helpee to helper, retelling their stories validates their experiences and reminds them, as well as other members, of their progress" (p. 524). This transformation from helpee to helper also appears to help support group members gain a sense of personal control when discussing their illness (Arntson & Droge, 1987; Cline, 1999). In addition, the mentor role helps to reinforce positive attitudes, beliefs, and behaviors about the particular health issue for support group members.

Summary

The social support we receive from others is important to our physical and mental health. However, our perceptions of whether or not the support we receive is appropriate, our coping styles, and our personal and social resources mediate the relationship between social support and health outcomes. Many individuals are able to obtain sufficient support from the members of their primary social network. Other people find it difficult to receive adequate support from family members and friends, and they may opt to seek support from weak ties, including members of support groups. Support groups offer many advantages to people who are facing health concerns. The ability to find a concentrated setting where people share similar problems and feelings and the opportunity to help others are major advantages of support groups for people facing health issues.

References

Adelman, M. B., & Frey, L. R. (1997). *The fragile community: Living together with AIDS.* Mahwah, NJ: Lawrence Erlbaum.

Adelman, M. B., Parks, M. R., & Albrecht, T. L. (1987). Beyond close relationships: Support in weak ties. In T. L. Albrecht & M. B. Adelman (Eds.), *Communicating social support* (pp. 126–147). Newbury Park, CA: Sage.

Albrecht, T. L., & Goldsmith, D. J. (2003). Social support, social networks, and health. In T. L. Thompson, A. M. Dorsey, K. I. Miller, & R. Parrott (Eds.), *Handbook of health communication* (pp. 263–284). Mahwah, NJ: Lawrence Erlbaum.

Albrecht, T. L., Burleson, B. R., & Goldsmith, D. (1994). Supportive communication. In M. L. Knapp & G. R. Miller (Eds.), *Handbook of interpersonal communication* (2nd ed., pp. 419–449). Newbury Park, CA: Sage.

Andrews, S. C. (2001). Caregiver burden and symptom distress in people with cancer receiving hospice care. *Oncology Nursing Forum, 28,* 1469–1474.

Aneshensel, C. S., & Stone, J. D. (1982). Stress and depression: A test of the buffering model of social support. *Archives of General Psychiatry, 39,* 1392–1396.

Antze, P. (1976). The role of ideologies in peer psychotherapy organizations: Some theoretical considerations and three case studies. *Journal of Applied Behavioral Science, 12,* 323–346.

Arntson, P., & Droge, D. (1987). Social support in self-help groups: The role of communication in enabling perceptions of control. In T. L. Albrecht, M. B. Adelman, & Associates (Eds.), *Communicating social support* (pp. 148–171). Newbury Park, CA: Sage.

Babrow, A. S. (2001). Uncertainty, value, communication, and problematic integration. *Journal of Communication, 51,* 553–573.

Bakas, T., Lewis, R. R., & Parsons, J. (2001). Caregiving tasks among family caregivers of patients with lung cancer. *Oncology Nursing Forum, 28*, 847–854.

Ballieux, R. E., & Heijen, C. J. (1989). Stress and the immune response. In H. Weiner, I. Floring, R. Murison, & D. Hellhammer (Eds.), *Frontiers of stress research* (pp. 51–55). Toronto: Huber.

Barbee, A. P. (1990). Interactive coping: The cheering-up process in close relationships. In S. Duck & R. Silver (Eds.), *Personal relationships and social support* (pp. 46–65). Newbury Park, CA: Sage.

Barnes, M. K., & Duck, S. (1994). Everyday communicative contexts for social support. In B. R. Burleson, T. L. Albrecht, & I. G. Sarason (Eds.), *Communication of social support: Messages, interactions, relationships, and community* (pp. 175–194). Thousand Oaks, CA: Sage.

Berkman, L. F., & Syme, L. S. (1979). Social networks, host resistance, and mortality: A nine-year follow-up study of Alameda County residents. *Journal of Epidemiology, 109*, 186–204.

Billings, A. G., & Moos, R. H. (1981). The role of coping responses and social resources in attenuating the impact of stressful life events. *Journal of Behavioral Medicine, 4*, 139–157.

Bloom, J. R. (1982). Social support, accommodation to stress and adjustment to breast cancer. *Social Science Medicine, 16*, 1329–1338.

Bloom, J. R., & Spiegel, D. (1984). The relationship of two dimensions of social support to the psychological well-being and social functioning of women with advanced breast cancer. *Social Science Medicine, 19*, 831–837.

Brashers, D. E., Neidig, J. L., & Goldsmith, D. J. (2004). Social support and the management of people living with HIV or AIDS. *Health Communication, 16*, 305–331.

Burleson, B. R. (1990). Comforting as social support: Relational consequences of supportive behaviors. In S. Duck & R. C. Silver (Eds.), *Personal relationships and social support* (pp. 66–82). Newbury Park, CA: Sage.

Burleson, B. R. (1994). Comforting messages: Significance, approaches, and effects. In B. R. Burleson, T. L. Albrecht, & I. G. Sarason (Eds.), *Communication of social support: Messages, interactions, relationships, and community*. Newbury Park, CA: Sage.

Chesler, M. A., & Barbarin, O. A. (1984). Difficulties of providing help in a crisis: Relationships between parents of children with cancer and their friends. *Journal of Social Issues, 40*, 113–134.

Cline, R. J. (1999). Communication within social support groups. In L. R. Frey (Ed.), D. S. Gouran, & M. S. Poole (Assoc. Eds.), *The handbook of group communication theory and research* (pp. 516–538). Thousand Oaks, CA: Sage.

Clow, C. (2001). The physiology of stress. In F. Jones & J. Bright (Eds.), *Stress: Myth, theory, and research* (pp. 47–61). Harlow: Prentice-Hall.

Cobb, S. (1976). Social support as a moderator of life stresses. *Psychosomatic Medicine, 38*, 300–314.

Cohen, S. (1988). Psychosocial models of the role of support in the etiology of physical disease. *Health Psychology, 7*, 269–297.

Cohen, S., & Wills, T. A. (1985). Stress, social support, and the buffering hypothesis. *Psychological Bulletin, 98*, 310–357.

Crockett, W. H. (1965). Cognitive complexity and impression formation. In B. A. Maher (Ed.), *Progress in experimental personality research* (Vol. 2, pp. 47–90). New York: Academic Press.

Cwikel, J. M., & Isreal, B. A. (1987). Examining mechanisms of social support and social networks: A review of health-related intervention studies. *Public Health Review, 15*, 159–193.

Dainton, M., & Zelly, E. D. (2006). Social exchange theories: Interdependence and equity. In D. O. Braithwaite & L. A. Baxter (Eds.), *Engaging theories in family communication: Multiple perspectives* (pp. 243–259). Thousand Oaks, CA: Sage.

Dakof, G. A., & Taylor, S. E. (1990). Victim's perceptions of social support: What is helpful from whom? *Journal of Personality and Social Psychology, 58*, 80–89.

Davison, K. P., Pennebaker, J. W., & Dickerson, S. S. (2000). Who talks? The social psychology of illness support groups. *American Psychologist, 55*, 205–217.

Dean, A., & Lin, N. (1977). The stress buffering role of social support: Problems and prospects for systematic investigation. *Journal of Health and Social Behavior, 32*, 321–341.

Deutsch, M. (1985). *Distributive justice: A social psychological perspective*. New Haven, CT: Yale University Press.

DiMatteo, M., & Hays, R. (1981). Social support and serious illness. In B. Gottlieb (Ed.), *Social networks and social support* (pp. 117–148). Beverly Hills, CA: Sage.

Edwards, H., & Noller, P. (1998). Factors influencing caregiver–care receiver communication and the impact on the well-being of older care receivers. *Health Communication, 10*, 317–342.

Edwards, J. M., & Trimble, K. (1992). Anxiety, coping, and academic performance. *Anxiety, Stress, and Coping, 5*, 337–350.

Endler, N. S., & Parker, J. D. A. (1990). Multidimensional assessment of coping: A critical evaluation. *Journal of Personality and Social Psychology, 58*, 844–854.

Festinger, L. (1954). A theory of social comparison processes. *Human Relations, 2*, 117–140.

Frank, J. D., & Frank, J. B. (1991). *Persuasion and healing*. Baltimore: Johns Hopkins University Press.

Fritz, G. K., Williams, J. R., & Amylon, M. (1988). After treatment ends: Psychosocial sequelae in pediatric cancer survivors. *American Journal of Orthopsychiatry, 54*, 552–561.

Goffman, E. (1963). *Stigma: Notes on the management of spoiled identity*. Englewood Cliffs, NJ: Prentice-Hall.

Goldsmith, D. J. (2004). *Communicating social support*. Cambridge: Cambridge University Press.

Goldsmith, D. J., & Fitch, K. (1997). The normative context of advice as social support. *Human Communication Research, 23*, 454–476.

Grainger, K. (1995). Communication and the institutionalized elderly. In J. F. Nussbaum & J. Coupland (Eds.), *Handbook of communication and aging research* (pp. 417–436). Mahwah, NJ: Lawrence Erlbaum.

Granovetter, M. S. (1973). The strength of weak ties. *American Journal of Sociology, 78,* 1360–1380.

Heady, B. W., & Wearing, A. J. (1990). Subjective well-being and coping with adversity. *Social Indicators Research, 22,* 327–349.

Helgeson, V. S., & Gottlieb, B. H. (2000). Support groups. In S. Cohen, L. G. Underwood, & B. H. Gottlieb (Eds.), *Social support measurement and intervention* (pp. 221–245). New York: Oxford University Press.

Helgeson, V. S., Cohen, S., Schultz, R., & Yasko, J. (2000). Group support interventions for women with breast cancer: Who benefits from what? *Health Psychology, 19,* 107–114.

Hughes, H. (2005). Work stress differentials between psychiatric and general nurses. *British Journal of Nursing, 14,* 802–808.

Jones, D. N., & Reznikoff, M. (1989). Psychosocial adjustment to a mastectomy. *Journal of Nervous and Mental Disease, 177,* 624–631.

Katz, A. H. (1993). *Self-help in America: A social movement perspective.* New York: Twayne.

Katz, A. H., & Bender, E. I. (1976). Self-help groups in Western society: History and prospects. *Journal of Applied Behavioral Science, 12,* 265–282.

Kessler, R. C., Mickelson, K. D., & Zhao, S. (1997). Patterns and correlates of self-help group membership in the United States. *Social Policy, 27,* 27–46.

Kohn, P. M. (1996). On coping adaptively with daily hassles. In M. Zeidner & N. S. Endler (Eds.), *Handbook of coping* (pp. 181–201). New York: John Wiley & Sons.

Krause, N. (1990). Stress, support, and well-being in later life: Focusing on salient social roles. In M. A. Stephens, J. H. Crowther, S. E. Hobfoll, & D. L. Tennenbaum (Eds.), *Stress and coping in later-life families* (pp. 71–97). New York: Hemisphere.

La Gaipa, J. J. (1990). The negative effects of informal support systems. In S. Duck & R. C. Silver (Eds.), *Personal relationships and social support* (pp. 122–139). Newbury Park, CA: Sage.

Laizner, A. M., Yost, L. M., Barg, F. K., & McCorkle, R. (1993). Needs of family caregivers of persons with cancer: A review. *Seminars in Oncology Nursing, 9,* 114–120.

LaRocca, J., House, J., & French, J. R. (1980). Social support, occupational health, and stress. *Journal of Health and Social Behavior, 21,* 201–218.

Lepore, S. J., Allen, K. A. M., & Evans, G. W. (1993). Social support lowers cardiovascular reactivity to an acute stressor. *Psychosomatic Medicine, 55,* 518–524.

MacDonald, L. D., & Anderson, H. R. (1984). Stigma in patients with rectal cancer: A community study. *Journal of Epidemiology and Community Health, 38,* 284–290.

Magen, R. H., & Glajchen, M. (1999). Cancer support groups: Client outcome and the context of group process. *Research on Social Group Practice, 9,* 541–554.

Mathieson, C. M., Logan-Smith, L. L., Phillips, J., MacPhee, M., & Attia, M. L. (1996). Caring for head and neck oncology patients: Does social support lead to better quality of life? *Canadian Family Physician, 42,* 1712–1720.

Mok, B. H. (2001). Cancer self-help groups in China: A study of individual change, perceived benefit, and community impact. *Small Group Research, 32,* 115–132.

Mok, E., & Martinson, I. (2000). Empowerment of Chinese patients with cancer through self-help groups in Hong Kong. *Cancer Nursing, 23,* 206–213.

Pierce, G. R., Sarason, I. G., & Sarason, B. R. (1996). Coping and social support. In M. Zeidner & N. S. Endler (Eds.), *Handbook of coping* (pp. 434–451). New York: John Wiley & Sons.

Pitula, C. R., & Daugherty, S. R. (1995). Sources of social support and conflict in hospitalized depressed women. *Nursing and Health, 18,* 325–332.

Rappaport, J. (1993). Narrative studies, personal stories, and identity transformation in the mutual help context. *Journal of Applied Behavioral Science, 29,* 239–256.

Riessman, F. (1965). The "helper" therapy principle. *Social Work, 10,* 27–32.

Rosenberg, P. P. (1984). Support groups: A special therapeutic entity. *Small Group Behavior, 15,* 173–186.

Roter, D., & Hall, J. A. (1992). Improving talk through interventions. *Doctors talking with patients/patients talking with doctors: Improving communication in medical visits.* Westport, CT: Auburn House.

Sarason, B. R., Sarason, I. G., & Pierce, G. R. (1990). *Social support: An interactional view.* New York: Wiley.

Sarna, L., & McCorkle, R. (1996). Burden of care and lung cancer. *Cancer Practice, 4,* 245–251.

Schimmel, S. R. (1999). *Cancer talk: Voices of hope and endurance from "The Group Room," the world's largest cancer support group.* New York: Broadway Books.

Spiegel, D. (1992). Effects of psychosocial support on patients with metastatic breast cancer. *Journal of Psychosocial Oncology, 10,* 113–121.

Spiegel, D., & Bloom, J. R. (1983). Pain in metastatic breast cancer. *Cancer, 52,* 149–153.

Spiegel, D., Bloom, J. R., & Yalom, I. (1981). Group support for patients with metastatic cancer: A randomized prospective outcome study. *Archives of General Psychiatry, 38,* 527–533.

Sullivan, C. F., & Reardon, K. K. (1985). Social support satisfaction and health locus of control: Discriminators of breast cancer patients' style of coping. In M. L. McLaughlin (Ed.), *Communication yearbook* (Vol. 9, pp. 707–722). Beverly Hills, CA: Sage.

Thoits, P. (1982). Conceptual, methodological, and theoretical problems in studying social support as a buffer against life stress. *Journal of Health and Social Behavior, 23,* 145–159.

Turner, R. A., King, P. R., & Tremblay, P. F. (1992). Coping styles and depression among psychiatric outpatients. *Personality and Individual Differences, 13,* 1145–1147.

Uchino, B. N., Cacioppo, J. T., & Kiecolt-Glaser, J. K. (1996). The relationship between social support and physiological processes: A review with emphasis on underlying mechanisms and implications for health. *Psychological Bulletin, 119,* 488–531.

Walsh-Burke, K. (1992). Family communication and coping with cancer. Impact of the We Can Weekend. *Journal of Psychosocial Oncology, 10,* 63–81.

Weber, B. A., Roberts, B. L., & McDougall, G. J. (2000). Exploring the efficacy of support groups of men with prostate cancer. *Geriatric Nursing, 41,* 250–253.

Wills, T. A. (1985). Supportive functions of interpersonal relationships. In S. Cohen & S. L. Syme (Eds.), *Social support and health* (pp. 61–82). New York: Academic Press.

Wortman, C., & Dunkel-Schetter, C. (1979). Interpersonal relationships and cancer. *Journal of Social Issues, 35,* 120–155.

Wright, K. B. (1997). Shared ideology in Alcoholics Anonymous: A grounded theory approach. *Journal of Health Communication, 2,* 83–99.

Wright, K. B. (2000). The communication of social support within an on-line community for older adults: A qualitative analysis of the SeniorNet community. *Qualitative Research Reports in Communication, 1,* 33–43.

Wright, K. B. (2002). Social support within an on-line cancer community: An assessment of emotional support, perceptions of advantages and disadvantages, and motives for using the community from a communication perspective. *Journal of Applied Communication Research, 30,* 195–209.

Wright, K. B., & Bell, S. B. (2003). Health-related support groups on the Internet: Linking empirical findings to social support and computer-mediated communication theory. *Journal of Health Psychology, 8,* 37–52.

Yalom, I. (1995). *The theory and practice of group psychotherapy.* New York: Basic Books.

Chapter 5

Culture and Diversity Issues in Healthcare

[Culture refers to the] shared beliefs, values, and practices of a group of people. A group's culture includes the language or languages used by group members as well as the norms and rules about how behavior can appropriately be displayed and how it should be understood.

(O'Hair, Friedrich, Wiemann, & Wiemann, 2002, p. 9)

Culture permeates all aspects of life and it influences our perceptions and experiences of life events, including health-related situations. Conceptions of health and illness as well as ways to treat illness vary from culture to culture within the United States and around the world. As more and more people from different cultures have immigrated to the United States in recent years, there is greater diversity among patients than ever before. Providers can no longer approach healthcare from a single cultural perspective and be effective in treating patients from other cultures in a competent manner. As we will explore in this chapter, culture conceptions of illness and health can be radically different as people from different cultures come together in healthcare settings. Ignoring cultural differences in conceptions of illness and health can lead to a variety of problems between providers and patients, including culturally inappropriate medical decision-making, increased anxiety, fear, and anger, and patient dissatisfaction with overall healthcare.

In addition to the greater use of translators, many healthcare organizations are now implementing intercultural communication training programs. Cultural diversity has become more and more important in healthcare settings among providers. While healthcare settings have traditionally excluded women and minorities, healthcare provider diversity has increased in recent years. In addition, providers exhibit a great deal of professional diversity due to differences in training and expertise. In recent years, healthcare organizations have attempted to capitalize on the strength of diverse provider perspectives to help solve complex patient health issues through interdisciplinary healthcare teams.

This chapter will explore these issues and a variety of other communication concerns related to culture and diversity within health settings. Specifically, it will examine a variety of topics related to diversity and culture in healthcare, including patient diversity in the US healthcare system, cultural differences in concepts of health and medicine, the need to recognize cultural diversity in healthcare, alternative medicine, social implications of disease, spirituality and health, provider diversity, and interdisciplinary healthcare teams.

Patient Diversity

The United States is becoming more culturally diverse as a nation. Over 47 million people ·speak a language other than English in the United States (US Census Bureau, 2005). Traditionally, most patients in the US healthcare system have been white. However, in the last decade, the population of white Americans grew at about 3.5 percent while other racial and ethnic groups increased by over 43 percent (Ndiwane, Miller, Bonner et al., 2004). By 2030, the population of many minority groups in the US is expected to increase while the population of white Americans is expected to decrease by 10 percent. This presents a number of challenges to healthcare providers, who lack important knowledge about the groups and how to effectively communicate with them (Ndiwane et al., 2004). Currently, people of Mexican origin are the largest minority group in the United States, followed by people from various Asian countries and Central America (US Census Bureau, 2005). In addition, various co-cultures within the US differ in terms of level of education, income, and housing status, all of which impact perceptions of health and access to healthcare services. There are many different problems related to patient diversity that affect quality healthcare and provider–patient communication. For example, many minority groups and recent immigrants often lack access to adequate healthcare or cannot afford these services. Members of many ethnic groups mistrust the healthcare system for a variety of reasons, including historical injustices such as the mistreatment of Native Americans and African Americans (Ferguson et al., 1998) and the preponderance of Caucasian providers. A number of patients have trouble understanding the English language, and language barriers can lead to many problems such as misunderstandings between providers and patients, misdiagnoses, inappropriate treatments, and poor adherence to suggested treatments for medical problems (Hornberger, Itakura, & Wilson, 1997; Johnson, Roter, Powe, & Cooper, 2004; Rivadeneyra, Elderkin-Thompson, Silver, & Waitzkin, 2000). In addition to language barriers, many immigrants are unfamiliar with the US healthcare system. Given the complexities of managed care, referrals, medical terminology, and many other aspects of the healthcare system, even for people who grew up with it, you can easily understand how an immigrant might find healthcare in the US confusing and intimidating.

Cultural Differences in Concepts of Health and Medicine

Our understanding of the world and our experiences of illness and health are heavily influenced by our day-to-day communication with others. Some communication scholars have argued that people *create* reality through communication (Gergen, 1999; Pearce, 1995). This is not to say that physical reality is created through communication, but rather that our understanding of reality evolves from interaction with others and is based on and informed by previous interactions. In terms of health, when individuals discuss their conceptions of illness and health again and again, they learn about these concepts through repeated interaction. People who are socialized within a particular culture come to understand illness and health through repeated interactions with others. All cultures have beliefs about illness and health that are passed down from generation to generation (Galanti, 1991; Lupton, 1994).

Perspectives of health and illness in western society are largely dominated by the biomedical model of health. Biomedicine refers to medical practices and beliefs derived from the western scientific tradition, including germ theory, biology, biochemistry, and biophysics, and it is focused primarily on establishing physical causes for illness (Gillick, 1985; Sharf & Vanderford, 2003). However, the biomedical view of health is just one of many cultural conceptions of health around the world and within the United States (Galanti, 1991; Spector, 1996). *Ethnomedical belief systems* are culturally unique beliefs and knowledge about health and disease (Witte, 1991). In addition, Airhihenbuwa and Obregon (2000) argue that communicating about health risks (such as the risk for HIV/AIDS) in ways that are based upon western cultural assumptions, such as privileging the individual over the group or culture as a whole and linear types of thinking (which have their base in the western scientific tradition), are often inadequate when communicating with people from certain regions and cultures, such as South America, Central America, the Caribbean, and Africa. Unfortunately, many providers lack adequate training in understanding the ethnomedical belief systems of their patients from other countries and co-cultures within the United States. Ignorance or misunderstanding of these different belief systems can lead to a host of communication problems between providers and patients (O'Hair, O'Hair, Southward, & Krayer, 1987).

Cultural differences in attributions of illness/health

Many cultures attribute illness to spiritual forces, and this is in direct conflict with the western biomedical model that attributes disease to microorganisms, such as viruses, or to lifestyle influences. For example, some cultures, such as the Hmong from Southeast Asia, often attribute disease to spiritual forces such as malevolent spirits or ghosts who bring ill health, or to the lack of protective spirits of ancestors (Johnson, 2002). Some cultural groups, such as Mexican immigrants, often exhibit strong cultural tendencies towards fatalism when it comes to health issues (Barron, Hunter, Mayo, & Willoughby, 2004), or the belief that health problems are meant to be or caused by God/supernatural forces. Individuals with fatalistic views of health often feel that they have no control over health problems, and they may perceive little personal ability or responsibility for the success or failure of health outcomes. Therefore, individuals from cultures that promote fatalistic views of health may have a more difficult time adhering to biomedical treatments suggested by healthcare providers or making significant lifestyle changes that influence health risks (Lupton, 1994).

Medical procedures that are commonplace in western culture, such as surgery, blood transfusions, and blood tests, are not part of some cultures around the world (such as the Hmong), and these often provoke fear and mistrust among immigrants (Helman, 2000; Smith, 1997). In terms of medical treatment options, some cultures value biomedical solutions to health problems while others prefer more natural remedies for health problems or spiritual solutions to them. For example, researchers have found that a large number of immigrants from Mexico use herbal medications, massage, and relaxation techniques, which are often suggested by family members or *curanderos*, traditional Mexican folk healers (Hunt, Hamdi, & Arana, 2000; Keegan, 1996).

Acculturation

Immigrants often change their lifestyle in ways that can affect their health when they come to the United States. For example, mainstream US culture often promotes sedentary lifestyles, high fat/high food consumption, smoking, and a variety of other unhealthy behaviors. However, the cultures that many immigrants come from do not promote these lifestyles and diets, and taking on new diets and lifestyles can lead to a variety of health problems. For example, hypertension, diabetes, and substance abuse are becoming more common among immigrants from Southeast Asia and other countries who adopt US mainstream diets and lifestyles (Aldrich & Variyam, 2000; Cobas, Balcazar, Benini, Keith, & Chong, 1996; Popkin & Udry, 1998). Immigrants may find their ability to continue their traditional diet somewhat difficult to maintain, since some of the traditional foods to which they are accustomed may not be available in the US, and children can become "Americanized," so that they take on unhealthy lifestyle habits. Moreover, because immigrants from these countries often attribute disease to spiritual forces, they may not understand the connection between lifestyle behaviors and poor health (Helman, 2000; Johnson, 2002).

Informed consent

In the United States patients have the legal right to be fully informed about their health condition, and many Americans perceive this law as ethical and would insist on having full knowledge of their health situation, especially if they were at risk of dying from cancer or high blood pressure. However, beliefs surrounding the issue of informed consent vary by culture, and informed consent should be delivered to people in culturally sensitive ways (Carrese & Rhodes, 1995; Kakai, 2002). For example, the Hmong involve extended family in important decisions, including medical decisions if a family member becomes ill (Johnson, 2002). Moreover, Hmong culture is patriarchal, and decision-making is typically left to the oldest member of the family and male family members, such as a husband or father (Johnson, 2002).

Providers in the United States often pressure family members to make decisions about treatment options relatively quickly, but this can lead to problems for a Hmong patient if an older family member (such as a grandfather) or a high-status male family member is not nearby, and other family members may be hesitant to make a decision about healthcare treatment for a family member without consulting this person (Johnson, 2002). In Japan, providers historically concealed terminal cancer diagnoses from patients (Kakai, 2002). Although Japanese physicians have adopted a policy of disclosing terminal cancer diagnoses to patients in recent years, and the majority of Japanese say that they prefer to be informed by their physician if they have cancer (Long, 2000), many individuals still prefer indirect or ambiguous communication from a physician if a family member is diagnosed with cancer (Kakai, 2002). This indirect communication about a cancer diagnosis allows family members to be more hopeful about a loved one's recovery as opposed to viewing the diagnosis as a "death sentence." Complicating the issue of informed consent further, medical interpreters are required to interpret information for providers and patients without omitting or changing anything (Dysart-Gale, 2005). This can make it difficult to convey information to patients in a culturally sensitive way, especially if the physician or other provider who is attempting to convey information to the patient through an interpreter has little understanding of the health beliefs of the patient.

Cultural differences of people born in the United States

Cultural differences in health beliefs and influences on health behaviors do not just affect immigrants in the United States. There are many different co-cultures among people who were born in the United States, and these co-cultures can influence health beliefs and health behaviors in a variety of ways. For example, in the southern United States, many people eat foods that are high in calories and fat, such as barbeque, fried okra, and sweet tea (iced tea with large quantities of sugar), because this is often part of traditional Southern cuisine. However, these types of food can have a tremendous impact on health risks, such as obesity, diabetes, high blood pressure, and heart disease, especially if they are not consumed in moderation. Cultural issues implicate certain age groups as well. Older patients have a tendency to prefer a communication style that contains less detail and is jargon free, whereas younger and middle-aged adults expect more medical information in their messages (O'Hair, Behnke, & King, 1983).

Recognizing Cultural Diversity in Health Beliefs

As we have seen, healthcare organizations have witnessed a number of demographic shifts among patients in recent years (Dysart-Gale, 2005). As a result, healthcare workers must learn to communicate effectively with people from other cultures in order to provide competent and quality healthcare (Ulrey & Amason, 2001). In order for healthcare providers to be culturally sensitive, they must have knowledge about the varying cultural beliefs of their patient population, understand and respect the cultural beliefs, attitudes, and values of patients, and be willing to use cultural knowledge when interacting with patients and making decisions about treatment options (Brislin, 1993; Ulrey & Amason, 2001). Providers need to be aware of cultural differences in beliefs about the nature of illness and health as well as the relationship between cultural practices and health.

Learning to communicate more effectively with patients from diverse cultural backgrounds has a number of implications for business-related outcomes within healthcare settings (Voelker, 1995). For instance, as competition between healthcare organizations increases, individual organizations must find ways to attract new patient populations and keep patients satisfied so that they will not go to a competitor to obtain health-related services. Conversely, culturally insensitive or inappropriate communication behaviors on the part of providers can lead to a host of problems, including patient dissatisfaction with healthcare and malpractice lawsuits (Kreps & Thornton, 1992).

A continuing problem in healthcare settings is the assumption that all stakeholders, but particularly patients, share the same perceptions as the host culture. Several studies have offered a view of how Americans perceive themselves and are perceived by others. One such study, conducted by Protocol International, suggested Americans see themselves as efficient, direct, competitive, action-oriented, outgoing, open, and self-reliant. Conversely, people from other cultures saw Americans as abrupt, confrontational, materialistic, pushy, insincere, transparent, and self-centered. Central to competent intercultural communication is having cultural partners who understand the perspective held by each person (Leong & Schneller, 1997). Understanding how healthcare stakeholders view one another is a critical challenge, one that can be overcome with some effort. For instance, American student nurses found that as they learned more about Russian culture, their stereotypes broke down and it was easier for them to understand key cultural aspects that could lead to better healthcare (Heuer, Bengiamin, & Downey, 2001).

Barriers to providing culturally sensitive healthcare

Unfortunately, many barriers to providing culturally sensitive healthcare exist within the current US healthcare system. Many providers do not have adequate knowledge of how changes in lifestyle from one culture to another can affect the health of immigrants. The majority of hospitals and healthcare facilities in the United States today still do not have an adequate number of translators or personnel who understand the ethnomedical belief systems of patients (Schott & Henley, 1996).

Alternative Medicine

Alternative medicines, such as more holistic forms of medicine, have had a long history around the world and in the United States, and many of the practices that are known as western mainstream or orthodox medicine are relatively recent innovations compared to the use of herbal remedies, acupuncture, osteopathy, chiropractics, yoga, massage, guided imagery, and therapeutic touch. Some studies estimate that about 42 percent of the US population, or around 83 million people, have used some form of alternative medicine or holistic therapy within the last year, spending an estimated $27 billion on such therapies (Eisenberg et al., 1998). Studies also suggest that the majority of individuals who use alternative forms of medicine do not mention it to their physicians and other healthcare providers (Dunn & Perry, 1997). Despite the prevalence and use of alternative forms of medicine, many are hesitant to talk about their use of alternative medicine with providers because of the dominance of mainstream biomedical approaches to health in our culture (Goldner, 1998). US healthcare providers are aware of the growth in popularity of alternative medicines among patients, and there is greater interest among providers in talking with patients about the pros and cons of such approaches (Udani, 1998). For instance, there is concern among many physicians over the possible interaction effects that can occur when a patient is simultaneously using prescription medications and over-the-counter treatments (such as herbal remedies) for the same health problem.

As we saw in chapter 1, there is a fundamental tension between the biomedical model of health and psychosocial approaches, a tension which includes different perceptions about the efficacy of mainstream medical approaches as opposed to alternative approaches to treating disease and enhancing health. This tension can be seen in the history of medicine within the United States. For example, advances in the natural sciences and medical technology during the eighteenth and nineteenth centuries led physicians to begin to distinguish biomedical approaches to medicine from alternative forms of medicine (Schreiber, in press). For example, during this time, herbal remedies were popular treatments for a variety of illnesses, although their efficacy is difficult to document since people did not usually keep records of successes and failures. However, also during this time, there were a variety of traveling "medicine shows" that typically used performers to persuade audiences to purchase somewhat dubious remedies for their ailments (which often contained mostly alcohol).

To distance themselves from these sometimes questionable approaches to medicine, and to set themselves apart from other types of medical practitioners, biomedical practitioners began to form societies such as the American Medical Association and write medical books that detailed biomedical approaches. However, the language they used to make these distinctions often privileged the biomedical approach or talked about more holistic approaches to medicine in derogatory and negative terms, for example describing them as unprofessional, lacking standards, or erratic (Schreiber, in press). As a result, many holistic approaches to health that have value in enhancing physical, psychological, and spiritual health came to be seen as unorthodox, suspicious, and ineffective. Today, many people dismiss homeopathic medicine and other approaches as quackery, and alternative medicine often carries a negative social stigma. Even terms like "alternative medicine," "complementary medicine," and "integrative medicine" are not without problems. The word "alternative" carries the connotation of being out of the ordinary, while "complementary" and "integrative" imply that these approaches should be used in conjunction with other, biomedical approaches rather than on their own. Some scholars have argued that these terms help to privilege the biomedical approach to medicine (Schreiber, in press; Wardwell, 1994).

However, holistic medicines may offer some advantages and disadvantages over biomedicine, although what is perceived as an advantage or disadvantage by the patient largely depends on his or her values regarding health, illness, and quality of life. For example, biomedical approaches to a disease such as cancer typically involve the use of chemotherapy, radiology, and surgery. While these procedures offer a number of advantages in terms of destroying cancerous cells and tissue, they also have a great number of side effects. For instance, people who are on chemotherapy often experience fatigue, nausea, hair loss, and a variety of other problems. While one of the authors was conducting research at a cancer center in Memphis, Tennessee, one patient described chemotherapy as like "using an atomic bomb to kill a terrorist hiding in New York City."

In other words, chemotherapy may help to kill the cancer, but it also destroys a lot of healthy tissue in the process. Holistic approaches may be an attractive alternative to treating disease for individuals facing chemotherapy and other biomedical approaches in that they offer a less invasive type of treatment or one that does not negatively impact their quality of life in a significant way. It should be pointed out that many traditional herbal remedies used for centuries have been adapted by pharmaceutical researchers. For instance, the herb *Periwinkle vinca rosea* contains insulin that can be used in the treatment of diabetes, and *Rauwolfia serpentine* is an herb that contains respirine, which is commonly used as a tranquilizer by biomedical practitioners (Airhihenbuwa, 1995).

However, while pharmaceutical companies often use natural ingredients when developing medications, they also frequently develop synthetic versions of chemicals found in nature as well as ways to make these chemicals more concentrated. In addition, because many holistic approaches do not treat disease in an aggressive manner, individuals who are given a good prognosis by their physician for overcoming a disease may consider traditional biomedical treatments along with complementary holistic therapies. Other individuals who are facing a terminal illness and who have been told they may have a relatively short survival time may choose to forgo aggressive biomedical treatments and use holistic approaches to allow for some treatment of symptoms without threatening their overall quality of life.

Spirituality, Culture, and Health

Religion and spirituality are important influences on health beliefs and behaviors, and many health-related practices observed in cultures around the world and within the United States are rooted in religious and spiritual traditions. Religion and spirituality have had a profound influence on views of health and illness in many cultures, and they have a number of implications for health communication, although relatively few health communication scholars have examined the impact of religious and spiritual influences on health (Parrott, 2004). This section will explore the influence of religion and spirituality within a variety of health contexts.

Religious and spiritual beliefs can influence both generalized views about health and illness and specific behaviors. For example, fatalistic views about health among Mexican immigrants can be traced to the Roman Catholic religious worldview. According to Barron et al. (2004), "within this religious worldview, God controls all, and faith, not medical management, is essential to recovery from illness" (p. 333). Similarly, many Christian Scientists in the US avoid taking medications or seeing the doctor when they become ill. Instead, these individuals rely on their faith and prayer to help them through their health problems. In Japan, followers of Shintoism believe that the *kegare* is a source of spiritual contamination associated with events like death and terminal illness (Kakai, 2002). People in Japan who have these beliefs often avoid people who are terminally ill and their loved ones because they fear spiritual contamination. This belief leads many Japanese families to avoid publicly talking about their own or a family member's terminal illness.

Religion and psychological/physical health outcomes

Religious beliefs and practices are often associated with social and psychological mechanisms that can enhance health and well-being (Levin, 1996; Robinson & Nussbaum, 2004). Many religions encourage healthy lifestyles, such as avoiding smoking, excessive alcohol consumption, and promiscuous sex. Regular church attendance has been linked to increased morale, less depression, reduced likelihood of being hospitalized, and reduced mortality rates (Koenig & Larson, 1998; Koenig et al., 1999). Many providers are not prepared to discuss religious topics with patients, largely due to the emphasis on biomedical approaches to health during medical school, but medical schools are increasingly including courses on the influence of religion on health in the curriculum (Robinson & Nussbaum, 2004).

Religion and social support

Churches and other religious organizations are important sources of social support, which has been linked to a variety of positive psychological and physical health outcomes (see chapter 4). Church membership provides opportunities to expand one's social network and to give and receive different types of social support. In our increasingly mobile society, religious organizations provide opportunities for people to develop and expand their social network when they are new to a community. According to Robinson and Nussbaum (2004), church membership can "provide a sense of belonging, fellowship, and cohesiveness, as well as provide instrumental and emotional resources, such as monitoring others for illness and providing encouragement, hope, and aid" (p. 65). Church membership can also help reduce a person's sense of social isolation, and this has important implications for psychological well-being (Levin, 2001). Religion also encourages behaviors that are related to social support, such as staying married and spending time with family (Levin, 1996). Hospitals and other health facilities in the United States have had a long tradition of hiring clergy or using volunteers to provide patients with opportunities for spiritual guidance and support during times of illness. Finally, religious beliefs and spiritual talk are often extremely comforting to people who are dying from a terminal illness or who have experienced the death of a loved one (Keeley, 2004), and church social network members can provide instrumental help to people who are caregivers for a loved one facing an illness.

Many support groups are modeled after Alcoholics Anonymous (AA), an organization influenced by religious and spiritual thought (Jenson, 2000). AA was formed in 1935 by a New York stockbroker named Bill Wilson after what he referred to as a spiritual awakening resulting from his association with the Oxford Group, a Christian-based religious organization whose members believed in temperance and that belief in God was necessary to achieve sobriety.

People who join AA learn about the Twelve Steps to recovery from alcoholism. Many of the Twelve Steps have their roots in the teachings of the Oxford Group (Kassel & Wagner, 1993; Wright, 1997). The Twelve Steps stress the importance of relying on a Higher Power to help recovering alcoholics get through situations that may tempt them to drink and to help them manage problems in their daily lives. According to the AA worldview, recovering alcoholics are powerless over the temptation to drink, and a Higher Power is needed to help them through difficult situations. The AA literature stresses the idea that members can choose their own conception of a Higher Power (this idea is also reinforced during AA group meetings), and this spiritual pluralism allows people from different religious backgrounds to put aside individual differences in conceptions of a Higher Power in order to come together for the common purpose of recovery (Jenson, 2000; Wright, 1997).

Social Implications of Illness

Disease and illness not only affect us physically, they also have a variety of social implications. As we have seen, the ways in which we perceive health and illness are influenced by many different social forces, including the mass media, religion, institutions of higher learning, family and peers, and larger cultural perspectives of social life. These influences on our perceptions of health and illness, in turn, influence the way we communicate with others about health, and how we behave when we encounter health issues (O'Hair & Sparks, in press; Palmer, Kagee, Coyne, & DeMichele, 2004). In addition, health-related behaviors, such as diet, exercise, smoking, and alcohol consumption, and sexual behaviors take place in social settings and are reinforced through social interactions. This section examines negative perceptions of illness, then looks at ways in which people who are afflicted with health problems socially construct more positive ways to view them.

Stigma and disease

Some health problems are viewed negatively by society. Many diseases carry a social *stigma*, or a mark of shame, disgrace, or taboo that is attached to people and their problem (Goffman, 1963; O'Hair et al., 2003). In terms of health problems, we often view certain diseases and conditions negatively (and frequently the people who have them) because of the ways that society has influenced our perceptions. Cultural beliefs about the nature of diseases and stereotypes about the individuals who have them both influence the stigma of disease, and stigmatized individuals often face prejudice and discrimination as a result of their illness (Kreps & Thornton, 1992). While all health conditions have social implications, in the following sections we examine some of the many social issues surrounding four health concerns: HIV/AIDS, cancer, alcoholism, and mental illness.

HIV/AIDS

According to Schwalbe and Staples (1992), US culture influences our perceptions of HIV/AIDS and our behaviors surrounding the disease in a variety of ways, including an obsession with sexuality (promoted by advertising and the media in general), a culture of homophobia, reluctance to openly discuss sexual matters, limited technical knowledge of HIV/AIDS among laypersons, and a tension between secular, scientific views and religious (often punishment-based) perceptions of HIV. In an effort to sell products, advertisers, filmmakers, and television producers regularly use sexual content to attract our attention. Unfortunately, this has had the secondary effect of helping us to become a culture that is preoccupied with sex. In an effort to gain the social rewards of being sexually active, many people engage in sexual behaviors without considering many of the dangerous consequences.

Because of the cultural norm to not openly discuss sexual matters, many couples are reluctant to talk about condom usage, previous sexual partners, or other highly relevant information about sexual history that may influence risk for HIV/AIDS. Moreover, there is often confusion among laypersons about the ways in which the HIV virus can be transmitted, the course of the disease, and ways that it can be treated. Some religious groups still see HIV/AIDS as a curse from God as opposed to the scientific view that HIV is caused by a retrovirus. In addition, because HIV/AIDS was first seen among gay men and intravenous drug users, and these groups have traditionally been perceived by many in mainstream America as unnatural or undesirable, HIV/AIDS carries a social stigma with it (Adelman & Frey, 1997).

Cancer

While not to the same degree as HIV/AIDS, cancer has also been found to carry a social stigma. Cancer is one of the most significant health challenges facing our society, being the second leading cause of death in the United States (American Cancer Society, 2001). Over 9,000,000 US citizens are currently living with some form of cancer, with about 1,000,000 new cases diagnosed each year. Spiegel, Bloom, and Yalom (1981) contend that individuals within the social network of a person with cancer "often in subtle but unmistakable ways distance themselves from the dying" (p. 528) as a result of societally induced fears about disease and death. Ironically, members of social networks sometimes withdraw from us during times when we need them the most. For example, Samarel and Fawcett (1992) reported that a diagnosis of cancer often leads to difficulty maintaining the previous quality of interpersonal relationships and creates dissatisfaction with traditional sources of support (O'Hair & Sparks, in press). There are many reasons for the stigma associated with cancer. One reason is that cancer is often associated with death and dying, both of which are difficult subjects for people to talk about in our culture. Few individuals like to bring up the subject, even when the person with cancer would like to talk about it (O'Hair et al., 2003; Wortman & Dunkel-Schetter, 1979). The stigma attached to someone dying of a disease like cancer can lead to social isolation, which has been linked to both depression and mortality among cancer patients (Reynolds & Kaplan, 1990).

Our research has suggested that there is a need for a paradigm shift among patients and practitioners in the cancer communication context. Patients who find themselves at the mercy of a complex and overwhelming delivery and recovery system often adopt an acquiescence profile in managing their cancer care (O'Hair, Kreps, & Sparks, in press). Instead, we must find ways to promote a more proactive or "agency" approach to cancer care (O'Hair & Sparks, in press; O'Hair et al., 2003; O'Hair, Scannell, & Thompson, 2005). Agency is a strategy that promotes emotional and informational management processes that facilitate uncertainty management. Once patients manage their uncertainty, they position themselves to realize self-empowerment and to make decisions that correspond to their goals. Some patients come to terms with their terminal illness and make decisions that make them feel more comfortable and empowered (palliative care). Others exert agency by insisting on enrollment on the latest clinical trial that offers hope for a cure. The key to agency is being in control of information and emotions in order to make an informed and empowered decision. Health communication stands as the most obvious option for putting forth *patient agency*.

Alcoholism

The disease model of alcoholism (Jellinek, 1952), which has been adopted by the medical profession, is a relatively new idea. Prior to the conceptualization of alcohol problems as a disease, they were seen primarily as a moral issue and were most often associated with individuals who were stigmatized as having a "low character" (Lender & Martin, 1987). When "normal" drinkers encounter individuals who cannot control their drinking behavior or who behave irresponsibly while drinking, they often view this type of behavior as abnormal, despite the fact that many people who experience alcohol problems have a physical dependence on alcohol coupled with a psychological craving that makes consumption difficult to control (Jellinek, 1952). Problem drinkers may be seen by "normal" drinkers as people who should be able to control their drinking, despite the fact that once an alcohol-dependent individual takes a drink, he or she may have little control over behaviors. When the body is deprived of alcohol, the alcohol-dependent person typically experiences intense cravings for drink, even when they may know that they won't be able to stop once this first drink is consumed (Jellinek, 1952).

Mental illness

Over 44 million Americans suffer from a diagnosable mental disorder. The most common types of mental illness include major depression, bipolar disorder, schizophrenia, and obsessive-compulsive disorder (Regier, Narrow, Rae et al., 1993). Mental illness carries a social stigma for a variety of reasons. In addition, eating disorders such as anorexia nervosa, bulimia nervosa, and binge-eating disorder are often classified as types of mental illness. The mass media often portray mental illness in negative ways, such as showing people who are mentally ill as dangerous or out of control, despite the fact that these types of incidents are very rare among mentally ill individuals. In addition, there are a number of misconceptions about mental illness in our society, especially because for many Americans their primary exposure to mental illness is through the entertainment media. Negative words such as "loony," "psycho," and "crazy" are commonly used to describe mentally ill individuals in the mass media and are a common part of our society's vernacular. Not surprisingly, these negative perceptions of mental illness can cause a variety of social problems for mentally ill people, who are often feared or shunned when others discover they are dealing with a mental illness.

Changing Social Perceptions of Health Issues through Communication

Communication often plays a vital role in determining how people perceive health issues (Cline, 2003; Lupton, 1994). Individuals with alcoholism, cancer, HIV/AIDS, and a variety of other diseases and conditions often attempt to alter social perceptions of these health concerns in their interactions with others. Communication is important for helping people construct new health-related identities, especially in interactions between individuals sharing the same disease or health concern. For example, the term "cancer survivor" has largely replaced earlier designations like "cancer victim," largely due to people with cancer redefining the disease in light of their own experiences. Many people with cancer object to terms like "cancer victim" because it places them in a powerless position, preferring instead the more positive connotations of "cancer survivor" (O'Hair et al., 2003). Language can be very powerful in altering cultural perceptions about health concerns. Through terms like "cancer survivor," many people facing the disease have attempted to use language to change cultural beliefs and attitudes towards the disease.

One common way that individuals facing similar health conditions can transform their own and others' perceptions is through the use of narrative. Narratives are essentially stories that people tell each other, but they can be any verbal or nonverbal account of a sequence of events (Fisher, 1987). Storytelling is a common human activity in all facets of life, including health situations (Smyth, Gould, & Slobin, 2000). While it is easy to think of narratives as "just stories," they can be a powerful influence on the way that we see the world. Narratives are rarely neutral. When people tell stories, they frame events and the way they experience them in specific ways. This involves sequencing and interpreting events in meaningful ways that make sense to them. According to Fisher (1987), we process our lives as a series of events in an unfolding narrative — one with characters, a particular setting, and a plot. Narratives are also commonly used to communicate experiences to others, and when stories are told again and again, they can influence the way that large groups of people (and even whole cultures) interpret everyday life events. In terms of health, narratives can be used to create, recreate, and sustain cultural beliefs about health issues (Harter, Japp, & Beck, 2005; Japp, Harter, & Beck, 2005; O'Hair, Scannell et al., 2005).

For example, people who are living with cancer often have a unique perspective of what it is like to live with disease on a daily basis. Even though oncologists may know much more about cancer than the patients they treat, if they have not lived with cancer themselves they likely have a much different perspective of the disease than someone who has had to cope with fear associated with a cancer diagnosis, the sickness associated with chemotherapy, or changes in relationships with others. When people coping with the same type of disease or health condition meet one another, they often share stories about their experiences and can influence one another's perceptions about their common health issue in a variety of ways. Someone who has been recently diagnosed with cancer might identify more with long-term cancer survivors than with her oncologist as a result of sharing common thoughts and feelings related to living with cancer. Similarly, most recovering alcoholics remember what it was like to live with an alcohol addiction and the problems associated with it, and this allows them to identify with the thoughts and feelings of someone who is attempting to get sober. Through storytelling, recovering alcoholics are often able to tell people struggling with an alcohol addiction how they felt when they were first trying to get sober and the types of thoughts, feelings, and behaviors that help them to stay sober.

In some cases, a newly diagnosed cancer patient or a newly recovering alcoholic may perceive people who have been dealing with these health issues for a long period of time as being more credible than a healthcare provider. A person who has actually lived with a health problem can often be very significant in influencing the thoughts and behaviors of someone with a similar health problem due to the enhanced credibility associated with "having been there." This is one of the reasons why peer support groups can be so influential in helping people to cope with health problems and maintain healthy behaviors.

According to Rappaport (1993), members of self-help groups use narrative as a way of forming a social identity. As we have discussed, people with cancer and other life-threatening diseases and conditions often experience feelings of isolation. Support groups provide an environment in which these individuals feel they share a common identity with others. Some of the messages exchanged within cancer support groups appear to be useful in changing members' perceptions of the disease. As we have also seen, society tends to attach a negative stigma to cancer because many people equate it with death and dying, despite the fact that there are many forms of cancer and that the prognoses for different types vary widely.

The widespread societal perception of the hopelessness of recovery from cancer may lead some individuals to view themselves as victims of the disease, which may result in passive coping strategies (Kreps, 1993) or a type of self-fulfilling prophecy, in which they do not actively seek treatment for the disease or adhere to lifestyle changes that may improve their chances of survival. In cancer support groups, members learn to identify with others' experiences and feelings about cancer through sharing narratives, and this appears to both validate their own experiences and feelings and lessen their sense of isolation (Mok & Martinson, 2000; Wright & Bell, 2003).

Communication researchers have suggested that narratives play an important role in changing the worldview of support group members when it comes to dealing with health-related issues (Anderson & Geist-Martin, 2003; Arntson & Droge, 1987; Cline, 1999). According to Davison, Pennebaker, and Dickerson (2000), "each individual account contributes to a larger collective narrative that paints a portrait of identity by diagnosis" (p. 210). By helping to form such collective understandings, the storytelling process within support groups is important for establishing a sense of community among members (Adelman & Frey, 1997). Moreover, stories told in support groups are a way of conveying advice in a nondidactic fashion, which means that people often do not give each other advice directly (Arntson & Droge, 1987; Wright, 1997). Instead, people tell their stories about their personal experiences and what types of thoughts and behaviors helped them to cope. In this way, individuals are free to follow or disregard advice from others (Arntson & Droge, 1987). Support groups for alcoholics, such as AA, recognize the social stigma attached to problem drinking and use communication to help members overcome the stigma of alcohol abuse (Wright, 1997).

People with similar health concerns can also use narratives to create and sustain a culture that offers a unique perspective on the issues they face. Cancer survivors, recovering alcoholics, and people with disabilities have been influential in changing public perceptions of these health issues by telling their stories to each other and through the mass media. For example, alcoholics were once seen as being morally weak, but through the stories of members of organizations such as AA, recovering alcoholics have been instrumental in promoting the idea that alcoholism is a physical disease rather than a moral failing.

Table 5.1 Select healthcare provider occupations

Child life specialist	Pharmacy technician
Dentist	Phlebotomist
Dental assistant	Psychologist
Dental hygienist	Physician
Hospital administrator	Physician assistant
Medical sonographer	Registered nurse
Occupational therapist	Surgical technologist

Provider Diversity

As we have seen, patients exhibit a great amount of diversity in the current US healthcare system. Unfortunately, the racial and ethnic diversity of providers has not kept pace with the diversity of patients in recent years, and as we have discussed, this may lead to a number of communication problems. However, there is also considerable diversity among healthcare providers in terms of occupation, education levels, areas of expertise, and socioeconomic status (see table 5.1 for a list of some of the many healthcare provider occupations). This section briefly explores healthcare provider diversity.

The amount of training for jobs in the healthcare system varies widely. For example, phlebotomists can often receive a certificate after about 6 months of training, while radiologists and other types of medical personnel have much more extensive training. Nurses and physicians obviously require more advanced levels of education and training. In addition, the training specific to each type of provider and interactions among providers having the same occupation contributes to a variety of unique co-cultures within many healthcare settings. Even among medical doctors there is a great deal of diversity and status difference in medical specialty. Some medical doctors, such as pathologists, have little interaction with patients, and physicians often attribute a higher professional status to surgeons and other specialties due to the amount and sophistication of the training they receive.

Much like patients, providers are socialized into unique cultures based upon factors such as education and training. Even within a relatively small healthcare organization, there are a wide variety of cultural conceptions of health and healthcare among providers. These differences can lead to conflict between providers from different backgrounds (see chapter 6) and can affect communication with patients. For example, many physicians gravitate towards recommending certain procedures and medications as a result of their training, and may have relatively low tolerance for alternative treatments recommended by other providers or by the patient. While cultural differences among providers can often lead to negative outcomes, health organizations can capitalize on provider diversity in an effort to provide more comprehensive care. For example, Wright and Frey (in press) studied a state-of-the-art cancer center in Memphis, Tennessee, where oncologists provide patients with traditional bio-medical cancer treatments along with complementary herbal treatments, relaxation therapy, and group/individual counseling. In addition, many of the larger modern healthcare organizations rely on an interdisciplinary team approach to patient care. With this approach, administrators within a healthcare organization assemble a team of providers with different types of training and experience in an effort to gain a more holistic understanding of a patient's health issues. For example, interdisciplinary teams are often composed of a wide range of providers, such as physicians, nurses, pharmacists, physical therapists, psychologists, and social workers. Moreover, interdisciplinary team members collaborate with each other to find holistic ways to treat patients, taking into account medical and social factors. We examine interdisciplinary healthcare teams in much greater depth in chapter 11.

Summary

This chapter has taken on a topic – namely, diversity – that is often emphasized in mission and vision statements and frequently recognized as an essential component of comprehensive healthcare delivery. Many healthcare organizations have succeeded in addressing diversity issues with grace and enthusiasm. However, organizations still face the many challenges that diversity presents in relation to disease management, provider–patient relationships, and quality healthcare delivery. In this chapter we have promoted an agency approach to diversity whereby patients or consumers of healthcare services impose their rights to information and uncertainty management processes to achieve empowerment, which in turn provides increased options for making decisions about their healthcare.

We recognize that diversity in healthcare is a dynamic and constantly challenging factor that healthcare professionals are expected to consider. Diversity issues will impose their will on the delivery system regardless of preference or preparedness. Organizations will find that embracing an open and integrative approach to diversity will maximize their effectiveness for patient care and at the same recognize the value-added nature of diversity sensitivity.

References

Abramson, J. S., & Mizrahi, T. (1996). When social workers and physicians collaborate: Positive and negative interdisciplinary experiences. *Social Work*, *41*, 270–281.

Adelman, M. B., & Frey, L. R. (1997). *The fragile community: Living together with AIDS*. Mahwah, NJ: Lawrence Erlbaum.

Airhihenbuwa, C. O. (1995). *Health and culture: Beyond the Western paradigm*. Thousand Oaks, CA: Sage.

Airhihenbuwa, C. O., & Obregon, R. (2000). A critical assessment of theories/models used in health communication for HIV/AIDS. *Journal of Health Communication*, *5*, 5–16.

Aldrich, L., & Variyam, J. N. (2000). Acculturation erodes the diet quality of US Hispanics. *Diet Quality*, *23*, 51–55.

American Cancer Society. (2001). *Cancer statistics*. Retrieved November 1, 2002, from www.cancer.ogr/cancerinfo/.

Anderson, J. O., & Geist-Martin, P. (2003). Narratives and healing: Exploring one family's stories of cancer survivorship. *Health Communication*, *15*, 133–143.

Arntson, P., & Droge, D. (1987). Social support in self-help groups: The role of communication in enabling perceptions of control. In T. L. Albrecht, M. B. Adelman, & Associates (Eds.), *Communicating social support* (pp. 148–171). Newbury Park, CA: Sage.

Barron, F., Hunter, A., Mayo, R., & Willoughby, D. (2004). Acculturation and adherence: Issues for health care providers working with clients of Mexican origin. *Journal of Transcultural Nursing*, *15*, 331–337.

Berteotti, C. R., & Seibold, D. R. (1994). Coordination and role-definition problems in health-care teams: A hospice case study. In L. R. Frey (Ed.), *Group communication in context: Studies of natural groups* (pp. 107–131). Hillsdale, NJ: Lawrence Erlbaum.

Brislin, R. W. (1993). *Understanding culture's influence on behavior*. Fort Worth, TX: Harcourt Brace.

Carrese, J. A., & Rhodes, L. A. (1995). Western bioethics on the Navajo reservation. Benefit or harm? *JAMA*, *274*, 826–829.

Cline, R. J. (1999). Communication within social support groups. In L. R. Frey (Ed.), D. S. Gouran, & M. S. Poole (Assoc. Eds.), *The handbook of group communication theory and research* (pp. 516–538). Thousand Oaks, CA: Sage.

Cline, R. J. W. (2003). Everyday interpersonal communication and health. In T. L. Thompson, A. M. Dorsey, K. I. Miller, & R. Parrott (Eds.), *Handbook of health communication* (pp. 285–313). Mahwah, NJ: Lawrence Erlbaum.

Cobas, J. A., Balcazar, H., Benini, M. B., Keith, V. M., & Chong, Y. (1996). Acculturation and low-birthweight infants among Latino women: A reanalysis of HHANES data with structural equation models. *American Journal of Public Health*, *86*, 394–396.

Cooley, E. (1994). Training an interdisciplinary team in communication and decision making skills. *Small Group Research*, *25*, 5–25.

Coopman, S. J. (2001). Democracy, performance, and outcomes in interdisciplinary health care teams. *Journal of Business Communication, 38,* 261–284.

Davison, K. P., Pennebaker, J. W., & Dickerson, S. S. (2000). Who talks? The social psychology of illness support groups. *American Psychologist, 55,* 205–217.

Dunn, L., & Perry, B. L. (1997). Where your patients are. *Primary Care, 24,* 715–721.

Dysart-Gale, D. (2005). Communication models, professionalization, and the work of medical interpreters. *Health Communication, 17,* 91–103.

Eisenberg, D., Davis, R., Ettner, S., Appel, S., Wilkey, S., Van Rompay, M., & Kessler, R. (1998). Trends in alternative medicine use in the United States, 1990–1997: Results of a national follow-up study. *Journal of the American Medical Association, 280,* 1569–1575.

Ferguson, J. A., Weinberger, M., Westmoreland, G. R., Mamlin, L. A., Segar, D. S., Green, J. Y., Martin, D. K., & Tierney, W. M. (1998). Racial disparity in cardiac decision making: Results from patient focus groups. *Archives of Internal Medicine, 158,* 1450–1453.

Fisher, W. R. (1987). *Human communication as narration: Toward a philosophy of reason, value, and action.* Columbia, NC: University of North Carolina Press.

Galanti, G. (1991). *Caring for patients from different cultures: Case studies from American hospitals.* Philadelphia, PA: University of Pennsylvania Press.

Gergen, K. J. (1999). *An invitation to social construction.* London: Sage.

Gillick, M. (1985). Common-sense models of health and disease. *New England Journal of Medicine, 313,* 700–703.

Goffman, E. (1963). *Stigma: Notes on the management of spoiled identity.* Englewood Cliffs, NJ: Prentice-Hall.

Goldner, M. A. (1998). *Explaining the success of the alternative health care movement: How integrative medicine is expanding Western medicine.* Unpublished doctoral dissertation, Ohio State University, Columbus, OH.

Harter, L. M., Japp, P. M., & Beck, C. S. (Eds.). (2005). *Narratives, health, and healing: Communication theory, research, and practice.* Mahwah, NJ: Lawrence Erlbaum.

Helman, C. G. (2000). *Culture, health, and illness.* Oxford: Butterworth Heinemann.

Heuer, L., Bengiamin, M., & Downey, V. (2001). The impact of an international cultural experience on previously held stereotypes by American student nurses. *Multicultural Education.* Accessed September 26, 2006, from www.findarticles.com/p/articles/mi_qa3935/is_200110/ai_n8960443/pg_7.

Hornberger, J., Itakura, H., & Wilson, S. (1997). Bridging language and cultural barriers between physicians and patients. *Public Health Reports, 112,* 410–417.

Hunt, L. M., Hamdi, A., & Arana, L. L. (2000). Herbs, prayer, and insulin: Use of medical and alternative treatments by a group of Mexican American diabetes patients. *Journal of Family Practice, 49,* 216–223.

Japp, P. M., Harter, L. M., & Beck, C. S. (2005). Vital problematics of narrative theorizing about health and healing. In P. Japp, L. Harter, & C. Beck (Eds.), *Narratives, health, and healing: Communication theory, research, and practice* (pp. 7–30). Mahwah, NJ: Lawrence Erlbaum.

Jellinek, E. M. (1952). *The disease concept of alcoholism.* Highland Park, NJ: Yale Center of Alcohol Studies Press.

Jenson, G. H. (2000). *Storytelling in Alcoholics Anonymous: A rhetorical analysis.* Carbondale, IL: Southern Illinois University Press.

Johnson, R., Roter, D., Powe, N. R., & Cooper, L. A. (2004). Patient race/ethnicity and quality of patient–physician communication during medical visits. *American Journal of Public Health, 94,* 2084–2091.

Johnson, S. K. (2002). Hmong health beliefs and experiences in the Western health care system. *Journal of Transcultural Nursing, 13,* 126–132.

Kakai, H. (2002). A double standard in bioethical reasoning for disclosure of advanced cancer diagnosis in Japan. *Health Communication, 14,* 361–376.

Kassel, J. D., & Wagner, E. F. (1993). Processes of change in Alcoholics Anonymous: A review of possible mechanisms. *Psychotherapy, 30,* 222–234.

Keegan, L. (1996). Use of alternative therapies among Mexican Americans in the Texas Rio Grande Valley. *Journal of Holistic Nursing, 14,* 277–294.

Keeley, M. P. (2004). Final conversations: Survivors' memorable messages concerning religious faith and spirituality. *Health Communication, 16,* 87–104.

Kirkman-Liff, B. (1999). Medicare managed care and primary care of elderly people. In F. Netting & F. Williams (Eds.), *Enhancing primary care of elderly people* (pp. 3–23). New York: Garland.

Koenig, H. G., & Larson, D. B. (1998). Use of hospital services, religious attendance, and religious affiliation. *Southern Medical Journal, 91,* 925–932.

Koenig, H. G., Hays, J. C., Larson, D. B., George, L. K., Cohen, H. J., McCullough, M. E., et al. (1999). Does religious attendance prolong survival? A six-year follow-up study of 3,968 older adults. *Journal of Gerontology, 54A,* M370–M376.

Kreps, G. L. (1993). Refusing to be a victim: Rhetorical strategies for confronting cancer. In G. L. Kreps & B. C. Thornton (Eds.), *Perspectives on health communication* (pp. 42–47). Prospect Heights, IL: Waveland Press.

Kreps, G. L., & Thornton, B. C. (1992). *Health communication: Theory and practice* (2nd ed.). Prospect Heights, IL: Waveland Press.

Lefley, H. (1998). Training professionals for rehabilitation teams. In P. Corrigan & D. Giffort (Eds.), *Building teams and programs for effective psychiatric rehabilitation* (pp. 13–23). San Francisco: Jossey-Bass.

Lender, M. E., & Martin, J. K. (1987). *Drinking in America.* New York: Free Press.

Leong, F. T. L., & Schneller, G. (1997). White Americans' attitudes toward Asian Americans in social situations: An empirical examination of potential stereotypes, bias, and prejudice. *Journal of Multicultural Counseling and Development, 25,* 68–78.

Levin, J. S. (1996). How religion influences morbidity and health: Reflections on natural history, salutogenesis and host resistance. *Social Science and Medicine, 43,* 849–864.

Levin, J. S. (2001). *God, faith, and health: Exploring the spirituality–healing connection.* New York: Wiley.

Long, S. O. (2000). Public passages, personal passages, and reluctant passages: Notes on investigating disclosure practices in Japan. *Journal of Medical Humanities, 21,* 3–13.

Lupton, D. (1994). *Medicine as culture: Illness, disease, and the body in Western societies.* Thousand Oaks, CA: Sage.

Mok, E., & Martinson, I. (2000). Empowerment of Chinese patients with cancer through self-help groups in Hong Kong. *Cancer Nursing, 23,* 206–213.

Ndiwane, A., Miller, K. H., Bonner, A., et al. (2004). Enhancing cultural competencies of advanced practice nurses: Health care challenges in the twenty-first century. *Journal of Cultural Diversity, 11,* 118–121.

O'Hair, H. D., & Sparks, L. (in press). Relational agency in life threatening illnesses. In K. Wright & S. Moore (Eds.), *Readings in health communication.* Mahwah, NJ: Lawrence Erlbaum.

O'Hair, H. D., Behnke, R., & King, P. (1983). Age-related patient preferences for physician communication behavior. *Educational Gerontology, 9,* 147–158.

O'Hair, H. D., Friedrich, G., Wiemann, J., & Wiemann, M. (2002). *Competent communication.* New York: Bedford St. Martin's Press.

O'Hair, H. D., Kreps, G. L., & Sparks, L. (in press). Conceptualizing cancer care and communication. In H. D. O'Hair, G. L. Kreps, & L. Sparks (Eds.), *Handbook of communication and cancer care.* Cresskill, NJ: Hampton Press.

O'Hair, H. D., O'Hair, M., Southward, M., & Krayer, K. (1987). Patient compliance and physician communication. *Journal of Compliance in Health Care, 2,* 125–128.

O'Hair, H. D., Scannell, D., & Thompson, S. (2005). Agency through narrative: Patients managing cancer care in a challenging environment. In L. Harter, P. Japp, & C. Beck (Eds.), *Narratives, health, and healing: Communication theory, research, and practice* (pp. 413–432). Mahwah, NJ: Lawrence Erlbaum.

O'Hair, H. D., Sparks, L., & Thompson, S. (2005). Negotiating cancer care through agency. In E. B. Ray (Ed.), *Health communication in practice: A case study approach* (pp. 81–94). Mahwah, NJ: Lawrence Erlbaum.

O'Hair, H. D., Villagran, M., Wittenberg, E., Brown, K., Hall, T., Ferguson, M., & Doty, T. (2003). Cancer survivorship and agency model (CSAM): Implications for patient choice, decision making, and influence. *Health Communication, 15,* 193–202.

Palmer, S. C., Kagee, A., Coyne, J. C., & DeMichele, A. (2004). Experience of trauma, distress, and posttraumatic stress disorder among breast cancer patients. *Psychosomatic Medicine, 66,* 258–264.

Parrott, R. (2004). "Collective amnesia": The absence of religious faith and spirituality in health communication research and practice. *Health Communication, 16,* 1–5.

Pearce, W. B. (1995). A sailing guide for social constructionists. In W. Leeds-Hurwitz (Ed.), *Social approaches to communication* (pp. 88–113). New York: Guilford.

Poole, M. S., & Real, K. (2003). Groups and teams in health care: Communication and effectiveness. In T. L. Thompson, A. M. Dorsey, K. I. Miller, & R. Parrott (Eds.), *Handbook of health communication* (pp. 369–402). Mahwah, NJ: Lawrence Erlbaum.

Popkin, B. M., & Udry, J. R. (1998). Adolescent obesity increases significantly in second and third generation US immigrants: The National Longitudinal Study of Adolescent Health. *Journal of Nutrition, 128,* 701–706.

Rappaport, J. (1993). Narrative studies, personal stories, and identity transformation in the mutual help context. *Journal of Applied Behavioral Science, 29,* 239–256.

Regier, D. A., Narrow, W. E., Rae, D. S., et al. (1993). The de facto mental and addictive disorders service system. Epidemiologic Catchment Area prospective 1-year prevalence rates of disorders and services. *Archives of General Psychiatry, 50,* 85–94.

Reynolds, P., & Kaplan, G. A. (1990). Social connections and risk for cancer: Prospective evidence from the Alameda County study. *Behavioral Medicine, 16,* 101–110.

Rivadeneyra, R., Elderkin-Thompson, V., Silver, R. C., & Waitzkin, H. (2000). Patient centeredness in medical encounters requiring an interpreter. *American Journal of Medicine, 108,* 470–474.

Robinson, J. D., & Nussbaum, J. F. (2004). Grounding research and medical education about religion in actual physician–patient interaction: Church attendance, social support, and older adults. *Health Communication, 16,* 63–85.

Samarel, N., & Fawcett, J. (1992). Enhancing adaptation to breast cancer: The addition of coaching to support groups. *Oncology Nursing Forum, 19,* 591–596.

Schott, J., & Henley, A. (1996). *Culture, religion, and childbearing in a multiracial society: A handbook for health professionals.* Oxford: Butterworth Heinemann.

Schreiber, L. M. (in press). The importance of precision in language: Communication research and (so-called) "alternative" medicine. *Health Communication.*

Schwalbe, M. L., & Staples, C. L. (1992). Forced blood testing: Role taking, identity, and discrimination. In J. Huber & B. E. Schneider (Eds.), *The social context of AIDS.* Newbury Park, CA: Sage.

Sharf, B. F., & Vanderford, M. L. (2003). Illness narratives and the social construction of health. In T. L. Thompson, A. M. Dorsey, K. I. Miller, & R. Parrott (Eds.), *Handbook of health communication* (pp. 9–35). Mahwah, NJ: Lawrence Erlbaum.

Smith, L. S. (1997). Critical thinking, health policy, and the Hmong culture group, Part I. *Journal of Cultural Diversity, 4,* 5–12.

Smyth, J., Gould, O., & Slobin, K. (2000). The role of narrative in medicine: A multi-theoretical perspective. *Advances in Mind–Body Medicine, 16,* 186–194.

Spector, R. (1996). *Culture and diversity in health and illness.* Stamford, CT: Appleton Lange.

Spiegel, D., Bloom, J. R., & Yalom, I. (1981). Group support for patients with metastatic cancer: A randomized prospective outcome study. *Archives of General Psychiatry, 38,* 527–533.

Udani, J. (1998). Integrating alternative medicine into practice. *Journal of the American Medical Association, 280,* 1620.

Ulrey, K. L., & Amason, P. (2001). Intercultural communication between patients and health care providers: An exploration of intercultural communication effectiveness, cultural sensitivity, stress, and anxiety. *Health Communication, 13,* 449–463.

US Census Bureau. (2005). 2005 American community survey data: Race and ethnicity. Retrieved February 21, 2007, from www.factfinder.census.gov.

Voelker, R. (1995). Speaking the language of medicine and culture. *JAMA, 273,* 1639–1642.

Wardwell, W. I. (1994). Alternative medicine in the United States. *Social Science and Medicine, 38,* 1061–1068.

Witte, K. (1991). The role of culture in health and diseases. In L. Samovar and R. Porter (Eds.), *Intercultural communication: A reader* (6th ed., pp. 199–207). Belmont, CA: Wadsworth.

Wortman, C., & Dunkel-Schetter, C. (1979). Interpersonal relationships and cancer. *Journal of Social Issues, 35,* 120–155.

Wright, K. B. (1997). Shared ideology in Alcoholics Anonymous: A grounded theory approach. *Journal of Health Communication, 2,* 83–99.

Wright, K. B., & Bell, S. B. (2003). Health-related support groups on the Internet: Linking empirical findings to social support and computer-mediated communication theory. *Journal of Health Psychology, 8,* 37–52.

Wright, K. B., & Frey, L. R. (in press). Communication and care in an acute cancer center: The effects of patients' willingness to communicate about health, healthcare environment perceptions, and health status on information seeking, participation in care practices, and satisfaction. *Health Communication.*

Chapter 6

Communication and Healthcare Organizations

Several years ago, a friend of the second author received new lungs for a much-needed and long-awaited transplant. It was not until the twenty-third month of the two-year waiting period that she finally received them. Interestingly, this woman would never have received her new lungs if a nurse who had befriended her had not argued on her behalf. The nurse played a pivotal role in influencing the hospital administration, who would not have given her the lungs were it not for the strategic communication the nurse provided to the decision-makers. The nurse was asked how the patient was doing in the hospital, to which the nurse answered, "Oh, she's doing quite well," which was a bit of a stretch. However, if the nurse had answered more bluntly, for example "She's having trouble breathing," then it is near certain that our friend would not be living today. She still has to take more than 30 pills a day, but she is alive and well nearly 9 years after the transplant – and that is a miracle! Communication played a significant role in the health outcome (i.e., the life) of this incredible woman.

Most of the health communication situations we experience take place within some type of healthcare organization. Our interactions with physicians, dentists, nurses, laboratory technicians, and many other types of providers are often influenced by characteristics of the larger healthcare organization and that organization's relationship with stakeholders in networks of other organizations. While we have seen that provider–patient communication can be quite complex even when it occurs between just you and your doctor, it is important to remember that these interactions are embedded within the norms and practices of a larger healthcare system.

Few organizations are more complex than modern-day healthcare organizations, such as hospitals, nursing homes, and health insurance companies, and communication is an essential part of an organization's ability to function effectively.

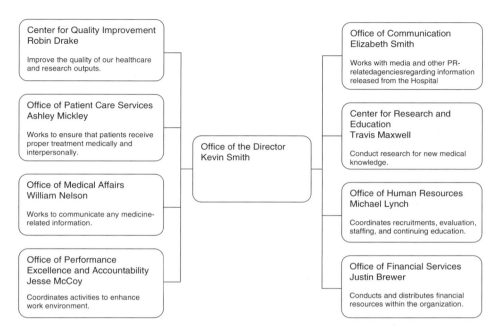

Figure 6.1 Health organizational hierarchy 1: Oklahoma General Health Care Center.

This chapter examines a variety of communication issues related to healthcare organizations, including communicative characteristics of organizations, types of healthcare organizations, and some of the major influences on communication within healthcare organizations in today's healthcare system.

Healthcare Organizations as Systems

One helpful way to examine healthcare organizations is to view them as systems. O'Hair, Friedrich, and Dixon (in press) define a system as an interdependent collection of components that are related to one another and combine their relative strengths to respond to internal changes and external challenges. For example, a hospital can be viewed as a complex system that contains many smaller systems or interrelated units, such as the hospital's administration, radiology department, and nursing department. In addition, hospitals are typically embedded within larger systems that oversee or influence the daily operations of the hospital (e.g., government agencies) or provide it with necessary resources, such as medical supplies (e.g., pharmaceutical companies).

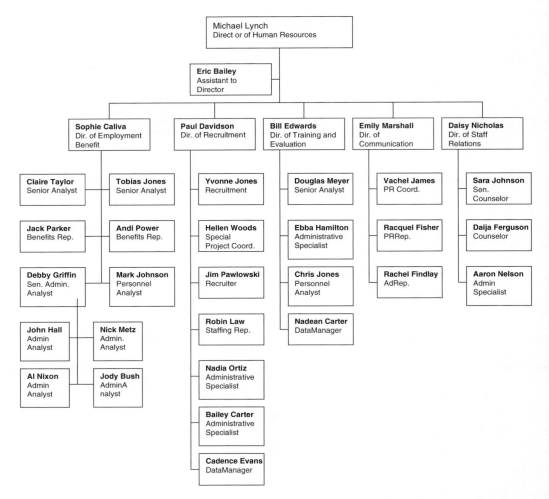

Figure 6.2 Health organizational hierarchy 2: Oklahoma General Health Care Center, Office of Human Resources.

The ways in which healthcare systems function have important implications for patient care. For example, another dear friend of the second author has been fighting fourth-stage esophageal cancer with a nearly three-inch malignant tumor that has metastasized to the liver. The surgeon at one hospital told him to have the difficult and aggressive chemotherapy and radiation treatment to shrink the tumor down enough to do surgery. The surgeon said, "We can do it. It will be difficult, but if you do your part I can definitely get the tumor out of the esophageal area, move the stomach up and you will survive. The average survival rate is around five years, but you are younger and stronger than those statistics." The surgeon continued to explain the ways in which the tumors have to shrink, particularly the ones in the liver, which may be more difficult depending on where they are located and how much they shrink from the chemotherapy and radiation, but he further expressed that "this operation is absolutely doable." However, the "system" in which a surgeon operates may not be as optimistic about a patient's prognosis due to the cost of such procedures. For example, the "system" at another hospital where the author's friend obtained a "second opinion" told him to get his affairs in order, and that no chemotherapy or radiation would help. Many hospital administrators and other key decision-makers within healthcare systems often find they must focus on the bottom line, while patient care that is tailored to the individual rather than to the system can often take a back seat.

Characteristics of systems

According to *systems theory*, systems have certain characteristics that can influence the communication behaviors of individuals within them. Complex systems such as healthcare organizations are more than the sum of their individual parts. Different units of a system are *interdependent*, and they interact in ways that create outcomes that would not be possible otherwise.

A hospital could not function if it relied only on the services of providers. A physician would have trouble diagnosing and treating a patient's health problems if he or she did not have medical supplies or support from other units in the organization (e.g., nurses, technicians, laboratory personnel), a patient could not treat his or her health problem without the services of pharmacies and health insurance organizations, and the hospital itself could not exist without proper licensing from government health agencies and an administration that managed the business and legal aspects of the hospital (e.g., managing costs, ordering supplies, handling malpractice lawsuits). Each of these units (as well as many others) must work together and coordinate its actions for the hospital to function, and communication within and between different elements of the organization is vital to the organization's ability to function effectively.

Systems have other qualities, such as *homeostasis*, or the ability of a system to self-regulate or achieve a sense of balance when faced with changing conditions. Similar to the thermostat in your home that adjusts to changing temperatures by turning on and off the heater or air conditioner, systems such as healthcare organizations must adapt to changing situations. For example, a normally busy medical clinic that finds itself with fewer patients than average for several months must advertise its services or make other arrangements to attract a suitable number of patients for the business to function. During the cold and flu season, a department of public health may need to take steps to insure a steady supply of flu shots to keep up with the increased demand. In both cases, the organizations are reacting to shifts in the system.

In addition, systems exhibit a characteristic known as *equifinality*, which can be defined as the "many different ways by which a system may reach the same end state" (Infante, Rancer, & Womack, 1997, p. 92). In other words, systems such as healthcare organizations often use many different strategies to achieve a desired goal or outcome. For example, if a hospital is faced with a high nursing turnover rate, it can hire new nurses to replace those who have left the organization or find ways to retain existing nurses in an attempt to improve the situation. Increased medical costs within a healthcare organization can be addressed by laying off staff, finding more efficient ways to provide care, and/or focusing on preventive measures to reduce the number of patients who require costly services to treat certain illnesses.

Communication among members of a system is important to achieving homeostasis and the process of equifinality. In order to achieve a sense of balance or improve the situation when faced with challenging conditions, healthcare organizations rely on input from their members. Individuals and units of an organization are needed to provide solutions to issues that threaten the normal functioning of the organization when they arise. While we have seen that there are often many ways an organization can solve problems or meet goals, healthcare organizations need to find the best strategy for reducing costs and providing quality healthcare. This can be an extremely difficult task for healthcare organizations in today's dynamic and competitive healthcare environment. We will examine how members of healthcare organizations communicate with one another to adapt to changing conditions later in this chapter.

Types of Healthcare Organizations

There are currently more types of healthcare organizations than at any other time in history, ranging from small clinics and practices to large government agencies. The growth of these organizations in the modern-day healthcare system is due to many factors, including increased specialization, competition in the healthcare marketplace, managed care, changing professional and legal standards, and the diverse health needs of the US population.

Lammers, Barbour, and Duggan (2003) identify some of the many types of healthcare organizations that we see today (see table 6.1). Some of these organizations are primarily concerned with financing and regulating health services and products, while others are important in terms of accrediting hospitals and other healthcare delivery organizations or influencing healthcare standards and

Table 6.1 Types of healthcare organizations

Organizations concerned with financing and regulating health services and products
Centers for Medicare and Medicaid
Insurance and managed care
Organizations concerned with healthcare delivery
Departments of public health
Hospice centers
Hospitals
Medical groups
Nursing homes
Parish nurse programs
Physicians' offices
Pharmaceutical and biotechnological organizations
Professional organizations that influence other healthcare organizations
Accreditation organizations
Trade and professional associations

Source: Adapted from Lammers et al. (2003).

practices, and many are important in terms of healthcare delivery. In addition to these organizations, other organizations are focused on health-related research. It is important to remember that many of these organizations are interdependent or are influenced by one another in other significant ways.

Health insurance organizations are important for helping consumers to access healthcare services, managing the costs of healthcare, and paying providers for their services. The federal government also provides health insurance through Medicaid and Medicare to serve older adults and individuals with lower incomes. We will examine health insurance, Medicare, and Medicaid in more depth later in this chapter.

Healthcare delivery service organizations exist in both the public and private sector, and they can range from small physicians' offices to large hospitals. While some physicians still work out of private offices, many cannot afford the tremendous costs of running an office, paying staff, and using outside services (such as diagnostic laboratories). These costs have led many doctors to join medical groups where they can share the costs with a small number of other physicians by pooling together resources. Investor–owned and nonprofit hospitals and hospital systems are important healthcare delivery organizations that bring together even more resources than medical groups. Other healthcare organizations include nursing homes, teaching hospitals, hospice services for chronically ill patients, and parish nurse programs in which nurses are hired by churches and other religious organizations to service the needs of their members.

The federal government provides healthcare services for veterans through the Veterans' Administration Healthcare System and it supports other types of hospitals through federal income tax revenue. Federal government organizations overseen by the Department of Health and Human Services, such as the Center for Disease Control and Prevention and the National Cancer Institute, engage in various types of research that influence healthcare practices within healthcare delivery organizations. State and many local governments have departments of public health or other agencies that provide vital services, such as immunizations, HIV and other sexually transmitted disease screening, pre-natal care, and psychological counseling. Pharmaceutical and biotechnology organizations as well as hospital supply companies support all of these health-care delivery organizations.

Finally, organizations such as the Joint Commission on the Accreditation of Healthcare Organizations (JCAHO) make sure that hospitals and other healthcare facilities meet certain standards of quality healthcare on a two-to three-year basis. JCAHO assesses and accredits almost 15,000 healthcare organizations in the United States in a variety of care delivery functions (JCAHO, 2006). According to Lammers et al. (2003), "JCAHO accreditation is important to health organizations because it is required by many third-party payers, state licensing agencies, managed care organizations, and financial institutions" (p. 324). In addition to accreditation, professional associations such as the American Medical Association, the American Hospital Association, and the American Nurses Association influence healthcare organizations by advocating certain standards of practice and lobbying for their interests in Congress.

Communication within Healthcare Organizations

Organizational information theory and healthcare organizations

Healthcare organizations must confront many challenges on a daily basis at both the macro and micro levels, such as finding ways to cut costs by efficiently managing resources, taking decisions about how to improve healthcare for con-sumers, making efforts to retain staff, and promoting the organization in an effort to attract consumers and improve business conditions. Communication is central to successfully meeting these and a host of other challenges typically faced by healthcare organizations. Healthcare organizations must use communication to acquire, manage, disseminate, evaluate, and act upon various types of information to function effectively, and communication is a vital component of the interre-lationships within an organization (e.g., administrator–provider relationships, provider–provider relationships, and provider–patient relationships) and the interrelationships among healthcare organizations and other organizations within the healthcare system, such as relationships among hospitals, diagnostic laboratories, pharmaceutical companies, and health insurance organizations.

Organizational information theory is a useful framework to assess the various ways in which healthcare organizations use information to function on a daily basis and to meet organizational goals. Karl Weick (1979) developed organizational information theory to describe the process by which organizations collect, manage, and use information they receive. Two important tenets of this theory are that change is a constant within organizations, and that confronting change successfully is necessary for the survival of organizations. For example, in the last 50 years, we have seen hospitals and other healthcare organizations respond to many changes in the health landscape, including provider specialization, the rise of managed care, healthcare legislation (such as the Health Insurance Portability and Accountability Act), an increase in the number of female physicians, nursing shortages, an aging population, diseases like HIV and Severe Acute Respiratory Syndrome (SARS), and the threat of biological terrorism. Healthcare organizations cannot ignore significant changes and trends such as these in health and healthcare and expect to remain competitive in today's healthcare market. Organizations must adjust to these types of changes as they occur, and communication plays an important role in the process of adapting to them.

Organizations rely on members within the organization who are skilled in certain areas to interpret information, or the organization can find people outside of the organization (i.e., using affiliations with other organizations or resources) to help interpret the information. Based upon the interpretation of the information, organizations first decide whether the information is relevant or useful to the goals of the organization, then they must decide how to use the information or adapt to it so that organizational goals are met. For example, suppose hospital administrators learn that poor physician handwriting has led to a high percentage of mistakes in filling prescriptions at the hospital pharmacy. While it may be relatively easy to interpret that this information is relevant to the organization and poses a problem to organizational goals (such as providing quality patient care and avoiding lawsuits), finding ways to solve the problem can be somewhat ambiguous. By consulting with a team of experts within the organization, a computer specialist might suggest that physicians use a personal data assistant (PDA) device, where they could select from a list of medications when prescribing for patients, and then the information could be sent by wireless technology from the PDA directly to a computer in the pharmacy. The administrators might conclude that this is the best way to manage the issue, or after consulting with other experts within the organization (such as an accountant) they may feel that this option would be too expensive, and they may continue to seek other information about ways to solve the problem.

According to Weick (1979), organizations engage in communication patterns known as *cycles*, which include an action, a response, and an adjustment. An action might be a question someone within the organization raises when confronted with an ambiguous problem he or she encounters, such as if a nurse asks why so many children are coming into the clinic with otitus media (an ear infection). A response to this action might be: "I saw this problem last winter during flu season" from a fellow nurse. The first nurse might adjust to this information by alerting physicians that they might expect to see a number of cases in the near future. Of course, when the physicians hear about this problem, it may lead to additional cycles (e.g., more questions, responses, and adjustments). These multiple cycles are known as *double interact loops* according to Weick (1979).

Most healthcare organizations have formal rules and policies for interpreting and acting upon ambiguous information as it surfaces. In organizations with formal organizational structures, ambiguous information is typically delegated to individuals who specialize in certain areas of knowledge, and many healthcare organizations rely upon hierarchical structures to process information. Hierarchies often have the advantage of processing information quickly and efficiently, but they can be problematic if organizations rely too much on individuals at the top of the hierarchy, such as managers, directors, and administrators, to interpret, process, and disseminate equivocal information. Ambiguous information is often encountered at various levels of organizations. For example, sometimes issues that can affect an entire hospital are first encountered by administrators, while at other times they are first recognized by people on the "front lines" of healthcare, such as nurses and receptionists. Other times pertinent information about an issue that will have a major impact on the organization can come from a particular department within the organization, such as the hospital security department.

O'Hair, O'Rourke, and O'Hair (2001) identify three common forms of message flow within healthcare organizations. When upper managers or administrators identify issues and messages are then communicated to the lower levels of the hierarchy, this is known as *downward communication*. Conversely, when people at the lower levels of the hierarchy, such as maintenance personnel, encounter information that may be useful to the organization and communicate messages to people at higher levels, this is known as *upward communication*. When messages are communicated among individuals who share a similar status within the organization, such as information exchanged among nurses, this is known as *horizontal communication*. Healthcare organizations with traditional hierarchical structures tend to privilege downward communication, and this can be detrimental to the organization since people at lower levels of healthcare organizations often possess important information about day-to-day operations and events that the higher levels of the organization may not be aware of, even though this information can be vital to the organization's success. For example, charge nurses are some of the most vital members of hospital organizations since they assist other nurses, order medicine, and organize schedules and other duties that appear out of the blue. All too often these important organizational resources are not consulted on the very issues they deal with on a daily basis. Instead, they receive emails and memos dictating policy for the very floors of the hospital they serve.

Messages can also be communicated through *formal and informal organizational communication networks* (Kreps & Thornton, 1992). Formal communication networks are tied to the structure of the organization, and messages may include emails, memos, handbooks, and other forms of written or oral communication, while informal channels tend to be more interpersonal and are linked to workers' need for additional information about organizational events and issues. Informal communication networks often consist of relationships that develop within the organization through day-to-day interactions. For example, supervisors make friends with subordinates, employees from different areas of the organization eat lunch and go to happy hour together, and people begin to rely on one another for various types of organizational information, including everyday gossip about personalities and opinions about policy changes and regulations. While a hospital memo might announce that the administration is considering hiring a new director of nursing from within the organization, employees may use friends in different departments or among the administration to find out which individuals might be the best candidates.

Informal leaders can emerge from these networks, and these individuals can sometimes become more powerful than formal leaders, especially when people trust them more than formal leaders. As we will see in the next section, informal networks are an important part of organizational culture, and administrators need to be aware of the influence of informal networks on employee perceptions of the organization and behaviors.

Healthcare Organization Culture

Healthcare organizations use communication for more than processing information and managing uncertainty: communication is central to the development and maintenance of relationships and the creation of organizational culture. A culture can be defined as the beliefs, assumptions, attitudes, and values a group of individuals share about the world based upon common experiences. In other words, when people share similar experiences on a regular basis, they often develop similar ways of seeing the world. All of us are members of many different cultures that are based upon common interests or shared realities due to common experiences (e.g., communication majors, sororities and fraternities, religious organizations, clubs), and like the cultures of these groups, members of healthcare organizations develop unique ways of seeing the organization and their experiences within it through day-to-day interactions.

Communication scholars who take a cultural approach to organizations argue that individuals within organizations create meanings for everyday events that occur in organizations, and they ultimately develop a unique sense of organizational reality (Eisenberg & Riley, 2001; O'Reilly, Chatman, & Caldwell, 1991; Pacanowsky & O'Donnell-Trujillo, 1982). These scholars contend that organizational members constantly create meanings for the behaviors they observe within the organization in an attempt to make sense of their world. The meanings that individual members create are shared with others through different forms of communication within the organization, such as symbols, stories, and rituals. These messages as well as the physical layout of hospitals, clinics, and other healthcare organizations can reflect the beliefs, attitudes, and values of an organization.

For example, in a hospital that values a holistic approach to healthcare, such as addressing patients' emotional needs in addition to providing care for physical health problems, stories about organizational heroes, such as a story about a nurse who called a patient at home on several occasions following a mastectomy to see how she was coping emotionally after the procedure, might be frequently told by members. Such a story would legitimize the organization's culture value of going beyond physical health when providing patient care, and by portraying the nurse's actions as heroic or favorable the story suggests that her behavior should be emulated by other employees. Other stories, such as those about organizational "villains" or individuals who behaved in ways that were contrary to the beliefs, attitudes, and values of the organization, might also be told to indirectly disseminate information about culturally undesirable behaviors.

Several years ago, one of the authors conducted a study (Wright & Frey, in press) that examined a comprehensive cancer center in Memphis, Tennessee. This cancer center wanted to create a "home-like" environment for its clients as opposed to a more institutionalized medical setting (such as the sterile environment that is often seen in large hospitals). This desire to create a warm and friendly environment at the center was reflected in the physical surroundings, which resembled a comfortable living room, including a kitchen and meeting rooms for clients, rather than the look of a traditional medical clinic. The clients indicated that they perceived the center to be more like a home than an institution, and this perception influenced their communication with staff members and satisfaction with the center.

Insights into the beliefs, attitudes, and values of other healthcare organizations can often be gained by examining organizational promotional materials, such as pamphlets and television commercials. In several cities, hospitals and medical centers have purchased state-of-the-art medical technology and often advertise these services as a way of conveying to potential patients that they have the ability to provide "cutting-edge" medical care. However, because technology is often perceived as cold and inhuman in our culture, many of these organizations also wish to convey to consumers that they still value caring relationships with patients despite the technology. For example, one hospital in Oklahoma City uses advertising slogans such as: "We provide the touch beyond the technology."

In addition to the overall cultural values of healthcare organizations, numerous co-cultures, or smaller groups of individuals with their own unique system of beliefs, attitudes, and values, exist within them. As we will discuss in greater detail in chapter 11, healthcare organizations consist of individuals from a wide variety of backgrounds in terms of education and training. The unique socialization of administrators, physicians, nurses, technicians, and other healthcare workers creates distinct co-cultures within health organizations, and differences in worldviews between each of these co-cultures can lead to misunderstandings, different expectations of healthcare, and sometimes conflict between groups (O'Hair, Thompson, & Gilchrist, 2004).

Influences on Healthcare Organization Communication

Pharmaceutical and biotechnology companies

Pharmaceutical companies are an important influence on healthcare organizations because they are the main suppliers of the prescription drugs that are commonly used to treat a multitude of health conditions. Major pharmaceutical companies, such as Pfizer, Merck, and Bristol Myers Squibb, are under tremendous pressure to generate quarterly profits for their investors, and the promotion of prescription drugs represents a growing source of pharmaceutical marketing. These companies market new prescription drugs to providers through the use of pharmaceutical sales representatives and to consumers through direct-to-consumer advertising (see chapter 8).

Pharmaceutical companies spend a substantial portion of their marketing budgets promoting prescription medications to health organizations. Physicians and other providers frequently attend seminars, lunches, and other promotional events sponsored by drug companies, and pharmaceutical sales representatives make frequent visits to hospitals, clinics, and other major health facilities in an effort to persuade providers to prescribe their company's medications. Many pharmaceutical companies do not necessarily rely on convincing medical arguments to persuade physicians to adopt their products. Pharmaceutical companies often try to hire attractive individuals as sales representatives who provide physicians and other providers with free sample packets of medications. Many of the events sponsored by drug companies are designed to "wine and dine," or persuade providers by offering free lunches and other perks for attending a sales event. For example, one of the authors worked as a researcher at a family medicine center in Oklahoma City and was invited to a free pharmaceutical company luncheon that included a huge barbeque buffet, including ribs, fried chicken, and free cocktails. The purpose of the event, ironically, was to promote a new appetite suppressant medication.

Direct-to-consumer marketing is an effective marketing tool for pharmaceutical companies (Holmer, 1999). Direct-to-consumer advertising urges consumers to "ask your doctor about" a particular medication. Undoubtedly you have seen some of the many direct-to-consumer advertisements for various medications on television in recent years, including Viagra, cholesterol-reducing medications, allergy pills (such as Claritan), hormone replacement therapy (HRT) drugs for women facing menopause, and a host of anti-anxiety and depression medications. Both pharmaceutical sales representatives and direct-to-consumer advertising appear to influence provider prescribing behaviors. For example, Ubel, Jepson, and Asch (2003) found that physician prescription practices were associated with the provision of free samples of medications by pharmaceutical representatives. We will examine drug advertisements in more depth in chapter 10.

While patients certainly need these medications for treating their health problems and providers need them to help patients, the rising cost of many of these medications (particularly newer ones) has raised many questions about whether more expensive drugs are more effective than cheaper drugs, and about ethical issues surrounding the process of prescription drug marketing.

For example, many health problems, such as certain types of heart disease, can be treated with relatively inexpensive medications such as beta-blockers, but cardiologists and other physicians often continue to favor more expensive medications like angiotensin-converting enzyme (ACE) inhibitors and calcium channel blockers as their first choice for treating patients largely due to the influence of pharmaceutical sales representatives who promote these higher-priced drugs (Ubel et al., 2003). Prescribing more expensive drugs increases profits for pharmaceutical companies, but it can have a negative impact on patients in a variety of ways. The practice of prescribing higher-priced medications can unfairly favor higher-income patients who can pay for them. Lower-income patients and older patients on fixed incomes often find it difficult to afford prescription medications. Medicaid and Medicare are two organizations that were created to help lower-income and older patients, but they often only pay for a small percentage of drug costs, resulting in more money the patient has to spend to purchase the medication. This may lead to lower compliance on the part of the patient when it becomes too expensive to continue taking the drug.

One questionable practice that occurs in many hospitals and medical centers is clinical *preceptorships*. During a preceptorship, a pharmaceutical company representative spends the day with the physician seeing patients "as an educational experience," but the physician receives an honorarium (often hundreds of dollars) from the drug company in return. While sales representatives may indeed learn much about medicine during a preceptorship, the primary reason for this activity is ultimately to build relationships between sales representatives and providers for the purpose of selling the company's medications.

In addition, patients who learn about medications through direct-to-consumer marketing may influence their providers to prescribe medications they don't really need. The over-prescribing of antibiotics in the United States is related to patient requests during office visits for these drugs, and many times providers will prescribe them even when they know the medication will have little effect. While direct-to-consumer marketing of medications may be educational for patients and facilitate communication between providers and patients when they are discussed, these medications can have unwanted side effects or may be inappropriate for patients in other ways, and this can lead to other health problems if the doctor feels pressured by the patient to prescribe them.

Providers often do not question the practices of pharmaceutical marketing or do not critically examine conflicts of interest that may develop as a result of their relationships with drug sales representatives. For example, one study found that medicine residents and faculty had relatively low levels of knowledge about physician–pharmaceutical industry relationships (Watkins & Kimberly, 2004). Research suggests that pharmaceutical companies will most likely continue these marketing strategies in the future (Holmer, 1999), and more education about the many ethical issues surrounding the relationships between pharmaceutical companies and health organizations is needed.

HIPPA

In 1996 the US Congress passed the Health Insurance and Accountability Act (HIPPA), which was designed to lower healthcare costs, safeguard identifiable patient data, and promote e-commerce in health. The law required that healthcare organizations identified by HIPPA be compliant by April of 2003. The implementation of HIPPA has affected healthcare organizations in a variety of ways.

Patient privacy

Efforts to become compliant with the patient privacy section of HIPPA have been very costly for healthcare organizations. The patient privacy section of HIPPA requires healthcare organizations to protect verbal, written, and electronic patient data. Health organizations have had to spend billions of dollars making changes to the way that patient information is handled in order to comply with these standards. For example, HIPPA requires health organizations to hire a privacy officer (who coordinates efforts to meet privacy regulations), to set up new privacy policies and procedures, to train employees to safeguard identifiable patient data, and to periodically review daily operations to insure that the privacy standards are being met. Verification of organizational compliance can occur through random unannounced visits by the Department of Health and Human Services, the Office of Civil Rights, or through health information privacy complaints filed against an individual or the organization (Bradley, 2004).

According to Gunter (2002), "the privacy rule is estimated to have a $3 billion financial impact on the US economy over the next 10 years" (p. 50). These costs will ultimately be passed on to consumers in the form of higher health insurance premiums. Failure to comply with HIPPA privacy protocols can be expensive, including fines for wrongful disclosure of health information ranging from $50,000 to $250,000 and imprisonment from one to ten years (Gunter, 2002). The law also allows for civil lawsuit awards up to $25,000 per violation.

While HIPPA privacy standards are costly for healthcare organizations, the privacy section offers benefits to patients. In recent years, many consumers have become concerned about third parties gaining access to their health records. Sensitive information within health records, including HIV status or history of other diseases and conditions, unhealthy lifestyle information (such as whether or not a patient smokes or drinks), and personal information, are typically not the types of information most people want revealed to insurance companies, researchers, hospital staff, or other third parties such as pharmaceutical companies and marketing firms. Physicians and other healthcare workers frequently write notes about patients in medical charts, particularly information about patient behaviors, such as when they are confrontational, moody, or perceived to be problem patients. In the past, receptionists, nurses, and other individuals working within the organization could easily access this information. Under HIPPA, sensitive patient information is more secure than in the past, although the law has not completely eliminated all third parties from seeing this type of information.

HIPPA's effect on medical research

Hospitals and medical facilities are not only places where people come to be treated for health problems, they are also sites for medical research. Researchers need access to patient populations to test new medications, medical procedures, and new approaches to healthcare delivery (including health communication studies). Under HIPPA, researchers must obtain detailed written permission from patients to use individually identifiable patient data, and this new rule is making it more costly for healthcare organizations to conduct research. Prior to HIPPA, researchers could access patient records and other information more easily, requiring in many cases only a brief review by the organization's Institutional Review Board. According to Kulynych and Korn (2002), "Erecting new regulatory barriers to the use or disclosure of medical information imposes costs, not only in terms of real dollars, but also in terms of research delayed or perhaps forgone" (p. 204). However, the more stringent policies towards protecting patient data in the research process may encourage greater patient participation because potential participants will have assurances that sensitive information will remain private.

HIPPA's effect on providers and patients

Under HIPPA, doctors are required to obtain a patient's permission before sending their information to pharmacies, laboratories, and insurance companies. Patients can also request a report of all parties who have seen their health information, and patients must be permitted to review and amend their medical records. Providers are required to explain privacy issues to every patient they treat and answer any questions a patient may have about the HIPPA privacy policies. Many providers feel that this new requirement may take time away from other activities during appointments with patients. As we have seen earlier, providers face a number of time constraints during provider–patient interactions, and many providers feel that the HIPPA requirements add to an already heavy workload. However, Ross and Lin (2003), in a review of studies that examined the effects of patient access to medical records due to HIPPA, found that the increased opportunities for providers and patients to talk about the patient's medical records could enhance provider–patient communication.

Medicare and Medicaid

The US government provides health insurance to about 74 million Americans through the Centers for Medicare and Medicaid. The Centers for Medicare and Medicaid were created in 1965 and provide a safety net for US citizens who may find it difficult to obtain health insurance from other sources due to factors such as living on a fixed income, difficulty obtaining employment because of a disability, and living beneath the poverty level. Individuals 65 years of age and older are eligible for Medicare benefits as well as people (old or young) with a permanent disability, while Medicaid provides health insurance to lower-income individuals and their children. The Centers for Medicare and Medicaid impose many rules and regulations on providers in terms of how they will be reimbursed for healthcare services. Each US state is allowed to determine eligibility requirements for Medicare and Medicaid, and the health services that are reimbursed by these programs vary from state to state (Lammers et al., 2003).

There is great concern over the ability of the federal government to continue covering medical expenses through Medicare and Medicaid due to rising healthcare costs and the aging of the US population. Medicare currently covers two-thirds of the healthcare costs for older adults in the United States, and with the number of individuals 65 and older projected to grow substantially over the next decade, the Medicare program will need to find new ways to assure quality healthcare services for US citizens. Medicare currently has a number of restrictions on types of services that individuals can obtain from providers, and many individuals on Medicare find it difficult to afford prescription drugs because in many cases Medicare will only reimburse individuals for a small portion of the cost of these medications. This problem is exacerbated by the rising cost of prescription drugs and the tendency for pharmaceutical companies to promote more expensive products. Many hospitals and other health facilities provide only limited services to individuals being reimbursed by Medicaid, and during financial downturns certain Medicaid services can be eliminated as a cost-cutting measure (Vock, 2005).

In 1985 the US Congress passed legislation to extend Medicare benefits to people living in nursing homes, and under this newer legislation Medicare now covers the costs of approved hospice programs for terminally ill individuals. However, these services are often underused because of delayed referrals and lack of information about them (Miller & Mor, 2001). Medicare and Medicaid restrictions on the reimbursement of providers, medical procedures, and medications will likely continue to influence the practices of health organizations in the future.

Insurance and managed care

The introduction of managed care in the United States has transformed healthcare delivery from an activity controlled by providers to one controlled by healthcare bureaucracies (Hafferty & Light, 1995; Moore, O'Hair, & Ledlow,

2002). According to Anthony (2002), "the purpose of managed care is to effectively coordinate and oversee the delivery of care such that excessive and possibly unnecessary care is eliminated, thereby improving quality while reducing costs" (p. 2033). Managed care organizations help bring providers and patients together in a way that is financially beneficial to both parties (and to the managed care organization). These organizations help providers gain access to consumers by offering consumers attractively priced health plans, advertising the plans, and working with employers who offer health plans to recruit potential consumers. In addition, managed care organizations create binding contracts with physicians, other providers, hospitals, and other health facilities, making them legally obligated to participate in managed care health plans, but the contracts also insure that they will be reimbursed for their services. Consumers prepay for services through monthly premiums, but they have the benefit of being able to access providers and health facilities when needed, while providers and health facilities have the advantage of being able to rely on a steady inflow of patients who need their services.

There are many types of managed care organizations today. According to Street (2003), "as we enter the 21st century, managed care has grown into a complex and multifaceted phenomenon with no singular identity." However, Street goes on to say that "practically all medical care is 'managed' in some way" (p. 72). Consumers can choose many types of managed care plans, ranging from traditional prepaid indemnity insurance policies that cover catastrophic events to access (albeit limited by the stipulations of the health plan) to networks of providers, facilities, and services for a fixed amount of money per year. This section discusses three major types of managed care: traditional health insurance, health maintenance organizations, and preferred provider organizations. Of course, there are many hybrid managed care plans, and these often combine features of each of these types of managed care.

Traditional health insurance, similar to car or home insurance, can be expensive for most consumers, although there are many different plans that are currently offered in today's market. Most of these plans pay for services in times of severe need, such as if an individual needs an operation or if he or she has been in an accident. These plans typically carry a deductible, and consumers have to pay a premium for the insurance. Like other types of insurance, the amount of premium will typically rise as a consumer makes more insurance claims. These types of plans are helpful for disastrous events, but they may not be ideal when less costly health services are needed for preventive health services, such as check-ups and diagnostic tests (e.g., blood tests).

Health maintenance organizations (HMOs) are an example of an early type of managed care organization, and they are still a popular option for consumers today. HMOs typically allow consumers access to a hospital system or a relatively small network of providers, facilities, and services. Consumers prepay a set amount for access to the HMO, and they can obtain healthcare when necessary. One disadvantage of HMOs is that patients are typically assigned a primary care physician, who serves as a gatekeeper allowing patients to access services and other providers (such as specialists). Typically, a patient must obtain a referral from his or her primary physician in order to gain access to services and other providers within the HMO. In some cases patients must call in to a triage center where a health professional determines their level of care and makes a recommendation (Ledlow, O'Hair, Moore, 2003). In addition, patients are only allowed to access providers, facilities, and services that are within the domain of the HMO, and they are not covered if they use services outside of the HMO. The HMO Act of 1973 required larger employers to make an HMO plan available for workers, and this led to the rapid rise of these organizations (Lammers et al., 2003). However, newer managed care options have provided consumers with other choices besides HMOs.

Preferred provider organizations (PPOs) "are a less unified form of managed care that offers patients wider (though still limited) choices of physicians and hospitals at varying levels of costs reflecting discounts providers are willing to give to attract patients" (Lammers et al., 2003). Under PPO plans, consumers are allowed to choose from a list of providers and services, including specialists. One advantage of PPOs is that consumers do not need to see a primary care physician when they require health services. If a patient is experiencing foot problems, she is free to choose a podiatrist from a list of podiatrists offered by the PPO rather than having to see a primary care physician first. The list of providers offered by most PPO plans typically includes most types of specialists and several providers working within each specialty. The wider amount of health service choices within PPOs has led to an increase in their popularity. However, like HMOs, providers are often limited by the plan to certain treatment options, and consumers are penalized financially or not covered in some cases if they choose a provider or service that is outside of the PPO services network.

Effects of managed care on provider–patient relationships

While managed care has made health insurance more affordable for consumers, many patients feel their provider's behaviors (e.g., treatment decisions) are dictated by managed care organizations, and this has negatively affected patient perceptions of trust towards providers (Davies & Rundall, 2000). Costs are often contained under managed care by managing the number of referrals made to specialists (Halm, Causino, & Blumenthal, 1997). Because specialty care is associated with higher medical costs (Greenfield et al., 1992), providers often play the role of gatekeeper by limiting patient access to specialists and more expensive procedures through the referral process. Under managed care, primary care providers are limited to a list of approved providers to whom they can refer patients. Patients and providers often resent the restrictions on health services that are placed upon them by managed care plans. Patients want to have more choices in terms of which providers they can see and the services they can obtain, and providers often desire greater flexibility in referring patients to the best specialists and services possible. As we will see in the next section, the rise of managed care has had a major impact on provider stress and relationships with patients.

Provider Stress, Conflict, and Support within Healthcare Organizations

Healthcare organizations can be very stressful environments for providers. For example, stressors that have traditionally existed within healthcare organizations include staff shortages, work overload, time pressures, having to answer to multiple supervisors, administrative and co-worker conflict, dealing with organizational bureaucracy, lack of support from superiors and peers, and uncertainty concerning ability to treat patients (Simoni & Patterson, 1997; Tyler & Cushway, 1995).

Communicating with patients can be stressful for providers in a variety of ways. Patients may be worried or anxious about their health condition, embarrassed by questions asked by providers, angry or abusive, and they may have difficulty expressing their thoughts and feelings to providers (Maslach & Jackson, 1982). Providers may find it difficult to discuss emotional topics, deliver bad news to the patient, or deal with the patient's family members (O'Hair et al., 2003).

A major contributor to healthcare provider job stress is role conflict and role ambiguity. According to Apker and Ray (2003), *role conflict* "refers to a person having to engage in two or more incompatible roles simultaneously," while *role ambiguity* "refers to a lack of clarity regarding the definition and expectations for a particular role" (p. 351). For example, nurses may experience role conflict when taking on the role of patient advocate (e.g., protecting the rights of patients and being sensitive to their needs) while simultaneously playing the role of a "good employee" who needs to answer to physicians and administrators. In terms of role ambiguity, under managed care practices nurses are being asked to perform more administrative duties, such as documenting insurance information for patients, and they may question whether the main focus of their job is to care for patients' physical and emotional needs or to take care of their insurance needs. Many other duties that nurses are sometimes expected to perform, such as answering telephones and admitting new patients, are not clearly defined by hospital administrators as part of their job description, and nurses often find it frustrating when asked to perform duties that are incompatible with their expectations of what their job actually entails.

Additionally, stress among healthcare workers can result from *emotional labor*, or the job-related need to display socially appropriate emotions when interacting with others within healthcare contexts (Apker & Ray, 2003). For example, providers such as nurses often must display empathy and concern for patients in an effort to comfort them, and have to suppress emotions such as anger when interacting with uncooperative patients or sadness when interacting with a terminally ill patient (so they do not upset the patient further), and they must suppress other emotions in an effort to act "professional" when communicating with co-workers. Management of these emotions can be a difficult task to accomplish for providers, and it can lead to stress and emotional exhaustion. Many providers also must contend with managing their emotions outside of the workplace. After a stressful day, providers often do not want to display emotions such as anger, sadness, or frustration to their family members or loved ones.

In recent years a variety of changes have redefined the healthcare profession, and in many cases these changes have led to increased stress for healthcare workers. The increased surveillance of medical expenses by managed care organizations has led to a situation where providers must think more about the costs of procedures and medications, a patient's insurance coverage, and administrative duties (documenting adherence to managed care regulations), and these changes can negatively affect the quality of provider–patient communication (Lammers & Geist, 1997). Under managed care, providers may feel they have less time to address patients' emotional concerns, their communication with patients may become more formal, and patients often feel more dehumanized (Lammers & Geist, 1997). In addition, according to Buiser (2000), current trends such as case management, downsizing, restructuring of the workforce, and changes in patient profile have negatively affected job satisfaction among healthcare workers.

Stress and conflict

Stress and conflict within healthcare organizations are often interrelated. Managing the multiple demands placed upon healthcare workers inside and outside of the workplace (e.g., incompatible personalities in the workplace, financial problems, family problems) increases stress and can lead to conflict among healthcare workers and between healthcare workers and their loved ones outside of the workplace (Decker, 1997; Miller & Gilles, 1996). Conflict, in turn, tends to produce more stress for healthcare workers, and this may lead to additional conflict. Healthcare workers tend to work closely together in a fast-paced environment where they often have to deal with multiple patients, carry out unpleasant duties (e.g., removing bedpans from hospitalized patients), perform administrative duties, cope with the bureaucracy of the healthcare organization (e.g., forms and procedures set forth by administrators), and work in an environment where people vary widely in terms of status and education (Apker & Ray, 2003).

Individuals differ in the way they handle conflict and tend to exhibit patterns of conflict that are trait-like, or relatively stable and consistent over time (Hample, 1999). Some people tend to be argumentative, which involves focusing on issues (presenting and defending one's own position and refuting another's), while other individuals tend to be verbally aggressive (using personal attacks as opposed to focusing on the issues) or conflict avoidant (refusing to engage in an argument or withdrawing from the setting). (For reviews of this research see Deutsch & Coleman, 2000; Infante & Wigley, 1986; Rahim, 2001.) When individuals with different conflict traits engage in conflict, this can lead to unsatisfying outcomes. For example, a radiology technician who is argumentative will find it frustrating when arguing with a physician who tends to be verbally aggressive, and she may resent the physician for making personal attacks rather than focusing on the issues.

In addition, healthcare workers frequently encounter unpleasant patients or patients who are unhappy because of their fear of seeing a provider or uncertainty over their health status, and this can lead to conflict between providers and patients. Like any other workplace, unpleasant personalities, inflated egos, and other interpersonal issues can lead to conflict among workers, but these problems are often magnified in stressful healthcare settings.

Effects of job stress

Stress appears to be inevitable in healthcare organizations, and stress can lead to many negative outcomes for healthcare workers, including, fear, uncertainty, insecurity, frustration, resentment, anger, sadness, depression, guilt, betrayal, and distrust (Young & Brown, 1998). One effect of job stress is *burnout*, or a "syndrome of emotional exhaustion, depersonalization, and reduced personal accomplishment" (Maslach & Jackson, 1982, p. 228). When healthcare workers experience burnout, they may see little value in their job or no longer care about performing their duties well. Stress and burnout can lead to higher job dissatisfaction, and dissatisfaction may exhibit itself in the form of lower productivity, higher absenteeism, increased work errors, poor judgment, defensive behavior, hostility, reduction in creativity, and higher job turnover (Buiser, 2000). For example, in recent years there has been a shortage of nurses in the

United States, and a major contributing factor to the nursing shortage is dissatisfaction with stressful conditions in the workplace (Apker, 2001; Nursing World, 2001). Bacharach, Bamberger, and Conley (1991) found that high levels of role conflict experienced by nurses at work were predictive of higher levels of job burnout and lower levels of satisfaction. This situation has become especially acute among younger nurses (Shrader, Marion, Broome, West, & Nash, 2001).

In addition, low job satisfaction may adversely affect the quality of patient care (Douglas, Meleis, Eribes, & Kim, 1996). Preventable medical errors are the eighth most common cause of death in the United States (Sexton, Thomas, & Helmreich, 2000), and when healthcare workers are dissatisfied, they may become less sensitive to patient needs, and less concerned or neglectful in terms of performing duties. Moreover, dissatisfaction in the workplace and job stress can lead to other problems that can affect patient care. Substance abuse, for example, is common among healthcare workers and is often related to job stress and job dissatisfaction (Shattner & Coman, 1998).

Support and stress in the workplace

Support networks in the workplace have been found to protect healthcare workers from adverse mental and physical health consequences of job stressors (Dignam & West, 1988). Perceived availability of support in hospitals has been linked to a reduction in emotional exhaustion and burnout among healthcare workers (Cronin-Stubbs & Rooks, 1985; Firth, McIntee, McKeown, & Britton, 1986; Hare, Pratt, & Andrews, 1988; Ogus, 1990). Studies have found that both social support and positive coping activities (such as problem-focused coping, see chapter 4) are associated with the ability to solve problems more effectively and fewer sick days in healthcare organizations (Koleck, Bruchon-Schweitzer, Thiebaut, Dumartin, & Sifakis, 2000).

Summary

Healthcare organizations are an integral part of healthcare delivery and an important context for examining health communication. Healthcare organizations facilitate healthcare by pooling together many resources, and these resources are used by organizations to adapt to changing conditions. In addition, healthcare organizations can be viewed as cultures with their own unique beliefs, attitudes, and values. Interactions at the smallest levels of healthcare organizations, such as talk between providers and patients, are often influenced by forces at higher levels of the organization and the larger healthcare system. Pharmaceutical companies, government agencies, and managed care organizations have considerable influence on the day-to-day operations of healthcare organizations. Finally, healthcare organizations are stressful and demanding environments for healthcare workers, and this can lead to many negative outcomes, such as health problems, burnout, and conflict. However, social support networks within these organizations can help individuals cope with stress.

References

Anthony, D. (2002). Changing the nature of physician referral relationships in the US: The impact of managed care. *Social Science and Medicine, 56*, 2033–2044.

Apker, J. (2001). Role development in the managed care era: A case in hospital-based nursing. *Journal of Applied Communication Research, 29*, 117–136.

Apker, J., & Ray, E. B. (2003). Stress and social supporting health care organizations. In T. L. Thompson, A. M. Dorsey, K. I. Miller, & R. Parrott (Eds.), *Handbook of health communication* (pp. 347–368). Mahwah, NJ: Lawrence Erlbaum.

Bacharach, S., Bamberger, P., & Conley, C. (1991). Work–home conflict among nurses and engineers: Mediating the impact of role stress on burnout and satisfaction at work. *Journal of Organizational Behavior, 12*, 39–53.

Bradley, D. (2004). HIPPA compliance efforts. *Pediatric Emergency Care, 20*(1), 68–70.

Buiser, M. (2000). Surviving managed care: The effect on job satisfaction in hospital-based nursing. *MEDSURG Nursing, 9*, 129–134.

Cronin-Stubbs, D., & Rooks, C. A. (1985). The stress, social support, and burnout of critical care nurses: The results of research. *Heart and Lung, 14*(1), 31–9.

Daft, R. L., & Lengel, R. H. (1986). Organizational information requirements, media richness, and structural design. *Management Science, 22*, 554–571.

Davies, H., & Rundall, T. (2000). Managing patient trust in managed care. *Milbank Quarterly, 778*, 609–624.

Decker, F. H. (1997). Occupational and nonoccupational factors in job satisfaction and psychological distress among nurses. *Research in Nursing and Health, 20*, 453–464.

Deutsch, M., & Coleman, P. T. (Eds.). (2000). *The handbook of conflict resolution: Theory and practice*. San Francisco: Jossey-Bass.

Dignam, J. T., & West, S. G. (1988). Social support in the workplace: Tests of six theoretical models. *American Journal of Community Psychology, 16*, 701–724.

Douglas, M. K., Meleis, A. I., Eribes, C., & Kim, S. (1996). The work of auxiliary nurses in Mexico: Stressors, satisfiers, and coping strategies. *International Journal of Nursing Studies, 33*, 495–505.

Eisenberg, E., & Riley, P. (2001). Organizational culture. In F. Jablin & L. Putnam (Eds.), *The new handbook of organizational communication* (pp. 291–322). Beverly Hills, CA: Sage.

Firth, H., McIntee, J., McKeown, P., & Britton, P. (1986). Burnout and professional depression: Related concepts? *Journal of Advances in Nursing, 11*(6), 633–641.

Greenfield, S., Nelson, E., Zubkoff, M., Manning, W., Rogers, W., Kraviz, R., Keller, A., Tarlov, A., & Ware, J. E. (1992). Variations in resource utilization among medical specialties and systems of care. *Journal of the American Medical Association, 267*, 1624–1630.

Gunter, K. P. (2002). The HIPPA privacy rule: Practical advice for academic and research institutions. *Healthcare Financial Management, 56*, 50–54.

Hafferty, F., & Light, D. (1995). Professional dynamics and the changing nature of medical work. *Journal of Health and Social Behavior, 35*, 132–153.

Halm, E. A., Causino, N., & Blumenthal, D. (1997). Is gatekeeping better than traditional care? A survey of physicians' attitudes. *Journal of the American Medical Association, 278*, 1677–1681.

Hample, D. (1999). The life space of personalized conflicts. In M. E. Roloff & G. D. Paulson (Eds.), *Communication yearbook 22* (pp. 172–201). Thousand Oaks, CA: Sage.

Hare, J., Pratt, C. C., & Andrews, D. (1988). Predictors of burnout in professional and paraprofessional nurses working in hospitals and nursing homes. *International Journal of Nursing Studies, 25*(2), 105–115.

Hinshaw, A. S., Smeltzer, C. H., & Atwood, J. R. (1987). Innovative retention strategies for nursing staff. *Journal of Nursing Administration, 17*, 8–16.

Hollon, M. F. (1999). Direct-to-consumer marketing of prescription drugs: Creating consumer demand. *Journal of the American Medical Association, 281*, 382–384.

Holmer, A. F. (1999). Direct-to-consumer prescription drug advertising builds bridges between patients and physicians. *Journal of the American Medical Association, 281*, 380–382.

Infante, D., & Wigley, C. (1986). Verbal aggressiveness: An interpersonal model and measure. *Communication Monographs, 53*, 61–69.

Infante, D. A., Rancer, A. S., & Womack, D. F. (1997). *Building communication theory* (3rd ed.). Prospect Heights, IL: Waveland Press.

Joint Commission on Healthcare Organizations (JCAHO). (2006). Facts about the Joint Commission. Retrieved September 2, 2006, from www.jointcommission.org/AboutUs/joint_commission_facts.htm.

Koleck, M., Bruchon-Schweitzer, M., Thiebaut, E., Dumartin, N., & Sifakis, Y. (2000). Stress, coping, and burnout among French general practitioners. *European Review of Applied Psychology, 50*, 309–314.

Kreps, G. L. (1990). *Organizational communication: Theory and practice* (2nd ed.). White Plains, NY: Longman.

Kreps, G. L., & Thornton, B. C. (1992). *Health communication: Theory and practice* (2nd ed.). Prospect Heights, IL: Waveland Press.

Kulynych, J., & Korn, D. (2002). The effect of the new federal medical-privacy rule on research. *New England Journal of Medicine, 346*, 201–204.

Lammers, J. C., & Geist, P. (1997). The transformation of caring in the light and shadow of "managed care." *Health Communication, 9*, 46–60.

Lammers, J. C., Barbour, J. B., & Duggan, A. P. (2003). Organizational forms of the provision of health care: An institutional perspective. In T. L. Thompson, A. M. Dorsey, K. I. Miller, & R. Parrott (Eds.), *Handbook of health communication* (pp. 319–345). Mahwah, NJ: Lawrence Erlbaum.

Ledlow, G., O'Hair, H. D., & Moore, S. (2003). Predictors of communication quality: The patient, provider, and nurse call center triad. *Health Communication*, *15*, 431–455.

Maslach, C., & Jackson, S. E. (1982). Burnout in health professions: A social psychological analysis. In G. S. Sanders & J. Suls (Eds.), *Social psychology of health and illness*. Hillsdale, NJ: Lawrence Erlbaum.

Miller, D., & Gilles, P. (1996). Is there life after work? Experiences of HIV and oncology health staff. *AIDs Care: Psychological and Socio-Medical Aspects of AIDS/HIV*, *8*, 167–182.

Miller, S. C., & Mor, V. (2001). The emergence of Medicare hospice care in US nursing homes. *Palliative Medicine*, *15*, 471–480.

Moore, S. D., O'Hair, H. D., & Ledlow, G. (2002). The effects of health delivery systems and self-efficacy on patient compliance and satisfaction. *Communication Research Reports*, *19*(4), 362–371.

Nursing World. (2001, November 5). American Nurses Association applauds introduction of Nurse Retention and Quality of Care Act 2001. Retrieved January 20, 2004, from www.nursingworld.org/rnrealnew.

Ogus, E. D. (1990). Burnout and social support systems among ward nurses. *Issues in Mental Health Nursing*, *11*(3), 267–281.

O'Hair, H. D., Friedrich, G., & Dixon, L. (in press). *Strategic communication in business and the professions* (6th ed.). Boston: Houghton Mifflin.

O'Hair, H. D., O'Rourke, J., & O'Hair, M. (2001). *Business communication*. Cincinnati, OH: South-Western.

O'Hair, H. D., Thompson, S., & Gilchrist, E. (2004). *Physician referral: Exploring the culture*. Paper presented at the annual meeting of the International Communication Association, New Orleans.

O'Hair, H. D., Villagran, M., Wittenberg, E., Brown, K., Hall, T., Ferguson, M., & Doty, T. (2003). Cancer survivorship and agency model (CSAM): Implications for patient choice, decision making, and influence. *Health Communication*, *15*, 193–202.

O'Reilly, C., Chatman, J., & Caldwell, D. (1991). People and organizational culture: A Q-sort approach to assessing person–organization fit. *Academy of Management Journal*, *34*, 487–516.

Pacanowsky, M. E., & O'Donnell-Trujillo, N. (1982). Organizational communication and organizational cultures. *Western Journal of Speech Communication*, *46*, 115–130.

Rahim, M. A. (2001). *Managing conflict in organizations* (3rd ed.). Westport, CT: Quorum Books.

Ross, S. E., & Lin, C. T. (2003). The effects of promoting patient access to medical records: A review. *Journal of the American Medical Informatics Association*, *10*, 129–138.

Sexton, J. B., Thomas, E. J., & Helmreich, R. L. (2000). Error, stress, and teamwork in medicine and aviation: Cross-sectional surveys. *British Medical Journal*, *320*, 745–749.

Shattner, P., & Coman, G. (1998). The stress of metropolitan general practice. *Medical Journal of Australia*, *169*, 133–137.

Shrader, K., Marion, E., Broome, C. D., West, M. E., & Nash, M. (2001). Factors influencing satisfaction and anticipated turnover for nurses in an academic medical center. *Journal of Nursing Administration*, *3*(4), 210–216.

Simoni, P. S., & Patterson, J. J. (1997). Hardiness, coping and burnout in the nursing workplace. *Journal of Professional Nursing*, *13*, 178–185.

Street, R. L., Jr. (2003). Communication in medical encounters: An ecological perspective. In T. L. Thompson, A. M. Dorsey, K. I. Miller, & R. Parrott (Eds.), *Handbook of health communication* (pp. 63–80). Mahwah, NJ: Lawrence Erlbaum.

Tyler, P. A., & Cushway, D. (1995). Stress in nurses: The effects of coping and support. *Stress Medicine*, *11*, 243–251.

Ubel, P. A., Jepson, C., & Asch, D. A. (2003). Misperceptions about beta-blockers and diuretics: A national survey of primary care physicians. *Journal of General Internal Medicine*, *18*, 997–983.

Vock, D. C. (2005). Medicaid cuts could target drug costs. Stateline.org. Retrieved September 10, 2006, from www.stateline.org/live/ViewPage.action?siteNodeId=136&languageId=1&contentId=53376.

Watkins, R. S., & Kimberly, J., Jr. (2004). What residents don't know about physician–pharmaceutical industry interactions. *Academic Medicine*, *79*, 432–437.

Weick, K. (1979). *The social psychology of organizing* (2nd ed.). Reading, MA: Addison-Wesley.

Wright, K. B., & Frey, L. R. (in press). Communication and care in an acute cancer center: The effects of patients' willingness to communicate about health, healthcare environment perceptions, and health status on information seeking, participation in care practices, and satisfaction. *Health Communication*.

Young, S., & Brown, H. N. (1998). Effects of hospital downsizing on surviving staff. *Nursing Economics*, *16*, 258–262.

Part IV

Influences of Technologies
and Media

Chapter 7

New Technologies and Health Communication

Have you ever looked up information about an illness on WebMD or used your health insurance company website to find a physician who is in your provider network? If so, you are one of millions of people who search for health information on the Internet each day. Health communicative activities on the Internet include everything from pop-ups about new pharmaceutical products to on-line support groups for almost every imaginable disease and condition.

The US healthcare system has a long and distinguished history of innovation, and when new technological advances are found to benefit healthcare delivery and the prevention of disease, it is often on the cutting edge of adopting them. In recent years we have witnessed the growth of a variety of new communication technologies that have led to many changes in health communication. The development of the Internet, wireless computer technology, global satellite positioning, and software that allows for the tailoring of messages are just a few examples of the high-tech revolution that has led to communication changes within the health delivery system. In addition, many of these technologies are converging in interesting ways, allowing for unique applications of technology to healthcare settings. For example, computers have integrated wireless technology, allowing for wireless access to other computers via the Internet, and global satellite positioning components are now being embedded in computer chips and everyday products which will eventually allow for physical tracking of medications, medical equipment, and people carrying portable computers. The extent to which these newer technologies will transform health communication remains to be seen, but it appears that technology will continue to be used by the healthcare system in the future.

Healthcare organizations hope that the application of these technologies will reduce the costs associated with traditional channels of communication (e.g., telephone, paper-based patient charts, memorandums from healthcare organization administrators) and increase convenience and efficiency. New technologies can also be used in health prevention and education efforts to disseminate and access health information as well as facilitate relationships (provider–provider, provider–patient, and patient–patient). The costs of the current US healthcare system were estimated to be over $1 trillion in 2001 (US Census Bureau, 2001) and are projected to rise over the next decade.

New communication technologies have the ability to impact health communication both positively and negatively (Neuhauser & Kreps, 2003). In some cases the cost of adopting them may not be beneficial to health practitioners, so it is important for health communication scholars to understand the advantages and disadvantages these technologies offer in terms of disseminating health information and facilitating interaction among different stakeholders in the health arena. This chapter examines some of the prominent ways in which new communication technologies are currently being used in the US healthcare system and their potential impact on health outcomes.

Health Information on the Internet

More and more Americans are using the Internet to search for health information than ever before. Surveys of Internet usage patterns have revealed that health information is one of the most popular topics that individuals search for on a daily basis (Fox & Rainie, 2000; Harris Interactive, 2001; UPI, 1999). While the growth and popularity of using the Internet for health information may provide consumers with up-to-date information about various aspects of disease prevention, illness, treatment, and control, there are many questions concerning the vast difference in credibility and quality of health-related information that is currently on-line. In addition, there are many concerns about access to the Internet, particularly among traditionally underserved segments of the population.

Health information access

At no other point in history has access to health information been so convenient for both providers and consumers (Eng, 2001). Every day, people can gain access to much of the same information as healthcare providers on government and research institution websites or electronic databases on the Internet that are free or charge a fee (e.g., MedLine), but few take advantage of them for financial, cultural, and educational reasons. Instead, most consumers limit their search for health information to the use of search engines that find health-related websites (Fox & Rainie, 2000). Consumers can find a variety of websites sponsored by government organizations, such as the National Institutes of Health (NIH) and the Center for Disease Control (CDC), and on-line medical journals, and they can even pose questions and receive information from healthcare specialists on some websites (e.g., WebMD). Access to health information via the Web has led to patients bringing information they have found there to discussions with their physicians during office visits (Aspden & Katz, 2001), more talk about information acquired from the Internet during medical interviews (Aspden & Katz, 2001; Ferguson, 1998), and greater patient ability to discuss more specific details of diseases and conditions (Napoli, 2001). Moreover, patients often act upon health advice obtained from the Internet (Bass, 2003). However, relatively little research has examined how health information from the Internet influences the decision-making process and outcomes in medical encounters. It has also failed to explore other communicative aspects of provider–patient relationships, such as issues of power and control, or the effects of how knowledge about health topics obtained from the Internet influences patient communication.

Current search engines (e.g., Yahoo and Google) often lack an efficient way to access specific health-related websites. A keyword search for a specific disease, such as HIV/AIDS, will result in links to hundreds of sites that may vary in terms of their intended audience, information quality, and specificity of information about the disease (Bass, 2003). People accessing information about HIV/AIDS are often interested in very different aspects of the disease. For example, some people are interested in HIV prevention, while others might be concerned about specific treatment options or finding an on-line support group for people living with the disease. Other individuals interested in HIV/AIDS, such as physicians and researchers, frequently obtain information from HIV/AIDS websites dealing with highly technical aspects of the disease. The major search engines make it difficult to locate information about health that is tailored specifically to the education level and interests of individuals. This makes it extremely cumbersome to sift through hundreds of links to websites that may not provide the desired information, or information may be presented in language that is too technical or too basic depending upon the background of the searcher (Eng, 2001).

In addition, just because people have access to information does not necessarily mean they will use it, understand it, or change their attitudes and behaviors because of it. For years people have had access to health information from university libraries and many other sources, but they have not necessarily used the information, had the capacity to understand it, or they have lacked the motivation to enact the suggested behaviors for improving health outcomes.

Credibility

It is often difficult to assess the credibility of health information found on the Internet. Anyone who has access to a web page authoring program and server space can potentially upload web pages or a website dedicated to a health-related topic. While some websites are created by government organizations, such as the CDC, others are designed by people who have an interest in a certain disease or illness (such as individuals coping with cancer). A number of researchers have expressed concerns about credibility in evaluating information on health-related websites (Barnes et al., 2003; Cummins et al., 2003). While government, university, and research organization-sponsored websites typically provide the most credible information, some websites created by interest groups and individuals can also contain credible information. For example, sometimes a cancer survivor or a person who is a caregiver for someone with Alzheimer's disease may have credible information to offer others because of his or her first-hand experience with the disease. Complicating the issue further, consumers often differ in terms of what they perceive to be credible information. Some people find scientific studies about a disease to be credible whereas others think that accounts of personal experience have more credibility.

Unfortunately, studies have found that much of the health information on the Internet is either inaccurate or incomplete (Bierman, Golladay, and Baker, 1999; Hersch, Gorman, and Sacherek, 1998), and many websites do not conform to standards set by professional medical associations, such as the American Medical Association (Rice, 2001). Typically, standards for credible websites include the provision of informed consent for consumers, editorial control over messages (e.g., controlling spam and other unwanted messages through the use of moderators or website content editors), and disclosure of all website sponsors, such as pharmaceutical companies or other health-related businesses (Rice, 2001). In addition, websites that are affiliated with established research institutions, medical research firms, and government agencies are typically seen as more credible than those that do not have such an affiliation. Assessing the credibility of websites is often a difficult task for laypersons, and even for researchers and health professionals there are currently few consistent guidelines. Some researchers have attempted to create guidelines for health information on the Internet (see Cummins et al., 2003; Kim, Eng, Deering, & Maxfield, 1999; Weiler & Pealer, 2000), but whether or not these will ultimately be adopted on a large scale remains questionable.

Literacy issues/underserved populations

Despite the large amount of health information that is currently available on the Internet, there are many underserved populations, including older adults, individuals from lower socioeconomic households, people with low literacy levels or little experience with technology, individuals with disabilities, and people living in rural areas who cannot access the Internet or who have limited access. Although the digital divide has become smaller in recent years due to a decline in the cost of computers and access to the Internet, many members of underserved populations still have difficulty gaining access to health information on-line (Rice, 2001). Unfortunately, these individuals are often also members of high-risk groups for many diseases and conditions, and they would benefit most from the health information that exists on the Internet.

Efforts have been made to reach members of underserved populations, including organizations such as SeniorNet that attempt to provide access to computers and computer training for older individuals within senior centers and other locations within communities, software applications that allow people with disabilities (e.g., people who are visually impaired) to use web browsers, and corporate programs that provide donations of older computers and Internet access to poor communities. However, a great deal of work still needs to be done in order to reduce the digital divide in the United States. Addressing this problem will take efforts on many fronts, including making improvements to the Internet infrastructure to allow access in a variety of locations, computer literacy programs, and community efforts to provide locations where individuals can access the Internet for free, such as libraries and community centers. In addition, public health campaigns need to be directed towards helping individuals find information that is tailored to their health needs and helping them make sense of the health information that exists on-line.

New Technologies and Patient–Patient Communication

Health-related web communities and computer-mediated support groups

The development of the Internet has created possibilities for increased patient–patient communication, mostly through health-related web communities and computer-mediated support groups. Computer-mediated support groups have become more prevalent in recent years as a source of information and support for numerous health concerns as a result of the Internet's increasing popularity and its ability to connect people who have similar health issues (Ferguson, 1998; UPI, 1999). A number of scholars, including health communication researchers, have recently focused their attention on these groups in an attempt to study their benefit to participants and to understand how the nature of supportive communication is affected by both the constraints and advantages of the computer medium (Alexander, Peterson, & Hollingshead, 2003; Braithwaite, Waldron, & Finn, 1999; Galinski, Schopler, & Abell, 1997; Wright, 1999, 2000a, 2000b).

Advantages and disadvantages of computer-mediated support groups

Query and Wright (2003) developed a model of on-line support group participation for people facing health concerns to help explain why some people use these groups while others do not. Not everyone who is concerned about a health issue seeks social support: some people choose individually based strategies for coping with stressful events, while others are more socially oriented in coping with stressful situations, such as seeking various types of social support (Kohn, 1996; Pierce, Sarason, & Sarason, 1996). Many people feel that they have sufficient support from family and friends, and they may never feel the need to join an on-line support group. However, as we saw in chapter 4, there are times when people facing an illness find it difficult to communicate with close ties, such as family members and friends. For example, researchers have found that life-threatening illnesses are difficult topics for most people to discuss, especially when they affect a close relative or loved one, and family members and friends often minimize the concerns of people with a serious illness, avoid interacting with them, steer conversational topics away from emotional talk about the disease, or refrain from any discussion of illness (Dakof & Taylor, 1990; Helgeson, Cohen, Shultz, & Yasko, 2000).

Problems communicating about health with traditional face-to-face support network members may lead some individuals to seek support on-line. Papacharissi and Rubin (2000) concluded that individuals use computer-mediated communication as a "functional alternative" when face-to-face communication is perceived as difficult or not preferred. For individuals facing illness whose support needs are not met by their traditional support network, the Internet allows them to find other people with similar health concerns and provides an opportunity to obtain support from a much larger network than would be possible in the face-to-face world. The Internet is considered an *unbounded network* because, unlike the face-to-face world, on-line relationships are not hampered by temporal and geographical restrictions. Thus, it is possible for on-line support group participants to meet and obtain support from a large network of other people who come together to discuss very specific health concerns (e.g., prostate cancer groups, HIV/AIDS) as opposed to more general health issues. The Internet can also be seen as a weak tie support network (see chapter 4), and people may be able to obtain more diverse points of view about health-related problems and talk about difficult issues with less interpersonal risk.

Other features of the Internet may be advantageous to those who use on-line support groups. Wellman (1997) contends that reduced nonverbal and appearance cues in email and other popular text-based forms of computer-mediated communication facilitate relationships that may be inhibited in the face-to-face world. Many of us are reluctant to form relationships with people in the face-to-face world due to cues such as age, gender, race, and appearance. However, in text-based computer-mediated communication, people do not see these cues and relationships tend to form around topics in which people have a mutual interest.

Additionally, *social information processing theory* (Ramirez, Walther, Burgoon, & Sunnafrank, 2002; Walther, 1996) asserts that in computer-mediated communication, message senders portray themselves in a socially favorable manner to draw the attention of message receivers and foster anticipation of future interaction. Message receivers, in turn, tend to idealize the image of the sender due to overvaluing minimal, text-based cues. In addition, the asynchronous format of most computer-mediated interaction (and to some extent in synchronous formats, such as chat rooms) gives the sender and the receiver more time to edit their communication, making computer-mediated interactions more controllable and less stressful compared to the immediate feedback loop inherent in face-to-face interactions. Idealized perceptions and optimal self-presentation in the computer-mediated communication process tend to intensify in the feedback loop, and this emphasis often leads to what Walther (1996) labels "hyperpersonal interaction," or a more intimate and socially desirable exchange than face-to-face interactions.

Hyperpersonal interaction is enhanced when no face-to-face relationship exists, so that users construct impressions and present themselves "without the interference of environmental reality" (Walther, 1996, p. 33). Hyperpersonal interaction has been found to skew perceptions of relational partners in positive ways, and in some cases computer-mediated relationships may exceed face-to-face interactions in intensity, including within on-line support groups (King & Moreggi, 1998; Ramirez et al., 2002; Walther, 1996; Wright & Bell, 2003).

The text-based nature of computer-mediated communication has other advantages. Weinberg, Schmale, Uken, and Wessel (1995) argue that the therapeutic value of writing down problems in text-based computer-mediated support groups may allow for more reflection and distance from others without worrying about other people's immediate responses. In addition, writing down problems creates distance between people and their dilemmas (Diamond, 2000), and this may help people view their health concerns more objectively.

All of these features of computer-mediated support groups, along with the anonymity and 24-hour availability of these groups, may lead people to a support network that fulfills their needs. In addition, some people may augment their support network using on-line support groups rather than replacing their traditional face-to-face network members with virtual ones. Preliminary research on health-related computer-mediated support groups indicates that the people who use these groups tend to be satisfied with the support they receive, and they are often able to obtain more (and better-quality) support than would be possible within their face-to-face network (Braithwaite et al., 1999; Sullivan, 2003; Wright, 2002a).

Of course, on-line support groups have their disadvantages, and researchers have found that there other sources of dissatisfaction among people using them (Galinski et al., 1997; King & Moreggi, 1998; Preece & Ghozati, 2001; Walther & Boyd, 2002; Wright, 2000b). Participants often find the lack of immediacy when communicating with others frustrating. Other reasons for dissatisfaction include difficulty when expressing and interpreting emotions due to reduced nonverbal cues; dissatisfaction with the inability to touch others; frustration with unwanted messages from unsolicited parties participating in the group (including spam messages); and increased opportunities for some individuals to misrepresent themselves to the group.

New Technologies and Provider–Provider Communication

The Internet and other new communication technologies are transforming provider interaction and access to information in a variety of health settings, such as hospitals, clinics, pharmacies, and research facilities. In the past, long-distance telephone calls, overnight letters, and creation and storage of patient records contributed to the tremendous costs of running a health organization (costs that are eventually passed along to consumers). New communication technologies may present cheaper, more convenient, and more efficient alternatives to traditional ways of communicating within health organizations. This section examines several ways that new communication technologies are facilitating communication among providers.

Email, wireless/satellite communication, and electronic records

Email and wireless communication

Email is a relatively simple computer application, but it has transformed communication among providers in many important ways. Physicians and other providers can now obtain information and opinions from other key health personnel within and between organizations. The attachment feature of email has allowed providers to send one another detailed information about patient histories, relevant research articles about specific conditions, insurance records, and other important information that can be used to facilitate the healthcare process. In addition, the asynchronous nature of email allows providers to transcend temporal and geographical barriers. Providers at rural health clinics can quickly and cheaply access information from larger urban hospitals and research facilities, consult with specialists, and keep up with current information regarding health conditions from websites sponsored by medical research institutions and government websites (e.g., the NIH and the CDC). Communication researchers have found that most providers have positive attitudes towards email and see its value in improving communication among providers, although there appears to be some resistance among many older physicians to adopt this technology (Aspden, Katz, & Bemis, 2001). However, in the future, more and more physicians and other providers are expected to use email as more Internet training programs are introduced and older physicians retire (Aspden et al., 2001).

Satellite technology

The convergence of satellite technology and the Internet has led to health information organizations such as HealthNet (www.healthnet.org/), which provides a global communication network that links healthcare workers around the world via email. HealthNet and similar organizations use email and satellite technology to connect healthcare providers and to provide them with access to information such as on-line medical journals and other health-related databases. This technology has been particularly useful to health professionals in the developing world. For example, HealthNet has helped healthcare professionals in Africa and in developing countries fight the HIV/ AIDS pandemic. In remote parts of developing countries, such access to medical journals and other up-to-date information sources can be vital for preventing and treating disease. Satellite/Internet technology is thus an important means of disseminating information to providers who work in these environments.

Wireless communication devices

Personal data assistants (PDAs) and similar wireless devices now allow providers to enter information about patients during or shortly after medical interviews and to send information via wireless email to other providers, pharmacologists, technicians, and other health professionals (Eder & Wise, 2001). Prescriptions for patients can be easily emailed to hospital pharmacies, and the process of making additional appointments and referrals is facilitated through wireless technology when messages can be sent quickly and conveniently to receptionists and other medical staff. In the past, physicians often made notes in charts after a meeting with patients, and then used transcription services to provide detailed information about patients. Wireless devices aid providers in supplying more detail about medical conditions for patient records, and also help to circumvent problems with poor handwriting or other difficulties associated with taking notes about patients.

Electronic records

According to Eder and Wise (2001), it has been estimated that "nearly 75% of all business activities in healthcare are related to the capture and manipulation of information, most of which is paper based" (p. 310). Among healthcare organizations that have not adopted electronic records, a patient's vital medical information is often scattered across medical records kept by many different caregivers in many different locations, and valuable information such as drug allergies and preexisting health conditions is often unavailable at the time of care. Electronic records and web-based technologies have tremendous potential in terms of capturing and storing information in healthcare settings. Over the next decade, US government agencies such as the NIH are urging healthcare organizations to move to electronic patient records. It is hoped that electronic records will ultimately improve healthcare quality by preventing medical errors, reducing healthcare costs, improving administrative efficiencies, reducing paperwork, and increasing access to affordable healthcare.

Electronic patient records can now be easily created through standardized electronic forms and stored in web-based programs on computer servers within health organizations. Many hospitals have computer programs that allow providers to enter information about the patient on computer within examination rooms, and prompts within the computer programs remind providers to ask patients about detailed aspects of their medical history, lifestyles, and health condition. X-rays and the results of other diagnostic tests can be quickly sent to providers or attached to electronic patient records.

Server storage of patient records takes up less space than rooms designated for paper charts, and computer programs allow physicians, receptionists, nurses, technicians, and other medical personnel to quickly and conveniently retrieve patient medical records. In addition, when referring patients to other healthcare providers, sending electronic patient records helps to save time and money because it allows for more detailed information to be transmitted due to the increased bandwidth of electronic formats. Information on patient charts that has been entered electronically is much easier to read than handwritten notes, and this appears to reduce misinterpretation of records and costly medical errors (Eder & Wise, 2001).

Disadvantages of new communication technologies

While there are numerous advantages of web-based communication and electronic medical records in terms of cost savings and greater efficiency for providers and health organizations, there are disadvantages as well. According to Eder and Wise (2001), "there is no single, universally accepted standard for formatting electronic health records" (p. 316). This may cause problems in accessing and interpreting information about patients when information is shared between organizations using different types of electronic records or systems for organizing and accessing patient data. Less is known about how the use of computers in the examination room affects the interaction between providers and patients. However, it is likely that using a computer to enter patient information detracts from direct interaction with patients both verbally and nonverbally. The health communication literature has documented a variety of interaction problems that can occur between providers and patients in examination rooms without computers, such as problems assessing patient cues, time constraints, and provider domination of the interaction (see Geist & Hardesty, 1990; Roter, Hall, & Katz, 1988; von Friedrichs-Fitzwater, Callahan, Flynn, & Williams, 1991; Zyzanski, Stange, Langa, & Flocke, 1998), and it is reasonable to assume that the introduction of computers will make provider–patient interaction even more complex and potentially problematic.

For example, electronic prompts to enter certain types of information about the patient (e.g., symptoms) in current medical interview software may distract a physician from asking more relevant information that comes up during a medical interview, such as risky lifestyle behaviors or psychosocial concerns. Moreover, eye contact, listening, and attention to the patient might be compromised by the use of computer programs to collect patient information. Future research would benefit from assessing the impact of the presence of computers or other electronic communication devices on provider–patient interaction.

In recent years there have been growing concerns over privacy and confidentiality issues surrounding the use of electronic patient records. According to Katz and Aspden (2001), there are a number of questions relating to patient privacy associated with the use of electronic records that need to be addressed. First, during medical interviews patients often disclose a great deal of sensitive information about their lifestyle behaviors, including substance abuse problems, psychological problems, and sexual history. This information can be potentially damaging financially to the patient if it is accessed by third parties such as insurance companies, who may decide to raise insurance premiums for the patient based upon what they might perceive to be increased risk factors from the information they access from his or her records. Also, other third-party access to patient information can be damaging to patients socially, particularly if a history of mental illness or the HIV status of a patient is inappropriately discussed by hospital staff and this information gets back to members of his or her social network. Moreover, there have been cases where attorneys have examined medical records to look for a history of malpractice claims among patients, which could be used to cancel insurance or deny access to healthcare. The Department of Health and Human Services (DHHS) has been collaborating in recent years with the private sector and other federal agencies to identify and endorse voluntary standards that are necessary for health information to be shared safely and securely among healthcare providers. The implementation of HIPPA (see chapter 6) has also set guidelines for the use of electronic records and patient information.

Finally, there is concern that certain information about patients, such as disease status, risk factors, and lifestyles, could be sold to marketing firms for pharmaceutical companies or other health-related industries, resulting in unwanted solicitations for products aimed at patients. Researchers and other individuals often request access to electronic patient information, and they should be concerned with the ethical issues involved when dealing with this type of sensitive information. These and other issues present challenges for the future of electronic record use, and ethical concerns about how patient information could be used inappropriately as this technology advances need careful consideration. Some health organizations have been experimenting with new forms of electronic security, such as digital signatures, encrypted data, or the use of improved Intranets, which are closed computer networks that limit access to information to certain health facilities.

Telemedicine and providers

During the past decade telemedicine has become an important means for increasing provider–provider communication, and various types of telemedicine are projected to increase dramatically over the next ten years (Turner, 2003). Telemedicine can be defined as "the use of telecommunications technologies to facilitate the delivery of healthcare at a distance for the direct benefit of patients" (Turner, 2003, p. 516). Telemedicine has traditionally used technologies such as videoconferencing, but with the advent of the Internet, web cameras, email, and the ability to attach multimedia files (such as X-rays and other diagnostic images), computer-mediated communication has become an attractive and lower-cost alternative. While some telemedicine initiatives have directly involved provider–patient communication, due to current barriers such as licensing and legal constraints, privacy and reimbursement issues, and lack of experience among providers in telemedicine applications, telemedicine has largely been limited to facilitating communication between providers (Turner, 2003).

For example, since in the United States a physician needs to be licensed to practice medicine in the state where he or she sees the patient, this creates legal problems when physicians and patients are in different states. In addition, it is difficult for managed care and insurance organizations to develop reimbursement policies for services rendered when providers are geographically dispersed. Turner (2003) argues that the question of how to reimburse providers for their services when using telemedicine represents one of the largest barriers to its growth. Insurance companies, managed care organizations, and legislative bodies will need to agree upon new policies for reimbursing providers in order for telemedicine to be used more routinely in the United States.

Advantages of telemedicine for providers

Despite the legal and financial constraints associated with telemedicine, it has many advantages for both patients and providers. This section focuses on advantages for providers, while the advantages for patients are discussed later in this chapter.

Telemedicine allows providers to benefit from the expertise offered by a health specialist or technician located outside of his or her organization. A specialist such as an oncologist practicing medicine in Maryland can be consulted by a primary physician in Los Angeles via an Internet chat or video application while he or she is examining a patient. Providers can use this technology to cheaply and conveniently communicate with experts to diagnose diseases and other health problems, to obtain a second opinion, to be given supervision while performing difficult medical procedures, and to have a consultation about treatment options, medications, and a host of other medical concerns. In addition, the Internet can be used to obtain patient data, such as reports from laboratories, pharmacies, and technicians, from any location. The use of the Internet for telemedicine is superior to traditional means of information exchange since it allows providers to send and receive data quickly and cheaply in real time, and it supports multiple users at different locations.

Continuing education

Most providers, including physicians, physician assistants, nurses, technicians, and other key health organization personnel, are required in most states to complete continuing education requirements in order to renew their license as a health provider. This is also true for many other types of health providers, including physical therapists, dentists and dental hygienists, and pharmacists. Most states require a certain number of continuing education hours each year, and providers must submit proof of continuing education hours when reapplying for state licensure. Continuing education credit is given for attending a variety of health-related courses offered by scholars and other experts in health-related topics at universities and other sites in communities across the country. In the past, providers have had to take continuing education courses on weekends or days off, or the health organization schedules time for providers to attend them.

Over the last several years a variety of web-based continuing education courses have appeared, and many allow providers to complete the course at their own pace, some even allowing providers to download a certificate of completion at the end of the course. According to Whitten, Eastin, and Cook (2001), "the Internet provides a very low-cost way of presenting CME [continuing medical education], avoiding expensive meeting spaces, the rental of audiovisual equipment needed, as well as travel expenses and accommodation costs for faculty and staff" (p. 265). Web-based continuing education courses support the use of multimedia, and they are relatively inexpensive to design, implement, and maintain. However, the variety and quality of Internet-based continuing education courses vary (Kim, 1998), and this needs to be assessed in future research along with other cost-cutting benefits these courses offer to the healthcare system.

New Technologies and Provider–Patient Communication

Potential for increased provider–patient interaction

Patients now have potentially greater access to physicians and other providers via the Internet than in the past, particularly through email and on-line health sites such as WebMD. However, despite the advantages that email offers in terms of facilitating communication between providers and patients, such as reduced expense, greater convenience, and the ability to attach documents containing health information, providers have largely been reluctant to adopt email as a means of communicating with patients (Rice & Katz, 2001). According to a study by Fox and Rainie (2000), only 9 percent of participants in their survey had ever contacted their physician via email. However, the same study found that 50 percent of participants reported that information from the Web led them to ask their doctor questions during regular medical visits, and this may mean that the Internet facilitates provider–patient interaction more indirectly, by assisting information exchange between providers and patients in face-to-face settings.

Physicians often view providing an email address to patients as like giving them a phone number, and many providers feel that letting patients have their email address is something of an invasion of privacy. Despite the widespread use of email in our culture, there is little evidence to suggest that provider–patient interaction has increased substantially as a result of this technology. According to Rice and Katz (2001), "The fact that these technologies were not adopted, we would argue, is not because the technology limits or permits access to physicians. Rather, it is the social structure that balances full access against managed boundaries" (p. 425). In other words, while email has the ability to increase doctor–patient communication, many physicians are reluctant to transcend traditional provider–patient relational boundaries because of such issues as social status, power, and control. In addition, given the many demands on physicians' time in most healthcare organizations, responding to multiple patient emails increases their workload and may be another reason why we have not seen substantial physician–patient interaction via email.

The use of email for provider–patient communication could potentially have a number of benefits for patients. The asynchronous nature of email might help apprehensive patients by giving them more time to compose their thoughts when asking questions or expressing concerns about their health. Attachments could be used to send and receive information about diseases and conditions, and patients could be easily linked via hypertext to government websites providing additional information or to sources of on-line social support. More research is needed to assess additional potential benefits of provider–patient email exchange. However, barriers between provider and patients, such as unequal power/status, as well as time constraints will likely continue to undermine the potential of using email to increase provider–patient communication.

Health websites, such as WebMD, regularly schedule chats with physicians and other providers or allow consumers to pose questions through the use of bulletin boards. These types of websites allow patients to obtain health information free of charge from providers who are willing to participate. Providers who interact with patients through these websites are often paid by the website administrators, who ultimately make their money from sponsors who pay for advertising on the website. Sponsors are typically organizations that provide health services (such as hospitals and specialized health clinics) or companies who sell health-related products, such as prescription drugs (e.g., Eli Lilly, Pfizer), diet products, or medical supplies. The commercial sponsorship of such websites raises a number of ethical concerns. For example, is the desire to raise revenue through these websites more important than the promotion of public health? While these websites may have both these goals, their heavy commercial sponsorship raises questions about whether products and services are in the best interest of the consumer, and low-cost health alternatives may not be promoted simply because the organizations offering these services have chosen not to advertise on these websites.

In addition, while providers who appear on WebMD and other health-related websites give consumers advice, they typically qualify the advice they provide with the recommendation that consumers see their primary physician. The advice consumers receive may help them to allay fears or manage uncertainties about their health status, and it may lead them to seek additional information or explore treatment options. However, since providers on these websites cannot diagnose illnesses or prescribe medications, it is essential that consumers follow up on the advice they receive with their physician. Problems may arise if consumers feel that they need not be concerned about their health as a result of interacting with providers on these websites or if the advice raises unwarranted fears. Because many diseases and conditions are difficult to diagnose without the use of laboratory tests, web-based providers can only make educated guesses about a consumer's health condition based upon the information given by the consumer. More research needs to be conducted on how consumers process and act upon (or do not act upon) advice received from providers on these websites.

Telemedicine and patients

Relatively little research exists on the implications of how telemedicine affects the provider–patient communication process. Initial studies suggest that patients are largely satisfied with the experience of telemedicine, and they appreciate the ability to communicate with specialists (Gutske, Balch, West, & Rogers, 2000; Turner, 2003). However, these studies also report that the majority of the interaction within telemedicine consultations tends to occur between the primary physician and the specialist, largely excluding the patient. While health communication researchers have identified problems in dyadic communication between providers and patients, such as providers ignoring the patient's psychosocial concerns, interrupting the patient, and dominating the conversation (Roter et al., 1988; Suchman, Markakis, Beckman, & Frankel, 1997; von Friedrichs-Fitzwater et al., 1991), little is known about communication involving multiple providers (three-way or higher) and a patient and how it affects the interaction. Yet, some literature suggests that the presence of multiple individuals in health encounters may have negative outcomes for patients, such as failure to address their concerns (Street, Wheeler, & McCaughan, 2000). These and many other communicative aspects of telemedicine need to be examined in future research.

Managed care organization efforts to reach patients via the Internet

Managed care organizations are increasingly using the Internet to provide information to patients. A central tenet of managed care is the reduction of cost to health organizations and the consumer by controlling access to health resources and through prevention efforts. The Internet offers managed care organizations a cheap and convenient way to provide patients with information about lifestyle changes, diagnostic testing for diseases, and other means of preventing susceptibility to health problems that can be costly to the organization. In addition, websites developed by these organizations often contain interactive features such as tutorials about diseases and conditions, risk factors, and diet and exercise, and they provide links to related websites. Consumers can access specific health information tailored to their needs by providing information about their lifestyles and health history, and interactive forms (similar to those used by search engines) direct them to information based upon their input.

However, interactive features on these websites tend to emphasize health information (on web pages) as opposed to interaction with actual providers. In an analysis of prominent health maintenance organization (HMO) websites in the United States, Witherspoon (2001) found that none of the websites in the study offered email links to specific doctors or other practitioners, and none offered a bulletin board or chat room where they could interact with providers. Instead, consumers are typically directed to web pages that provide information such as facts about diseases and conditions, information about exercise classes, and recipes for healthy diets. Most sites provided links to support groups for various health conditions or to government-sponsored websites (e.g., the CDC or the National Cancer Institute). While HMO and other managed care websites offer great possibilities for influencing health behaviors, few websites currently take advantage of the full potential of the multimedia and interactive features that current web technologies provide.

New Technologies and Health Campaigns

Tailoring health messages

Advances in computer programming and software have enabled individuals interested in health campaigns to use computers to tailor messages to specific characteristics of target audiences. According to Kreuter, Farrell, Olevitch, and Brennan (2000), *tailored health promotion materials* refer to "any combination of information and behavior change strategies intended to reach one specific person, based on characteristics that are unique to that person, related to the outcome of interest, and derived from an individual assessment" (p. 5). Rimal and Adkins (2003) contend that it is important to understand various aspects of the target audience, the channel(s) that will be used in the campaign, and the individual messages that participants will receive. These authors define *segmentation* as "dividing members of the target according to some meaningful criterion," *targeting* as "selecting the proper channel, based upon audience characteristics," and *tailoring* as "crafting health messages to reflect audience characteristics" (p. 500).

Computer tailoring of health messages can be used to produce materials for health campaigns using any communication channel, including print materials, television and radio advertisements, and Internet-based campaigns. Computers facilitate the tailoring of messages through the use of algorithms in computer programming that are used to create messages according to certain criteria designated by the researcher. Thus, a computer program can be written to create different messages depending upon whether participants in the target population are members of certain groups based on demographics, psychological characteristics, and communication behaviors (Rimal & Adkins, 2003), such as whether a person is male or female, belongs to a certain age group, or has scored high or low on a health self-efficacy measure.

Computer programs allow the creation of tailored messages by quickly linking together specific messages to targeted individuals through the use of algorithms created for the programming process. For computer programmers, creating a program based on algorithms does not typically require extensive programming skills. However, many health communication personnel working on campaigns do not have the computer science background to create message tailoring programs, and they often have to hire individuals to help with this part of the campaign.

Advantages of message tailoring

According to Kreuter et al. (2000) and Strecher and Kreuter (1999), tailored messages offer many advantages over more generic types of messages in health campaigns. First, tailored messages are more likely to be personally relevant to members of the target audience since they are created using demographic, psychological, and communication characteristics for specific individuals within the audience. For example, if 20 individuals out of 100 within a target audience scored high on a sensation–seeking measure prior to a campaign attempting to change risky sexual behaviors, only these 20 individuals would receive a message that specifically addressed high sensation-seeking tendencies. Second, Kreuter et al. (2000) maintain that people pay more attention to personally relevant information in health campaigns, and this is an important first step in changing attitudes and ultimately behaviors. Third, superfluous information found in more generic messages is eliminated, and only the information that matches the characteristics of a particular individual is used in the message for that person. When messages attend to the specific needs of individuals, Kreuter et al. (2000) argue that the information will be more thoughtfully processed, which is an important prerequisite for lasting attitudinal and behavioral change according to the elaboration likelihood model (Petty & Cacioppo, 1981).

Process of message tailoring

According to Kreuter et al. (2000), there is ideally a nine-step process for creating tailored messages, including extensive background research on target audience characteristics, creating assessment measures for demographic, psychological, and communication variables, designing appropriate messages for each possible segment of the target audience, creating algorithms and the computer program for the campaign, and implementing and evaluating the campaign.

In addition to creating specific messages for members of a target audience, another important issue to consider in health campaigns is how to best reach individuals. Rimal and Adkins (2003) argue that successful tailored health message campaigns offer an optimal balance between audience reach and specificity. According to these authors, more attention should be devoted to finding ways to use appropriate channels of communication based upon audience characteristics. For example, some people, such as college students, might pay more attention to health messages disseminated via the Internet, whereas older adults might pay more attention to print material given to them by their physician.

Summary

New communication technologies will most likely continue to influence how consumers seek health information and communicate with other consumers and providers about health issues. These technologies appear to offer health organizations and providers many advantages in terms of gathering, storing, and disseminating health information, such as electronic patient charts and information from diagnostic tests. In addition, telemedicine presents new opportunities for providers to collaborate during the process of caring for patients, and the Internet and other new computer technologies will continue to be used for public health campaigns. However, despite the optimism over these technologies for improving healthcare, many cultural, educational, financial, and legal barriers exist that will certainly shape the future of new technologies and health communication.

References

Alexander, S. C., Peterson, J. L., & Hollingshead, A. B. (2003). Help is at your keyboard: Support groups on the Internet. In L. R. Frey (Ed.), *Group communication in context: Studies of bona fide groups* (2nd ed., pp. 309–334). Mahwah, NJ: Lawrence Erlbaum.

Aspden, P., & Katz, J. E. (2001). Assessments of quality of health care information and referrals to physicians: A nationwide survey. In R. E. Rice & J. E. Katz (Eds.), *The Internet and health communication: Experiences and expectations* (pp. 99–106). Thousand Oaks, CA: Sage.

Aspden, P., Katz, J. E., & Bemis, A. (2001). Use of the Internet for professional purposes: A survey of New Jersey physicians. In R. E. Rice & J. E. Katz (Eds.), *The Internet and health communication: Experiences and expectations* (pp. 107–119). Thousand Oaks, CA: Sage.

Barnes, M., Penrod, C., Neiger, B., Merrill, R., Eggett, D., & Thomas, E. (2003). Measuring the relevance of evaluation criteria among health information seekers on the Internet. *Journal of Health Psychology, 8*, 71–82.

Bass, S. B. (2003). How will Internet use affect the patient? A review of computer network and closed Internet-based system studies and the implications in understanding how the use of the Internet affects patient populations. *Journal of Health Psychology, 8*, 25–38.

Biermann, J. S., Golladay, G., & Baker, J. (1999). Evaluation of cancer information on the Internet. *Cancer, 86*, 381–390.

Binik, Y. M., Cantor, J., Ochs, E., & Meana, M. (1997). From the couch to the keyboard: Psychotherapy in cyberspace. In S. Kiesler (Ed.), *Culture of the Internet* (pp. 71–100). Mahwah, NJ: Lawrence Erlbaum.

Braithwaite, D. O., Waldron, V. R., & Finn, J. (1999). Communication of social support in computer-mediated groups for people with disabilities. *Health Communication, 11*, 123–151.

Cummins, C., Prochaska, J. O., Driskell, M., Evers, K., Wright, J., Prochaska, J. M., & Velicer, W. (2003). Development of review criteria to evaluate health behavior change websites. *Journal of Health Psychology, 8*, 55–62.

Dakof, G. A., & Taylor, S. E. (1990). Victim's perceptions of social support: What is helpful from whom? *Journal of Personality and Social Psychology, 58*, 80–89.

Davison, K. P., Pennebaker, J. W., & Dickerson, S. S. (2000). Who talks? The social psychology of illness support groups. *American Psychologist, 55*, 205–217.

Diamond, J. (2000). *Narrative means to sober ends: Treating addiction and its aftermath.* New York: Guilford Press.

Dunham, P., Hurshman, A., Litwin, E., Gusella, J., Ellsworth, C., & Dodd, P. (1998). Computer-mediated social support: Single young mothers as a model system. *American Journal of Community Psychology, 26*, 281–306.

Eder, L. B. (2001). Web-enabled hospitals in the United States: Influences on adoption processes. In R. E. Rice & J. E. Katz (Eds.), *The Internet and health communication: Experiences and expectations* (pp. 309–327). Thousand Oaks, CA: Sage.

Eder, L. B., & Wise, D. E. (2001). Web-enabled hospitals in the United States: Influences on adoption processes. In R. E. Rice & J. E. Katz (Eds.), *The Internet and health communication: Experiences and expectations* (pp. 309–327). Thousand Oaks, CA: Sage.

Eng, T. R. (2001). *The eHealth landscape: A terrain map of emerging information and communication technologies in health and health care.* Princeton, NJ: The Robert Wood Johnson Foundation.

Evans, R. L., & Connis, R. T. (1995). Comparison of brief group therapies for depressed cancer patients receiving radiation treatment. *Public Health Reports, 110*, 306–312.

Ferguson, T. (1998). Digital doctoring: Opportunities and challenges in electronic patient–physician communication (Editorial). *Journal of the American Medical Association, 280*, 1261–1262.

Flatley-Brennan, P. (1998). Computer network home care demonstration: A randomized trial in persons living with AIDS. *Computers in Biology and Medicine, 28*, 489–508.

Fox, S., & Rainie, L. (2000). The online health care revolution: How the Web helps Americans take better care of themselves. A Pew Internet and American Life Project Online Report. Retrieved January 2, 2004, from www.pewinternet.org.

Galinski, M. J., Schopler, J. H., & Abell, M. D. (1997). Connecting group members through telephone and computer groups. *Health and Social Work, 22*, 181–189.

Geist, P., & Hardesty, M. (1990). Reliable, silent, hysterical, or assured: Physicans assess patient cues in their medical decision making. *Health Communication, 2*, 69–90.

Gutske, S., Balch, D., West, V., & Rogers, L. (2000). Patient satisfaction with telemedicine. *Telemedicine Journal, 6*, 5–13.

Harris Interactive. (2001). The increasing impact of eHealth on consumer behavior. *Health Care News, 21*, 1–9.

Helgeson, V. S., & Gottlieb, B. H. (2000). Support groups. In S. Cohen, L. G. Underwood, & B. H. Gottlieb (Eds.), *Social support measurement and intervention* (pp. 221–245). New York: Oxford University Press.

Helgeson, V. S., Cohen, S., Schultz, R., & Yasko, J. (2000). Group support interventions for women with breast cancer: Who benefits from what? *Health Psychology, 19*, 107–114.

Hersch, W., Gorman, P., & Sacherek, L. (1998). Applicability and quality of information for answering clinical questions on the Web. *Journal of the American Medical Association, 280*, 1307–1308.

Katz, J. E., & Aspden, P. (2001). Networked communication practices and the security and privacy of electronic health care records. In R. E. Rice & J. E. Katz (Eds.), *The Internet and health communication: Experiences and expectations* (pp. 393–415). Thousand Oaks, CA: Sage.

Kim, H. (1998, August). CME: A whole new World (Wide Web). *American Medical News*, pp. 1–3.

Kim, P., Eng, T. R., Deering, M. J., & Maxfield, A. (1999). Published criteria for evaluating health-related web sites: Review. *British Medical Journal, 318*, 647–649.

King, S. A., & Moreggi, D. (1998). Internet therapy and self-help groups: The pros and cons. In J. Gackenbach (Ed.), *Psychology and the Internet: Intrapersonal, interpersonal, and transpersonal implications* (pp. 77–109). San Diego, CA: Academic Press.

Kohn, P. M. (1996). On coping adaptively with daily hassles. In M. Zeidner & N. S. Endler (Eds.), *Handbook of coping* (pp. 181–201). New York: John Wiley & Sons.

Kreuter, M., Farrell, D., Olevitch, L., & Brennan, L. (2000). *Tailoring health messages: Customizing communication with computer technology.* Mahwah, NJ: Lawrence Erlbaum.

Napoli, P. M. (2001). Consumer use of medical information from electronic and paper media: A literature review. In R. E. Rice & J. E. Katz (Eds.), *The Internet and health communication: Experiences and expectations* (pp. 79–98). Thousand Oaks, CA: Sage.

Neuhauser, L., & Kreps, G. L. (2003). Rethinking communication in the e-health era. *Journal of Health Psychology, 8*, 7–23.

Papacharissi, Z., & Rubin, A. M. (2000). Predictors of Internet use. *Journal of Broadcasting and Electronic Media, 44*, 175–196.

Petty, R. E., & Cacioppo, J. T. (1981). *Attitudes and persuasion: Classic and contemporary approaches.* Dubuque, IA: William C. Brown Company.

Pierce, G. R., Sarason, I. G., & Sarason, B. R. (1996). Coping and social support. In M. Zeidner & N. S. Endler (Eds.), *Handbook of coping* (pp. 434–451). New York: John Wiley & Sons.

Preece, J. J., & Ghozati, K. (2001). Experiencing empathy on-line. In R. E. Rice & J. E. Katz (Eds.), *The Internet and health communication: Experiences and expectations* (pp. 237–260). Thousand Oaks, CA: Sage.

Query, J. L., Jr., & Wright, K. B. (2003). Assessing communication competence in an on-line study: Towards informing subsequent interventions among older adults with cancer, their lay caregivers, and peers. *Health Communication, 15*, 203–218.

Ramirez, A., Walther, J. B., Burgoon, J. K., & Sunnafrank, M. (2002). Information-seeking strategies, uncertainty, and computer-mediated communication. Toward a conceptual model. *Human Communication Research, 28*, 213–228.

Rice, R. E. (2001). The Internet and health communication. In R. E. Rice & J. E. Katz (Eds.), *The Internet and health communication: Experiences and expectations* (pp. 5–46). Thousand Oaks, CA: Sage.

Rice, R. E., & Katz, J. E. (2001). Concluding thoughts. In R. E. Rice & J. E. Katz (Eds.), *The Internet and health communication: Experiences and expectations* (pp. 417–429). Thousand Oaks, CA: Sage.

Rimal, R. N., & Adkins, D. A. (2003). Using computers to narrowcast health messages: The role of audience segmentation, targeting, and tailoring in health promotion. In T. L. Thompson, A. M. Dorsey, K. I. Miller, & R. Parrott (Eds.), *Handbook of health communication* (pp. 497–513). Mahwah, NJ: Lawrence Erlbaum.

Roter, D. L., Hall, J. A., & Katz, N. R. (1988). Patient–physician communication: A descriptive summary of the literature. *Patient Education and Counseling, 12*, 99–119.

Scott, C. R. (1999). Communication technology and group communication. In L. R. Frey (Ed.), *The handbook of group communication theory and research* (pp. 432–472). Thousand Oaks, CA: Sage.

Sharf, B. F. (1997). Communicating breast cancer on-line: Support and empowerment on the Internet. *Women and Health, 26*, 65–84.

Shaw, B., McTavish, F., Hawkins, R., Gustafson, D., & Pingree, S. (2000). Experiences of women with breast cancer: Exchanging social support over the CHESS computer network. *Journal of Health Communication, 5*, 135–159.

Smith, L., & Weinert, C. (2000). Telecommunication support for rural women with diabetes. *Diabetes Educator, 26*, 645–655.

Spiegel, D. (1992). Effects of psychosocial support on patients with metastatic breast cancer. *Journal of Psychosocial Oncology, 10*, 113–121.

Spiegel, D., Bloom, J. R., & Yalom, I. (1981). Group support for patients with metastatic cancer: A randomized prospective outcome study. *Archives of General Psychiatry, 38*, 527–533.

Strecher, V. J., & Kreuter, M. W. (1999). Health risk appraisal from a behavioral perspective: Present and future. In G. C. Hyner, K. W. Peterson, J. W. Travis, J. E. Dewey, J. J. Foerster, & E. M. Framer (Eds.), *Society of Prospective Medicine handbook of health assessment tools* (pp. 75–82). Pittsburgh, PA: Society of Prospective Medicine.

Street, R. L., Wheeler, J., & McCaughan, W. (2000). Specialist–primary care provider–patient communication in telemedical consultations. *Telemedicine Journal, 6*, 45–54.

Suchman, A. L., Markakis, K., Beckman, H. B., & Frankel, R. (1997). A model of empathic communication in the medical interview. *Journal of the American Medical Association, 277*, 678–683.

Sullivan, C. F. (2003). Gendered cybersupport: A thematic analysis of two on-line cancer support groups. *Journal of Health Psychology, 8*, 83–103.

Turner, J. W. (2003). Telemedicine: Expanding health care into virtual environments. In T. L. Thompson, A. M. Dorsey, K. I. Miller, & R. Parrott (Eds.), *Handbook of health communication* (pp. 515–535). Mahwah, NJ: Lawrence Erlbaum.

UPI. (1999). Harris poll: Most net users want health information (Press Release). Louis Harris & Associates, February 11, 1999, New York, pp. 1–6.

US Census Bureau. (2001). Press release. Retrieved January 15, 2004, from www.census.gov/Press-Release/www/2003/cb03-08.html.

von Friedrichs-Fitzwater, M. M., Callahan, E. J., Flynn, N., & Williams, J. (1991). Relational control in physician–patient encounters. *Health Communication, 1,* 17–36.

Walther, J. B. (1996). Computer-mediated communication: Impersonal, interpersonal, and hyperpersonal interaction. *Communication Research, 23,* 3–43.

Walther, J. B., & Boyd, S. (2002). Attraction to computer-mediated social support. In C. A. Lin & D. Atkins (Eds.), *Communication technology and society: Audience adoption and uses* (pp. 153–188). Cresskill, NJ: Hampton Press.

Weiler, R. M., & Pealer, L. N. (2000). The sitelegend: Twelve components of a new strategy for providing website documentation. *Journal of School Health, 70,* 148–152.

Weinberg, N., Schmale, J. D., Uken, J., & Wessel, K. (1995). Computer-mediated support groups. *Social Work with Groups, 17,* 43–55.

Wellman, B. (1997). An electronic group is virtually a social network. In S. Kiesler (Ed.), *Culture of the Internet* (pp. 179–205). Mahwah, NJ: Lawrence Erlbaum.

Whitten, P. S., Eastin, M. S., & Cook, D. (2001). The role of the organization in the success of web-based continuing medical education programs. In R. E. Rice & J. E. Katz (Eds.), *The Internet and health communication: Experiences and expectations* (pp. 261–285). Thousand Oaks, CA: Sage.

Witherspoon, E. (2001). A pound of cure: A content analysis of health information on web sites of top-ranked HMOs. In R. E. Rice & J. E. Katz (Eds.), *The Internet and health communication: Experiences and expectations* (pp. 189–212). Thousand Oaks, CA: Sage.

Wright, K. B. (1999). Computer-mediated support groups: An examination of relationships among social support, perceived stress, and coping strategies. *Communication Quarterly, 47,* 402–414.

Wright, K. B. (2000a). Social support satisfaction, on-line communication apprehension, and perceived life stress within computer-mediated support groups. *Communication Research Reports, 17,* 139–147.

Wright, K. B. (2000b). Computer-mediated social support, older adults, and coping. *Journal of Communication, 50,* 100–118.

Wright, K. B. (2002a). Social support within an on-line cancer community: An assessment of emotional support, perceptions of advantages and disadvantages, and motives for using the community from a communication perspective. *Journal of Applied Communication Research, 30,* 195–209.

Wright, K. B. (2002b). Motives for communication within on-line support groups and antecedents for interpersonal use. *Communication Research Reports, 19,* 89–98.

Wright, K. B., & Bell, S. B. (2003). Health-related support groups on the Internet: Linking empirical findings to social support and computer-mediated communication theory. *Journal of Health Psychology, 8,* 37–52.

Zyzanski, S. J., Stange, K. C., Langa, D., & Flocke, S. A. (1998). Trade-offs in high volume primary care practices. *Journal of Family Practice, 46,* 397–402.

Chapter 8

Mass Communication and Health

Grey's Anatomy, House, Scrubs, Extreme Makeover, and *ER*. It is very likely that you have watched one or several of these popular television shows in recent years. As you have probably noticed, the lives of healthcare providers and people facing health issues are regularly the subject of shows on television. In fact, these shows are so popular that they have generated millions of dollars for television networks, and several have been nominated for Emmy awards. Television and other mass media play an important role in influencing our perceptions of health and our health behaviors in a variety of ways. In addition to entertainment, television, films, newspapers, the Internet, and other media regularly convey information that can influence our health, such as advertisements for fast food, popular film characters engaging in unhealthy behaviors, celebrities who may influence unrealistic body images, and news stories about medical breakthroughs. Americans are avid consumers of the mass media, and our exposure to media content begins when we are young children. Many of our perceptions about health, illness, medicine, and healthcare professionals are shaped by what we see, hear, and read in the mass media. While our family members, peers, and educators also are strong social influences on our health perceptions and behaviors, what we learn from these sources interacts with the mass media to socialize us about health in very complex ways.

This chapter explores the role of mass media in influencing our perceptions of health and our health behaviors. It primarily focuses on traditional mass media, such as television, film, radio, and print. We begin by discussing two popular theories of media influence and research linking mass media images of health and portrayals of health situations to health behaviors. Next, we explore issues concerning how health-related stories are presented in the news media and the implications of reporting practices on public conceptions of health and health behaviors.

Two Perspectives of Media Influence

Most communication scholars feel that the mass media influence our perceptions and behaviors in a number of ways, including those related to health. However, it is has been difficult for researchers to demonstrate a direct link between specific media content and health behaviors. As you will see in this chapter, the relationship between mass media content and behaviors is complex, and many variables mediate the degree to which the mass media influence our behaviors. This chapter presents two broad perspectives of the relationship between media usage and behaviors. These theoretical frameworks are important to understand before talking about specific health behaviors that appear to be influenced by the mass media, such as eating habits, substance abuse, and violence, which we will explore later in this chapter.

Cultivation theory

A popular theory that has been used to explain the effects of mass media (particularly television) is *cultivation theory* (Gerbner, 1998; Gerbner & Gross, 1972; Gerbner, Gross, Morgan, & Signorelli, 1982). Cultivation theorists argue that the reality portrayed in the mass media influences our perceptions of reality in the real world over an extended period of time. In other words, cultivation theory posits that long-term repeated exposure to mass media messages shapes our understanding of the world in ways that are consistent with how reality is portrayed in the media. Cultivation theory holds that television can have a "normalizing" effect in terms of influencing perceptions, and televised behaviors may become perceived as acceptable or desirable over time (Shrum, 1999). Most cultivation theorists have examined the influence of television on behaviors because Americans use television more than any other medium, and because television is relatively inexpensive compared to other media (e.g., the Internet) and does not require consumers to be literate (Gerbner, Gross, Jackson-Beeck, Jeffries-Fox, & Signorelli, 1978).

Heavy viewers of television often tend to have attitudes and beliefs about the world that are congruent with the reality promoted by television, a concept known as *mainstreaming* (Gerbner, 1998). Television can also influence perceptions of reality in subtle ways. For example, *first-order effects* refer to information about a topic that people learn by watching television, and *second-order effects* are more generalized perceptions about topics and the world that people learn from television (Gerbner, Gross, Morgan, & Signorelli, 1986). For example, a heavy viewer of *ER* might learn some basic terminology used in emergency room settings (a first-order effect), but she might also come to believe that biomedical and technological solutions to health problems (used most often in the show) are the most effective ways to deal with them (a second-order effect).

Similar to other perceptions of reality, our perceptions of health are most likely influenced in a variety of ways by our exposure to media content. Given the high prevalence of health-related dramatic entertainment in the mass media and health-related news stories, the mass media present a version of reality surrounding health issues that is often much different than what occurs in the real world (Turow & Coe, 1993). Yet, just because certain images of health are presented in the mass media, critics of cultivation theory argue that this does not necessarily mean that people will pay attention to all of these messages, interpret them, or react to them in the same way. In other words, for some individuals, the effects of encountering media content may be limited due to the reasons they use media. In the next section, we present an alternative framework for examining the influence of the mass media on perceptions and behaviors.

Uses and gratifications theory

While early theories about the influence of television and other mass media on individual behavior proposed that the mass media are very powerful in changing behaviors, later theories began to examine the idea of how the effects of the mass media are mediated by audience members as active users of media and choice makers when it comes to interpreting media content. For example, *uses and gratifications theory* proposes that the effects of media are tempered by the ways in which people use them. Specifically, the theory posits that people actively choose certain types of media and media content to gratify various psychological and social needs or to accomplish certain goals (Katz, Blumler, & Gurevitz, 1974). The reasons why individuals choose one type of media over another or choose specific media content are as diverse as people themselves, but what we choose to view, read, and listen to mediates the influence of the mass media. In the next section, we will explore various needs that the mass media fulfill concerning health.

Needs Fulfilled by the Mass Media Concerning Health

Information seeking

Media fulfill the need for information about the world or specific interests. Given the rapid changes we have experienced in society in recent years, with the advent of diseases such as HIV and Severe Acute Respiratory Syndrome (SARS) and health threats due to terrorism, most people desire up-to-date news and accurate information about health-related events. The mass media help to fulfill our desire to reduce uncertainty about health issues by gathering information that will help us to make better choices about how we should respond to daily events. Some people may gratify their information-seeking needs about health by paying attention to health stories on CNN or their local television news station. For other individuals, radio, newspapers, and magazines such as *Time* or *Men's Health* or Internet sources such as WebMD may be more important sources of news and information than television.

Entertainment, diversion, and tension release

Others may learn about health issues by watching shows such as *Grey's Anatomy* or *Scrubs* for entertainment or as a diversion from the stress of everyday life. While people may initially watch a show like *ER* to fulfill entertainment needs, they can often learn about a variety of health-related issues that are part of the story of the program episode. For example, *ER* deals with many timely health issues (albeit sometimes indirectly) as part of the show's stories, including medical malpractice litigation, advanced care directives, and a variety of up-to-date medical procedures. For many people, television shows like *ER* or *Grey's Anatomy* are one of the few places where they acquire information about the world of medicine and current health issues, particularly if they tend to avoid news stories about health on television or other media.

Individuals may also develop expectations about provider–patient interaction based on this type of entertainment, and characters on television often serve as role models for the ways individuals are expected to behave in health encounters. This may be problematic if people identify with providers who tend to be paternalistic towards patients, and this influences their behaviors when they actually visit their physicians and other providers in real life. However, shows like *Grey's Anatomy* sometimes show patients behaving in assertive ways, and the stories often give an insight into the stressful lives of healthcare professionals. In these cases, watching such programs can provide people with positive role models or help them see the perspective of providers. These programs also provide a venue for social comparison to others. According to social comparison theory (Festinger, 1954; see also chapter 4), individuals compare themselves to other individuals in society and make a variety of judgments about their own lives, such as their abilities, opinions, and behaviors. For example, people may perceive themselves to be more or less healthy than the people they see on television. This can sometimes motivate people to engage in diet and exercise programs or be proactive about their health in other ways if they feel that they are relatively unhealthy compared to the people they see on television. However, as we have seen, negative aspects of television and other media, such as advertisements for fast food or role models engaging in unhealthy behaviors, can negatively affect health behaviors.

The media also provide content that can help us divert our attention from the stress of everyday life and fulfill various affective needs, including the need to appreciate aesthetic, emotional, and pleasurable experiences. Watching a situation comedy or emotional drama can help people temporarily forget about their problems and elevate their moods. There is some evidence that humor is linked to positive health outcomes (du Pre', 1998; Lambert & Lambert, 1995). Humor tends to lift a person's mood and reduce stress levels, both of which are linked to positive psychological and physical health outcomes. However, while experiencing pleasure through using media can have a positive effect on health, diverting attention from problems does not make them go away, and avoidance of problems can sometime create more stress for individuals in the long run. In addition, spending too much time using passive media like television may lead to a sedentary lifestyle in which people limit their physical and mental activity. Sedentary lifestyles have been linked to obesity and other health problems, and there is some evidence that choosing to watch television over more mentally challenging activities (e.g., reading) on a long-term basis may lead to cognitive problems over time (Friedland et al., 2001).

Media use to fulfill social needs

Television and other mass media provide people with the substance for conversations with members of their social network. Katz, Gurevitch, and Haas (1973) referred to this as the *personal integrative function*. The personal integrative function of media occurs when the knowledge we gain from the media about the world, current events, or happenings in the lives of media characters helps to enhance our credibility and status in conversations with others. For example, media provide us with content about health issues for conversations with members of our social network, such as sharing information from a news story about a new medical procedure.

Interactive media such as the Internet can fulfill interpersonal needs. In the last decade, on-line health communities have become important places where people can meet others with similar health concerns and obtain health information from healthcare professionals and other consumers, as well as emotional support and encouragement when coping with health problems (see chapter

7). Even noninteractive media help to foster a sense of connection with others, particularly when people view the same content on a television program. For example, after the terrorist attacks on 9/11, watching television stories on CNN about how people were coping with the threat of terrorism helped many people feel that they were not alone, and this may have helped them to feel less anxious.

Convenience

Finally, people often choose a certain medium to fulfill their needs because it is convenient to do so. For example, some individuals may find navigating the Internet to be cumbersome, so they prefer to obtain health information from health-related news stories on television, in newspapers, and in magazines. Other people find the Internet to be a cheap and convenient way to discuss health issues with other people, particularly when they are geographically separated from their conversational partner(s). In addition, some people are more active than others when seeking health information, and this may motivate them to use resources like the Internet to find a variety of sources of health information, for example www.cdc.gov, instead of consulting one or two articles in a magazine.

Media Usage, Health Portrayals, and Health Behaviors

The mass media play a significant role in their ability to influence health behaviors. Americans are keen consumers of the mass media, and they are exposed to many different messages and images of health through media content. By the time an average American reaches 19 years of age, he or she will have spent more time watching television than most people spend at a full-time job in a year (Dworetzky, 1993). According to Bahk (2001), "because health occupies an essential part of human living, dramatic media presentations frequently depict health-related events for developing their story lines" (p. 188). In addition, the popular media are an important source of health-related information for most Americans (Atkin & Arkin, 1990; Signorelli, 1993), even when health information comes in the form of entertainment. As we have mentioned, information about health issues encountered through entertainment programs such as *ER* can potentially raise awareness about health issues and risks, and this information can sometimes motivate positive behavioral changes (Montgomery, 1990; Scharf, Freimuth, Greenspon, & Plotnick, 1996).

However, portrayals of health situations in the mass media are often unrealistic, and they tend to emphasize certain messages about health while excluding others. The following sections explore unrealistic portrayals of health situations and unhealthy role models associated with the entertainment media.

Unrealistic portrayals of health situations

While some television and film dramas have somewhat accurate portrayals of healthcare settings, the mass media can also distort our perceptions of health situations in a variety of ways. Medical procedures and other solutions to health problems are presented as being far more successful in the media than in real life (Diem, Lantos, & Tulsky, 1996; Wallack & Dorfman, 1992). Key healthcare organization members such as administrators, physician assistants, laboratory technicians, and other medical personnel are rarely seen in media portrayals of healthcare situations, while physicians are the healthcare professional that viewers see most frequently. Constraints on providers imposed by managed care and other bureaucratic influences are seen much less than they occur in real healthcare situations. Healthcare teams, telemedicine, and other newer approaches to healthcare are also rarely seen in media portrayals of health situations. Patients on television are more likely to be depicted as having acute medical conditions rather than long-term chronic health conditions (which are more common), and most discussion between providers and patients centers on biomedical rather than psychosocial issues (Turow & Coe, 1993). Individuals with mental illness are often portrayed in stereotypical ways (du Pre', 2005), promoting the idea that people with mental illness are dangerous and unstable. Characters with disabilities in the media, when they do appear at all, are rarely depicted as living ordinary lives (Signorelli, 1993). Instead, the media often focus too much attention on a character's disability or portray people with disabilities in stereotypical ways. Older individuals dealing with health problems are often disproportionately underrepresented in health-related film and television content (Turow & Coe, 1993). When they do appear, health problems are often attributed to age rather than disease, and issues common among older patients, such as polypharmacy or the impact of companions on provider–older patient interaction, do not appear in media portrayals of healthcare situations as often as they occur in real life. Despite these problems, film and television audience members frequently identify with characters who portray physicians and other healthcare professionals. The popularity of television shows like *Grey's Anatomy*, *Scrubs*, *Nip/Tuck*, and other health-related programs reflects the enormous interest many Americans have in healthcare situations.

Unhealthy role models and the promotion of unhealthy behaviors in advertising

Most sources of entertainment and advertising in the mass media have been criticized for promoting unhealthy perceptions of health and health behaviors among media consumers (Bahk, 2001; Terre, Drabman, & Speer, 1991; Signorelli, 1993). The media characters that are most attractive to media consumers often serve as role models for a variety of health behaviors, but unfortunately many of the health-related behaviors they engage in are negative (Kline, 2003). For example, central characters in popular television shows and movies often engage in a variety of unhealthy behaviors, including smoking, drinking alcohol, practicing unsafe sex, and eating unhealthy foods. In many cases it makes little difference whether media role models are real or fictitious in terms of influencing health behaviors (Kline, 2003). People often look up to television and film actors due to their attractiveness and celebrity status. The media often send competing messages when it comes to health.

For example, while we may often want to look like Angelina Jolie, Sarah Jessica Parker, or Brad Pitt, we also associate these actors with behaviors we see them performing in the media. When the characters these actors portray eat unhealthy foods, smoke, drink alcohol, or engage in other unhealthy behaviors, it sends audience members an indirect message that these behaviors are desirable since they are associated with characters to whom we are attracted. To be fair, it should be pointed out that popular films such as *Patch Adams* and *Lorenzo's Oil* and television shows like *Grey's Anatomy* do show positive aspects of healthcare, such as humor and health, alternative medicines, and provider commitment to quality healthcare. Yet, positive portrayals of health situations are often offset by unhealthy role models in health-related entertainment as well as unhealthy lifestyles promoted by advertisements in the media. The following sections explore research on the effects of encountering unhealthy role models on a regular basis in the mass media.

The influence of media on eating habits

Obesity

Obesity has become a major public health concern in the United States. Approximately 280,000 adult deaths in the United States each year are related to obesity (Allison, Fontaine, Manson, Stevens, & VanItallie, 1999). Obesity is linked to a number of health problems, including diabetes, heart disease, hypertension, and cancer (Allison et al., 1999; Mokdad et al., 1999; Must et al., 1999). The risk for obesity often begins at an early age. In the US, nearly 15 percent of children between the ages of 6 and 11 years can be classified as obese, a percentage that has nearly tripled since the 1960s (Ogden, Flegan, Carroll, & Johnson, 2002). Many aspects of the mass media are related to obesity. According to Byrd-Bredbenner, Finckenor, and Grasso (2003), television actors "constantly talk about, handle, or consume foods and alcoholic beverages, but almost none are overweight or suffer the consequences of over-consumptions" (p. 336).

In addition, television advertisements routinely promote unhealthy food products, and the popularity of television and related media in the US has contributed to sedentary lifestyles for many Americans. For children, there has been a significant shift over the last several decades from physical activities to sedentary behavior that has been linked to media usage, particularly the increased use of computers, DVDs, and electronic games (Hofferth & Sandberg, 2001). Almost 60 percent of American adults are currently over-weight (Flegal, Carroll, Ogden, & Johnson, 2002). And while there are many other factors related to obesity, including genetics, socioeconomic variables, and a family history of obesity, sedentary activities coupled with an increase in consuming unhealthy fast foods promoted by the mass media appear to be a major contributor to the problem.

Eating disorders

The standard of beauty for men and women has changed throughout history. However, in the past century, the media have perpetuated the thin ideal for women. While fewer than 5 percent of people in the United States suffer from anorexia and bulimia, there has been an increase in these types of eating disorders over the last several decades, particularly among women (Becker, Grinspoon, Klibanski, & Herzog, 1999). Although some men suffer from eating disorders, only an estimated 5 to 15 percent of people with anorexia or bulimia and an estimated 35 percent of those with a binge-eating disorder are male. People with anorexia feel distress about eating and are compelled to avoid eating or take other actions to keep from gaining weight (such as exercise or diet medications), despite the fact that they are in danger of being under-weight. Individuals with bulimia have the compulsion to purge after eating in an effort to lose weight. Both types of eating disorders can lead to a variety of serious health problems, including cardiac arrest, kidney failure, severe malnutrition, and death.

While there are many factors that may contribute to a person developing anorexia or bulimia, there is some evidence that the mass media influence unhealthy eating habits by distorting perceptions of ideal body weight, especially given the thin body images of characters on television, films, and in fashion magazines (Harrison, 2000; Harrison & Cantor, 1997). Brown and

Walsh-Childers (2002) contend that research over the past 20 years has shown that the women who appear in the media are substantially thinner (typically 25% thinner) than the average American woman. Brown and Walsh-Childers (2002) also found in a study that nearly all the *Playboy* centerfolds and three-fourths of fashion industry models had body mass indexes (BMI) of 17.5 or below – the American Psychological Association's criteria for anorexia nervosa.

Consistent with uses and gratifications theory, there is some evidence that the type of media people use is related to healthy and unhealthy eating habits. For example, Dutta-Bergman (2004) found that healthy eating habits were associated with newspapers, magazines, and the Internet, particularly when individuals used these media for information-seeking purposes. However, the same author found that watching sports and comedy on television and using the Internet for entertainment purposes was associated with unhealthy eating habits. It is also important to note that this study did not provide evidence that these types of media necessarily *cause* unhealthy eating habits, and the results can also be partially explained by other variables associated with using media for information purposes, such as age, gender, and education level, which are also linked to unhealthy eating habits (Dutta & Youn, 1999; Swenson & Wells, 1995).

Media content and cosmetic surgery

Have you ever wanted to have Angelina Jolie's lips or Brad Pitt's stomach? We are born with certain features, but more and more people are altering the cards that genetics has dealt them through cosmetic surgery. The popularity of television shows such as *Nip/Tuck*, *Extreme Makeover*, and *The Swan* reflect our culture's obsession with cosmetic surgery. It is not abnormal to want to be physically attractive in our society. Perceptions of physical attractiveness are associated with a variety of other favorable perceptions, such as intelligence, honesty, and persuasiveness (Hatfield & Sprecher, 1986), despite the fact that physically attractive people may be unintelligent, dishonest, and relatively unskilled at influencing others. While there is evidence that some aspects of what human beings find attractive is innate (Langlois, Roggman, & Rieser-Danner, 1990), our perceptions of what we find attractive are largely based upon culture and appear to be heavily influenced by the mass media (Hatfield & Sprecher, 1986).

In recent years researchers have become interested in the relationship between perceptions of attractiveness in the media and cosmetic surgery (Sarwer, 1997), especially given the rise of the "reality television" programs that promote plastic surgery as a transformative practice in the lives of women. Many of these shows, such as *The Swan*, promote the idea that women need to have cosmetic surgery in order to achieve a high sense of self-esteem and happiness. The problem, of course, is that stereotypical notions of beauty are promoted, such as being ultra-thin or having a small nose and large lips for women, and these shows tend to downplay the risks associated with cosmetic surgery. As with any operation there are risks, ranging from bad reactions to anesthesia to technical problems that may arise during surgery. Many people who have cosmetic surgery are dissatisfied with the results (especially when they find they do not necessarily look like the supermodel or movie star they admire). As a result, some individuals opt for additional cosmetic surgery to "correct" these problems. In extreme cases individuals may develop body dys-morphic disorder, in which an individual has cosmetic surgery multiple times in an effort to achieve an unrealistic ideal of beauty.

Media content and acts of violence

Researchers have estimated that most children will witness 8,000 murders and 100,000 other types of violent acts before finishing elementary school (Donnerstein, Slaby, & Enron, 1994). Some of the first images we see on television as children are violent acts, such as the abusive behaviors between characters in popular cartoons, and we continue to witness violence as our cognitive development takes place and our preferences shift to programs such as dramas and news programs. Communication researchers have been interested in the effects of television violence on children for decades. In recent years, violent acts such as the killing spree at Columbine High School in Littleton, Colorado, have spurred a renewed interest in the impact of media violence on violent behavior. Yet, despite exposure to violent content, a number of variables, including cognitive and emotional maturity, intelligence, gender, and viewing habits, mediate the effects of violent content on aggressive or violent behavior (Atkin, Greenberg, Korzenny, & McDermott, 1979; Robinson & Bachman, 1972; Van Erva, 1998). Less is known about the relationship between other media, such as video games, and aggressive or violent behavior. Funk (1993) found that 50 percent of video games contained some form of violence against human or fantasy characters. In addition, the *interactive* nature of video games, or the ability of children to be an active participant in the game, is thought to have negative effects on children when playing violent types of games (Dill & Dill, 1998) since children are more involved with the mediated characters compared to more passive media (e.g., television).

The relationship between media and substance abuse

Alcohol

A number of researchers have found that alcohol advertising plays an important role in shaping perceptions of alcohol use, including the idea that drinking alcohol is a normal, exciting, and favorable activity (Fleming, Thorson, & Atkin, 2004; Wallack, Grube, Madden, & Breed, 1990). In addition, alcohol advertising regularly associates alcohol usage with images of wealth, prestige, power, and social approval (Cassell, 1995; Fleming et al., 2004). Alcohol advertisers typically direct a far greater number of advertisements towards younger consumers in an attempt to influence drinking behaviors early (Fleming et al., 2004; Grube & Wallack, 1994). The use of alcohol is also highly prevalent in the mass media, particularly among characters in television programs and films. Christenson, Henriksen, and Roberts (2000) found that 71 percent of prime-time television programs during the 1998–1999 season had characters who consumed alcoholic beverages or made reference to alcohol.

Other researchers have found similar patterns for the prevalence of alcohol use in prime-time television, feature films, and music videos (Durant et al., 1997; Everett, Schnuth, & Tribble, 1998; Kean & Albada, 2003; Mathios, Avery, Bisogni, & Shanahan, 1998). Drinking in the media is portrayed as sophisticated and intelligent, and it usually occurs among characters who are well liked, attractive, and wealthy (Mathios et al., 1998). In addition, female characters who drink alcohol are often portrayed more positively than male characters (Mathios et al., 1998). For example, on the popular HBO series *Sex and the City*, the lead character Carrie Bradshaw and her friends regularly drink large quantities of alcohol in glamorous surroundings. However, despite the plethora of television shows, films, and other media that glamorize alcohol consumption, there are relatively few cases where popular media present content that emphasizes the harmful effects of long-term alcohol usage or problems related to alcohol abuse (Signorelli, 1993).

When the alcoholic beverage industry does caution consumers about alcohol abuse in advertisements, it often promotes the idea of self-control and responsibility in consuming alcoholic beverages. However, this perspective ignores many individuals, such as alcoholics, who often feel they have little control over the amount of alcohol they consume once they begin drinking, and who report engaging in behaviors that they would not consider while sober (Wright, 2001).

Tobacco products

Researchers have identified a relationship between tobacco advertising and consumption of tobacco products (Biener & Siegel, 2000; Gilpin & Pierce,

1997). Essentially, as tobacco product advertising increases, so does consumption of these products. While cigar smoking was once associated with blue-collar workers, in recent years it has been promoted by the media as a glamorous and sophisticated type of smoking behavior, and this has led to an increase of over 250 million cigar sales a year (DeSantis & Morgan, 2003; Satcher, 1999). Magazines like *Cigar Aficionado* (which sells over 400,000 copies a year) regularly link cigar smoking with being wealthy and living the "good life," and they have become an important outlet for cigar advertisers to reach consumers (DeSantis & Morgan, 2003). In a study of *Cigar Aficionado* magazine, DeSantis and Morgan (2003) found that cigar advertisements often attempt to pitch the idea that cigars are qualitatively superior to cigarettes (with the implication that cigarette smoking is more of a lower-class activity). In addition, advertisers presented the argument that cigar smoking is inherently less dangerous than other types of behaviors (such as eating junk food), reduces stress, and is fine in moderation, and also made claims refuting scientific evidence that has linked smoking with cancer. However, these claims were based on questionable evidence, and more reputable studies have found that cigar smoking is actually linked to the same cancers and other health problems as cigarette smoking (Baker et al., 2000).

Media and sexual behavior

One in four Americans will become infected with a sexually transmitted disease (STD) during his or her lifetime, and the United States has the highest rate of non-HIV STDs in the industrialized world (Institute of Medicine, 1997). The cost of treating STDs within the US healthcare system amounts to more than $10 billion each year (Institute of Medicine, 1997). The mass media may be particularly significant in influencing perceptions about sex and sexual behavior, especially given the high prevalence of sexual activity in television shows and films. Popular media portrayals of sexual behavior often emphasize its positive aspects while ignoring the potential consequences, such as pregnancy and STDs (Lowry & Towles, 1989; Olson, 1995). For example, sexual activity with multiple partners is often associated with popular characters and rewards (popularity, being macho, etc.) in television shows and films. However, it is rare to see discussions about the use of condoms or other safe-sex practices. While some films and television programs have characters who are HIV-positive, the behaviors that led to their HIV-positive status are rarely discussed. In addition, other types of STDs that are common in the United States, such as syphilis, herpes, the human papilloma virus (which causes genital warts), and chlamydia, are rarely discussed in the entertainment media.

Direct-to-consumer advertising of prescription medications

Medications such as Prozac, Viagra, and Claritin have become household names, largely because they have been aggressively promoted by pharmaceutical companies through direct-to-consumer advertisements in the mass media (Holmer, 1999; Nelkin, 1995). Direct-to-consumer marketing attempts to create consumer demand for medications by constructing advertising messages in the popular media that promote the attractiveness of the product to the public along with messages encouraging people to ask their doctor about the drug (Bradley & Zito, 1997; Hollon, 1999). Direct-to-consumer marketing first emerged as a marketing strategy in the pharmaceutical industry in 1981, and it has since become a multi-billion dollar industry (Cline & Young, 2004; Wilkes, Bell, & Kravitz, 2000). Like all advertisements, direct-to-consumer advertisements serve to sell a particular product, which may or may not be useful to the audience.

The question of whether the advent of direct-to-consumer advertising has had a positive or negative effect on consumers is a subject of debate among health professionals and health scholars (Wilkes et al., 2000). Proponents of direct-to-consumer marketing cite greater consumer awareness of health conditions, increased knowledge of medications, and the ability of such advertisements to stimulate discussions between providers and patients and to promote more active patient roles as positive outcomes of this type of marketing (Cline & Young, 2004; Pines, 2000). Those who are concerned about the negative effects of direct-to-consumer advertisements have focused on the cost of advertised medications vis-à-vis less expensive drugs that are just as effective in treating consumer health problems, misleading or inaccurate information about the benefits and risks of the medications, unrealistic expectations about treatment outcomes, conflicts with patients who demand medications, and unnecessary visits to providers (Cline & Young, 2004; Pinto, 2000; Sellers, 2000).

In terms of message characteristics of direct-to-consumer advertisements, Cline and Young (2004) found that direct-to-consumer advertisements tend to be directed towards white consumers, and most advertisements do not use characters that reflect members of minority groups or older adults. In addition, these advertisements tend to be aimed at individuals with higher incomes. While legally drug advertisements that make positive claims about products also have to present negative information (du Pre', 2005), advertisers often use tactics such as promoting the positive aspects of the product for the majority of the television commercial, then quickly mentioning the list of potential side effects at the end of the commercial (Hunter & Thompson, 2004). Some advertisers present ambiguous information about the product and avoid directly making positive claims so that they do not have to mention negative aspects (du Pre', 2005). For example, a recent marketing campaign for the non-prescription male enhancement drug Enzyte showed a character named "Bob" being happy in several facets of his life, presumably due to Enzyte helping him to have a more satisfying sex life. However, the advertisement made no scientific claims about the efficacy of the product, nor did it discuss any potential side effects.

The promotion of medications through direct-to-consumer advertising has strongly influenced patient preferences and prescribing patterns (Holmer, 1999). For example, one study found that while overall office visits to US doctors in 1998 remained stable, visits for health conditions targeted by direct-to-consumer advertising campaigns rose substantially (Maguire, 1999). For example, during 1998, following aggressive advertising of Viagra, doctor visits for impotence rose by 113 percent (Maguire, 1999). Sales of Viagra, Prozac, and other heavily marketed drugs have skyrocketed in recent years, resulting in billions of dollars in sales for pharmaceutical companies.

Health News Stories in the Media

Health-related stories are highly prevalent in the news media. In fact, stories dealing with health issues are among the most frequent types of stories in television news, newspapers, and magazines (Kline, 2003). In addition, the news media have a long-standing relationship with health promoters at the national, state, and local level, and the news media have been actively involved in promoting a variety of health campaigns and initiatives during the last several decades (Boutwell, 1995; Cooper, Burgoon, & Roter, 2001; Dubren, 1977). However, Cooper et al. (2001) found that audience members do not remember much of the health information they encounter through the news media, and attention to health-related news media stories is influenced by variables such as the personal relevance of a news story, whether or not the story is novel, and its shock value. In addition, the types of health-related stories and the way these stories are presented are influenced by the needs and agendas of news media organizations. The following section takes an in-depth look at problems associated with the reporting of health-related stories in the news media.

Problems in the reporting of health news stories

Agenda-setting theory

Agenda setting refers to how the daily selection and display of news stories by the media influences audience perceptions about the importance of news topics and issues (Protess & McCombs, 1991). The decision to select or not to select a news story is dependent on a number of factors, including the perceived importance of the story by the public and members of media organizations, time constraints, and whether a story is ongoing or "breaking news." *Media gatekeepers* are members of news media organizations who make decisions about which stories will be disseminated to the public and how the information will be presented. According to agenda-setting theory, these individuals play an important role in shaping public perceptions about which issues, including health issues, are important. Gatekeeper decisions to tell or not to tell a story are often linked to political views and news coverage policies that are part of the culture of media organizations. By making conscious decisions to cover some health issues and not others, news organizations can influence public perceptions of the relative importance of these issues. Agenda-setting theory is a useful framework for understanding how the *underreporting* or *overreporting* of a health problem or issue (or inaccuracies when reporting it) by a news organization can ultimately affect the public's understanding of the issue and their behaviors towards it.

A good example of how underreporting of a health problem by the media can impact public perceptions and behaviors is the HIV/AIDS epidemic in the United States. James Kinsella's (1989) study of AIDS and the American media demonstrates the agenda-setting practices of media organizations in the early years of the HIV/AIDS epidemic in the US. According to Kinsella, news organizations avoided covering AIDS stories because the infected population at that time was primarily gay men. Gatekeepers within news organizations did not want to offend mainstream audiences with stories about individuals who may have contracted the disease through what the gatekeepers perceived to be deviant sexual behaviors. Unfortunately, because HIV/AIDS first spread among people whose behaviors mainstream America found to be somewhat offensive (e.g., gay men having sex, intravenous drug use), when stories did appear in the mainstream media they tended to be ambiguous about the risk behaviors for the disease (even though they were known at the time). As the HIV/AIDS epidemic began to spread, the media eventually gave it more coverage. However, Kinsella (1989) argues that most AIDS stories that did receive news coverage dealt with individuals who acquired the disease through heterosexual contact or through blood transfusions (so-called "innocent victims" of HIV/AIDS).

By limiting the coverage of HIV/AIDS stories in the early days of the epidemic, many heterosexual people did not perceive HIV/AIDS to be an issue they needed to worry about, and many heterosexuals continued to engage in unsafe sexual behaviors despite the fact that they were at risk for the disease. In addition, by downplaying the crisis in the media, money for HIV/AIDS research from the government was stalled (Dearing & Rogers, 1992). Even as new antiviral medications for HIV begin to be developed, media organizations are accused of not disseminating information about how these drugs may prolong the life of people with HIV, provided that they get tested for the disease while it is in its early stages (Kahn, 1993).

Of course, the media have underreported many other health problems as well. Deaths from asthma, diabetes, heart disease, stroke, tobacco-related problems, and environmental and occupational influences on health tend to be underreported in the US relative to their incident rates in the population (Frost, Frank, & Maiback, 1997; Seale, 2002; Signorelli, 1993). Davidson and Wallack (2004), in a content analysis of popular print news media, found substantial underreporting of STDs, particularly STDs other than HIV/AIDS. In addition, they found that most articles dealing with STDs did not cover routes of transmission, causes, or signs and symptoms of various STDs. Underreporting of health problems tends to occur even more often when the problems affect minority populations in the United States (Kline, 2003; Vargas & dePyssler, 1999).

Overreporting of health-related issues is also quite common in the mass media (Kline, 2003). For example, while catastrophic events such as tornadoes, homicides, and motor vehicle accidents claim many lives each year in the United States, the number of people who die in these events is relatively small compared to deaths from diseases such as heart disease and cancer (Frost et al., 1997). However, news stories are much more likely to report deaths resulting from catastrophic events than deaths resulting from diseases and other common health problems (Frost et al., 1997; Singer, 1990). One of the reasons for the overreporting of tornadoes, homicides, and other traumatic events is that they tend to be more sensational and attention-grabbing than stories about people dying from diseases and health problems (who tend to die less dramatically in healthcare facilities). Compared to natural disasters and homicides, the way that most people die from health problems may appear somewhat mundane. The producers of mass media news stories, who are interested in attracting the attention of audience members to gain advertising revenue, typically choose health-related stories that are more visually stimulating, graphic, or sensational. For example, you may have heard the news media saying: "If it bleeds it leads." Unfortunately, overreporting of traumatic events may lead people to overestimate their risk of dying from a catastrophic event (Singer, 1990).

When the news media decide to focus their attention on more common health problems, health risks are sometimes overreported. For example, although more people die of lung and colon cancer than skin cancer or breast cancer each year, many US media sources run a much higher percentage of skin cancer and breast cancer stories than stories about lung and colon cancer (Gerlach, Marino, & Hoffman-Goetz, 1997; Lantz & Booth, 1998; Kline, 2003). Women's magazines often devote excessive attention to diet, fitness, and reproductive health at the expense of major health risks for women, such as heart disease (Seale, 2002). One of the reasons why these types of stories tend to be overreported may be due to our culture's obsession with appearance and youth. For example, surgery for skin cancer and breast cancer can often lead to changes in physical appearance, such as visible scars left behind after the removal of melanomas or the removal of a breast due to a mastectomy, and because these changes are tied to cultural conceptions of beauty and sexuality, many women fear these types of cancer. Because of these fears, mass media organizations know that women will pay attention to stories about these types of cancer. However, this can be problematic when other types of cancers and health problems that pose greater risks to women are not given as much attention.

Media bias and inaccuracies in reporting health issues

Related to agenda-setting theory is the *framing* of news stories, or the "selection and emphasis of certain aspects of issues" (Andsager & Powers, 2001, p. 163). In other words, even when the news media decide to cover a particular story, they tend to discuss certain aspects of the issue while excluding other aspects. Although the news media often strive for "fair and balanced" reporting of issues, the reporting of news stories is influenced by a variety of social, cultural, and economic factors within news organizations and news organization personnel that can shape the way a particular story is presented (Andsager & Powers, 2001; Parrott & Condit, 1996). For example, news stories often emphasize the biomedical perspective of health and/or dominant cultural conceptions of health while downplaying psychosocial issues and alternative viewpoints (Parrott, 1996; Ruzek, Olesen, & Clarke, 1997). Since pharmaceutical companies and other corporations with vested interests in biomedical approaches to medicine are often sponsors of media news programming, these organizations have a vested interest in promoting the biomedical model of healthcare.

Exposure to health-related news stories may have second-order effects, or more subtle effects due to long-term exposure, on audience member perceptions. For example, health-related stories tend to emphasize the idea that avoiding health problems is largely in the control of the individual, and messages tend to focus on individual solutions to health problems while downplaying health issues that are largely outside of most people's control (Seale, 2002), such as health problems related to the environmental waste practices of corporations. In addition, few news stories emphasize collective responses to public health issues, such as ways to organize political efforts to deal with health issues facing larger communities.

The news media often rely heavily on sources for health-related stories, such as government officials, key members of the medical establishment, and members of the pharmaceutical industry, to bolster the credibility of their stories (Shaw & McCombs, 1989; Shoemaker & Reese, 1996). However, these sources often have a somewhat narrow and privileged view of health issues, and they may be interested in preserving the status quo and/or financial interests when discussing health concerns (Dearing & Rogers, 1992; Wright, 1999). In addition, health-related news stories often pay little attention to risks involved with certain "breakthrough" medical procedures, or they may emphasize harmful aspects of some procedures while downplaying benefits if it provides a more sensational story (Ruzek et al., 1997; Vanderford & Smith, 1996). News stories about new pharmaceutical products rarely present a balanced view of the benefits and the potential risks of these medications, and information about new drugs that is provided in the media tends to emphasize their potential benefits while downplaying problems, such as side effects and cost vis-à-vis competing medications (Entwistle & Sheldon, 1999).

While news organizations strive to present accurate information to the public, inaccuracies in the reporting of health-related news stories are quite common in the media (Carlson, Li, & Holm, 1997; Kline, 2003). Due to the limited amount of time and space the news media can devote to any story, there is always the potential that some information will be left out of a health-related item. In addition, news reporters may find it difficult in some cases to accurately convey a health-related story because of a variety of factors, including the nature of the story, the amount of medical or scientific expertise required to understand the health-related event, a reporter's level of education, or the experience a reporter has with a health issue. News story inaccuracies can have wide-reaching effects on public perceptions of health issues. For example, Freed, Katz, and Clark (1996) found that many people began to perceive some vaccinations as risky (and subsequently avoided them) after news reports that the former 1994 Miss America, Heather Whitestone, was deaf as a result of receiving a vaccination, even though her condition was later confirmed by her pediatrician to be the result of contracting meningitis when she was a child.

Summary

The mass media influence our perceptions of health and health-related issues in a variety of ways. Some communication theorists contend that the mass media influence us by altering our perceptions of the world through repeated long-term exposure to the reality portrayed through media content. Other researchers argue that the reasons behind why we use media and the ways in which we use them ultimately mediate the effects of mass media messages. However, researchers have found a relationship between exposure to health-related images and messages in the mass media and both positive and negative health outcomes. Unfortunately, despite the potential of the media to influence healthy behaviors, they tend to be more of a negative influence, leading to problems such as poor eating habits, substance abuse, and sometimes the tendency to accept violence or aggressive behavior. We rely heavily on the news media for up-to-date and accurate information about health issues. However, news media organizations often have their own agendas when presenting the news that may influence the way health stories are covered. In addition, these organizations are also influenced by larger social norms surrounding health issues. Finally, the limited amount of time and space that media organizations can devote to health stories may lead to inaccuracies and other problems in the reporting of health-related news.

References

Allison, D. B, Fontaine, K. R., Manson, J. E., Stevens, J., & VanItallie, T. B. (1999). Annual deaths attributable to obesity in the United States. *Journal of the American Medical Association, 282*, 1530–1538.

Andsager, J. L., & Powers, A. (2001). Framing women's health with a sense-making approach: Magazine coverage of breast cancer and implants. *Health Communication, 13*, 163–185.

Atkin, C., & Arkin, E. B. (1990). Issues and initiatives in communicating health information. In C. Atkin & L. Wallack (Eds.), *Mass communication and public health: Complexities and conflicts* (pp. 13–40). Newbury Park, CA: Sage.

Atkin, C., Greenberg, B., Korzenny, F., & McDermott, F. (1979). Selective exposure to televised violence. *Journal of Broadcasting, 23*, 5–14.

Bahk, C. M. (2001). Drench effects of media portrayal of fatal virus disease on health locus of control beliefs. *Health Communication, 13*, 187–204.

Baker, F., Ainsworth, S. R., Dye, J. T., Crammer, C., Thun, M. J., Hoffman, D., et al. (2000). Health risks associated with cigar smoking. *Journal of the American Medical Association, 284*, 735–747.

Becker, A. E., Grinspoon, S. K., Klibanski, A., & Herzog, D. B. (1999). Eating disorders. New England Journal of Medicine, *340*, 1092–1098.

Biener, L., & Siegel, M. (2000). Tobacco marketing and adolescent smoking: More support for a causal inference. *American Journal of Public Health, 90*, 407–411.

Boutwell, W. B. (1995). The under cover skin cancer prevention project: A community-based program in four Texas cities. *Cancer, 75*, 657–660.

Bradley, L. R., & Zito, J. M. (1997). Direct-to-consumer prescription drug advertising. *Medical Care, 35*, 86–92.

Brown, J. D., & Walsh-Childers, K. (2002). Effects of media on personal and public health. In. J. Bryant & D. Zillman (Eds.), *Media effects: Advances in theory and research.* Mahwah, NJ: Lawrence Erlbaum.

Byrd-Bredbenner, C., Finckenor, M., & Grasso, D. (2003). Health-related content in prime-time television programming. *Journal of Health Communication, 8,* 329–341.

Carlson, E. S., Li, S., & Holm, K. (1997). An analysis of menopause in the popular press. *Health Care Women International, 18,* 557–564.

Cassell, S. (1995). Public discourse on alcohol: Implications for public policy. In H. Holder & G. Edwards (Eds.), *Alcohol and public: Evidence and issues* (pp. 190–211). Oxford: Oxford University Press.

Christenson, P. G., Henriksen, L., & Roberts, D. F. (2000). *Substance use in popular prime time television.* Retrieved from www.mediascope.org/pubs/supptt.pdf.

Cline, R. J. W., & Young, H. N. (2004). Marketing drugs, marketing health care relationships: A content analysis of visual cues in direct-to-consumer prescription drug advertising. *Health Communication, 16,* 131–157.

Cooper, C. P., Burgoon, M., & Roter, D. L. (2001). An expectancy-value analysis of viewer interest in television prevention news stories. *Health Communication, 13,* 227–240.

Davidson, A. E., & Wallack, L. (2004). A content analysis of sexually transmitted diseases in the print news media. *Journal of Health Communication, 9,* 111–117.

Dearing, J. W., & Rogers, E. M. (1992). AIDS and the media agenda. In T. Edgar, M. A. Fitzpatrick, & V. S. Freimuth (Eds.), *AIDS: A communication perspective* (pp. 165–189). Hillsdale, NJ: Lawrence Erlbaum.

DeSantis, A. D., & Morgan, S. E. (2003). Sometimes a cigar [magazine] is more than just a cigar [magazine]: Pro-smoking arguments in *Cigar Aficionado,* 1992–2000. *Health Communication, 15,* 457–480.

Diem, S. J., Lantos, J. D., & Tulsky, J. A. (1996). Cardiopulmonary resuscitation on television: Miracles and misinformation. *New England Journal of Medicine, 334,* 1578–1582.

Dill, K. E., & Dill, J. C. (1998). Video game violence: A review of the empirical literature. *Aggression and Violent Behavior, 3,* 407–482.

Donnerstein, E., Slaby, R. G., & Enron, L. D. (1994). The mass media and youth aggression. In L. D. Enron, J. H. Gentry, & P. Schlegel (Eds.), *Reason to hope: A psychological perspective on violence and youth* (pp. 219–250). Washington, DC: American Psychological Association.

Dubren, R. (1977). Evaluation of a televised stop-smoking clinic. *Public Health Reports, 92,* 81–84.

du Pre', A. (1998). *Humor and the healing arts: A multimethod analysis of humor use in health care.* Mahwah, NJ: Lawrence Erlbaum.

du Pre', A. (2005). *Communicating about health: Current issues and perspectives* (2nd ed.). Boston: McGraw-Hill.

Durant, R. H., Rome, E. S., Rich, M., Allred, E., Emans, S. J., & Woods, E. R. (1997). Tobacco and alcohol use behaviors portrayed in music videos: A content analysis. *American Journal of Public Health, 87,* 1131–1135.

Dutta, M. J., & Youn, S. (1999). Profiling healthy consumers: A psychographic approach to social marketing. *Social Marketing Quarterly, 5,* 5–21.

Dutta-Bergman, M. J. (2004). Reaching unhealthy eaters: Applying a strategic approach to media vehicle choice. *Health Communication, 16,* 493–506.

Dworetzky, J. P. (1993). *Introduction to child development* (5th ed.). St. Paul, MN: West.

Entwistle, V., & Sheldon, T. (1999). The picture of health? Media coverage of the health service. In B. Franklin (Ed.), *Social policy, the media and misrepresentation.* London: Routledge.

Everett, S. A., Schnuth, R. L., & Tribble, J. L. (1998). Tobacco and alcohol in top-grossing American films. *Journal of Community Health, 23,* 317–324.

Ferris, J. E. (2003). Parallel discourses and "appropriate" bodies: Media constructions of anorexia and obesity in the cases of Tracy Gold and Carnie Wilson. *Journal of Communication Inquiry, 27,* 256–263.

Festinger, L. (1954). A theory of social comparison processes. *Human Relations, 2,* 117–140.

Flegal, K. M., Carroll, M. D., Ogden, C. L., & Johnson, C. L. (2002). Prevalence and trends in obesity among US adults, 1999–2000. Journal of the American Medical Association, 288, 1723–1727.

Fleming, K., Thorson, E., & Atkin, C. K. (2004). Alcohol advertising exposure and perceptions: Links with alcohol expectancies and intentions to drink or drinking in underaged youth and young adults. *Journal of Health Communication, 9,* 3–29.

Freed, G. L., Katz, S. L., & Clark, S. J. (1996). Safety of vaccinations: Miss America, the media, and public health. *Journal of the American Medical Association, 276,* 1869–1872.

Friedland, R. P., et al. (2001, March). Patients with Alzheimer's disease have reduced activities in midlife compared with healthy control-group members. *Proceedings of the National Academy of Sciences, 98,* 3440.

Frost, K., Frank, E., & Maiback, E. (1997). Relative risk in the news media: A quantification of misrepresentation. *American Journal of Public Health, 87,* 842–845.

Funk, J. B. (1993). Reevaluating the impact of video games. *Clinical Pediatrics, 32,* 86–90.

Gerbner, G. (1998). Cultivation analysis: An overview. *Mass Communication and Society, 1,* 175–194.

Gerbner, G., & Gross, L. (1972). Living with television: The violence profile. *Journal of Communication, 26,* 173–199.

Gerbner, G., Gross, L., Jackson-Beeck, M., Jeffries-Fox, S., & Signorelli, N. (1978). Cultural indicators: Violence profile No. 9. *Journal of Communication, 28,* 176–206.

Gerbner, G., Gross, L., Morgan, M., & Signorelli, N. (1982). Charting the mainstream: Television's contribution to political orientations. *Journal of Communication, 32,* 100–127.

Gerbner, G., Gross, L., Morgan, M., & Signorelli, N. (1986). Living with television: The dynamics of the cultivation process. In J. Bryant & D. Zillman (Eds.), *Perspectives on media effects* (pp. 17–40). Hillsdale, NJ: Lawrence Erlbaum.

Gerlach, K. K., Marino, C., & Hoffman-Goetz, L. (1997). Cancer coverage in women's magazines: What information are women receiving? *Journal of Cancer Education, 12,* 240–244.

Gilpin, E. A., & Pierce, J. P. (1997). Trends in adolescent smoking initiation in the United States: Is tobacco marketing an influence? *Tobacco Control, 6,* 122–127.

Grube, J., & Wallack, L. (1994). Television beer advertising and drinking knowledge, beliefs, and intentions among school children. *American Journal of Public Health, 84,* 254–259.

Hatfield, E., & Sprecher, S. (1986). *Mirror, mirror: The importance of looks in everyday life.* Albany: State University of New York at Albany Press.

Harrison, K. (2000). The body electric: Thin-ideal media and eating disorders in adolescents. *Journal of Communication, 50*(3), 119–143.

Harrison, K., & Cantor, J. (1997). The relationship between media consumption and eating disorders. *Journal of Communication, 47,* 40–67.

Hatfield, E., & Sprecher, S. (1986). *Mirror, mirror: The importance of looks in everyday life.* Albany, NY: State University of New York Albany Press.

Hofferth, S. L., & Sandberg, J. F. (2001). How American children spend their time. *Journal of Marriage and Family, 63,* 295–308.

Hollon, M. F. (1999). Direct-to-consumer marketing of prescription drugs: Creating consumer demand. *Journal of the American Medical Association, 281,* 382–384.

Holmer, A. F. (1999). Direct-to-consumer prescription drug advertising builds bridges between patients and physicians. *Journal of the American Medical Association, 281,* 380–382.

Hunter, K. M., & Thompson, S. R. (2004, November). *Mass media medicine: A weighted content analysis and effects assessment of direct-to-consumer pharmaceutical ads.* Paper presented at the annual National Communication Association Convention, Chicago.

Institute of Medicine. (1997). *The hidden epidemic: Confronting sexually transmitted diseases.* Washington, DC.

Kahn, A. D. (1993). *AIDS: The winter war.* Philadelphia: Temple University Press.

Katz, E., Blumler, J. G., & Gurevitz, M. (1974). Utilization of mass communication by the individual. In J. G. Blumler & E. Katz (Eds.), *The uses of mass communication: Current perspectives on gratifications research* (pp. 19–32). Beverly Hills, CA: Sage.

Katz, E., Gurevitch, M., & Haas, H. (1973). On the use of mass media for important things. *American Sociological Review, 38,* 164–181.

Kean, L. G., & Albada, K. F. (2003). The relationship between college students' schema regarding alcohol use, their television viewing patterns, and their previous experiences with alcohol. *Health Communication, 15,* 277–298.

Kinsella, J. (1989). *Covering the plague: AIDS and the American media.* New Brunswick, NJ: Rutgers University Press.

Kline, K. N. (2003). Popular media and health: Images, effects, and institutions. In T. L. Thompson, A. M. Dorsey, K. I. Miller, & R. Parrot (Eds.), *Handbook of health communication* (pp. 557–581). Mahwah, NJ: Lawrence Erlbaum.

Lambert, R. B., & Lambert, N. K. (1995). The effects of humor on secretory immunoglobulin A levels in school-aged children. *Pediatric Nursing, 21,* 16–19.

Langlois, J. H., Roggman, L. A., & Rieser-Danner, L. A. (1990). Infant's differential social responses to attractive and unattractive faces. *Developmental Psychology, 26,* 153–159.

Lantz, P. M., & Booth, K. M. (1998). The social construction of the breast cancer epidemic. *Social Science Medicine, 46,* 907–918.

Lowry, D., & Towles, D. (1989). Prime time TV portrayals of sex, contraception and venereal diseases. *Journalism Quarterly, 66,* 347–352.

Maguire, P. (1999). How direct-to-consumer advertising is putting the squeeze on physicians. *ACP-ASIM Observer* [On-line]. Retrieved August 21, 2004, from www. aconline.org/journals/news/mar99/squeeze.htm.

Mathios, A., Avery, R., Bisogni, C., & Shanahan, J. (1998). Alcohol portrayals on prime time television: Manifest and latent messages. *Journal of Studies on Alcohol, 59,* 305–310.

Mokdad, A. H., Serdula, M. K., Dietz, W. H., Bowman, B. A., Marks, J. S., & Koplan, J. P. (1999). The spread of the obesity epidemic in the United States, 1991–1998. *Journal of the American Medical Association, 282,* 1519–1522.

Montgomery, K. C. (1990). Promoting health through entertainment television. In C. Atkin & L. Wallack (Eds.), *Mass communication and public health: Complexities and conflicts.* Newbury Park, CA: Sage.

Must, A., Spadano, J., Coakley, E. H., Field, A. E., Colditz, G., & Dietz, W. H. (1999). The disease burden associated with overweight and obesity. *Journal of the American Medical Association, 282,* 1523–1529.

Nelkin, D. (1995). *Selling science: How the press covers science and technology.* New York: W. H. Freeman.

Ogden, C. L., Flegan, K. M., Carroll, M. D., & Johnson, C. L. (2002). Prevalence and trends in overweight among US children and adolescents, 1999–2000. *Journal of the American Medical Association, 28,* 1728–1732.

Olson, B. (1995). Sex and the soaps: A comparative content analysis of health issues. *Journalism Quarterly, 71,* 840–850.

Parrott, R. L. (1996). A women-centered "sense-making" approach to communicating about women's reproductive health. In R. L. Parrott & C. M. Condit (Eds.), *Evaluating women's health messages* (pp. 414–425). Thousand Oaks, CA: Sage.

Parrott, R. L., & Condit, C. M. (1996). Priorities and agendas in communicating about women's reproductive health. In R. L. Parrott & C. M. Condit (Eds.), *Evaluating women's health messages* (pp. 1–11). Thousand Oaks, CA: Sage.

Pines, W. L. (2000). Direct-to-consumer advertising. *Annals of Pharmacology, 34,* 1341–1344.

Pinto, M. B. (2000). On the nature and properties of appeals used in direct-to-consumer advertising of prescription drugs. *Psychological Reports, 86,* 597–606.

Protess, D. L., & McCombs, M. E. (1991). *Agenda-setting: Readings on media, public opinion, and policy-making.* Hillsdale, NJ: Lawrence Erlbaum.

Robinson, J., & Bachman, J. (1972). Television viewing habits and aggression. In G. Comstock & E. Rubenstein (Eds.), *Television and social behavior: Television and adolescent aggressiveness* (pp. 372–382). Washington, DC: US Government Printing Office.

Ruzek, S. B., Olesen, V. L., & Clarke, A. E. (1997). *Women's health: Complexities and differences*. Columbus, OH: Ohio State University Press.

Sarwer, D. B. (1997). The "obsessive" cosmetic surgery patient: A consideration of body image dissatisfaction and body dysmorphic disorder. *Plastic Surgical Nursing, 17*, 193–209.

Satcher, D. (1999). Cigars and public health. *New England Journal of Medicine, 340*, 1829–1831.

Scharf, B. F., Freimuth, V. S., Greenspon, P., & Plotnick, C. (1996). Confronting cancer on *Thirty Something*: Audience response to health content on entertainment television. *Journal of Health Communication, 1*, 133–138.

Seale, C. (2002). *Media and health*. Thousand Oaks, CA: Sage.

Sellers, J. A. (2000). The two faces of direct-to-consumer advertising. *American Journal of Health-Systems Pharmacy, 51*, 1401.

Shaw, D. L., & McCombs, M. E. (1989). Dealing with illicit drugs: The power, and limits, of mass media agenda-setting. In P. J. Shoemaker (Ed.), *Communication campaigns about drugs: Government, media, and the public* (pp. 113–120). Hillsdale, NJ: Lawrence Erlbaum.

Shoemaker, P. J., & Reese, S. D. (1996). *Mediating the message: Theories of influences on mass media content* (2nd ed.). White Plains, NY: Longman.

Shrum, L. J. (1999). Television and persuasion: Effects of the programs between the ads. *Psychology and Marketing, 16*, 119–140.

Signorelli, N. (1993). *Mass media images and impact on health*. Westport, CT: Greenwood Press.

Singer, E. (1990). A question of accuracy: How journalists and scientists report research on hazards. *Journal of Communication, 40*, 102–116.

Swenson, M. R., & Wells, W. D. (1995). Target marketing for health communication. *Social Marketing Quarterly, 2*, 5–9.

Terre, L., Drabman, R. S., & Speer, P. (1991). Health-relevant behaviors in the media. *Journal of Applied Social Psychology, 21*, 1303–1319.

Turow, J., & Coe, L. (1993). Curing television's ills: The portrayal of health care. In B. C. Thornton & G. Kreps (Eds.), *Perspectives on health communication* (pp. 130–145). Prospect Heights, IL: Waveland.

Vanderford, M. L., & Smith, D. H. (1996). *The silicone breast implant story*. Mahwah, NJ: Lawrence Erlbaum.

Van Erva, J. P. (1998). *Television and child development* (2nd ed.). Mahwah, NJ: Lawrence Erlbaum.

Vargas, L. C., & dePyssler, B. J. (1999). US Latino newspapers as health communication resources: A content analysis. *Howard Journal of Communications, 10*, 189–205.

Wallack, L., & Dorfman, L. (1992). Health messages on television commercials. *American Journal of Health Promotion, 6*, 190–196.

Wallack, L., Grube, J., Madden, P. R., & Breed, W. (1990). Portrayals of alcohol on prime-time television. *Journal of Studies on Alcohol, 51*, 428–433.

Wilkes, M. S., Bell, R. A., & Kravitz, R. L. (2000). Direct-to-consumer advertising: Trends, impact, and implications. *Health Affairs, 19*, 110–128.

Wright, K. B. (1999). AIDS, the status quo, and the elite media: An analysis of the guest lists of "The MacNeil/Lehrer News Hour" and "Nightline." In W. N. Elwood (Ed.), *Power in the blood: A handbook on AIDS, politics, and communication.* Mahwah, NJ: Lawrence Erlbaum.

Wright, K. B. (2001). *Perceptions of responsibility, stigmatization, and control in college student drinking situations: An analysis of undergraduate student perceptions of alcohol issues on campus.* Paper presented at the annual Southern States Communication Association Convention, Lexington, KY.

Part V

Risk, Campaigns, Communities, and Teams

Chapter 9

Risk and
Crisis Communication

"Terror threat orange," "A category four hurricane is heading toward Florida," "Eat foods that are high in fiber," and even "Put on sunscreen before you go outside today!" are common preventive risk messages we all frequently hear. Even at college you have likely heard your friends sending messages to you or other friends such as "Don't drink too much," "Be sure to have a designated driver," and "Take condoms just in case." As you get older, you are likely to hear more and more messages about changing diet and exercise habits, and messages about mammograms, colonoscopies, and prostate cancer exams as preventive measures for disease when you reach a high-risk age group. While many individuals in the United States may not perceive that they are at risk for health problems, we are all vulnerable to some type of physical, psychological, or social health threat. From the examples given above, you may have noticed that health threats range from widespread threats (global and regional) to community and individual threats. As a result, health communication researchers have become increasingly interested in identifying groups of people who are at the greatest risk for specific types of threats and finding ways to design appropriate messages to help individuals avoid or reduce them.

In recent years, we have seen the world at greater risk for global and large-scale health threats, such as HIV/AIDS, environmental threats (e.g., pollution and toxic waste), and politically motivated threats, such as bioterrorism. The terrorist attacks on September 11, 2001, the anthrax mailings in the months following September 11, and viruses such as SARS and avian 'bird" flu have made many people in the United States realize just how vulnerable they are to health threats in our ever-shrinking world. Communication between government agencies, media sources, scientists, and healthcare providers around the world is crucial during times of health-related crises and in order to cope with pandemics, such as HIV/AIDS. In addition, health communicators must now be conscious of disseminating messages about some health risks to a worldwide audience.

In addition to these health threats, there are many populations within the United States and all over the world who are at risk for various health problems due to reasons such as poverty, age, race, hunger, inadequate education, insanitary environmental conditions, and lack of access to appropriate healthcare. Many of these populations are marginalized groups who are at risk for health problems due to larger social issues, including political and cultural conditions, racial injustice, and lack of financial and social resources. Increasingly, we are seeing a greater divide between those who have the resources to deal with these health issues and those who do not. Communicating health risk and coordinating disease prevention and control efforts within these populations can be complex and challenging situations for healthcare promoters.

This chapter explores health risk and crisis communication issues at the global/large-scale, community, and individual levels. Specifically, it begins by defining risk communication and crisis communication. This is followed by a discussion of global threats to health, including HIV and terrorism, as well as communication strategies for coping with these threats. Next it examines several factors that are related to being at risk for health problems in the United States and strategies for communicating about risk at the community level. Finally, it examines strategies for communicating about risk at the provider–patient level.

Defining Risk Communication

Risk communication, or discourse about physical hazards, has been an academic field of study roughly since the time of the 1984 Bhopal disaster, an accidental chemical release that killed more than 2,000 people in Bhopal, India. The Bhopal disaster awakened many groups to the realization that we need to coordinate our communication and emergency management efforts in big and small towns throughout the United States, as well as industrial sites throughout the world. The need for coordinating communication between emergency agencies became all too apparent in the days following the Hurricane Katrina disaster in New Orleans (and surrounding areas) in 2005. Furthermore, beginning in the 1980s, there was increasing awareness that physical hazards were not necessarily those that caused the greatest numbers of illnesses and deaths. An additional source of interest in risk communication has come from the existence of frightening diseases such as cancer and AIDS. Scientific uncertainty about these diseases sometimes leads people to wonder about the possible ways in which they may have contracted them. Moreover, during this time period, people also began to realize that physical hazards, diseases, and other health problems often have a much greater impact on individuals in society who have lower incomes, less education, and who are often members of marginalized groups. For example, the people who were most adversely affected by the Katrina disaster tended to be poor African Americans. Consequently, groups as diverse as trade associations, medical associations, public relations offices, and many government groups currently devote considerable effort to learning how best to communicate with the public about risk and safety.

Our era has fueled interest in risk communication for still more reasons. First, despite this last century being one of the "safest of times," in one sense it was also one of the most dangerous. Half of the twentieth century's worst industrial accidents (those killing more than 50 people) occurred since 1977 (Shrivasta, 1987). In addition, while many newly synthesized chemicals and procedures make our lives infinitely safer, healthier, and more comfortable than we would be without them, these same substances frighten us because we often lack the specialized scientific knowledge to understand the potential risks these products may contain (e.g., toxins, side effects). Moreover, they frighten us because we do not always trust industry or the government to operate in connection with these potential hazards in ways that are motivated by our best interests. However, as Rowan (2004) points out, during this same period the mass media's tools for alerting us to disasters, accidents, and harmful substances have also increased.

Although they are often used interchangeably, risk communication differs from *crisis communication* in one important sense. Risk communication deals only with communication about physical hazards such as tornadoes, toxic chemicals, and so forth. Crisis communication may, but does not have to, concern physical hazards. For example, an unexpectedly negative news article could constitute a crisis for an organization, or an unexpected disaster such as Hurricane Katrina could constitute a crisis for Louisiana and the entire country by raising awareness of a nation lacking in preparedness and effective communication exchange among officials and the affected communities. Another important goal of health communication scholars is to raise public awareness of the importance of communication following a crisis, why communication about hurricanes, terrorist attacks, health epidemics, and other unknown disasters can be so difficult, and what people can do to improve these communication processes.

Global and Large-Scale Health Threats

This section explores some of the major threats to health around the world, including environmental threats, hunger, pandemics, and terrorism. In addition, we will explore several responses to these threats posed by health communication scholars.

Environmental threats/world hunger

Environment-related diseases and injuries cause millions of preventable deaths each year. Hazardous waste disposal, overpopulation, smog, and pollution are just a few of the many adverse environmental factors that have been linked to health problems. As we discussed earlier in this chapter, people who are poor and/or marginalized tend to be at most risk for many of these health problems. Overpopulation is most common in developing countries, many of which already lack sufficient financial and structural resources. In countries with overpopulation problems, more people mean that there are greater demands on farm land, water supplies, and other natural resources, many of which are often affected by pollution due to the number of people. Around the world, millions of tons of hazardous waste are produced annually by industries, and these materials are often linked to many different health problems. Unfortunately, minority and/or low-income populations within many countries face *environmental injustice*, or disproportionate exposure to environmental dangers due to race, ethnicity, or socioeconomic status (Anderton, Anderson, Oakes, & Fraser, 1994). Hazardous waste disposal often occurs in locations that are in close proximity to where minority and/or low-income populations live, areas which are considered "undesirable" by higher-income individuals within the greater community. While most of these hazardous materials are contained within landfill, toxic emissions from landfills, such as methane gas, can create health risks for people in the surrounding areas. For example, methane and other gases emitted by landfills are carcinogenic, leading to long-term health problems.

Environmental injustice appears to be a global phenomenon. Ethnic minorities in Central Asia, Australia, Africa, and South America have all suffered acute and prolonged health problems caused by radiation tests, toxic waste from the petroleum industry, and many other hazardous materials (Bullard, 1993). In the United States, several studies have found evidence of toxic waste materials being dumped near minority and/or low-income neighborhoods (Rowan, 1996).

More than 840 million people in the world suffer from hunger or are malnourished, and while hunger is certainly a problem in the United States, most people facing hunger live in developing nations (Care.org, 2006). Millions of children suffer from hunger around the world, putting them at risk for developmental problems associated with malnutrition, such as stunted growth, susceptibility to disease, cognitive impairment, and early mortality rates. About 5 million children around the world die from problems related to malnutrition each year. In addition, hunger affects an individual's productivity, sense of hope, and overall well-being. There are many causes of world hunger, including the economic condition of countries and regions, land rights and ownership, inefficient agricultural practices, war, famine, drought, poor crop yields, and environmental problems.

As you can imagine, dealing with problems such as environmental injustice and world hunger is no easy task. At the very least, health communication scholars and other individuals can help to raise awareness about environmental problems and environmental injustice by conducting more studies that demonstrate the link between industry waste disposal practices and health problems, by interventions designed not only to raise awareness of these issues among people living in communities where these practices occur but also to give them the tools to promote change, and through health campaigns designed to change industry practices or that create new legislation that will end them.

While the world has the capacity to produce enough food for everyone, we are well short of achieving this goal. A variety of economic, political, educational, and cultural issues, such as the wealth of a region, rights to land, racism, and knowledge about agricultural practices, contribute to the inability of regions to produce and distribute food to everyone. Donating food as aid or charity in non-emergency situations is more or less a short-term solution to world hunger. While such donations can be crucial during emergency situations, the long-term solution to hunger may lie in economic, educational, and political reform efforts. Again, campaigns designed both to raise the awareness of those individuals who have the greatest needs and to improve economic and educational conditions are ways in which health communication scholars can help to make a long-term impact on hunger.

Pandemics

A pandemic is a global epidemic of a disease or health problem. The world is more vulnerable to pandemics than ever before due to increased travel around the world and immigration. The HIV/AIDS threat is the most prominent pandemic the world faces today. However, other diseases have the potential to become pandemics if efforts are not taken to contain them. We will focus on the impact of HIV/AIDS and the emergence of new threats, such as SARS and avian flu, and responses to these threats below.

HIV/AIDS

More than 20 million people worldwide have died of AIDS since the beginning of the pandemic, and 38 million people were estimated to be living with

HIV/AIDS by the end of 2003 (Joint United Nations Program on HIV/AIDS, 2004). Women now account for about half of the number of people with HIV worldwide. Young people (between the ages of 15 and 24) account for most of the new HIV infections worldwide.

Africa is the continent that has been hit the hardest by the HIV/AIDS pandemic, followed by South and Southeast Asia. Nearly 25 million individuals with HIV/AIDS live in African countries, while over 6 million live in Asian countries (Joint United Nations Program on HIV/AIDS, 2004). A large proportion of individuals living with HIV/AIDS are from low-income countries, such as many countries in Sub-Saharan Africa and Asia, and lack access to antiviral medications that could prolong their lives. Even within higher-income countries, such as the United States and a number of European countries, people who have reduced economic means typically lack access to these medications and are at greater risk for developing opportunistic infections associated with HIV/AIDS and dying from the disease sooner. The number of people with HIV/AIDS is expected to rise despite increased knowledge about prevention and treatment of the disease.

Patterns of infection vary among regions of the world. The populations that are at greatest risk for HIV/AIDS include pregnant women between 15 and 24 in African countries (Joint United Nations Program on HIV/AIDS, 2004). In many Asian countries, injecting drug users, sex workers and their partners, and men who have sex with men are the most vulnerable to the disease (Steinfatt & Mielke, 1999). Within Europe and the United States, injected drug use and sex between men are currently the greatest risk factors for contracting HIV. However, infection due to heterosexual sex is on the rise in the United States, particularly among minority groups. These at-risk behaviors are associated with socioeconomic issues. Many people in Southeast Asian countries become sex workers because it is often a better economic alternative than other types of employment in economically depressed areas (Steinfatt & Mielke, 1999; Wenniger et al., 1991). In some cases, young women are forced by their family members to engage in sex work in order to financially support their family. Many people who inject heroin and other drugs often cannot afford clean needles, and so sharing needles (and the chance of contracting HIV) is more prevalent among low-income populations. In addition, lack of education about HIV/AIDS and low condom usage in many countries contribute to high incident rates.

Communicating about HIV/AIDS risks to vulnerable populations around the world has proven to be a difficult task. The risk factors for HIV/AIDS vary by region and culture around the world, and many at-risk behaviors are related to cultural beliefs and behavioral norms. These beliefs and behaviors are shaped by an array of complex social, economic, and political factors (Amaro, 1995), all of which health risk communicators need to take into consideration.

For example, Cameron, Witte, and Nzyuko (1999) found that the high prevalence of HIV infection in Kenya was related to the cultural practice of prostitution among young women and truck drivers on the Trans-Africa highway. Young women in this part of Kenya are often drawn to prostitution because of their economic situation. Cameron et al. (1999) found that it was the cultural norm among male truck drivers in this culture to have sex with multiple partners, and they tended to have fatalistic beliefs about contracting HIV (e.g., the belief that everyone has to die of something, so what difference does HIV make?), and many held the belief that sex with a condom was not "real" sex. The women interviewed in this study said that they found it difficult to verbalize their desire to use condoms due to male/female power differentials in the culture (e.g., women are not typically assertive when interacting with men). In addition, economic and structural issues within the culture contributed to a shortage of available condoms or condoms that were damaged due to inadequate storage procedures.

In other parts of Africa and many cultures around the world, men are admired for having multiple sex partners, they often demand sex with females, or they forcibly engage in (unprotected) sexual intercourse with women (du Pre, 2005; Kamwendo & Kamowa, 1999). In China, knowledge about HIV/AIDS is related to the restricted control of media. In recent years the Chinese government has not perceived HIV/AIDS as a major health threat despite the fact that over a half-million people have been diagnosed with AIDS (Geist-Martin, Ray, & Sharf, 2003), and many people are unaware of the disease or lack basic information about how it is spread (Rosenthal, 2001).

SARS/avian flu

While few diseases have had the global impact of HIV/AIDS, there is always potential for the spread of disease worldwide. In February of 2003, we witnessed the advent of Severe Acute Respiratory Syndrome (SARS), a viral respiratory illness that quickly spread from Asia to more than 24 countries in North and South America and Europe before it was contained. According to the World Health Organization (WHO), a total of 8,098 people worldwide became sick with SARS during the 2003 outbreak, and 774 people died from the disease (WHO, 2004). One of the frightening aspects of SARS was that rather than being spread by sexual contact or through the exchange of blood (such as HIV/AIDS), the disease could be contracted by casual human-to-human contact. People traveling to different countries were able to spread the disease to different continents relatively quickly. It is not difficult to imagine how similar types of viruses that are more lethal than SARS could spread around the world in the future.

More recently there has been growing concern over avian "bird" flu around the world. Avian flu caused numerous deaths among people who were in close contact with poultry or other types of birds. However, there is great concern among members of WHO that the virus may go through a series of genetic mutations in the future, causing the disease to spread from human-to-human contact. While the United States was somewhat slow in responding to the avian flu threat, other countries, such as China, engaged in widespread campaigns to alert people about the potential threat of this virus and steps that could be taken to prevent it. Recently, when the first author of this book was in Hong Kong, he saw hundreds of posters in subways, billboards, and other public places warning individuals of this new threat.

Communication played a vital role in helping to contain the SARS outbreak of 2003 and avian flu. The Centers for Disease Control (CDC) and WHO set up an Emergency Operations Center shortly after the SARS outbreak and avian flu were recognized. In addition, these organizations deployed medical officers, epidemiologists, and other specialists to assist with on-site investigations around the world. Information about the disease was communicated to clinicians who conducted extensive laboratory tests to identify the causes of the disease. Today, the CDC has developed recommendations and guidelines to help public health and healthcare officials plan for and respond quickly to the reappearance of SARS and avian flu. These guidelines are an example of a *crisis management plan*, which involves advanced planning and rehearsal for a health-related crisis. The CDC and WHO have a number of these plans in place to help prepare for other diseases and health risks. For example, WHO has developed the Global Outbreak Alert and Response Network (GOARN), which is a collaboration of health-related institutions and networks that pool human and technical resources for the rapid identification and confirmation of and response to outbreaks of international importance (WHO, 2004). However, in cases like SARS or avian flu where it is a new threat, communication between healthcare systems around the world can be challenging, especially given the availability and quality of health resources in different regions of the world. In the next section, we will examine how crisis management plans are also being used to prepare for terrorist attacks.

Terrorism

Over the last several decades, terrorism has emerged as a significant threat to the lives of people around the world. The United States has witnessed relatively few terrorist attacks compared to other regions of the world. For example, terrorist attacks have occurred more frequently in African, Latin American,

Asian, and Middle Eastern countries than in the United States (US Department of State, 2001). Yet, as a nation, the United States has become increasingly aware of domestic and foreign terrorist threats in recent years following the Oklahoma City bombing in 1995, the 9/11 attacks, and attacks by Al-Qaeda and other terrorist groups around the world (such as the many attacks on US troops in Iraq and the 2004 train bombing in Madrid, Spain). Scholars differ considerably in how they define terrorism. However, O'Hair and Heath (2005) provide a definition of terrorism based upon some of the most prevalent definitions in the terrorism literature:

> First, fear is the ultimate goal. Second, the violence only has to be threatened. Third, the victims are not always the ultimate targets. Fourth, primary audience members are those who observe the terrorist act. Fifth, political or social change are the primary objectives of terrorists. Terrorism, then, means deliberately exacting pain, suffering, and death on civilians for the purpose of accomplishing specific goals without regard for human rights and creating a climate of fear through violent means. (p. 12)

O'Hair and Heath (2005) argue that terrorism is essentially a communicative act in which terrorists send others a message designed to communicate fear in order to achieve their goals.

Besides the obvious threat to loss of life, terrorism affects health in many other ways. Prolonged periods of stress related to terrorist acts (or threats) can lead to negative stress-related health outcomes. Terrorist attacks are characterized by uncertainty and intense emotional responses (Sparks, 2005; Sparks, Kreps, Botan, & Rowan, 2005a, 2005b; Step, Finucane, & Horvath, 2002). In the months following the September 11 attacks, there was a reported increase in post-traumatic stress disorder (PTSD) and depression (Lacy & Benedek, 2003), particularly among people who were friends and relatives of those who died in the attacks and among people who lived in close geographic proximity to New York City and Washington, DC. Moreover, Ahern et al. (2002) found that heavy viewing of negative images of the 9/11 attacks in the mass media, such as people jumping out the World Trade Center towers, was also associated with post-traumatic stress disorder and depression.

In terms of threats to physical health, the US population has become more vulnerable to acts of bioterrorism, or the release of chemical, biological, or radiological hazards into the environment, in recent years due to the rise of domestic and foreign terrorist groups (Kreps et al., 2005a, 2005b). For example, as with the use of chemical weapons (e.g., anthrax and Serin gas), diseases such as smallpox create serious threats to public health. A large-scale act of bioterrorism has the potential to severely challenge the available resources of our emergency response and healthcare systems.

At-Risk Communities within the United States

In addition to these large-scale threats, there are many different communities within the United States where people are at significant risk for physical, psychological, and social health problems. Physical health problems include diseases and other threats to the body, while psychological health problems often consist of a variety of conditions, such as increased stress, anxiety, and low self-esteem. Social health problems include limited availability of social support or resources to help individuals cope with problems and feelings of social isolation. This section identifies several variables that are associated with being at risk in America and some of the groups that are most vulnerable to health threats in the United States.

Risk factors

As we have seen, people who are at risk for poor health often face disparities in access to healthcare and the quality of care they receive due to their social status. In addition, they often live within communities that have limited social resources, such as social capital or human capital. These social factors often put members of such groups at higher risk for health problems such as environmental health threats, susceptibility to disease, substance abuse, mental illness, and depression (Aday, 2001; Wyshak & Modest, 1996). We will examine each of these risk factors and how they are related to health problems.

Social status

Social status refers to disparities in political and personal power and access to resources in a society due to differences between people based on characteristics such as age, gender, race and ethnicity, and income. Moreover, social norms and institutions within a society reinforce power and access to resource differences between groups based on these characteristics. Social status is associated with health risks in the United States. For example, infants, children, the elderly, single females who are living alone or as the head of a household, several racial and ethnic groups (primarily African Americans, Hispanics, Native Americans, and Asian Americans), and individuals who are unemployed or have lower incomes are at the most risk for health problems in the United States. In addition, homeless individuals and many recent immigrants/refugees suffer from health problems due to their social status. These individuals often have difficulty affording or gaining access to healthcare, and they are often targets of discrimination due to the prevalence of ageist, sexist, and racist beliefs in our culture. Moreover, some groups such as illegal immigrants avoid seeking preventive care and/or help for many types of health problems because they fear facing legal action or deportation.

Members of these groups are often *marginalized*, or ignored, trivialized, unheard, perceived as inconsequential, or threatened due to processes within a society that privilege some groups over others based on their social status and negative societal perceptions of their status (Ford & Yep, 2003). When groups are marginalized, they are typically denied privileges, rights, and access to resources and the power to influence social structures in society, including access to adequate healthcare or the political process by which discriminatory practices in the healthcare system can be changed. According to Ford and Yep (2003), "individuals and groups that do not conform to the mythical norm, or 'the standards of normality' in society, are marginalized and devaluated, and their health concerns are treated differently than those in the dominant culture" (p. 244).

For example, in the early 1980s, during the first months of the HIV/AIDS epidemic in the United States, gay men in California were the first group to encounter the disease. Because much of the United States at that time held relatively negative attitudes about gay men and their lifestyles, early reports of HIV/AIDS were downplayed or ignored by the mainstream US media. Largely due to prejudices against gay men, the HIV/AIDS epidemic was trivialized in our culture as "the gay plague," and many people did not feel that the disease was something that they should be concerned about. Although health officials at that time were extremely concerned about the severity of the disease and how quickly it seemed to be spreading, much of mainstream America initially saw the epidemic as a problem within the gay community (if they thought about it all). It was not until the mid-1980s that the US media and mainstream America became concerned about HIV/AIDS. When stories began to break such as that of Ryan White, a child from Indiana who contracted the HIV virus, many people in the US started to pay attention to HIV/AIDS for the first time. Even then, children, hemophiliacs, and people who contracted the virus through blood transfusions were perceived as "innocent victims" of the disease while gay men were (and still largely are) seen as responsible for contracting the disease due to their own (undesirable) behaviors.

Of course, many groups of people, including gay men, continue to be marginalized in the United States. Gay men still experience discrimination due to their lifestyle choices and in terms of healthcare coverage for their partners. Other groups of people are marginalized due to a wide variety of characteristics, including gender, race and ethnicity, social class, and disability (Ford & Yep, 2003). Political and legal issues can also lead to marginalization. For example, many illegal immigrants living in the United States do not seek treatment for health problems for themselves or their family members because they fear deportation. As a result, many of the health concerns of this particular population go unnoticed by mainstream society.

Social capital

Social capital can be defined as the quantity and quality of interpersonal ties among people within a community, and the resources that these network members make available to individuals (Aday, 2001; Dearing, 2003). Social capital often takes the form of informational, tangible, and social support. According to Dearing (2003), "availability of social capital is dependent on one's position within a network; network structure both enables and constrains one's opportunity to access and use resources" (p. 214).

People who have the most social capital within a community benefit physically, psychologically, and socially due to having greater availability of resources for coping with physical and psychological problems, and a greater sense of well-being and belonging. According to Aday (2001), individuals who have the least social capital include those who live alone, those who are not married or in committed relationships, individuals who do not belong to voluntary social organizations (e.g., interest groups, churches), and people who have a limited number (or no) family or friends. People with limited social capital tend to be at greater risk for poor physical, psychological, and social health. Many populations or communities who are at risk for health problems have a high concentration of people with low social capital. For example, communities with a large number of people of lower socioeconomic status, people who are marginalized due to racial discrimination, and communities with people who may have few social connections, such as elderly people living alone or recent immigrants from other nations, often have less social capital than high-income communities or communities that have an infrastructure that better supports the development of social networks.

In terms of social capital, communities tend to benefit the most when their members are diverse, share similar social status, tie together organizations within the community, span other communities, and when individuals and organizations continue to create new network ties and bring resources to segments of the community that previously did not have them (Dearing, 2003; Flora, 1998). By contrast, communities with low social capital do not share these characteristics, and they tend to be much less organized, with fewer interrelationships among organizations and people, which typically often results in less overall access to resources. Homeless individuals often have few social support ties in their environment, and this may contribute to higher levels of stress and fewer tangible resources during times of need.

In addition, recent immigrants to the United States often experience problems adjusting to life in a new culture. They may find few supportive ties in the communities where they reside to help buffer the stress of adjustment (which often takes years). Not surprisingly, there is a high prevalence of stress-related health problems among immigrants, including gastrointestinal disorders and greater susceptibility to illness due to suppressed immune systems (Kim & Grant, 1997). Some immigrants, such as the Hmong from Laos and people from Bosnia, are refugees who have had their lives disrupted by war and other political conflicts. Some individuals from these groups suffer from post-traumatic stress disorder and depression (Ackerman, 1997; Wein et al., 1995), and they may find relatively few sources of emotional support within their community (e.g., people who can identify with their situation).

Human capital

Human capital refers to a community's investments in people's skills and capabilities (such as vocational training or public education) that enable them to act in new ways (such as mastering a trade) or enhance their ability to be productive members of society (Aday, 2001). Communities with higher unemployment rates, substandard schools or housing, and fewer opportunities for the creation of social ties among their members may be associated with lower human capital. In other words, some communities lack the resources or are otherwise unwilling or unable to invest in social structures that empower their members or enhance their quality of life. Lack of human capital may exacerbate problems such as homelessness, crime, and poverty.

A variety of issues may contribute to the lack of human capital in a community. In some communities, problems such as substandard housing, poor schools, and few employment opportunities often lead individuals to flee from the community in an effort to find better housing, schools, and employment elsewhere. In an attempt to find conditions that will better their lives, people living in communities with low human capital often move to nearby communities within a city or within the geographic area (Aday, 2001). Poor human capital conditions in a community can also contribute to an increase in crime, such as drug trafficking and gang violence, which in turn may motivate other citizens to leave who have the means to do so. Unfortunately, this may lead to even fewer job opportunities, worse school conditions, and more substandard housing as small business owners, teachers, and people who can invest in other types of human capital leave the community.

When this type of pattern occurs within a community, the members who are left behind typically have even fewer social resources to cope with problems, such as stress due to unemployment, higher crime rates, and other problems associated with the lack of human capital. People may cope with this stress in negative ways, such as drug and alcohol abuse, which can further exacerbate the community's problems. Higher stress levels coupled with fewer opportunities for social support may lead to psychological and physical health problems (see chapter 4). Lower incomes associated with few job and educational opportunities limit the type and quality of healthcare community members can obtain. In addition, higher-quality hospitals, clinics, and other health services are often reluctant to stay in poorer communities or build new facilities there. Worse still, poorer communities can suffer from environmental injustice, such as when they become the dumping grounds for environmental waste, which can lead to other types of health problems (Rowan, 2004).

Communication Strategies for Addressing Health Risks

While finding solutions to health threats is challenging because of multiple economic, cultural, and political issues, in recent years researchers have become interested in addressing these problem at a variety of levels, including targeting communities, organizations, and individuals. This section briefly explores the use of such initiatives in the areas of HIV/AIDS, terrorism, community-based initiatives for marginalized at-risk populations within the US, and provider–patient interventions. While it is unrealistic to think that the approaches described in this section are capable of resolving all of the issues related to at-risk populations, they represent examples of responses to such threats by risk and crisis communication researchers.

Dealing with the threat of HIV/AIDS

Efforts to communicate about the risk of HIV/AIDS have had varying degrees of impact (Brinson & Brown, 1997; Siska, Jason, & Murdoch, 1992). Early interventions often focused on rational arguments for changing behaviors rather than considering emotional, social, and everyday life concerns of target audiences (Freimuth, Hammond, Edgar, & Monahan, 1990). Brinson and Brown (1997) suggest using culturally appropriate narratives when constructing HIV/AIDS campaign messages. In other words, based on narrative theory (Fisher, 1985), Brinson and Brown contend that campaign messages should convey a story to target audience members that is believable, relevant, well structured, and that provides culturally based "good reasons" for the audience to accept the campaign message. In many parts of the world and among a number of co-cultures in the United States, storytelling is an important means for disseminating information (Airhihenbuwa, 1995), and thus it may be helpful in terms of raising awareness about HIV/AIDS and changing behaviors. However, more studies need to be conducted to assess the impact of campaigns using a narrative approach versus those that use more traditional types of persuasive messages.

Everett Rogers was a communication scholar who extensively researched HIV/AIDS in the US and other countries. He had some success using his *diffusion of innovations* model (Rogers, 1995) in HIV/AIDS campaigns (Dearing et al., 1996). The diffusion of innovations model holds that innovations, including new information about HIV/AIDS prevention or medical technologies that can treat the disease, are spread through a serious of stages. According to Roger's theory, *innovators* are those individuals who first acquire new knowledge. For example, when HIV/AIDS first appeared in the US, the researchers from the CDC who first discovered that the virus was being spread sexually were innovators in the HIV/AIDS epidemic. This information was then passed to *opinion leaders*, such as the news media, government officials, and other individuals who shared the responsibility for disseminating this information to the public. Those individuals who first received information about HIV/AIDS and acted on the public are known as the *early majority*, followed by the *late majority*, or people who learned about the disease (or acted upon this information) later. Finally, according to Rogers's theory, *laggards* were those individuals who were among the last to learn (or act on information) about HIV/AIDS.

Researchers learn new information about HIV/AIDS every day, but the problem is that it takes a great deal of time for such information to spread through the diffusion model. For example, in recent years, people with HIV have been able to prolong their lives by taking antiviral medication, especially if they were tested for HIV while the disease was in its early stages. Unfortunately, many people are still unaware of the advances that have been made in treating HIV, especially if they are in the late majority or are laggards in terms of exposure to this information, and they may avoid getting tested if they still perceive an HIV diagnosis as being equivalent to a death sentence.

It is important to have an understanding of where populations are in the diffusion process of information about HIV/AIDS. A number of at-risk populations within the US may be laggards in terms of awareness about how HIV/AIDS is spread. In addition, many places around the world lack access to new information about HIV/AIDS and/or to medications and medical advances that can treat it, and these regions are often in the beginning stages of the diffusion process as far as medical advances are concerned. This is especially true in countries where people do not have access to the mass media, or in cultures where interpersonal channels are more effective than the mass media in disseminating information due to literacy issues or cultural practices that privilege face-to-face communication over mediated channels (Airhihenbuwa, 1995), and in places that do not have a well-defined healthcare system infrastructure.

Dealing with the threat of terrorism

Communication and crisis management following a terrorist attack

When a terrorist attack occurs anywhere in the world, communication plays a crucial role in responding to it (Seeger, Vennette, Ulmer, & Sellnow, 2002). Specifically, developing crisis management strategies can help to reduce the number of casualties, increase the effectiveness of first-response personnel, and contain certain threats so that they do not affect larger numbers of people. According to Coombs (2005), risk is a driving force behind crisis management. Crisis management includes measures to identify and reduce the threat of a risk and to prepare organizations for when a risk becomes a crisis.

Coombs contends that crisis management is a four-step process: prevention, preparation, response, and learning. *Prevention* includes actions organizations take to reduce risks and vulnerabilities to a crisis. *Preparation* involves creating a crisis management plan, forming and training a crisis management team, and rehearsing the crisis management plan. For example, following the 9/11 attacks many local and state government organizations developed crisis management plans to deal with a bioterrorist attack. Mock terrorist attacks were then staged in an attempt to rehearse and evaluate how well the plan might work if a real attack were to occur. Rehearsing for such terrorist attacks can help to reduce the impact of an attack when it occurs. Coombs argues that many more lives would have been lost on 9/11 if employees had not been planning and practicing evacuations following the bombing of the World Trade Center in the early 1990s. *Response* refers to the actual measures taken when a crisis occurs. *Learning* is a review of what went right and wrong in the crisis management effort in an attempt to understand how future plans can be improved. For example, after the 9/11 attacks, police and fire department officials examined the failure of two-way radio systems during the crisis and have since taken steps to improve these communication systems in the event of future attacks.

Within the United States, significant steps have been taken since 9/11 to develop crisis management plans for a terrorist attack, most notably the creation of the Department of Homeland Security. The Department of Homeland Security has emphasized the need for industries that deal with chemicals, radioactive material, and other potential threats to the environment to develop emergency preparedness plans in the event of a terrorist attack. In addition, the Department of Homeland Security has required state and local governments to develop crisis management plans. According to Coombs (2005), the job of crisis managers is to identify and prioritize risks, which are then assessed in terms of the impact they can have on the organization and the likelihood of the risk occurring. Part of calculating the terrorist risk is the physical location of a facility, materials stored there, and the strategic importance of the facility. For example, many chemical facilities are located near densely populated areas in the United States and other countries, and crisis managers should be involved in assessing the risk of terrorists attacking these facilities, the impact such an attack would have on the surrounding community, and emergency response plans if an attack should occur.

According to Scholl, Williams, and Olaniran (2005), the media, as the disseminators of important crisis-related information, play a significant role in the success or failure of crisis management, including management of a terrorist attack. The public often looks to the media as an important source of information about the effect of long-term hazards, significant disaster threats, and recommended actions in response to certain threats. According to Nacos (2003), the constant flow of information provided by print, radio, and television makes the public feel more involved with the unfolding events. In addition, the news media are a valuable resource in assisting crisis managers with communicating vital information during an attack. Finally, the dissemination of news provides individuals with public spaces where they can engage in discussions with experts and each other about the terrorist acts, their aftermath, and their implications.

Scholl et al. (2005) recommend the creation of crisis communication center (CCC) teams to help disseminate appropriate messages to the public in the event of a terrorist attack, to circumvent any aversive outcomes from news coverage, and to provide messages that can assist the community during crisis (Crelinsten, 1994). Ideally, a CCC team should consist of community and municipal members who have a working knowledge of industrial, technical, and agricultural elements of the community that might potentially become terrorist targets. The CCC team should establish and maintain a good relationship with the media, develop plans for getting important messages about risks and resources out quickly to the public through the media, and select a credible spokesperson to deliver these messages in the event of an attack.

Coping with the psychological effects of terrorism

As we have seen, the threat of terrorism also impacts our psychological health by increasing our stress levels. Crisis communication researchers have examined a variety of strategies that may help to reduce stress following a terrorist attack or due to the threat of an attack. According to Becker (2005), supportive interpersonal communication can help people make sense of terrorist attacks and transform the meaning and significance of such events. Viewing television coverage of a terrorist attack appears to heighten individuals' emotional involvement with the televised content, which is related to a stronger need for interpersonal connections (Step et al., 2002). Becker (2005) recommend increasing one's reliance on social support networks and viewing television with others as coping strategies to improve psychosocial health. As we saw in chapter 4, social support networks can help us to buffer stress and facilitate positive forms of coping. In addition, as in other stressful periods, friends and family members can help us following a terrorist attack by elevating our mood and comforting us. However, long-term significant stress and depression following a terrorist attack may need to be treated by a skilled mental health professional. Sparks (2005) suggests that it is the media that strengthen the impact of terrorism and aid in the creation and redefinition of individual and collective identities. She further argues that it is important to understand the powerful role played by the media, especially television and new media such as the Internet, in defining, redefining, negotiating, renegotiating, and creating such social identities, which are continually formed and shaped via conversations surrounding the events. Understanding how social support groups shape our social identities during such times of crisis is a key element in coping with the crisis (Sparks, 2005).

Community-Based Health Initiatives for At-Risk or Marginalized Populations

Efforts to communicate information to vulnerable communities about health risks started with the work of people in business, such as the nuclear power industry, and with public health researchers with scientific backgrounds who were interested raising awareness about risk levels for a variety of health issues (Scherer & Juanillo, 2003). In addition, according to Scherer and Juanillo (2003), early attempts to influence at-risk communities were somewhat elitist and paternalistic due to the fact that people in power (e.g., individuals from large corporations and government agencies) attempted to influence at-risk communities by providing them with scientific evidence regarding risk factors without considering the larger cultural beliefs, attitudes, and needs of the communities they were trying to influence. Early risk communication interventions largely relied upon providing communities with risk-related statistics or other scientific data, and researchers initially thought that this information would be persuasive enough to promote behavioral change. However, many people have a difficult time interpreting this type of information and understanding what the scientific data mean in terms of everyday behaviors (Tinker, 1996). Even after attempts to explain what the statistics meant to at-risk communities, many early risk communicators found that their strategies to promote health behavior change had only weak or moderate impact (Scherer & Juanillo, 2003).

These interventions rested on the assumption that individuals will behave rationally and change their behaviors when they are exposed to information about health risks. However, follow-up studies have found that many people often continue to smoke, eat high-fat foods, practice unsafe sex, and perform a host of other unhealthy behaviors despite being exposed to information about these health risks. People do not change their health behaviors simply by being exposed to more information about their risk for a health problem. Increasingly, risk communicators have come to recognize that health behavior change is influenced by a multitude of individual perceptions about health and health risks as well as by a variety of cultural and social influences. The failure of early risk communication campaigns has led to a growing appreciation of the critical role of psychosocial and cultural factors that influence the public's understanding and assessment of, as well as responses to, health risks (Scherer & Juanillo, 2003).

For example, layperson judgments of risk are often much different than expert judgments. People with low levels of education or who are unfamiliar with scientific methods may not understand the process by which risk factors are assessed through surveys and available data or how health risk statistics are calculated. Just saying that 33 percent of Latino adolescents in a certain suburb of Los Angeles are estimated to have HIV may not be sufficient to change risky behaviors within this community. Although this HIV prevalence rate would be considered high for a specific group of people within a relatively small geographic area, some adolescents may not see the relationship between their own behaviors and the risk, they may not believe that this statistic is credible, or the statistic may not be believed because it does not resonate with their personal experience (e.g., the majority of their friends and family do not have HIV).

In addition, risk factors may be linked to cultural beliefs and behavioral norms within a community. For example, drinking alcohol, eating certain types of food, and many other health-related behaviors are often linked to the culture of a group. Harwood and Sparks's (2003) research on social identity and health supports the notion that our health behaviors are often linked to our group identities (and vice versa). This research further argues that our group memberships with positive health behaviors (e.g., healthy diet and exercise) will likely lead to healthier and thus increased longevity, whereas our group memberships that carry out unhealthy behaviors (e.g., smoking, sunbathing without protection, poor diet, couch potato life, heavy alcohol consumption) will likely lead to decreased health across the life span. Some communities may not trust the motives of intervention researchers, or they may be resistant to persuasive attempts to change health behaviors (Guttman, 2000; Parrott & Steiner, 2003), especially marginalized groups, who may distrust federal, state, and local government sources of information due to past patterns of discrimination or neglect (Ford & Yep, 2003).

Several risk communication researchers have argued that risk communication efforts are most successful when people within at-risk communities are empowered by campaigns (Rowan, 1996, 2004), when they are involved in the risk communication campaign process (Ford & Yep, 2003), and when campaigns dealing with health risks are framed within the worldview of the individuals who constitute an at-risk community or population (Ford & Yep, 2003). In other words, these researchers argue that risk communication efforts need to move beyond simple dissemination of information, and risk communication campaigns work best when they empower people within a community and incorporate a community effort (e.g., involvement of community leaders and concerned citizens) towards promoting change.

Many scholars have found that community involvement is essential in influencing the health behaviors of marginalized groups (Airhihenbuwa, 1995; Ford & Yep, 2003). Ford and Yep (2003) suggest using community advisory boards, or a group of individuals from within the marginalized community who meet with health risk campaign promoters to discuss the health issue or issues facing the community on a regular basis. A community advisory board's involvement in early stages of risk campaigns is essential to the risk communication process. Since the board consists of people who are members of the at-risk community, it can provide unique insights into the worldview of community members and the ways in which these cultural views shape perceptions of the health issue, responses to it, and how effective preventive efforts or health interventions can be developed from the standpoint of the community members.

In addition, a community forum, or a meeting where concerned citizens can interact with experts and informed laypersons from the community, can help risk communication campaigns and increase opportunities for dialogue between health promoters and members of the community. This type of interaction may help to merge scientific and community perceptions of health risk, and it may facilitate greater understanding and trust between the two parties. In addition, the use of lay health advisors, or members of the community who can provide insights into unique problems and barriers in the community, and who can be trained by risk communication specialists to help carry out the campaign, may improve the campaign's effectiveness.

Risk Communication Strategies at the Provider–Patient Level

There is a great need for health communication researchers to develop risk communication strategies at the provider–patient level. As trusted health authorities, providers are in an excellent position to motivate patients to reduce risky lifestyle behaviors and to engage in preventive screenings for diseases. As patients we are frequently encouraged to talk with our physicians about the risky choices we make in terms of our personal health (Rowan, Sparks, Pecchioni, & Villagran, 2003). While there exist lists of risk communication strategies (Covello & Allen, 1988) and disease risk communication guidelines (Arkin, 1999), these materials are not typically designed for physician–patient interaction. Instead, existing risk communication guidelines typically assume that communicators are speaking at a scientific meeting or press conference and that the principal communication goal is to explain the meaning of research findings as they pertain to groups or populations. This focus makes sense for press conferences and scientific meetings. It does not, however, reflect agendas that are typical in physician–patient consultations.

Moreover, advances in medical science often lead to new discoveries about health risks that can impact provider–patient communication. Consider, for example, the challenges endocrinologists, gynecologists, and internal medicine specialists faced when women on hormone replace therapy learned in July 2002 that there was a 26 percent increase in breast cancer among individuals taking this therapy as opposed to those in a control group (Rossouw et al., 2002). The Women's Health Initiative was halted because the combination estrogen-progestin therapy was increasing, not decreasing, women's chances of both breast cancer and heart attack. These findings meant that many women wanted to consult with their physicians about their best course of action. But doctors' responses to these women varied. According to the *Washington Post*, some doctors rejected the findings of the Women's Health Initiative. Other physicians accepted these findings completely. Still others urged consideration of each woman's individual health history (Connelly, 2002).

In part, this range of varied responses reflects the difficulty of translating findings about population groups facing health risks into practical advice for individuals. Physicians need help in both translating population findings into advice for individuals and in determining how best to communicate cancer risk with patients. Books such as that by oncologist Daniel Rosenblum (1993) show that patients vary in terms of whether and when they want physicians mainly to listen and empathize with feelings, mainly to explain complexities, or mainly to make recommendations and support behavioral change (also see Dickson, Hargie, & Morrow, 1989; Jones, Kreps, & Phillips, 1995; Roter & Hall, 1992).

To help physicians meet challenges involved in communicating cancer risk during patient consultations, Rosenblum (1993) summarizes key findings on cancer risk communication and on physician–patient interaction. Specifically, his book presents a "cancer risk communication aid" that (1) draws from research to alert physicians to likely barriers associated with communicating about cancer risk; (2) directs physicians to research-supported ways of overcoming these barriers through listening, empathizing, explaining, or per-suading; and (3) is packaged for easy recall during patient interaction.

Summary

People are vulnerable to many types of health threats both around the world and within the United States. Health risk communicators attempt to raise awareness of these threats among the individuals who are most at risk as well as provide them with information or resources to avoid or reduce the impact of these threats. In all parts of the world, including the US, people who have fewer economic, educational, political, and social resources are often at the greatest risk for health threats. Many of these groups suffer from issues like racism or are marginalized for a variety of other reasons. Some health threats are global in nature, including environmental threats, HIV/AIDS, and terror-ism. While these problems are challenging to address, health communicators can play a role in ameliorating them through interventions and other measures that help to raise awareness about the problems and provide resources for individuals.

References

Ackerman, L. K. (1997). Health problems of refugees. *Journal of the American Board of Family Practice, 10*, 337–348.

Aday, L. A. (2001). *At risk in America: The health and health care needs of vulnerable popu-lations in the United States.* San Francisco: Jossey-Bass.

Ahern, J., Galea, S., Resnick, H., Kilpatrick, D., Bucuvalas, M., Gold, J., & Vlahov, D. (2002). Television images and psychological symptoms after the September 11 terrorist attacks. *Psychiatry, 65*, 289–300.

Airhihenbuwa, C. O. (1995). *Health and culture: Beyond the Western paradigm.* Thousand Oaks, CA: Sage.

Amaro, H. (1995). Love, sex, and power: Considering women's realities in HIV pre-vention. *American Psychologist, 50*, 437–447.

Anderton, D. L., Anderson, A. B., Oakes, J. M., & Fraser, M. R. (1994). Environ-mental equity: The demographics of dumping. *Demography, 31*, 229–248.

Arkin, E. B. (1999). Cancer risk communication: What we know. *Journal of the National Cancer Institute Monographs, 25*, 182–185.

Becker, J. A. H. (2005). The intersection of terrorism, interpersonal communication, and health. In H. D. O'Hair, R. Heath, & G. Ledlow (Eds.), *Communication pre-paredness and response to terrorism: Communication and the media* (pp. 47–64). Westport, CT: Praeger.

Brinson, S. L., & Brown, M. H. (1997). The AIDS risk narrative in the 1994 CDC campaign. *Journal of Health Communication, 2*, 101–112.

Bullard, R. D. (Ed.). (1993). *Confronting environmental racism: Voices from the grassroots.* Boston: South End Press.

Cameron, K. A., Witte, K., & Nzyuko, S. (1999). Perceptions of condoms and barriers to condom use along the Trans-Africa Highway in Kenya. In W. N. Elwood (Ed.), *Power in the blood: A handbook on AIDS, politics, and communication* (pp. 149–163). Mahwah, NJ: Lawrence Erlbaum.

Care.org. (2006). World hunger statistics. Retrieved October 25, 2006, from www.care.org/campaigns/world-hunger/facts.asp.

Connelly, C. (2002, July 28). Doctors working to clear the fog of hormone study. *Washington Post,* pp. A-1, A-10.

Coombs, T. (2005). The terrorist threat: Shifts in crisis-management thinking and planning post-9/11. In H. D. O'Hair, R. Heath, & G. Ledlow (Eds.), *Communication preparedness and response to terrorism: Communication and the media* (pp. 211–226). Westport, CT: Praeger.

Covello, V. T., & Allen, F. W. (1988). *Seven cardinal rules of risk communication.* Washington, DC: US Environmental Protection Agency, Office of Policy Analysis.

Crelinsten, R. D. (1994). The impact of television on terrorism and crisis situations: Implications for public policy. *Journal of Contingencies and Crisis Management, 2*(2), 61–72.

Dearing, J. W. (2003). The state of the art and the state of the science of community organizing. In T. L. Thompson, A. M. Dorsey, K. I. Miller, & R. Parrott (Eds.), *Handbook of health communication* (pp. 207–220). Mahwah, NJ: Lawrence Erlbaum.

Dearing, J. W., Rogers, E. M., Meyer, G., Casey, M. K., Rao, N., Campo, S., & Henderson, G. M. (1996). Social marketing and diffusion-based strategies for communicating health with unique populations: HIV prevention in San Francisco. *Journal of Health Communication, 1*, 343–363.

Dickson, D. A., Hargie, O., & Morrow, N. C. (1989). *Communication skills training for health professionals.* New York: Chapman & Hall.

Du Pre, A. (2005). *Communicating about health: Current issues and perspectives* (2nd ed.). Boston: McGraw-Hill.

Fisher, W. R. (1985). The narrative paradigm: An elaboration. *Communication Monographs, 52*, 347–367.

Flora, J. L. (1998). Social capital and communities of place. *Rural Sociology, 63*, 481–506.

Ford, L. A., & Yep, G. A. (2003). Working along the margins: Developing community-based strategies for communicating about marginalized groups. In T. L. Thompson, A. M. Dorsey, K. I. Miller, & R. Parrott (Eds.), *Handbook of health communication* (pp. 241–261). Mahwah, NJ: Lawrence Erlbaum.

Freimuth, V. S., Hammond, S. L., Edgar, T., & Monahan, J. L. (1990). Reaching those at risk: Content-analytic study of AIDS PSAs. *Communication Research, 17*, 775–791.

Geist-Martin, P., Ray, E. B., & Sharf, B. F. (2003). *Communicating health: Personal, cultural, and political complexities.* Belmont, CA: Wadsworth.

Guttman, N. (2000). *Public health communication interventions: Values and ethical dilemmas.* Thousand Oaks, CA: Sage.

Harwood, J., & Sparks, L. (2003). Social identity and health: An intergroup communication approach to cancer. *Health Communication, 15*, 145–170.

Joint United Nations Program on HIV/AIDS. (July, 2004). 2004 report on the global AIDS epidemic. Retrieved August 28, 2004, from www.unaids.org/.

Jones, A., Kreps, G., & Phillips, G. (1995). *Communicating with your doctor: Getting the most out of health care.* Cresskill, NJ: Hampton Press.

Kamwendo, G., & Kamowa, O. (1999). HIV/AIDS and a return to traditional cultural practices in Malawi. In K. R. Hope, Sr. (Ed.), *AIDS and development in Africa: A social science perspective* (pp. 165–184). New York: Haworth.

Kim, Y., & Grant, D. (1997). Immigration patterns, social support, and adaptation among Korean immigrant women and Korean American women. *Cultural Diversity and Mental Health, 3*, 235–245.

Kreps, G. L., Alibek, K., Bailey, C., Neuhauser, L., Rowan, K. E., & Sparks, L. (2005a). Emergency/risk communication to promote public health and respond to biological threats. In M. Haider (Ed.), *Global public health communication: Challenges, perspectives, and strategies* (pp. 349–362). Sudbury, MA: Jones & Bartlett.

Kreps, G. L., Alibek, K., Bailey, C., Neuhauser, L., Rowan, K. E., & Sparks, L. (2005b). The critical role of communication in preparing for biological threats: Prevention, mobilization, and response. In H. D. O'Hair, R. Heath, & G. Ledlow (Eds.), *Community preparedness and response to terrorism: Communication and the media* (pp. 191–210). Westport, CT: Praeger.

Lacy, T. J., & Benedek, D. M. (2003). Terrorism and weapons of mass destruction: Managing the behavioral reaction in primary care. *Southern Medical Journal, 96*, 394–399.

Nacos, B. L. (2003). Terrorism as breaking news: Attack on America. *Political Science Quarterly, 118*(1), 23.

O'Hair, H. D., & Heath, R. (2005). Conceptualizing communication and terrorism. In H. D. O'Hair, R. L. Heath, & G. R. Ledlow (Eds.), *Community preparedness and response to terrorism: Communication and the media.* Westport, CT: Praeger.

Parrott, R., & Steiner, C. (2003). Lessons learned about pubic health collaborations in the conduct of community-based research. In T. L. Thompson, A. M. Dorsey, K. I. Miller, & R. Parrott (Eds.), *Handbook of health communication* (pp. 637–649). Mahwah, NJ: Lawrence Erlbaum.

Rogers, E. M. (1995). *Diffusion of innovations* (4th ed.). New York: Free Press.

Rosenblum, D. (1993). *A time to help, a time to hear: Listening to people with cancer.* New York: Free Press.

Rosenthal, E. (2001, December 30). With ignorance as fuel: AIDS speeds across China. *New York Times*, pp. A1, A8.

Rossouw, J. E., Anderson, G. L., Prentice, R. L., LaCroix, A. Z., Kooperberg, C., Stefanik, M. L., & Jackson, R. D. (2002). Risks and benefits of estrogen plus progestin in healthy postmenopausal women. *Journal of the American Medical Association, 288*(3). Retrieved online in the July 17 issue from www.jama.org.

Roter, D., & Hall, J. (1992). *Doctors talking with patients/patients talking with doctors: Improving communication in medical visits.* Westport, CT: Auburn House.

Rowan, F. (1996). The high stakes of risk communication. *Preventive Medicine, 25,* 26–29.

Rowan, K. E. (1995). What risk communicators need to know: An agenda for research. In B. R. Burleson (Ed.), *Communication yearbook, 18* (pp. 300–319). Thousand Oaks, CA: Sage.

Rowan, K. E. (2004). *Risk and crisis communication: Earning trust and productive partnering with media and public during emergencies.* Washington, DC: Consortium of Social Science Associations.

Rowan, K. E., Kreps, G. L., Botan, C. H., Sparks, L., Samoilenko, S., & Bailey, C. L. (in press). Risk communication, crisis management, and the CAUSE model. In H. D. O'Hair, R. Heath, K. J. Ayotte, & G. Ledlow (Eds.), *Terrorism: Communication and rhetorical perspectives.* Cresskill, NJ: Hampton Press.

Rowan, K. E., Sparks, L., Pecchioni, L., & Villagran, M. (2003). The "CAUSE" model: A research-supported guide for physicians communicating cancer risk. *Health Communication: Special Issue on Cancer Communication, 15,* 239–252.

Scherer, C. W., & Juanillo, N. K., Jr. (2003). The continuing challenge of community health risk management and communication. In. T. L. Thompson, A. M. Dorsey, K. I. Miller, & R. Parrott (Eds.), *Handbook of health communication* (pp. 221–239). Mahwah, NJ: Lawrence Erlbaum.

Scholl, J., Williams, D., & Olaniran, B. (2005). Preparing for terrorism: A rationale for the crisis communication center. In H. D. O'Hair, R. Heath, & G. Ledlow (Eds.), *Communication preparedness and response to terrorism: Communication and the media* (pp. 243–268). Westport, CT: Praeger.

Seeger, M. W., Vennette, S., Ulmer, R. R., & Sellnow, T. L. (2002). Media use, information seeking and reported needs in post crisis contexts. In B. S. Greenberg (Ed.), *Communication and terrorism* (pp. 53–63), Cresskill, NJ: Hampton Press.

Shrivasta, P. (1987). *Bhopal: Anatomy of a Crisis.* Cambridge, MA: Ballinger.

Siska, M., Jason, J., & Murdoch, P. (1992). Recall of AIDS public service announcements and their impact of ranking AIDS as a national problem. *American Journal of Public Health, 82,* 1029–1032.

Sparks, L. (2005). Social identity and perceptions of terrorist groups: How others see them and how they see themselves. In H. D. O'Hair, R. L. Heath, & G. R. Ledlow (Eds.), *Community preparedness and response to terrorism: Communication and the media* (pp. 13–28). Westport, CT: Praeger.

Sparks, L., Kreps, G. L., Botan, C., & Rowan, K. (2005a). Responding to terrorism: Translating communication research into practice. *Communication Research Reports, 22,* 1–5.

Sparks, L., Kreps, G. L., Botan, C., & Rowan, K. (Eds.). (2005b). Communication and terrorism [Special issue]. *Communication Research Reports, 22*(1).

Steinfatt, T. M., & Mielke, J. (1999). Communicating danger: The politics of AIDS in the Mekong region. In W. N. Elwood (Eds.), *Power in the blood: A handbook on AIDS, politics, and communication* (pp. 385–402). Mahwah, NJ: Lawrence Erlbaum.

Step, M. M., Finucane, & Horvath, C. W. (2002). Emotional involvement in the attacks. In B. S. Greenberg (Ed.), *Communication and terrorism: Public and media responses to 9/11* (pp. 261–274). Cresskill, NJ: Hampton Press.

Tinker, T. L. (1996). Recommendations to improve health risk communication: Lessons learned from the US Public Health Service. *Journal of Health Communication, 1*, 197–217.

Trumbo, C. W., & Rowan, K. E. (Eds.). (2000). Global climate change and the public [Special issue]. *Public Understanding of Science, 9*(3).

US Department of State. (2001). Patterns of global terrorism. Retrieved August, 2, 2004, from www.state.gov/.

Wein, S. M., Becker, D. F., McGlashan, T. H., Laub, D., Lazrove, S., Vojvoda, D., & Hyman, L. (1995). Psychiatric consequences of "ethnic cleansing": Clinical assessments and trauma testimonies of newly resettled Bosnian refugees. *American Journal of Psychiatry, 152*, 536–542.

Wenniger, B. G., Limparkarnjanarat, K., Ungchusak, K., Thanprasertuk, S., Choopanya, K., Vanichseni, S., et al. (1991). The epidemiology of HIV infection and AIDS in Thailand. *AIDS, 5* (Supplement 2).

Whitford, F., Feinberg, R., Earl, R., Doering, O., Rowan, K., Neltner, T., & Mysz, A. (2002). Pesticides and risk communication: Interactions and dialogue with the public. In F. Whitford (Ed.), *The complete book of pesticide management: Science, regulation, stewardship, and communication* (pp. 710–748). New York: John Wiley.

World Health Organization. (2004). Severe Acute Respiratory Syndrome (SARS). Retrieved August 17, 2004, from www.who.int/csr/sars/en/.

Wyshak, G., & Modest, G. A. (1996). Violence, mental health, and substance abuse in patients who are seen in primary care settings. *Archives of Family Medicine, 5*, 441–447.

Chapter 10

Health Campaigns and Community Health Initiatives

"This is your brain on drugs," "Think before you drink," and "Just Say No to Drugs." No doubt at some point in your life you have seen, heard, or read an advertisement attempting to get you to think about and/or change a health behavior. Health campaigns are an essential part of health promotion, or efforts to enhance health and prevent disease on a large scale. Health campaigns can be defined as a systematic effort to change health behaviors (or attitudes and beliefs about health and/or social and environmental conditions that mediate health behaviors) within a target population of people who are at risk for a health problem or problems (Bennett & Murphy, 1997; Salmon & Atkin, 2003).

Health campaigns have had a rich history in the United States (Paisley, 2001). However, there is a great need to study how to make health campaigns more effective. Although communication and public health researchers have learned more and more about how to effectively influence health behaviors in the past several decades, there is still much room for improvement. The literature on health campaigns suggests that the majority of campaigns conducted in recent years have had only limited success in changing targeted health behaviors (Kreps, 2001; Snyder, 2001; Snyder & Hamilton, 2002; Valente, 2002; Witte, Cameron, Lapinski, & Nzyuko, 1998). However, in many cases, researchers had unrealistic expectations in early health campaigns as well as poor implementation strategies. Nevertheless, changing any type of human behavior can be extremely difficult, and attempting to change health-related behaviors such as eating and exercise habits, alcohol and tobacco use, sexual practices, and compliance with recommended disease screenings can be particularly challenging.

Large-scale health campaigns often require considerable financial resources in order to pay campaign workers, conduct target audience research, create effective messages, and purchase advertising space in the mass media (although smaller campaigns can sometimes be accomplished for relatively little cost). Government agencies such as the National Institutes of Health (NIH) and the Centers for Disease Control and Prevention (CDC), university and medical researchers, and consumer advocacy groups are frequently involved in health campaigns.

Researchers who take a social scientific approach to health promotion draw from many disciplines when designing health campaigns, including public health, psychology, education, and communication. The communication discipline has played an instrumental role in the development of more effective health campaigns. Because health campaigns involve designing, disseminating, and evaluating messages about health, communication theory plays an integral role in the process of conducting a campaign. This chapter explores various levels of the health campaign process. Toward that end, it focuses on campaign goals, theoretical frameworks for campaigns, and the process of designing, implementing, and evaluating a health campaign.

Campaign Goals

Determining what you want to accomplish with a health campaign is an important first step in the process of developing it. These goals also help to determine the *target audience*, or those individuals that campaign designers attempt to influence with the campaign message(s). This section focuses on common goals of two broad types of health campaigns: Health awareness and behavioral change campaigns and public policy campaigns.

Health awareness and behavioral change campaigns

The goal of many health campaigns is to raise awareness about a health issue or to change individual health behaviors, attitudes, and beliefs. As we have seen in other chapters of this book, many diseases and health problems are linked to lifestyle choices, such as diet and exercise, and to other health problems that can be prevented through early screening efforts. A large number of health campaigns target the behaviors, attitudes, and beliefs that surround these areas. Campaigns dealing with smoking, diet, alcohol consumption, exercise, and sexual behaviors are common examples.

Public policy approaches

Other campaigns attempt to educate people about societal conditions or situations that promote health or healthcare inequities among marginalized groups in an effort to spur new legislation or grassroots efforts to improve healthcare. For example, as we have seen, people from certain ethnic groups and income levels are often at greater risk for health problems because of inadequate access to healthcare due to financial reasons or discrimination. Examples of this type of campaign are those that deal with improving social inequities in healthcare or with changing societal or institutional practices that disadvantage certain groups on account of race/ethnicity, economic status, gender, and age.

Theoretical Approaches to Health Campaigns

Prior to discussing the specifics of health campaign design and implementation, it is important to examine theories about how individuals' attitudes and behaviors can be influenced. Health communication researchers have found the theoretical frameworks discussed in this section to be important for understanding why some people are influenced by campaign messages while others are not. In addition, these theories help to provide crucial explanations for the links between cognitive processes, such as knowledge about a health problem and perceptions of health risk, and changes in health behaviors.

Social cognitive theory

Some health campaign researchers have attempted to understand how people learn about health-related issues, how they process health information, and how this information is linked to specific health-related behaviors. *Social cognitive theory* (Bandura, 1977, 1986) assumes that behavior is the outcome of interaction between cognitive processes and environmental events. In other words, health-related behaviors are ultimately the result of a combination of an individual's thought processes and influences from his or her social network and life situation. This section explores these aspects of social cognitive theory.

Cognitive processes influencing health behavior

According to social cognitive theory, a number of cognitive processes, such as expectations, self-efficacy, attitudes, beliefs, and values, influence various health-related behaviors. It is important to remember that these cognitive processes are triggered by stimuli from a person's environment (discussed below). For example, we learn many attitudes about health by listening to our friends and family members as well as from what we see and hear through the mass media (see chapter 8).

A person's beliefs and expectations can have considerable influence over his or her behavior. However, human beings vary considerably in their beliefs and expectations. Beliefs can be accurate or inaccurate, and expectations can be realistic or unrealistic. Social cognitive theory posits that behaviors are guided by two sets of expectations: (1) *the expectation that an action will lead to a particular outcome* and (2) *the expectation a person has about his or her ability to perform this action*. In terms of the first expectation, suppose a male geriatric patient does not believe that engaging in vigorous physical exercise three times a week will reduce his risk for heart disease. Based upon this expectation, it is unlikely that he will follow such a recommendation in a health campaign.

Second, a person's expectation that she is capable of performing an action that will lead to a particular outcome influences whether or not she will ultimately change her behavior. This expectation is influenced by an individual's *self-efficacy*, or the belief in one's ability to exert personal control over a situation (Bandura, 1977). In terms of health behaviors, researchers have found that self-efficacy is an important determinant of health information–seeking practices (Rimal, 2001), health behavior change (Bagozzi & Warshaw, 1990; Schwarzer, 1994), and health maintenance behaviors. Self-efficacy can range from generalized beliefs about one's own ability to perform health-related behaviors (e.g., "I can avoid getting sick most of the time") to beliefs about one's ability to perform very specific health-related behaviors (e.g., "I can remember to get a mammogram once a year"). Health self-efficacy beliefs are often better predictors of behavior than more generalized self-efficacy beliefs. Therefore, it is crucial for health campaign designers to consider the specific health self-efficacy beliefs that members of a target audience have about a course of action when recommending it during a campaign.

For example, if a health campaign designer is interested in reducing the incident rates of HIV infection among high school students by informing them about risk factors for the disease and the use of condoms as a preventive measure, it is possible that self-efficacy beliefs about condom use might be more important in influencing behavior than other beliefs about HIV. A high school student may be aware that unsafe sex can increase the risk of contracting HIV/AIDS, and he may believe that condoms can reduce the risk of HIV/AIDS. However, if this student does not believe that he is capable of using a condom every time he has sex (e.g., due to not being able to plan when opportunities for sexual intercourse might occur), then this belief will most likely be more important than other beliefs in terms of whether or not he ultimately practices safe sex.

Attitudes and values can also influence health behaviors. While social cognitive theory recognizes the influence of attitudes on behaviors, it does not provide a detailed explanation of this relationship. Values can influence health behaviors in a variety of ways. For example, when exposed to messages designed to change health-related behaviors, individuals make value judgments about outcomes related to the proposed behavioral changes. Good health is generally a long-term value for most people. However, long-term health values often compete with many short-term values, such as pleasure, excitement, and wanting to "fit in" with others. These short-term values may cause people to lose sight of long-term health values. For example, while most people do not want to be obese or suffer from weight-related problems such as diabetes or heart disease in the future, short-term values such as the pleasure that comes from eating rich foods or the convenience of unhealthy fast food may override the long-term value of being healthy.

Environmental influences on health behavior

Human beings learn how to behave in various life contexts by observing and modeling the behavior of others, typically family members, peers, and what we see and hear through the mass media. Behaviors are also associated with social norms or rules for following behavior. People tend to be rewarded or punished socially for adhering to (or ignoring) these rules in social situations. Social rewards may take the form of approval and inclusion, and punishments may involve anger, disapproval, and exclusion from social circles. In general, individuals typically behave in ways that maximize rewards and minimize costs. For example, if a teenager wants to fit in with her peers (who are perceived as having a high social status due to the social rewards and punishments they can provide), and smoking cigarettes is important to the peer group, then these sources of information about how to behave may be more likely to influence her behaviors than lower-status sources (e.g., a teacher or younger sibling).

Theory of reasoned action

The theory of reasoned action (Ajzen & Fishbein, 1980) states that the primary predictor of a behavior is an intention to engage in that behavior. This theory posits that *behavioral intentions* can be predicted by two parallel cognitive processes: (1) a person's attitude towards the behavior under consideration and (2) his or her appraisal of relevant social norms. An individual's attitudes about a behavior (i.e., evaluation of the behavior as positive, negative, or neutral) are influenced by his or her beliefs about the behavior. For example, if you believe that eating a low carbohydrate diet is an effective way to lose weight, then it is likely that you will have a more positive attitude about someone suggesting a "low carb" item on a restaurant menu than someone who does not believe that this type of diet is effective.

In addition, the theory of reasoned action takes into account social norms, such as the approval of friends and family members, surrounding the behavior under consideration. While a woman may have a positive attitude towards the idea of eating better and exercising more in an effort to lose weight, her husband may enjoy sedentary or unhealthy activities such as watching television or eating fried foods. If the husband sees his wife's interest in eating better and exercising as an attempt to get him to change his behaviors, he may be unsupportive of her engaging in a diet and exercise program. Depending upon the husband's approval or disapproval of his wife's proposed lifestyle changes and the wife's motivation to comply with her husband's wishes, this may outweigh the positive attitude the wife has about dieting and exercise and ultimately influence her behavioral intentions.

The theory of reasoned action also takes into account an individual's resources, skills, self-efficacy, opportunities, and ability to engage in the proposed behavior. Some of these factors may be internal (e.g., skills) or external to the person (e.g., opportunities to change behavior), and they can either inhibit or facilitate a person's perceived control over the proposed behavior (Ajzen & Fishbein, 1980). According to the theory, all of these factors need to be considered when predicting a person's intentions to perform a behavior. Health campaign designers often assess these variables when analyzing a target audience in order to get a better idea of what might lead a person to ultimately engage in a health-related behavior. However, although behavioral intentions are often predictive of actual behaviors, there is no guarantee that behavioral intentions will ultimately lead to behavioral changes.

Health belief model

The health belief model (Becker, 1974) focuses on individuals' perceived threat of illness and their behavioral response to that threat. When confronted with information about a disease or illness, people generally assess their perceived susceptibility to the threat and attempt to gauge the severity of the threat were it to affect them. In addition, individuals assess threats to their health vis-à-vis the costs and benefits of changing their behaviors and make appraisals of their environment and resources when making decisions about how to avoid or manage the threat. Each of these factors combines in unique ways to influence decision-making about health issues, depending upon the health issue and the target audience.

For example, a campaign designed to promote preventive screenings for prostate cancer among men between the ages of 45 and 60 would need to take a number of issues into consideration. In terms of perceived threat, a target audience member would assess how likely he would be to develop prostate cancer. Younger audience members may perceive that prostate cancer is an "older man's disease," and they may not see it as particularly threatening despite the fact that early detection of risk factors (such as an enlarged prostate or high PSA levels) can prevent prostate cancer. In terms of perceptions of severity, target audience members may or may not assess the symptoms of prostate cancer to be severe. Many people perceive prostate cancer as a more manageable type of cancer than other types (e.g., pancreatic cancer or breast cancer), even though prostate cancer has a high morbidity rate compared to other cancers in the United States. In terms of behavioral responses to the threat, perceptions such as whether or not a person believes that screenings can prevent prostate cancer, perceptions of the prostate exam as an unpleasant experience, and assessments of the costs versus the benefits of taking the time to have a prostate exam may motivate or hinder a person from getting screened for prostate cancer. Resources, such as access to adequate healthcare, and environmental influences, such as the support of family or peers in terms of getting the exam, also might factor into a person's decision to participate in a preventive screening for the disease.

An important contribution of this theory is the concept of *cues to action*, or message features that prompt individuals to pay attention to the content of messages (Murray-Johnson & Witte, 2003). According to Murray-Johnson and Witte (2003), cues to action are important in triggering an individual's motivation to make assessments of his or her available resources when acting on campaign messages. In order to effectively motivate target audience members to change health behaviors, campaign designers need to incorporate cues to action within campaign messages. In addition, Murray-Johnson and Witte state that cues to action can be *internal*, meaning that they emerge from within the individual, such as if a person starts an exercise program because of feeling bloated or unenergetic from living a sedentary lifestyle, or they can be *external*, such as pressure from peer group members to exercise or celebrity testimonials on television about the positive effects of an exercise program (e.g., an advertisement saying, "Oprah Winfrey lost 25 pounds using our aerobics video"). Identifying appropriate internal and external cues to action for a target audience can be a challenging aspect of campaign design, but it can be accomplished through careful audience analysis (discussed later in this chapter).

Extended parallel process model

Witte's (1992) *extended parallel process model* examines fear appeals as a motivation for health behavior change. Undoubtedly you have been exposed to a health campaign that attempted to use fear to get you to think about HIV/ AIDS, the dangers of drug use, or other risky practices (e.g., not wearing a

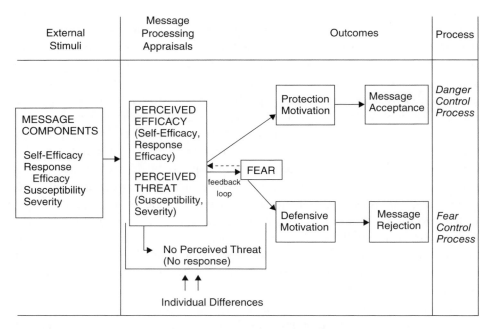

Figure 10.1 Extended parallel processing model (Witte 1992).

seatbelt or drunk driving). According to Murray-Johnson and Witte (2003), motivation is central to how a message is processed and acted upon, and fear has been used as a prominent motivating force in a variety of health-related campaigns because it is a common human emotion. According to the extended parallel process model, individuals exposed to a fear message engage in two sets of parallel cognitive processing (see figure 10.1). First, *danger control* refers to the appraisal of a threat and how it should be dealt with. Second, *fear control* involves an assessment of how to cope with the emotional reaction to a threat. Similar to other theories we have examined, individuals' self-efficacy and appraisals of their resources and environment play an important role in the process of thinking about how to cope with a threatening situation. Emotional responses to fear often involve increased anxiety and physiological responses, such as increased heart rate and perspiration. Both sets of processing lead to a behavioral response to the threat.

For example, after the terrorist attacks on September 11, 2001 and the deaths resulting from anthrax mailed to various people in the following months, many Americans became concerned about the threat of bioterrorism. In terms of danger control, some people, particularly those living in big cities, saw bioterrorism as a large threat whereas many people in rural parts of the United States felt it was less of a threat. Some people decided to deal with these threats by purchasing gas masks and other supplies that would be helpful in case of a bioterrorist act, while others did not see this threat as problematic enough to change their behaviors. These events also create a strong emotional impact. Some people attempted to control their emotional response to this threat through activities such as diversion (e.g., spending more time with family or engaging in pleasant activities), while others tried to reduce their fear by learning how to better prepare for such an attack in the future.

In terms of health campaigns, fear appeals need to be used with some degree of caution. Too much fear can lead to such intense emotional reactions that people become too preoccupied with their fear to think rationally about steps they can take to avoid the threat (Dillard & Peck, 2000; Dillard, Plotnick, Godbold, Freimuth, & Edgar, 1996; Stephenson & Witte, 2001). For example, a HIV/AIDS campaign that emphasizes death might produce such strong emotional reactions that individuals avoid thinking about the issue as a fear control response. This may prevent them from also thinking about ways in which they can reduce their susceptibility to the disease. Murray-Johnson and Witte (2003) advocate using high fear appeals only in cases where target audience members possess response efficacy, or the perceived ability to easily perform the recommended response behaviors promoted in the campaign. In addition, high fear appeals should be avoided with audiences who are already fearful of a threat since it can lead them to think less about the threat as a coping mechanism. In other cases the use of moderate fear appeals may be more appropriate to an audience (Hale & Dillard, 1995; Stephenson & Witte, 2001). Careful target audience analysis is needed to assess which type of fear appeal may be most effective for a specific population.

Stages of change models

Some researchers have developed theories of behavior change that take into account various stages of readiness that individuals pass through over time towards behavior change (Lippke & Ziegelmann, 2006; Prochaska & DiClemente, 1984; Schwarzer, 1992). The advantage of this approach is that it assumes people may be in different stages when it comes to changing their health behaviors. A prominent stage theory is the *transtheoretical model* (Prochaska & DiClemente, 1984), which describes five stages of behavioral change: precontemplation, contemplation, preparation, action, and maintenance/relapse. The HIV/AIDS pandemic is a helpful issue to illustrate this particular model, and examples from this crisis will be used to help explain it.

In the *precontemplation stage*, individuals are unaware of a health issue and subsequently do not think about making a behavioral change. For example, in the early 1980s many Americans were unaware of the looming threat of HIV/ AIDS because it was not being widely discussed in the mass media, and

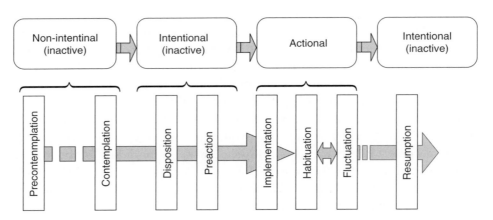

Figure 10.2   Multi-stage model of behavioral change (Lippke & Ziegelmann, 2006).

consequently, most people did not consider changing their sexual behaviors. In the *contemplation stage*, people are aware of a health issue but may still be weighing the pros and cons of adopting some type of behavioral change. Once stories about HIV/AIDS and its relationship to safe sex gained prominence in the mid- to late 1980s, many people began to examine their own sexual behaviors. However, many heterosexual people still questioned whether they were really at risk for the disease since HIV/AIDS was first seen within the gay community and among intravenous drug users. Even though people were thinking about the disease, many people continued to practice unsafe sex. In the *preparation stage*, individuals actively begin planning to change their behavior. As more and more reports of heterosexual people and non-intravenous drug users began to surface in the media, many Americans felt they were ready to begin practicing safe sex. In the *action stage*, behavioral change actually occurs, such as when people started using condoms when having sex. Finally, the *maintenance/relapse* stage refers to whether people stick with their behavior change or relapse into one of the previous stages. Since the 1980s many people have continued to practice safe sex in an effort to prevent the spread of HIV/AIDS.

Lippke and Ziegelmann (2006) have proposed the multi-stage model of health behavior change (MSM), which extends the number of stages in the transtheoretical model (see figure 10.2). Lippke and Ziegelmann distinguish between nonintentional inactive stages (precontemplation and contemplation) and the intentional (but still inactive) stages by adding the *disposition* stage, in which individuals implement certain goals for behavioral change, and the *preaction* stage, where people detail their plans for action. In addition, these researchers take into account the degree to which people stick to their behavioral changes (habituation), fluctuate, and resume behavioral changes following the decision to take action.

When using stages of change models to plan a health campaign, campaign designers need to assess the various stages at which individuals within a target population may be in regarding the campaign health issue. For example, different types of messages need to be constructed for people in the precontemplative stage versus the maintenance/relapse stage. For people who are in the precontemplative stage, campaign messages should be directed towards raising awareness of the health issue and influencing perceptions of susceptibility to it. By contrast, audience members who are in the maintenance/relapse stage should be encouraged through campaign messages to continue engaging in preventive behaviors and warned against the threat of relapse.

The Process of Conducting a Health Campaign

As we have seen, changing attitudes and beliefs about health and health–related behaviors can be extremely complex. Designing appropriate and effective messages that can lead to these goals in a health campaign requires a great deal of thought and planning. This section explores some of the key steps and considerations when conducting a health campaign.

Audience analysis

As with any attempt to inform or persuade a large group of people, health campaigns require a careful analysis of target audience characteristics. Having a thorough understanding of audience characteristics such as demographics, attitudes and beliefs, current behaviors, and reasons for current behaviors allows health campaign designers to appropriately segment audiences into smaller groups in order to produce messages that are appropriate to the characteristics of these subgroups within a target audience. As we will see, the greater the extent to which messages can be tailored to the characteristics of audience members, the more likely they will be to successfully influence attitudes, beliefs, and behaviors.

Conducting audience analysis research

Once a health campaign designer has decided upon a target audience for the campaign, he or she needs to conduct an *audience analysis*, or an assessment of a variety of characteristics of the audience members that are related to the campaign health issue, in order to gain a better understanding of how to influence them (Atkin & Freimuth, 2001). Analyzing a target audience typically requires research method skills, and while this topic is beyond the scope of this book, this section provides an overview of common ways in which campaign designers conduct target audience research. When conducting an audience analysis, campaign designers attempt to understand audience characteristics in a systematic way. The most common types of research methods for audience analysis are using available data, surveys, and interviews and focus groups. Each of these research methods is discussed below.

Using available data. In many cases information about target audience members already exists in the form of databases (Atkin & Freimuth, 2001). For instance, hospitals keep patient records, local and state governments compile health-related statistics about their regions, organizations keep employee records, and the federal government has databases about health-related variables through information provided on the US Census and through research efforts by organizations such as the CDC and the NIH. These databases allow campaign designers to examine characteristics of some target audiences without having to conduct primary research themselves. They can thus save campaign designers a great deal of time and money, since both are required to carry out interviews, focus groups, and surveys. However, these databases rarely contain all of the target audience characteristics that may be of interest to campaign designers. In addition, information gained from some databases can be dated (e.g., US Census data), and the information may no longer apply to the current target audience.

Surveys. Surveys are useful for collecting new information about a relatively large target audience through the use of questionnaires. Audience analysis surveys typically ask a variety of questions about audience demographics (e.g., age, gender, ethnicity, income), current health-related behaviors, attitudes and beliefs about health, efficacies and skills, and a variety of other questions that may help the campaign designer to better understand what will meet audience members' health needs and motivate them towards achieving the campaign goals (Atkin & Freimuth, 2001). Survey researchers rarely disseminate questionnaires to an entire target population because most populations are either too large or difficult to reach. Instead, audience researchers conduct surveys using a *sample* of individuals who are representative of the larger population, and they make inferences about the larger population based upon the findings from the sample.

A key aspect of samples is that they should be *representative* of the larger target population as much as possible. One way to be more confident about how representative a sample is of a population is to use a *probability sample*. *Sampling* is the process of obtaining a sample for a survey, and *probability sampling* involves randomly selecting participants for a sample from a *sample frame*, or list of population members. Each population member is given a number, and researchers use random number tables or random numbers generated by a computer to select certain numbers (and subsequently people) into the sample. It can be very difficult to find a sampling frame for many larger populations.

In many cases probability sampling is too difficult to accomplish, and researchers have to engage in *nonprobability sampling*, such as convenience samples (e.g., finding anyone who is willing to participate in the survey). When using a nonprobability sample, campaign designers need to be careful when segmenting the target audience based upon sample data results. However, in these cases, using a nonprobability sample is better than not conducting an audience analysis at all.

Interviews and focus groups. Interviews and focus groups are excellent methods for gaining a thorough understanding of target audiences' perceptions of a health issue and their health-related needs (Slater, 1995). Interviews and focus groups involve talking to a sample of target audience members and asking them various questions about their thought processes and behaviors relating to the campaign health issue. Interviews involve talking to individual audience members, whereas focus groups are group interviews with typically 8 to 10 people. When conducting interviews with individuals or within focus groups, it is important to try to make participants feel relaxed. The researcher should obtain informed consent, or permission from the participants after they have been informed about the purposes and potential risks of the study, prior to starting an interview or focus group. Focus groups should occur in comfortable surroundings, and the facilitator of the focus group should be skilled at getting people to express their opinions.

One advantage of focus groups over interviews is that one person's responses during a focus group can remind another participant of similar experiences or feelings with a health issue, and this can add to the richness of the data by allowing researchers to obtain multiple viewpoints on the subject. However, some individuals are more apprehensive about speaking up in a focus group compared to a one-on-one interview because they may feel that others in the group will judge them if they express a viewpoint. In addition, some individuals in groups tend to dominate the discussion, and this may take time away from other participants who are more reticent. Focus group facilitators should attempt to intervene in such situations and try to get all members of the group to talk if possible.

In addition, the researcher should ask participants' permission to tape record or videotape the interview or focus group. This will provide a record of the participant responses for data analysis. Videotape offers researchers the advantage of being able to assess nonverbal cues from participants that can give insights into how people feel about certain topics being discussed. Videotaping can be even more valuable for recording interactions during focus groups because it is often difficult to distinguish one participant from another on an audiotape. However, the researcher should protect the anonymity of all participants by using pseudonyms during the interview or focus group and when transcribing content from audio and videotape recordings, and the tapes should be stored in a locked facility so that people other than the researcher and his or her associates cannot access them.

Audience segmentation

Audience segmentation is the process of dividing the larger target audience population into smaller subgroups of individuals based upon some meaningful criteria (Rimal & Adkins, 2003; Slater, 1995), usually the demographic, psychological, and behavioral characteristics that were assessed during the audience analysis. Because people often differ considerably on these characteristics, it is difficult to design campaign messages that will influence an entire target population. Thus, the purpose of audience segmentation is to help maximize the impact of campaign messages. Generic health campaign messages (messages that apply to the majority of the population) tend to have limited impact on target audiences (Atkin & Freimuth, 2001), but more specific messages (i.e., messages tailored to unique characteristics of subgroups of the target population) tend to be much more effective in influencing attitudes, beliefs, and behaviors (Rimal & Adkins, 2003).

For example, communication researchers at the University of Kentucky have had a great deal of success segmenting audiences based on a psychological variable known as sensation seeking (Everett & Palmgreen, 1995; Palmgreen & Donohew, 2003; Palmgreen, Donohew, & Harrington, 2001). High sensation seekers are individuals who enjoy taking risks as well as vivid, exciting, and novel experiences, for example, people who like to bungee jump, sample exotic foods, and those who "like to live dangerously." In contrast, low sensation seekers tend to prefer mundane, everyday types of experiences, and they often feel more comfortable "playing it safe." According to Palmgreen et al. (2001), "high sensation seekers (HSSs) also have distinct and consistent preferences for particular kinds of messages based on their needs for the novel, the unusual, and the intense" (p. 301). For example, high sensation seekers like messages that are fast-paced and exciting, use close-up shots and music, and advertisements that employ rapid cutting. Using the SENTAR approach (a campaign approach based upon sensation-seeking tendencies), Palmgreen and associates have been successful in designing antidrug messages that appeal to high sensation seekers (who tend to be at high risk for drug abuse, risky sexual practices, and other negative health-related behaviors) and that have led to reductions in self-reported drug use.

Of course, sensation seeking is just one of many variables that can be used to segment target audiences. Other variables that can be used include (1) demographics (e.g., sex, race, socioeconomic status); (2) psychological variables (e.g., health beliefs, psychological tendencies, attitudes, values); and (3) health-related skills. Audience analysis and health-related theories play a crucial role in determining key variables that can be used to segment subgroups of target audiences. Segmentation helps campaign designers to maximize the potential of a campaign to influence positive health outcomes and to gain a careful understanding of important variables that can be used to improve the impact of future health campaigns.

Creating message content

Much of what appears in the specific content of messages during a health campaign is influenced by the characteristics of the target audience and the health issue itself. However, there are variables and considerations common to message content design in most campaigns that campaign designers should be familiar with. According to Salmon and Atkin (2003), "campaigns utilize three general communication processes to move a target audience toward a desired response: awareness, instruction, and persuasion" (p. 455). This section explores these aspects of message design and other important message content features, including gaining audience members' attention, variables associated with motivating audience members to action, and variables associated with the perceived personal and social resources for changing attitudes, beliefs, and behaviors among target audience members.

Gaining audience members' attention and motivating them to action

Health campaign message designers have to compete with many other types of messages in society, including advertisements, news, and entertainment (Murray-Johnson & Witte, 2003; Parrott, 1995; Salmon, 1989). Through the use of theoretical models of changing health-related cognitions and behaviors and a careful audience analysis, campaign designers can often identify key variables that have a high probability of motivating their target audience. Drawing on the health belief model, Murray-Johnson and Witte (2003) argue that campaign messages should contain cues to action, or message features that prompt individuals to pay attention to the content of messages. Recall from earlier in the chapter that cues to action are needed to trigger motivation, and they can be developed from sources internal to audience members, such as guilt or fear, or external sources, such as using credible spokespersons (e.g., the Surgeon General) to motivate change. During the audience analysis, campaign designers can assess the *salience* of certain types of messages, or the perceived importance of messages to audience members. Variables such as the perceived severity of a health threat, perceived susceptibility, and attitudes, beliefs, values, and perceived resources surrounding a health issue all influence the salience of messages.

Vividness, repetition, and how messages are placed in the media are also important factors in message design (Murray-Johnson & Witte, 2003). *Vivid messages*, such as messages that contain more exciting, colorful, or detailed images and/or audio cues, may motivate change because they are more memorable than less vivid messages. In addition, campaign messages that are novel or unexpected tend to motivate audience member involvement (Parrott, 1995). *Repetition of messages* can also stimulate motivation, and campaign designers should consider repeating key messages several times within campaign materials. Ideal placement of campaign messages should also be assessed during campaigns. Campaign designers can assess how target audience members respond to messages that vary in terms of vividness and repetition during the audience analysis phase of the campaign. *Placement* deals with where target audience members are most likely to see the message, and assessing ideal placement during the audience analysis phase helps campaign designers decide which media are best suited for disseminating the campaign messages.

Persuasive message appeals

There are a number of issues that campaign designers need to consider when constructing persuasive appeals for a health campaign. Individuals vary considerably in terms of the types of messages that influence their cognitions and behaviors.

Some individuals are influenced by messages emphasizing *credibility*, or the extent to which message content is believed to be accurate, and it is typically conveyed by the trustworthiness and competence of the person delivering the campaign message and through convincing evidence for a persuasive argument (Salmon & Atkin, 2003). According to Salmon and Atkin (2003), the *campaign messenger*, or the person who provides information and testimonials or demonstrates appropriate behaviors during a health campaign, is crucial in enhancing the message's credibility. Salmon and Atkin contend that when selecting a campaign messenger, he or she will be more credible and attractive (and subsequently more persuasive) to a target audience if he or she exhibits expertise, trustworthiness, familiarity, interpersonal attractiveness, and similarity to the target audience.

The messenger can be any person capable of conveying these characteristics to the target audience and does not necessarily need to be a celebrity, although for certain target audiences a celebrity such as Magic Johnson speaking about HIV/AIDS might embody these characteristics. Celebrity messengers can sometimes produce negative effects for a campaign, especially when stories emerge within popular media about their lifestyles or other controversial information that can undermine the campaign message. However, physicians, specialists, cancer survivors, and many other types of individuals may be good candidates for a campaign messenger. In addition to the campaign messenger, the credibility of a campaign can be enhanced by using evidence for cognitive and/or behavioral change that comes from credible sources, such as studies from established scientific journals (e.g., *Journal of the American Medical Association*) or trusted government sources (e.g., the CDC).

Other audiences are influenced by *logical appeals*, or persuasive messages that provide logical and convincing evidence for change, while others are influenced by *emotional appeals*, such as messages that emphasize strong emotions such as fear. Some researchers have found that messages that influence positive emotions in health campaigns, such as positive imagery and mood, tend to increase attention to messages, recall, positive attitudes, and compliance to recommended behaviors (Monahan, 1995). Less is known about other types of positive affect strategies in health campaigns, such as the use of humor. However, it appears that positive affect appeals tend to reduce psychological reactance, or the tendency of people to disregard messages that they find threatening or offensive.

When constructing campaign messages using these appeals, designers again need to consider many characteristics of the target audience that are found to be relevant during formative research and audience analysis procedures. For example, highly educated audiences may be more persuaded than less educated audiences by statistics or certain types of logical argument. For more educated audiences, *two-sided persuasive messages*, or messages that contain and refute counterarguments for the proposed behavioral change, may be more influential than one-sided messages (Salmon & Atkin, 2003). Depending upon the audience, emphasizing positive (e.g., health benefits) and/or negative (e.g., symptoms of a disease) incentives for change may be equally effective. One approach that draws upon presenting multiple arguments within a health campaign message is *inoculation theory* (McGuire, 1970; Pfau, 1995). Essentially, inoculation involves presenting audience members with weak arguments that are contrary to the goals of the campaign (e.g., reasons for drinking in an anti-drinking campaign) along with information that refutes these arguments. When these types of efforts are successful, target audience members are said to be inoculated to the influence of messages that run counter to the goals of the campaign. For example, a college student who has been exposed to a variety of arguments against binge drinking may be more likely to resist attempts by peers to engage in such behaviors.

In recent years, health communication scholars and health practitioners have utilized *prospect theory* by using message framing as a way to understand the communication involved in risky decisions (see, e.g., Kahneman & Tversky, 1979, 2000; Sparks, in press-a; Tversky & Kahneman, 1981). The landmark essays of Amos Tversky and Daniel Kahneman resulted in prospect theory, which suggests that individuals will react differentially to information presented as gains or losses. People encode information relevant to choice options in terms of potential gains or potential losses. Thus, factually equivalent information can be presented to people differently so that they encode it as either a gain or a loss (framing). A framing effect is demonstrated by constructing two transparently equivalent versions of a given problem, which nevertheless yield predictably different choices. The standard example of a framing problem, which was developed quite early, is the "lives saved, lives lost" question, which offers a choice between two public health programs proposed to deal with an epidemic that is threatening 600 lives: one program will save 200 lives, the other has a 1/3 chance of saving all 600 lives and a 2/3 chance of saving none. In this version, people prefer the program that will save 200 lives for sure. In the second version, one program will result in 400 deaths, the other has a 2/3 chance of 600 deaths and a 1/3 chance of no deaths. In this formulation most people prefer the gamble. Of course, these formulations present identical situations. The only difference is that in the first formulation the problem is framed in terms of lives saved, and in the second the situation is framed as a matter of lives lost. Thus, the message frame that a decision-maker adopts is controlled partly by the *formulation of the problem* and partly by the norms, habits, and personal characteristics of the decision-maker (Tversky & Kahneman, 1981, p. 453). Nearly all health-related information can be construed in terms of either gains (benefits) or losses (costs). For example, a gain-framed message would say that obtaining a mammogram allows tumors to be detected early, which maximizes treatment options. In contrast, the same message framed as a loss would say that if you do not obtain a mammogram, tumors cannot be detected early, which minimizes your treatment options. Thus, which frame works better?

The answer depends on whether the target health behavior is an illness detection behavior or an illness protection behavior (Rothman & Salovey, 1997). Detection behaviors (e.g., prostate exam) involve uncertainty – i.e., you may find a problem! Protection behaviors (e.g., using sunscreen) typically lead to relatively certain outcomes – i.e., you maintain your current healthy status.

The message-framing component of prospect theory has been utilized in health risk studies dealing with the uncertainty and risks involved in disease detection (Sparks, in press-a). Prospect theory predicts that loss-framed information leads to preference for uncertainty, whereas gain-framed information leads to preference for certainty. Research findings indicate that loss-framed messages were effective in promoting mammography, breast self-examinations, and HIV testing. Gain-framed messages were effective in promoting infant car restraints, physical exercise, smoking cessation, and sunscreen.

Other message considerations

Snyder and Hamilton (2002) examined the impact of several message characteristics in a wide variety of health-related campaigns. These researchers found that for some types of campaigns, especially health-related issues that have legal ramifications, such as driving under the influence, abuse of controlled substances like Oxycontin, and seat belt usage, *enforcement messages*, or messages that emphasize negative repercussions (e.g., fines, arrests) to target audience members as a result of not following laws, may be effective in motivating behavioral change. Snyder and Hamilton found that campaigns using enforcement messages influenced target audience members more than campaigns that did not include these types of messages. In addition, campaigns using messages that give audiences *new reasons to change* their behavior (e.g., new information about the importance of getting a mammogram) were more influential in terms of behavioral change than campaigns that relied on older information about a health topic.

Channels and message dissemination processes

One important consideration in designing a health campaign is the type of channel that will be used to disseminate the campaign message(s). Traditionally, health campaign designers have relied on traditional mass media when delivering campaign messages, such as television, radio, and print material (Atkin, 2001). In recent years researchers have started to investigate the efficacy of new media for disseminating health campaign messages, such as cell phones and the Internet. This section examines a number of different channel characteristics that have important implications for health campaign design.

Targeting is the process of selecting the best communication channel for disseminating a message (Rimal & Adkins, 2003). Again using information from the audience analysis, campaign designers need to make decisions about which channel or channels are appropriate for reaching and influencing the target audience. For example, campaign designers need to consider where target audience members are most likely to see campaign messages, the type of media they use, the ability of a channel to support specific types of messages, audience literacy levels, and the potential impact of various channels.

Some target audiences may be more likely to see television or radio messages, while other audiences are more likely to be exposed to a message when it comes to them through billboards, Internet advertisements, or interpersonal channels (e.g., peer group members). Among low literacy audiences, radio and television campaigns may be more influential than printed materials because radio and television can transcend the written word through audio messages and/or images that convey a message without words. Snyder and Hamilton (2002) found that campaigns with greater *reach*, or a higher percentage of people being exposed to the campaign message, were more influential in changing target audience behaviors than campaigns with a more limited reach. Messages on television and radio tend to have greater reach than messages disseminated through other channels. However, television and radio messages are typically more generic than printed materials or messages delivered in person (which are less expensive to produce and can be changed more easily for different segments of the target audience).

As we have seen, tailored messages tend to have greater impact than generic messages in campaigns. This aspect has to do with *specification*, or the ability of a channel to influence certain subgroups within the population (Atkin, 2001). In addition, using channels such as the Internet or a dialogue between a community spokesperson and target audience members in a face-to-face meeting invites greater audience participation and involvement than radio or television advertisements. All of these features of channels, as well as the cost and efficiency of the channel, need to be assessed by campaign designers (Salmon & Adkins, 2003).

However, researchers have recently been paying more attention to multi-pronged approaches to health campaigns. These advocate an interpersonal theory-based approach to changing health behaviors when it is appropriate and possible to implement (Rogers, 2003; Sparks, in press-a), particularly with specialized populations that do not use mediated sources, such as older adults and those from cultural and socioeconomic backgrounds with little access to technologies (Sparks & McPherson, in press; Sparks & Turner, in press). Health behavior and health communication scholars study messages and interventions that encourage patients to be active participants in health communication contexts. In addition to designing mediated health messages, researchers are also focusing on effective interpersonal message strategies that will prove effective given the unique complexities and barriers patients and their family members often face (see, e.g., Sparks, in press-b). Researchers can no longer ignore the unique cognitive and emotional processes different populations often experience. Interpersonal messages are more likely to reach such specific populations, one patient and one family at a time (Sparks, in press-b).

As we have seen, while it is always possible to create a more generalized or generic message that will be communicated to an audience, generalized messages often lack the impact of more specific messages. Traditionally, health campaign materials have been generic, and the creators of campaign messages have attempted to provide as much information as possible within a single communication without considering the specific characteristics of an audience (Kreuter & Wray, 2003; Kreuter, Farrell, Olevitch, & Brennan, 2000; Strecher, Rimer, & Monaco, 1989). However, *tailored* health messages, or messages designed to influence specific subgroups of a target audience based on individual member characteristics (Rimal & Adkins, 2003), tend to be more effective than generic messages in influencing cognitive and behavioral changes in target audiences (Davis, Cummings, Rimer, Sciandra, & Stone, 1992; Kreuter, Oswald, Bull & Clark, 2000; Rimal & Adkins, 2003; Rosen, 2000; Sparks & Turner, in press).

According to Salmon and Atkin (2003), "a typical health campaign might subdivide the population on a dozen dimensions (e.g. age, ethnicity, stage of change, susceptibility, self-efficacy, values, personality characteristics, and social context), each with multiple levels" (p. 453). In many cases, while it is possible to segment target audiences into literally thousands of subgroups, the majority of health campaigns create substantially fewer groups, due to financial and logistical constraints. Yet, even segmenting audiences into relatively few small subgroups can increase the precision of messages over generic messages.

It is now possible to create *personalized* messages in a health campaign through the use of computer programs (Kreuter, Farrell, et al., 2000) that use algorithms to match the characteristics of *each* individual in a target audience to a specific, individually tailored message. However, this method can increase the complexity and cost of a campaign. In addition, according to Schooler, Chaffee, Flora, and Roser (1998), there is always a tradeoff between the specificity of a health message and its reach. In other words, generic messages tend to have greater reach than tailored messages, which means that because the message is more generalized it can appeal to greater numbers of individuals who are exposed to it than tailored messages. Tailored messages, on the other hand, provide more specific information, but they may have limited reach because they are so specialized.

Atkin (2001) pinpoints a variety of other channel considerations when designing health campaigns. These include *accessibility* of the channel for the target audience (e.g., some individuals may have limited access to the Internet), *depth*, or the ability of the channel to convey complex information, *economy*, or the cost of using a particular channel, and *efficiency*, or the amount and quality of information a channel can deliver vis-à-vis the cost of using it. As you can see, there are many decisions a health campaign designer needs to make regarding the most appropriate and useful channel for the target audience.

Formative Campaign Evaluation

As we have seen, the process of creating a health campaign can be complex, especially when dealing with certain health issues and hard-to-influence audiences, and this may lead to many things that can potentially go wrong with a campaign. Larger campaigns can be quite expensive given the amount of time that is needed to analyze the audience, the cost of creating campaign materials, and the cost of using different media. Therefore, it is important for campaign designers to take measures to minimize possible campaign shortcomings. One way to identify and potentially minimize problems prior to launching a campaign is to engage in formative campaign evaluation (Atkin & Freimuth, 2001; Valente, 2002). Formative campaign evaluation research refers to the activities conducted prior to the start of a campaign. Valente (2002) outlines the objectives and the specific research activities that are important during the formative evaluation stage. Objectives in this stage include (1) understanding the target audience's barriers to action, (2) learning the appropriate language to develop messages, and (3) developing a conceptual model. Specifically, focus group discussions and/or in-depth interviews are conducted to determine knowledge, attitudes, and behaviors of the target population. This is particularly important prior to message development because evaluation data are useful in identifying target audience characteristics and predispositions, specifying intermediate response variables and behavioral outcomes, assessing channel exposure patterns, and determining receptivity to potential message components (Atkin & Marshall, 1996).

There are many ways that health campaigns can be evaluated, including some of the research methods that are mentioned in the section on audience analysis procedures in this chapter. Available data, interviews, focus groups, and surveys can all be used to assess the degree to which campaign goals were met, although these methods are not without limitations.

Pilot testing

By using a sample of the target population, campaign designers can gauge what aspects of the campaign work and do not work with a group of people who are similar to the larger population. When obtaining feedback about the campaign from the pilot sample, campaign designers should measure the degree to which the campaign messages led to cognitive and/or behavioral changes in the group, and potential problems with the campaign, such as determining whether messages were noticed, salient, or understandable to the audience, reasons why some people may not have been influenced by the messages, and the appropriateness of the spokesperson, medium, and message content.

Launching the campaign, process evaluation, and outcome evaluation

After making additional adjustments to campaign messages following formative evaluation and pilot testing, campaign designers are then ready to launch the campaign. The length of a health campaign will largely depend upon the goals of the campaign, such as if the campaign is targeting awareness about a health issue or behavioral outcomes related to it, the budget and resources available to the campaign designers, and other pragmatic issues, such as the amount of time that campaign designers can devote to it.

Determining whether or not a campaign is successful can be assessed by conducting outcome evaluation research. However, the question of why a campaign was or was not successful requires process evaluation research. Evaluation is widely understood to be conducted as a set of stages that require the systematic application of research procedures to assess the conceptualization, design, implementation, and utility of intervention programs (Rossi & Freeman, 1993; Shadish, Cook, & Leviton, 1991; Valente, 2002). Health campaign planners and researchers can rely on program evaluation strategies for assessment and improvement to inform future campaigns. In addition, evaluations serve as a means by which campaign planners and funding agencies can determine the effectiveness of a health campaign's promotion activities or treatments. Process evaluations tend to be easier to design and conduct when the campaign approach is derived from a strong theoretical framework. According to Valente (2002), "theory specifies how these factors relate to one another by constructing a conceptual model of the process of behavioral change" (p. 30). Ideally, campaign designers should integrate formative, process, and outcome evaluations into the campaign design (see figure 10.3).

However, there are a number of pragmatic barriers to conducting campaign evaluations within everyday types of health campaigns. For example, conducting additional research within a campaign for the purposes of evaluation can be costly and time consuming. In addition, some campaign planners believe that evaluation activities detract attention away from the actual campaign. While these barriers are certainly understandable from a practical standpoint, thorough process and outcome evaluations within campaigns help researchers

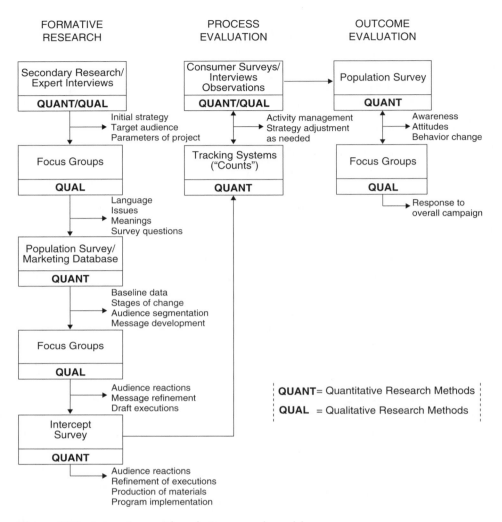

Figure 10.3 Integrative social marketing research model.

gain a better understanding of whether or not a certain campaign approach works and why.

Measuring behavioral changes within a target audience can take much more time than assessing awareness of the campaign messages. Campaign evaluators need to be aware of problems such as the *sleeper effect*, or when behavioral change due to being exposed to a campaign message occurs slowly. In some cases change may not occur for several months after a campaign, so it is often difficult for evaluators to find the optimal time to engage in an assessment of target audience change. When measuring awareness, campaign evaluators should ask for specific examples of what people saw, read, or heard about the campaign health issue during the period of the campaign, and what they remember about the issue. Of course, memory problems, leading questions by campaign evaluators in interviews or surveys, and other methodological issues can potentially create biases in terms of understanding actual awareness change.

Summary

Designing, implementing, and evaluating the effectiveness of a health campaign is a complex process, and campaign designers have to make numerous decisions that can ultimately lead to the success or failure of the campaign. Clear and realistic goals for a campaign are an important first step. Researchers have developed a number of theories about how to influence health attitudes, beliefs, and behaviors, and campaign designers can draw upon these theories when developing a campaign. After conducting a thorough audience analysis, campaign designers have numerous decisions to make about message design and message dissemination. Finally, campaigns should be pilot tested prior to implementation to assess any potential problems, and campaign designers need to conduct an evaluation of campaign processes and outcomes so that this information can be used to inform future campaigns.

References

Ajzen, I., & Fishbein, M. (1980). *Understanding attitudes and predicting social behavior*. Englewood Cliffs, NJ: Prentice-Hall.

Atkin, C. (2001). Theory and principles of media health campaigns. In R. E. Rice & C. K. Atkin (Eds.), *Public communication campaigns* (3rd ed., pp. 49–68). Thousand Oaks, CA: Sage.

Atkin, C., & Freimuth, V. S. (2001). Formative evaluation research in campaign design. In R. E. Rice & C. K. Atkin (Eds.), *Public communication campaigns* (3rd ed., pp. 125–145). Thousand Oaks, CA: Sage.

Atkin, C., & Marshall, A. (1996). Health communication. In W. Stacks & M. B. Salwen (Eds.), *An integrated approach to communication theory and research* (pp. 479–495). Newbury Park, CA: Sage.

Bagozzi, R. P., & Warshaw, P. R. (1990). Trying to consume. *Journal of Consumer Research, 17,* 127–140.

Bandura, A. (1977). Self-efficacy: Toward a unifying theory of behavioral change. *Psychological Review, 84,* 191–215.

Bandura, A. (1986). *Social foundations of thought and action: A social cognitive theory*. Englewood Cliffs, NJ: Prentice-Hall.

Becker, M. H. (1974). The health belief model and personal health behavior. *Health Education Monographs*, *2*, 324–508.

Bennett, P., & Murphy, S. (1997). *Psychology and health promotion*. Buckingham: Open University Press.

Davis, S. W., Cummings, K. M., Rimer, B. K., Sciandra, R., & Stone, J. C. (1992). The impact of tailored self-help smoking cessation guides on young mothers. *Health Education Quarterly*, *19*, 495–504.

Dillard, J. P., & Peck, E. (2000). Affect and persuasion: Emotional responses to public service announcements. *Communication Research*, *27*, 461–495.

Dillard, J. P., Plotnick, C. A., Godbold, L. C., Freimuth, V. S., & Edgar, T. (1996). The multiple affective outcomes of AIDS PSAs: Fear appeals do more than scare people. *Communication Research*, *23*, 44–72.

Everett, M. W., & Palmgreen, P. (1995). Influences of sensation seeking, message sensation value, and program context on effectiveness of anticocaine public service announcements. *Health Communication*, *7*, 225–248.

Hale, J., & Dillard, J. (1995). Fear appeals in health promotion: Too much, too little, or just right? In E. Maibach & R. Parrott (Eds.), *Designing health messages: Approaches from communication theory and public health practice* (pp. 65–80). Newbury Park, CA: Sage.

Kahneman, D., & Tversky, A. (1979). "Prospect theory": An analysis of decision under risk. *Econometrica*, *47*, 263–291.

Kahneman, D., & Tversky, A. (2000). *Choices, values, and frames*. Cambridge: Cambridge University Press.

Kreps, G. L. (2001). The evolution and advancement of health communication inquiry. In W. B. Gudykunst (Ed.), *Communication yearbook 24* (pp. 232–254). Newbury Park, CA: Sage.

Kreuter, M., & Wray, R. (2003). Tailored and targeted health communication: Strategies for enhancing information relevance. *American Journal of Health Behavior*, *27* (Supplement 3), S227–S232.

Kreuter, M., Farrell, D., Olevitch, L., & Brennan, L. (2000). *Tailoring health messages: Customizing communication with computer technology*. Mahwah, NJ: Lawrence Erlbaum.

Kreuter, M., Oswald, D. L., Bull, F. C., & Clark, E. M. (2000). Are tailored health education materials always more effective than non-tailored materials? *Health Education Research*, *15*, 305–315.

Lippke, S., & Ziegelmann, J. P. (2006). Understanding and modeling health behavior: The multi-stage model of health behavior change. *Journal of Health Psychology*, *11*, 37–50.

McGuire, W. J. (1970, February). A vaccine for brainwash. *Psychology Today*, *3*, 36–39, 63–64.

Monahan, J. (1995). Thinking positively: Using positive affect when designing health messages. In E. Maibach & R. L. Parrott (Eds.), *Designing health messages: Approaches from communication theory and public health practice* (pp. 81–98). Thousand Oaks, CA: Sage.

Murray-Johnson, L., & Witte, K. (2003). Looking toward the future: Health message design strategies. In T. L. Thompson, A. M. Dorsey, K. I. Miller, & R. Parrott (Eds.), *Handbook of health communication* (pp. 473–495). Mahwah, NJ: Lawrence Erlbaum.

Paisley, W. J. (2001). Public communication campaigns: The American experience. In R. E. Rice & C. K. Atkin (Eds.), *Public communication campaigns* (3rd ed., pp. 3–21). Thousand Oaks, CA: Sage.

Palmgreen, P., & Donohew, L. (2003). Effective mass media strategies for drug abuse prevention campaigns. In Z. Slobada & W. J. Bukoski (Eds.), *Handbook of drug abuse prevention: Theory, science, and practice* (pp. 27–43). New York: Plenum.

Palmgreen, P., Donohew, L., & Harrington, N. G. (2001). Sensation seeking in antidrug campaign and message design. In R. E. Rice & C. K. Atkin (Eds.), *Public communication campaigns* (3rd ed., pp. 300–304). Thousand Oaks, CA: Sage.

Parrott, R. L. (1995). Motivation to attend to health messages: Presentation of content and linguistic considerations. In E. Maibach & R. L. Parrott (Eds.), *Designing health messages: Approaches from communication theory and public health practice* (pp. 7–23). Thousand Oaks, CA: Sage.

Pfau, M. (1995). Designing messages for behavioral inoculation. In E. Maibach & R. L. Parrott (Eds.), *Designing health messages: Approaches from communication theory and public health practice* (pp. 99–113). Thousand Oaks, CA: Sage.

Prochaska, J. O., & DiClemente, C. C. (1984). *The transtheoretical approach: Crossing the traditional boundaries of therapy*. Homewood, IL: Dow Jones/Irvin.

Rimal, R. N. (2001). Perceived risk and self-efficacy as motivators: Understanding individuals' long-term use of health information. *Journal of Communication, 51,* 633–654.

Rimal, R. N., & Adkins, A. D. (2003). Using computers to narrowcast health messages: The role of audience segmentation, targeting, and tailoring in health promotion. In T. L. Thompson, A. M. Dorsey, K. I. Miller, & R. Parrott (Eds.), *Handbook of health communication* (pp. 497–513). Mahwah, NJ: Lawrence Erlbaum.

Rogers, E. V. (2003). *Diffusion of innovations* (5th ed.). New York: Free Press.

Rosen, C. S. (2000). Intergrating stage and continuum models to explain processing of exercise messages and exercise initiation among sedentary college students. *Health Psychology, 19,* 172–180.

Rossi, P. H., & Freeman, H. E. (1993). *Evaluation: A systematic approach*. Newbury Park, CA: Sage.

Rothman, A. J., & Salovey, P. (1997). Shaping perceptions to motivate healthy behavior: The role of message framing. *Psychological Bulletin, 12,* 3–19.

Rothman, A. J., Salovey, P., Antone, C., Keough, K., & Martin, C. D. (1993). The influence of message framing on intentions to perform health behaviors. *Journal of Experimental Social Psychology, 29*(5), 408.

Salmon, C. (1989). Campaigns for social "improvement": An overview of values, rationales, and impacts. In C. Salmon (Ed.), *Information campaigns: Balancing social values and social change*. Newbury Park, CA: Sage.

Salmon, C., & Atkin, C. (2003). Using media campaigns for health promotion. In T. L. Thompson, A. M. Dorsey, K. I. Miller, & R. Parrott (Eds.), *Handbook of health communication* (pp. 449–472). Mahwah, NJ: Lawrence Erlbaum.

Schooler, C., Chaffee, S. H., Flora, J. A., & Roser, C. (1998). Health campaign channels: Tradeoffs among reach, specificity, and impact. *Human Communication Research, 24,* 410–432.

Schwarzer, R. (1992). Self-efficacy in the adoption and maintenance of health behaviors: Theoretical approaches and a new model. In R. Schwarzer (Ed.), *Self-efficacy: Thought control of action* (pp. 217–243). Washington, DC: Hemisphere.

Schwarzer, R. (1994). Optimism, vulnerability, and self-beliefs as health-related cognitions: A systematic overview. *Psychology and Health, 9,* 161–180.

Shadish, W. R., Cook, T. D., & Leviton, L. C. (1991). *Foundations of program evaluation: Theories and practice.* Newbury Park, CA: Sage.

Slater, M. D. (1995). Choosing audience segmentation strategies and methods for health communication. In E. Maibach & R. L. Parrott (Eds.), *Designing health messages: Approaches from communication theory and public health practice* (pp. 186–198). Thousand Oaks, CA: Sage.

Snyder, L. B. (2001). How effective are mediated health campaigns? In R. E. Rice & C. K. Atkin (Eds.), *Public communication campaigns* (3rd ed., pp. 181–190). Thousand Oaks, CA: Sage.

Snyder, L. B., & Hamilton, M. A. (2002). A meta-analysis of US health campaign effects on behavior: Emphasizing enforcement, exposure, and new information, and beware the secular trend. In R. C. Hornik (Ed.), *Public health communication: Evidence for behavior change* (pp. 357–383). Mahwah, NJ: Lawrence Erlbaum.

Sparks, L. (in press-a). The SMILE health care communication model (SMILE-HCCM): An interpersonal theory-based approach to message framing in health care interventions. In S. S. Travis & R. Talley (Eds.), *Caregiving across the professions.* Oxford University Press. Project supported by a grant from Johnson and Johnson and the Rosalynn Carter Institute for Human Development.

Sparks, L. (in press-b). Cancer care and the aging patient: Complexities of age-related communication barriers. In H. D. O'Hair, G. L. Kreps, & L. Sparks (Eds.), *Handbook of communication and cancer care* (pp. 233–249). Cresskill, NJ: Hampton Press.

Sparks, L., & McPherson, J. (in press). Cross-cultural differences in choices of health information by older cancer patients and their family caregivers. In K. Wright & S. D. Moore (Eds.), *Applications in health communication* (pp. 179–205). Cresskill, NJ: Hampton Press.

Sparks, L., & Turner, M. M. (in press). Cognitive and emotional processing of cancer messages and information seeking with older adults. In L. Sparks, H. D. O'Hair, & G. L. Kreps (Eds.), *Cancer communication and aging.* Cresskill, NJ: Hampton Press.

Stephenson, M. T., & Witte, K. (2001). Creating fear in a risky world. In R. E. Rice & C. K. Atkin (Eds.), *Public communication campaigns* (3rd ed., pp. 88–102). Thousand Oaks, CA: Sage.

Strecher, V. J., Rimer, B. K., & Monaco, K. D. (1989). Development of a new self-help guide: Freedom from smoking for you and your family. *Health Education Quarterly, 16,* 101–112.

Tversky, A., & Kahneman, D. (1980). Causal schemata in judgments under uncertainty. In M. Fishbein (Ed.), *Progress in social psychology* (pp. 49–72). Hillsdale, NJ: Lawrence Erlbaum.

Tversky, A., & Kahneman, D. (1981). The framing of decisions and the psychology of choice. *Science, 211,* 453–458.

Valente, T. W. (2002). *Evaluating health promotion programs.* New York: Oxford University Press.

Witte, K. (1992). Putting fear back into fear appeals: The extended parallel process model. *Communication Monographs, 59,* 329–349.

Witte, K., Cameron, K. A., Lapinski, M. K., & Nzyuko, S. (1998). A theoretically based evaluation of HIV/AIDS prevention campaigns along the Trans-Africa Highway in Kenya. *Journal of Health Communication, 3,* 345–363.

Chapter 11

Interdisciplinary Healthcare Teams

You may have noticed that you can often accomplish more with a group of people when you are working on a project than when you work on it by yourself. For example, in one of your classes, a professor may have required you to participate in a group assignment, such as a research paper or presentation. Many students like group assignments because they can share the workload and each group member can concentrate on a specific part of the assignment. This allows them to research different facets of a topic in much greater detail than if it were an individual assignment. As you may have experienced, sometimes a group effort such as this can lead to a better-quality assignment when each group member contributes a substantial amount. However, when some group members do not pull their weight, if group members do not recognize the contributions of others, or if members do not understand a part of the assignment that another member focused on, then problems can occur which may lead to an unsatisfactory outcome. Group assignments such as these can give you an idea of what it is like to be a member of an interdisciplinary healthcare team. While there are many types of groups and teams within healthcare organizations, this chapter focuses on interdisciplinary teams, or what we will eventually term synergistic teams.

Diversity of Healthcare Professionals

Healthcare has become increasingly complex due to the specialized nature of the various disciplines that are part of the delivery system. As each discipline advances its art of caring based on increasingly evidence-based science, new opportunities for improved care are possible. Concomitant with the advancement in these disciplines is a renewed pride in itself that each discipline thinks is intrinsic to the care of patients. The increase in specialties creates a larger number of roles and players in the equation of care delivery. Examine just a *sampling* of healthcare disciplines represented in the following list.

Physicians	Registered nurses	Nutritionists
Health educators	Pharmacists	Clergy
Mental health providers	Physician assistants	Social workers
Interpreters	Dentists	Psychologists
Occupational therapists	Physical therapists	Families
Patient care assistants	Vocational nurses	Administrators

With specialization comes the challenge of coordinating and managing the multiple roles that professionals deliver to the context. Team-based processes have emerged as solutions for ensuring that all parties contributing to the care of the patient act in a nonduplicative, error-free manner.

Importance of Interdisciplinary Teams

Interdisciplinary teamwork has become central to modern healthcare organizations (Coopman, 2001), largely because of the growing belief within such organizations that no one person or discipline can have expertise in all the areas of specialty knowledge needed for the high-quality care of clients with complex conditions. According to Coopman (2001), "the very nature of health care is bringing providers from numerous disciplines together to address health care problems" (p. 262).

Interdisciplinary health teams capitalize on provider diversity within a healthcare organization by drawing together the unique perspectives of providers from a range of health-related disciplines. The perspective of each team member is influenced by the culture of the health-related discipline in which he or she was trained, and this often leads to very different perceptions about a patient and his or her health situation. Members of a team can often work more effectively with others rather than separately, and interdisciplinary teams can often draw upon the collective strength of team members' unique experiences and diverse perspectives on a health problem. Not all healthcare teams are interdisciplinary, but are rather a collection of individuals from different disciplines. In order for a healthcare team to be truly interdisciplinary, each team member must have some training in or some understanding of the other disciplines of other team members (Poole & Real, 2003). In other words, quality team members and effective team communication are important to the success of interdisciplinary teams, and just bringing people together from different disciplines does not necessarily guarantee successful outcomes for the patient (Rees, Edmunds, & Huby, 2005).

Interdisciplinary collaboration and teamwork offer a number of advantages in addressing the complexities of patient care, especially among patients with chronic multiple health problems (Coopman, 2001). For example, diverse interdisciplinary teams can target a patient's physical, psychosocial, and in some cases spiritual concerns with the goal of providing more comprehensive care. Targeting the multiple health issues and concerns of patients may lead to better outcomes than any single course of treatment, although successful outcomes are also influenced by the expertise of team members and the quality of group interaction (Poole & Real, 2003). There are many other reasons that favor effective teamwork over individual action or poorly executed teamwork, including a reduction in mortality due to fewer medical errors (Bleakley, Boyden, Hobbs, Walsh, & Allard, 2006; Langhorne, Williams, Gilchrist, & Howie, 1993). Teams also contribute to overall better care (Cooke, 1997), improved management of patient care (McHugh et al., 1996), and help to reduce the length of hospitalizations (Wieland, Kramer, Waite, & Rubenstein 1996). Teams also have a tendency to involve patients more in their own care, creating greater empowerment on the part of the care receiver (Grant & Finocchio, 1995). From a healthcare professions perspective, teams create greater learning opportunities (Edwards & Smith, 1998) and foster greater job satisfaction for the team members involved (Gage, 1998).

Just as team members must be ideally suited to address one or more of a patient's problems, the team should be able to work together well and have realistic goals for team meetings in order for it to be successful. Decision-making is central to interdisciplinary healthcare teams, and effective communication plays a crucial role in the decision-making process (Cooley, 1994; Lefley, 1998). Team members often require training in group communication and decision-making skills, especially since these skills are not always taught within the curriculum of some healthcare disciplines. Greater equality in decision-making during team meetings often leads to better patient care (Kirkmann-Liff, 1999). In other words, when each team member has the opportunity to participate equally in making decisions about the patient, then the diversity of team member viewpoints often leads to better decisions. However, other factors, such as the type and severity of the patient's health problems, available treatments, and organizational issues (e.g., managed care), also play an important part in the success of the team. In addition, interdisciplinary healthcare team members often vary in terms of their degree of involvement with the team. Some members are core members (usually a physician and a nurse), while other providers may be peripheral members, attending meetings only when necessary.

Determined and sustained efforts towards effective teamwork are unlikely to occur on their own. Fragmented, sporadic, and uncoordinated actions by diverse healthcare professionals are an inherent part of the status quo. Team-based medical care requires not only effort but training as well. That is why a number of policy and regulatory bodies (the Institute of Medicine, PEW

Health Professions Commission, the Joint Commission on Accreditation of Healthcare Organizations) have recommended or stipulated systematic training in team-based, interdisciplinary collaborative practices (Bokhour, 2006; Ladden, Bednash, Stevens, & Moore, 2006). A primary goal of this chapter is to propose a model that facilitates team-based communication for healthcare professionals.

Continuum of Healthcare Teams

Multiple models of healthcare teams have been designed and used in healthcare organizations for decades. A typical model is one where a healthcare professional, usually a physician, makes all decisions about patient care and communicates those decisions in a top-down communication mode (giving orders and directives to nurses, pharmacists, etc.). A completely opposite perspective is one in which all members of the healthcare context come together in a shared decision-making team where communication is multilateral, uninhibited, and interactive. These very different models of patient care can be placed on opposite sides of a continuum to better understand the various communication options during healthcare delivery. Based on previous research (Ellingson, 2003; Grant & Finocchio, 1995; Jones, 1997; Pike, 1991; Wieland et al., 1996), we can construct a continuum that allows us to understand the motives and operations of healthcare professionals as they come together to deliver care (see figure 11.1).

At the extreme left of the continuum is the model we mentioned above that views healthcare delivery from a *unidimensional* perspective. Physicians make decisions, tell others what their roles and duties are, and expect orders to be carried out without exception. As a more traditional model of care, this is often observed in physicians' offices where other members of the team are direct employees of the team leader (physician). Communication is often one-way and any sharing of decision-making is operationalized by the physician asking questions about conditions, lab results, or medication protocols.

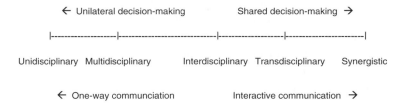

Figure 11.1 Continuum of healthcare teams.

A *multidisciplinary* approach to healthcare takes into consideration the expertise and experience of several healthcare professionals with an understanding that multiple viewpoints are possible. With this model it is still very likely that one individual, again usually a physician, makes most of the decisions and communicates her desires to other members of the team. Unlike the unidisciplinary model where the physician assumes an omnipotent role, input from other team members is likely to occur with some regularity. The extent to which the physician acts on such information and acknowledges it as a valuable contribution still remains her prerogative.

A third option is the popular *interdisciplinary* team model. Occupying the middle part of the continuum, the interdisciplinary team approach stresses the importance of each team member's contribution and strives to develop coordination and harmony among the diverse members of the team. The notion of coming together for the good of the patient is an important one to the interdisciplinary team, although ensuring the implementation of multiple approaches to care based on different medical disciplines can be challenging, if not problematic, with this approach. In some instances such teams find themselves in competition for the medical plan designed for the patient. Elements of negotiation and emergent leadership are observed. Ultimately, if the team experiences indecisiveness, a physician or charge nurse will intervene to make a unilateral decision on behalf of the patient.

Transdisciplinary teams are different from interdisciplinary teams in that they adopt more of an amalgamation model, where medical care emphasizes not so much the delivery of nursing, medicine, therapy, or other healthcare professional discipline as a blended approach that identifies the needs of the patient from a consultative and problem-solving perspective. Interdisciplinary teams evolve into transdisciplinary forms when team members develop trust among their colleagues and begin to share authority, responsibility, and expertise with other members (Wieland et al., 1996). In essence, the interdisciplinary effort becomes transformed into an integrated team working for the good of the patient rather than insisting on strict disciplinary influence. Clearly, effective and responsive communication is a key determinant for moving healthcare professionals into this transformative state.

At the other end of the continuum is the *synergistic* team. Like the transdisciplinary team that assumes a shared decision profile, this team model makes every effort to ensure that decisions not only involve the participation of all members of the team but that they are patient-centered. A synergistic team approach is not a common model for healthcare organizations, yet it offers the greatest opportunity for patient health and safety. In the next section we explore what a synergistic team is like and how it can succeed in highly complex healthcare organizations.

Model of Synergistic Healthcare Teams

Synergistic healthcare teams offer the greatest potential for improving patient outcomes and elevating organizational and system efficiency. Synergistic healthcare teams have three essential elements: (1) *instilling a sense of ownership*, (2) *becoming performance based*, and (3) *developing team synergy*. Marginalizing any one of these elements will limit the effectiveness of the team effort (see figure 11.2). Let us look at each of these elements in turn.

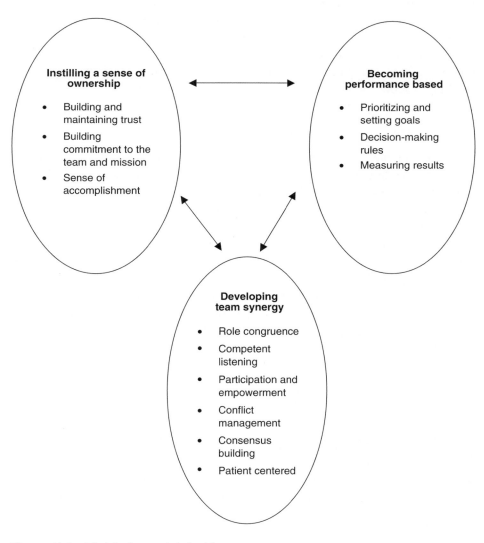

Figure 11.2   Model of synergistic healthcare teams.

Instilling a sense of ownership

Rosabeth Moss Kanter suggests in her book *Evolve!* (2001) that effective teams distinguish themselves from ineffectual ones through a feeling for and commitment to the greater good. Effective teams are those that take on a sense of ownership for the things they do, the decisions they make, and the ways that they feel. Medical teams are often under enormous pressure and find intrinsic fulfillment from personal accomplishments in delivering care. Personal achievement is critical to building confidence in oneself. However, the key to building effective, synergistic teams is inculcating a sense that what one does is part of a greater purpose that integrates personal goals into the good of the team and the patient. Accomplishing three goals instills this sense of team ownership: building and maintaining trust, building commitment to team and mission, and realizing a sense of accomplishment.

Building and maintaining trust

Drawing together a collection of healthcare professionals does not ensure a sense of devotion to the team or the care it delivers. This is especially true when team members hail from diverse backgrounds, groups, and locations (Rees et al., 2005). Having confidence in each member of the team is a challenging but necessary component of synergy. *Trust* is a key ingredient in developing ownership of the team. Trust comes in multiple forms. Trust in the group is the hope, belief, and confidence of team members that what is said and done in the group is both meaningful and appropriate. Team members expect that their efforts count for something. Trust in team colleagues comes from a history of communication that is open, sincere, and consistent. Team members trust those who are willing to say what they mean, have something valuable to say, and understand that what is said is honest and forthright. Team communication must ensure high levels of trust throughout the team process.

Trust can also be facilitated by:

- demonstrating that you do what you say and mean what you say;
- acting consistently;
- a willingness to listen to others and defer to their judgment;
- sharing information and asking for help;
- avoiding favoritism;
- disclosing personal things about self;
- acknowledging others' skills and talents (Kinlaw, 1991).

From these processes comes a greater sense of mutual respect for one another that promotes trust in teams, a key ingredient in acting on the patient's behalf in the absence of direct evidence. For example, if a charge nurse on a midnight shift reads a patient chart indicating the removal of oxygen therapy after two hours, she must have trust in the respiratory therapist in order to comply if her experience tells her to leave the oxygen in place.

Building commitment to team and mission (vision)

It is entirely possible that team members trust one another and still lack a strong commitment to the team and mission of the healthcare organization. Teams that exist primarily for social reasons are a good example of this phenomenon. To instill ownership in a healthcare team, *commitment* to the team and mission must also be present. Commitment is a state that reflects team members' willingness to care personally for the team and its members and to maintain a dogged determination to help the team succeed. This type of commitment is developed primarily through explicit clarification of the vision and mission entrusted to the team. Communication skills must include persuasive efforts to convince team members of the importance of the mission and vision, and providing feedback about how their efforts are making a difference within the larger organization. From this communication, team members come to assume a greater sense of identity with the team which can often become the focal point of their behaviors. Commitment can additionally be demonstrated by:

- caring personally about the team and its success;
- loyalty to the team, its members, and their mission;
- remaining focused on the team's mission and goals of patient care;
- maintaining high intensity levels for the team's efforts;
- demonstrating to others positive attitudes about the patient, organization, and healthcare in general;
- asking for commitment from other members of the healthcare team;
- taking pride in being part of the well-being of the patient (Kinlaw, 1991).

Once in place, commitment becomes easier to maintain because it is self-perpetuating through the sharing of common goals and a sense of needing one another to ensure positive health outcomes.

Sense of accomplishment

Healthcare professionals choose their profession for a multitude of reasons, but seeking a sense of accomplishment is an important goal. The feeling of contributing to the well-being of patients is more than a cliché. It is a sensation that rewards and motivates team members to assume ownership of the healthcare team. Not unlike sports teams who reach beyond normal expectations, healthcare teams take great pride in their accomplishments, whether large or small. It should be noted that team members can experience satisfaction with their own individual efforts as a team excels. It is that type of self-efficacy that causes healthcare professionals to seek additional experiences. However, experiencing a sense of team accomplishment can transcend even personal triumph precisely for the reasons teams exist – accomplishing more than individuals can. Taking ownership of team accomplishment feeds on itself and becomes a symbiotic experience for all involved. Inculcating a sense of accomplishment in team members can be achieved through:

- identifying and celebrating positive patient outcomes;
- demonstrating how the team is improving the healthcare organization;
- recognizing individual achievement within the context of team success;
- collective responsibility – holding the entire team accountable for its level of success.

It is through these levels of accomplishment that team members are able to address lingering uncertainties facing them during stressful times and understand that the team stands ready to offer encouragement and facilitation when the occasion arises.

Becoming performance based

Effective healthcare teams are those with an understanding that their performance counts and will be measured and rewarded accordingly. Not all rewards come in tangible ways, and teams do not necessarily anticipate that to be the case. However, what teams should expect is that their performance contributes to patient care and can be measured according to some acceptable standard. Three key factors are essential to instilling a performance-based team-building structure in healthcare organizations: prioritizing and setting goals, measuring results, and instilling strong decision-making procedures.

Prioritizing and setting goals

A first rule of thumb for basing a team's effort on its performance is through a process of goal setting. Teams must be allowed to take their charge from the office, clinic, or hospital and then prioritize and develop goals that are tangible, meaningful, and performance based. Some hospitals institute team-based structures to facilitate the collective management of patient care. Some of these contexts are more successful than others in developing the types of goals and the needed support to accomplish these goals. Besides setting the benchmark for success, goal setting/prioritization serves to focus team members' efforts on specific patient or organizational objectives, gives them a sense of direction, and helps them persist in their labors. One of the greatest concerns of hospitals, clinics, and long-term care facilities is patient safety. A mantra in healthcare, especially the facilities in which patients are cared for, is that they should do no harm to patients. Unfortunately, thousands of patients die each year in healthcare settings due to medical errors, poor safety practices, and ineffective coordination of patient care. For that reason healthcare organizations ask their teams to include patient safety in their goals for overall patient care.

Research has demonstrated that performance is enhanced when goals are specific, exciting, lofty, and prioritized (O'Hair, Friedrich, & Dixon, 2007). It is also important for teams to develop goals that allow some acceptable level of flexibility in their implementation and measurement, allowing for contingencies. Other strategies to keep in mind, according to O'Hair et al. (2007), include the following:

■ Goals should be problem based, not value based. Values are important, especially ethical values, but they must be practical and relevant and should explicitly state how they can be incorporated into immediate patient care.

■ Teams should set performance standards. How will the team know that it succeeded? Is length of hospital stay a good criterion? Is the control of pain a preeminent concern over a persistent physical therapy routine? Teams have to come to terms with diverse patient priorities.

■ Resources needed to accomplish goals (time, space, funds, etc.) should be identified. Generally, healthcare organizations are not going to volunteer resources without some driving impetus. Teams have to be ready to make credible requests for resources in order to accomplish their goals.

■ Teams will always need to recognize contingencies as they arise. Patients in critical care units will require adaptive plans for their care. Do all members of the team understand and interpret the goals and plans for the patient in a way where adjustments can be made with immediate notice?

Measuring results

Teams have a professional obligation to monitor and report their progress. Here we are not focusing on patient progress per se. That is accomplished through discharge reports and review committees. Instead, members must gauge their own performance as a team and how the activities of the team have contributed to positive outcomes. Therefore, teams must systematically assess their goals. It should be left up to the team how their results are measured, so long as they are accountable to the organization and the mission and vision of the team. Unfortunately, this is not always promoted in some healthcare organizations. Regardless, measurement or assessment techniques will vary according to the goals prioritized by the team, but should certainly include many of the standard criteria used for assessing performance. The key issue is that team members understand and appreciate the fact that their efforts are being measured on a systematic basis. The following guidelines are important:

- Results should be understood and accepted by the team.
- Results should be measured against the goals set by the team. Should goals be revised?
- Results should be compared to the mission of the organization.
- Results could be compared against other teams in the organization.
- How does the team feel about the results? Does it have a sense of accomplishment?
- How does the team feel about its level of commitment to the team and the mission?
- Were expectations set at the appropriate level? Were expectations violated?
- Do team members have confidence in themselves?
- Do team members seem to care about each other?
- Were facilitation efforts effective?
- How effective was the creative problem-solving process?
- How efficient was the group during its deliberations?

Decision-making procedures

Developing, understanding, and adhering to a set of rules for making decisions on patients' behalf comes under intense scrutiny from various sources within the organization. As an end point for just about everything that comes before it (analysis, assessment, evaluation, judgment), decision-making is influenced at every conceivable level (Koopman, 1998). Disciplinary norms influence how professionals make decisions, as do legal statutes and normative standards set by courts. The healthcare delivery system itself may weigh in on how decisions should be made in certain contexts ("do no harm," "do not over-medicate"). The healthcare organization where professionals practice no doubt has stipulations regarding certain decision-making rules and the team itself may impose

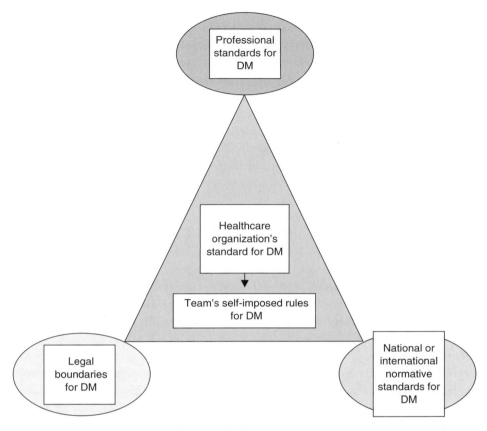

Figure 11.3 Decision–making (DM) standards.

decision–making rules that apply to its own activities. Figure 11.3 offers a simplified glimpse into how involved and potentially complicated decision–making procedures and stipulations can permeate the actions taken by health-care teams. Taken together, this system or culture of rules for decision–making (DM) offers important implications for team members, especially when deci-sion rules appear to conflict.

Similar to other organizations, healthcare facilities have a tendency to influ-ence decisions on lower units such as teams. A key reason behind this influence involves the focus on liability and litigation. As members of an organization, teams are afforded a reasonable degree of protection from legal implications through protection from their healthcare organization and from their own personal malpractice insurance. Hospitals may carry their own insurance or choose to self-insure, but regardless of their preferences they have a great deal at stake in how decisions are reached by healthcare teams. Therefore, health-care organizations have a role in the process that becomes manifested through decision rules that protect them from negligence. Like teams, organizations develop a strong sense of normative standards for decisions through environmental scanning (Sutcliffe, 2001) in order to avoid exposure to litigation claims based on unusual practices. Once normative and standardized guidelines are put in place for teams, it is the teams' own responsibility to develop rules for decision-making. These rules will vary according to the type of care they are delivering (e.g., acute, long-term palliative) and the composition of the team. However, some general guidelines based on the *functional perspective* (Gouran & Hirokawa, 1996; Hirokawa & Salazar, 1999) can be offered here to facilitate how teams make decisions (Dewey, 1933; Gouran & Hirokawa, 1999; O'Hair et al., 2007).

Problem identification. Not all medical conditions confronted by the medical team can be readily surmised. Unfamiliar symptoms or unexpected complications can create doubt about how to define the medical condition of a patient. Teams have much at stake in correctly identifying the condition and agreeing upon its etiology. Discussion and analysis will usually be required to make any conclusions about the medical problem. As much as possible, teams should be in solid agreement about the problem before moving to the next step.

Clarifying parameters and criteria. Teams will often move to subsequent steps after problem identification because time is short and deciding on a treatment regimen is an important intervening step in the process. However, teams need to ensure that they have adequately deliberated over what will constitute the standards by which they judge their decisions and the rules they will apply. In a cancer diagnosis, the team will want to set standards for care based on how the disease progresses and determine at what point aggressive treatment is continued or discontinued in favor of palliative care. It is better to make these decisions early on as guideposts rather than wait for symptoms and conditions to present, creating emotional conflict over treatment.

Generating alternatives. Teams have the advantage of being able to generate some creative options for medical care. Sometime known as "risky shift" or group polarization (Myers & Lamm, 1976; West, 1998), teams have a tendency to move away from neutral, normal, or expected alternatives towards decisions that are more extreme or unusual. Teams generate a sense of confidence that reduces their inhibitions to try something new. This can be good or bad. Innovative treatment options can save lives and reduce suffering for patients – when they work. Alternative treatment options that steer too far from the normal should probably come under the scrutiny of an outside party before moving forward (see the next phase). The point here is that as the touchstone phase for team decision-making, groups need to consider the opinions of all team members (including the patient) and to avoid being reticent in advancing strong and creative alternatives.

Evaluating alternatives. As an equally important step, team members must be ready to step up and offer their considered opinion about all of the alternatives generated by the prior step. It is within this phase that the ingenuity, care, and safety of the alternatives are carefully analyzed. Advantages and contraindications of all treatment alternatives should be exposed and weighed, and it is in this step that a diversity of team members can bring critical knowledge to bear on the options being tested. The best available evidence (referred to as evidenced-based medicine) should be applied to the alternatives and tested for strength. For example, a young patient with a protrusion on his midriff is being examined for the possibility of a tumor. Imaging has not reached a conclusion about the mass and two team members argue for the normal protocol of outpatient but invasive surgery to determine if the mass is malignant. Another team member argues that, based on the patient's age, it would be better to conduct a PET scan to determine if the growth is more cyst-like. A previous research article this team member read argues for the likelihood of such a mass and that further imaging would be less risky than surgery at this point.

Selecting the best option. In the previous case, a consensus may not be achieved among all team members. It is important that sufficient analysis and deliberation be pursued before reaching a final decision. Obviously, some medical conditions require a more rapid decision, such as in emergencies. In cases such as these it is likely that the physician will consider as much information and as many perspectives from the team as possible and then make a unilateral decision for care. When more time is available, generating as much agreement as possible for the treatment protocol is critical for several reasons. First, the evidence and experience that can be brought to bear in the case, the more likely it is that an option will be more valid. Second, team members want to know that what they are doing for the patient was a result of their input; they feel more invested in the decisions derived for the patient and develop that sense of ownership discussed earlier. Ultimately, a decision is usually made by the team leader based on due deliberation. Seldom do teams vote on a treatment option; a consensus is preferred when time allows.

Implementing the option. Putting the treatment option in place is much easier and teams have more confidence when all of the previous steps to decision-making have been followed. Many of the details and loose ends associated with treatment have been previously considered and steps for successful treatment have been laid out. The team will want to consider the most efficient pathways for care and develop a plan for implementation. As with any team-based decision involving complex processes, alternative options considered as part of the decision-making process must be kept in the background for handy reference should the original option fail the team. That is one of the more important reasons for arriving at medical decisions through a team-based format. Second- and third-place choices suggested by the team can be moved into place with confidence.

Evaluating the results. Teams can learn as much from their failures as they can from their successes. One of the hallmarks of effective team deliberation is taking advantage of hindsight as a learning tool. Known by many labels (after-action reviews, patient outcome reports, etc.), the process of understanding what worked and what didn't is invaluable to healthcare team members. Questions can be directed towards the evidence-based process of diagnosis and generation of alternatives. Did the systematic process of problem-solving work? Were some steps weaker than others? Was there a disconnect between the decisions reached by the team and the manner in which the treatment was implemented? How could the process have been improved? Teams have a functional and professional responsibility to bridge the gap between what occurred and what could have been better accomplished.

Developing team synergy

Group synergy is the phenomenon of groups performing in ways that reach beyond the collective efforts of individuals. "The whole is greater than the sum of its parts" is the typical phrase used to characterize group synergy. Group synergy is composed of role congruence, competent listening, participation and empowerment, conflict management, consensus building, and being patient centered.

Role congruence

Other problems within the team can lead to unsatisfactory outcomes. Role confusion as well as overlapping tasks and responsibilities can also inhibit interdisciplinary teamwork (Apker, Propp, & Ford, 2005; Berteotti & Seibold, 1994). Role congruence is important in terms of clarifying each team member's role, tasks, and responsibilities, and these should be clearly discussed during initial team meetings. What is well to remember is that while healthcare team members retain and promote their disciplinary professional roles (OTs, nurses, pharmacists, etc.), they are also very likely to take on team-based roles as well. Who is expected to set up meetings as needed? Who will act as the facilitator of the meetings? Who will be responsible for recording the deliberation of teams? Who will be in charge of communicating decisions to other organizational personnel? Who is responsible for follow-up through the treatment regimen? Responses to these questions provide essential substance for ensuring that team-based decisions and actions are efficient and complete.

Role congruence also involves the ability of members to suspend their personal inclinations for the good of the team. Roles are powerful forces in promoting an individual's identity in a professional organization. Identity is a key motivating force for why people behave in certain ways, and identity is all too often wrapped up in the specific roles medical professionals expect themselves to play (Lingard et al., 2006). When team members consider that their knowledge and expertise are intrinsically valuable to the patient and the team while at the same time perceiving that what they bring to the table is an integrated piece of the puzzle, it is easier to move towards role congruence that emulates synergy rather than unidisciplinary efforts.

Competent listening

Teams will succeed or fail based on their communication skills. In a way, all of the components of group synergy are communication based (Norris et al., 2005). However, championing the use of competent listening skills is clearly key. Listening is one of the most overlooked skills of team members and facilitators. As Stephen Covey said in his *Seven Habits* book (1986), seek to understand before you attempt to be understood. Make the effort to understand not only what a person is saying, but also why they are saying it (what are their true intent and motivation?). Try to understand their feelings. Determine whether they are communicating from a professional or a team-based role. Ask questions if you are unsure ("I am not sure I understand . . ."). Increase your tolerance for listening to others. Respect their input to the group. Give responsive nonverbal feedback when you are a listening (nodding, eye contact, forward lean, etc.) (O'Hair et al., 2007).

Approachability gives team members the impression that you are open and accessible to their ideas and opinions. Effective listening is one way to demonstrate approachability, as is an accessible nonverbal demeanor (smiling, eye contact, open body orientation, etc.) (Romig, 1996). Approachability can also be established by asking for opinions, commenting on ideas, and expressing positive regard for groups or team members.

Participation and empowerment

Medical teams do not automatically enjoy engaged, active, and creative participation. It takes clever facilitation skills to keep the team going and on track.

Beyond the normal questioning and responding, team members must probe, nurture, and encourage one another. In addition, it is important to stand ready to handle various dysfunctional roles that team members have a tendency to adopt.

Asking questions. Nothing is more important for team functioning than asking good questions. The following constitute some good rules for asking effective questions (O'Hair et al., 2007):

- Begin questions with "Who," "What," "Where," "When," and "How."
- Avoid questions requiring a yes or no answer.
- Ask questions that focus the medical team on the issues at hand (goals, mission).
- Phrase questions positively. Try not to be confrontational.
- Use secondary questions for elaboration or clarification.

Responding/feedback. One of the most effective ways to keep the discussion going is through effective responses or feedback. Responding is best accomplished through the following strategies:

- Paraphrasing: translating responses through summarizing, recapping in your own words.
- Evaluating: judging the effectiveness and appropriateness of responses in a constructive manner.
- Supporting: reassuring, encouraging, and sustaining responses of others.
- Probing: seeking additional information, provoking additional discussion.
- Interpreting: offering your own meaning (interpretation) for what someone has said.

Managing participation styles. Team members will not come to the table with similar inclinations and skills. Participation styles can be managed through effective facilitation skills (O'Hair, Friedrich, Wiemann, & Wiemann, in press). Examine the team communication styles that facilitate participation in table 11.1.

Conflict management

All teams will experience some level of conflict, and the success of interdisciplinary healthcare teams can be undermined by conflicts between different team members. Within any healthcare team, members will vary in terms of their social status and power. For example, physicians tend to have a higher

Table 11.1 Team communication styles that facilitate participation

Style	Description	Facilitation
Rambling	Much discussion except on the subject. Loses the point.	Raise hand slightly, get floor, refocus attention on the issue. Glance at watch.
Verbose	Excessive talkativeness, anxious to show off, very wordy.	Ask difficult questions to slow them down. Ask others to interpret the meaning. Ask for additional input.
Inarticulate	Can't put thoughts into a coherent form. Can't express themselves.	Paraphrase their comments. Ask others if they feel the same way.
Sidebar conversations	Two people talking privately during team discussion.	Call one by name and ask for their feelings on the discussion.
Avoiding	Noninvolvement, little participation.	Call on them by name. Ask for opinion.
Blocking	Indulges in negative or disagreeable comments.	Ask *why* they feel that way. Have them compare their view to the others.

social status and more power within healthcare organizations than nurses or social workers. Power differences may lead team members with less power to become apprehensive and contribute less to the group discussion. When this happens, ideas that may be beneficial in terms of treating the patient or meeting his or her needs may be lost. Power disparities can also lead to resentment among team members and impede successful collaboration (Abramson & Mizrahi, 1996).

Conflict between team members can arise in interdisciplinary teams for a variety of reasons, such as when people are not satisfied with the team discussion, if they feel that their viewpoint is being disregarded by other members, or because of personality differences (Coopman, 2001). Conflict can also be productive or unproductive. Conflict can lead to differing viewpoints about the nature of a problem, a healthy discussion of competing options for treating a patient, better-informed decisions, and reduction of oversights and redundancies that can be costly to the patient's health or the healthcare organization. Sometimes interpersonal conflict occurs due to personality differences and sometimes it is content oriented. Regardless, here are five steps to take to management conflict productively. (1) Openly state the cause of the conflict (is it personality based or differences of opinion?). (2) Discuss the goals of those in conflict. (3) Probe for areas of agreement. (4) Discuss means of resolving conflict through consensus. (5) Make a decision (O'Hair et al., in press).

Consensus building

Diversity of interests and styles in the team is a strength. Without diversity, there is no reason to form teams and individuals can be left to make decisions. Bringing diverse ideas to a consensual decision, however, is a challenge. One method of consensus building is through the process of normalizing norms. All groups will develop norms (regularized practices, behaviors) over time. Some are effective and others are not. Most experts agree that it is best to establish certain norms from the beginning of the group's existence. In this way, groups understand early on the ground rules for their deliberations. As a facilitation strategy, the first few sessions can begin by stating and agreeing on appropriate norms (e.g., being on time, turn-taking, no excessive speeches, no hostile remarks, active participation).

Coordination and collaboration among team members is also an ideal way to build consensus. Building upon one another's ideas, being supportive of the creative process, and engaging in reasoned skepticism contribute to consensus building. In addition, the following steps can be taken to reach consensual decisions in teams (O'Hair et al., 2007):

- Encourage team members to concede their personal positions when they are illogical or unworkable.
- Maintain an open mind about constructive conflict. Conflict can lead to better decisions when handled professionally. Use conflict to guide the team to a few remaining positions.
- Unless pressed for time, avoid voting or averaging as a means for decision-making.
- During stalemates, identify issues common to all positions and combine them into one integrated idea (decision) – known as the *common-denominator rule*.

For many people, team efficiency is a top priority among their "issues" concerning groups. Teamwork is often perceived as busy work or lost time, especially when team members have other responsibilities in the organization. Facilitation efforts that maintain an efficient team process are highly valued and contribute to consensus building. Consider the following steps to increasing efficiency in teams.

- Set an agenda and stick to it. Effective agendas are time bound (each item has a deadline associated with it).

- Employ a time monitor (timekeeper) to keep the group on track.
- Consider rules for participation (no speeches, comments to be one minute or less, etc.).
- Build in a reward system for maintaining efficiency.
- Do not hesitate to confront and challenge members when instances of inefficiency are observed.
- Demonstrate an energized level of communication as a model for efficient teamwork.

Patient-centered focus

Patients can also play a role in a synergistic team approach to healthcare, and many teams include the patient and/or his or her significant other(s) as team members (Poole & Real, 2003). Rather than being passive recipients of instructions and medications from their providers, healthcare teams should educate patients about the biological and psychological implications of their health issues and the various treatment options available to them (Coopman, 2001). As a form of patient agency (O'Hair et al., 2003), including patients in the process of decision-making can go a long way towards enriching the alternatives generated for care and investing the patient in the treatment regimen. As we have seen, allowing patients to become active and informed participants in their own wellness process maximizes the potential for successful treatment outcomes and patient satisfaction (Howe, 2006).

Summary

Healthcare teams are an indispensable part of the delivery system. Healthcare organizations that design and structure teams enjoy advantages over organizations that foster more unidisciplinary efforts towards patient care. These advantages come in the form of improved patient care and organizational efficiency, to name just a few. Healthcare teams do not happen on their own. Great efforts are necessary to instill the type of communication processes necessary for effective team-based care. The sheer number of healthcare professionals involved in care is a salient issue. Also, developing healthcare teams that suspend their own professional expectations for the good of the team and the patient presents a number of challenges, not the least of which is the tendency for professionals to promote their own knowledge and expertise over others. We argue that healthcare teams need to move to a perspective of care that takes advantage of the interdisciplinary strength represented by organizational members, a process we term synergistic healthcare teams.

The model for synergistic healthcare teams can be used by any healthcare organization hoping to improve the effectiveness and efficiency of its diverse interdisciplinary teams. The essential components of facilitation include instilling a sense of ownership, becoming performance based, and developing team synergy.

Team members can gain a sense of team ownership by developing trust with one another and with the team process. Trust leads to developing a commitment to the team and to the mission of the organization. Ownership is also assumed when team members gain a sense of accomplishment from their teamwork.

Medical team members can become performance based when they appropriately prioritize and set goals for themselves. These goals then lead to a process of creative problem solving where team members engage in innovative and critical thinking that leads to breakthrough results. These results are then measured to ensure that the team is on track and responsive to its mission. Recognizing and celebrating these results obviously contributes to instilling that sense of accomplishment mentioned earlier.

Group synergy is a result of ensuring that team members are employing competent communication skills. Group synergy is also a result of effective participation and empowerment of group members. These processes lead to consensus building which is so important to making team members feel like a "team." Finally, group synergy is maintained through efficient team processes, including a focus on patients as they become part of the synergistic team.

References

Abramson, J. S., & Mizrahi, T. (1996). When social workers and physicians collaborate: Positive and negative interdisciplinary experiences. *Social Work*, *41*, 270–281.

Apker, J., Propp, K. M., & Ford, W. S. Z. (2005). Negotiating status and identity tensions in healthcare team interactions: An exploration of nurse role dialectics. *Journal of Applied Communication Research*, *33*, 93–115.

Berteotti, C. R., & Seibold, D. R. (1994). Coordination and role-definition problems in health-care teams: A hospice case study. In L. R. Frey (Ed.), *Group communication in context: Studies of natural groups* (pp. 107–131). Hillsdale, NJ: Lawrence Erlbaum.

Bleakley, A., Boyden, J., Hobbs, A., Walsh, L., & Allard, J. (2006). Improving teamwork climate in operating theaters: The shift from multiprofessionalism to interprofessionalism. *Journal of Interprofessional care*, *20*, 461–470.

Bokhour, B. (2006). Communication in interdisciplinary team meetings: What are we talking about? *Journal of Interprofessional Care*, *20*, 349–363.

Cooke, C. (1997). Reflections on the healthcare team: My experiences in an interdisciplinary program. *Journal of the American Medical Association*, *277*, 1091–1092.

Cooley, E. (1994). Training an interdisciplinary team in communication and decision making skills. *Small Group Research*, *25*, 5–25.

Coopman, S. J. (2001). Democracy, performance, and outcomes in interdisciplinary health care teams. *Journal of Business Communication*, *38*, 261–284.

Covey, S. (1986). *Seven Habits Of Highly Effective People*. New York: McGraw-Hill.

Dewey, J. (1933). *How we think*. Lexington, MA: D. C. Heath.

Edwards, J., & Smith, P. (1998). Impact of interdisciplinary education in underserved areas: Health professions collaboration in Tennessee. *Journal of Professional Nursing*, *14*, 144–149.

Ellingson, L. L. (2003). Interdisciplinary health care teamwork in the clinical backstage. *Journal of Applied Communication Research*, *31*, 93–117.

Gage, M. (1998). From independence to interdependence: Creating synergistic health-care teams. *Journal of Nursing Administration*, *28*(4), 17–26.

Gouran, D. S., & Hirokawa, R. Y. (1996). Functional theory and communication in decision-making and problem solving groups. An expanded view. In R. Y. Hirokawa & M. S. Poole (Eds.), *Communication and group decision making* (2nd ed., pp. 55–80). Thousand Oaks, CA: Sage.

Grant, R. W., & Finocchio, L. J. (1995). California primary care consortium subcommittee on interdisciplinary collaboration. *Interdisciplinary collaborative teams in primary care: A model curriculum and resource guide*. San Francisco: Pew Health Professions Commission.

Hirokawa, R. Y., & Salazar, A. J. (1999). Task-group communication and decision-making performance. In L. Frey (Ed.), *Handbook of group communication theory and research* (pp. 167–191). Thousand Oaks, CA: Sage.

Howe, A. (2006). Can the patient be on our team? An operational approach to patient involvement in interprofessional approaches to safe care. *Journal of Interprofessional Care*, *20*, 527–534.

Jones, R. A. P. (1997). Multidisciplinary collaboration: Conceptual development as a foundation for patient-focused care. *Holistic Nursing Practice*, *11*(3), 8–16.

Kanter, R. K. (2001). *Evolve!* Boston: Harvard Business School Press.

Kinlaw, D. C. (1991). *Developing superior work teams*. San Diego, CA: Lexington Books.

Kirkman-Liff, B. (1999). Medicare managed care and primary care of elderly people. In F. Netting & F. Williams (Eds.), *Enhancing primary care of elderly people* (pp. 3–23). New York: Garland.

Koopman, P. (1998). Decision making. In N. Nicholson (Ed.), *Encyclopedic dictionary of organizational behavior* (pp. 128–133). Malden, MA: Blackwell.

Ladden, M. D., Bednash, G., Stevens, D. P., & Moore, G. T. (2006). Educating interprofessional learners for quality, safety and systems improvement. *Journal of Interprofessional Care*, *20*, 497–505.

Langhorne, P., Williams, B., Gilchrist, W., & Howie, K. (1993). Do stroke units save lives? *Lancet*, *342*, 395–398.

Lefley, H. (1998). Training professionals for rehabilitation teams. In P. Corrigan & D. Giffort (Eds.), *Building teams and programs for effective psychiatric rehabilitation* (pp. 13–23). San Francisco: Jossey-Bass.

Lingard, L., Whyte, S., Espin, S., Baker, G. R., Orser, B., & Doran, D. (2006). Towards safer interprofessional communication: Constructing a model of "utility" from preoperative team briefings. *Journal of Interprofessional Care, 20,* 471–483.

McHugh, M., West, P., Assatly, C., Duprat, L., Niloff, J., Waldo, K., et al. (1996). Establishing an interdisciplinary patient care team: Collaboration at the bedside and beyond. *Journal of Nursing Administration, 26*(4), 21–27.

Myers, D. G., & Lamm, H. (1976). The group polarization phenomenon. *Psychological Bulletin, 83,* 602–627.

Norris, E., Alexander, H., Livingston, M., Woods, K., Fischbacher, M., & Macdonald, E. (2005). Multidisciplinary perspectives on core networking skills. A study of skills and associated training needs for professionals working in managed clinical networks. *Journal of Interprofessional Care, 19,* 156–163.

O'Hair, H. D., Friedrich, G., & Dixon, L. (2007). *Strategic communication for business and the professions* (5th ed.). Boston: Houghton Mifflin.

O'Hair, H. D., Friedrich, G., Wiemann, J., & Wiemann, M. (in press). *Competent communication* (3rd ed.). New York: Bedford St. Martin's Press.

O'Hair, H. D., Villagran, M., Wittenberg, E., Brown, K., Hall, T., Ferguson, M., & Doty, T. (2003). Cancer survivorship and agency model (CSAM): Implications for patient choice, decision making, and influence. *Health Communication, 15,* 193–202.

Pike, A. W. (1991). Moral outrage and moral discourse in nurse–physician collaboration. *Journal of Professional Nursing, 7,* 351–363.

Poole, M. S., & Real, K. (2003). Groups and teams in health care: Communication and effectiveness. In T. L. Thompson, A. M. Dorsey, K. I. Miller, & R. Parrott (Eds.), *Handbook of health communication* (pp. 369–402). Mahwah, NJ: Lawrence Erlbaum.

Rees, G., Edmunds, S., & Huby, G. (2005). Evaluation and development of integrated teams: The use of Significant Event Analysis. *Journal of Interprofessional Care, 19,* 125–136.

Romig, D. A. (1996). *Breakthrough teamwork: Outstanding results using structured teamwork.* Chicago: Irwin.

Sutcliffe, K. M. (2001). Organizational environments and organizational information processing. In F. Jablin & L. Putnam (Eds.), *The new handbook of organizational communication* (pp. 197–230). Thousand Oaks, CA: Sage.

West, M. A. (1998). Risky shift/group polarization. In N. Nicholson (Ed.), *Encyclopedic dictionary of organizational behavior* (pp. 493–494). Malden, MA: Blackwell.

Wieland, D., Kramer, B. J., Waite, M. S., & Rubenstein, L. Z. (1996). The interdisciplinary team in geriatric care. *American Behavioral Scientist, 39,* 655–664.

Part VI

Contexts, Challenges, and Choices

Chapter 12

Emerging Health Communication Contexts and Challenges

As we saw in chapter 1, health communication is a relatively new and rapidly growing area of the communication discipline. As such, newer areas of health communication research are constantly attracting the attention of health communication scholars. While a discussion of all of these areas is well beyond the scope of this book, for this chapter we have selected three additional contexts of health communication that have received considerable attention in recent years. We focus on three rapidly growing areas of health communication research that have important implications for many of the other contexts we have examined in this book: (1) health literacy; (2) research on breaking bad news to patients in an appropriate way; and (3) older adult healthcare and health communication issues.

Health Literacy

Health literacy is defined by the US Department of Health and Human Services (DHHS) as the capacity to obtain, process, and understand basic health information and services needed to make appropriate health decisions. It is rapidly becoming an important health communication topic and has received national and international attention in the last few years (see www.health.gov/communication/literacy/).

Health literacy is increasingly recognized as a crucial issue affecting communication across the continuum of healthcare (Davis, Williams, Marin, Parker, & Glass, 2002). Recent research shows that on receiving diagnoses of illnesses such as cancer and Alzheimer's disease, patients and their families often face decisions for which they are usually unprepared. Surprisingly, healthcare providers and the medical establishment are often equally unprepared to help patients and their families make decisions that are right for them. In other words, health literacy is an issue for both patients and providers. Treatment choices are often made in an environment of uncertainty, ambiguity, misinformation, high emotion, and anguish, and the outcome ends up being less favorable than recent medical advances could allow (O'Hair, Kreps, & Sparks, in press; Pecchioni & Sparks, in press; Sparks, 2003a, 2003b; Sparks, O'Hair, & Kreps, in press).

Health literacy has been found to affect the health outcomes of individuals. While there is no consensus about the most appropriate way to measure health literacy, it typically deals with four important aspects: (1) cultural and conceptual knowledge; (2) listening and speaking (oral literacy); (3) writing and reading (print literacy); and (4) numeracy (knowledge of statistics and other numeric data used in healthcare). As Merriman, Ades, and Seffrin (2002) point out, most formulas for literacy base their results on sentence length and word difficulty, while word difficulty typically translates to word length. In other words (no pun intended), words of over two syllables are viewed as more difficult than those with fewer syllables. The results are usually expressed as a reading grade level, sometimes as a decimal or fraction (e.g., "8th RGL" or "12.5 RGL"). The authors further note that there is usually no correspondence between the highest grade level completed and the literacy skills of an individual. Although most adults in the United States have completed high school, the average reading grade level is eighth to ninth grade, which is the level of reading most newspapers and television news broadcasts attempt to write. Of course, similar to many other skills, reading skills atrophy if not used regularly, so people who are not reading consistently after they finish school will have correspondingly lower reading levels (Merriman et al., 2002).

Patients with poor health literacy have a complex array of difficulties with written and oral communication that may limit their understanding of preventive screening and symptoms of diseases like cancer, adversely affecting their stage at diagnosis (Davis et al., 2002). In addition, these barriers impair communication and discussion about risks and benefits of treatment options, as well as patient understanding of informed consent for routine procedures and clinical trials. More research is needed to identify successful methods for educating and communicating with patients who have limited health literacy.

Health-literate physicians tend to be better at communicating with patients. Patients increasingly desire to know more about the state of their health and related diagnoses, and a provider's ability to deliver health information in an appropriate way is now considered a crucial skill (Gillotti & Applegate, 1999; Sparks, 2003a, 2003b). Unfortunately, physicians often still take a routine approach to medicine and patients rather than using an approach tailored to each individual case and patient needs.

Yet, it is important to realize that health literacy is not a one-way street (i.e., the responsibility of healthcare providers). Patients must learn how to gather credible health information from a variety of providers. Consumer health literacy can be quite confusing and daunting. Patients must come to healthcare situations prepared with as much credible information as possible. The healthcare system can be a maze of misinformation. It is the health consumer's job to acquire as much information as possible. When reading health information or talking to health authorities, it is important to understand that statistics about your particular health issue may not necessarily apply to your particular case. Each individual patient has different characteristics that may result in a stronger health outcome (e.g., overall physical health status, genetic predispositions, tolerance for certain medications and treatments). However, it is not surprising that people who simply look at the numbers associated with a certain disease often lose hope, give up, and die without any real knowledge about how they might have responded to certain treatment options that may have resulted in gaining several years or more. Because health literacy is such a complex issue for patients, a variety of patient and caregiver advocacy groups have been formed in recent years (see, e.g., www.pancan.org) in an effort to raise awareness about particular diseases.

Breaking Bad News

The past several years have been associated with a sharp increase in interest among researchers, educators, and practitioners in how to most effectively communicate bad news to patients (Ptacek & Ellison, 2000; Hoy, 1985; Mast, Kindlimann, & Langewitz, 2005; Yedidia et al., 2003). Health communication scholars in recent years have been paying more attention to how healthcare providers break bad news in healthcare settings (Gillotti & Applegate, 1999; Gillotti, Thompson, & McNeilis, 2002; Sparks, Villagran, Parker-Raley, & Cunningham, in press; Thompson, 1994). Health information is the critical resource derived from successful health communication (Kreps, 1988a, 1988b, 2003). Effective and timely communication enables patients and their families to gather relevant health information about significant threats to health, and helps them identify strategies for avoiding and responding to these threats (Kreps, 2003). An increasing concern for physicians is how to effectively and appropriately communicate health information that is bad news to patients (Mast et al., 2005; Ptacek & Eberhardt, 1996).

Although the task of breaking bad news is a fundamentally important part of many healthcare interactions, it can be intimidating to providers (Barnett, 2004). Delivering bad news is difficult for physicians; therefore, phrases like "dropping the bomb" are often used to describe the daunting task (Baile et al., 2000; Mueller, 2002). Although delivering bad news is challenging, it can be done effectively, creating increased patient satisfaction and decreased patient emotional responses (Mast et al., 2005).

Although physicians have always been the bearers of bad news, the increase in chronic illness and in issues related to quality of life (see chapter 3) heightens the importance of understanding how the delivery of bad news affects patients and providers. The manner in which this type of communication occurs can significantly impact the patient's level of satisfaction with his or her interaction with hospital staff and overall treatment by the healthcare providers (Whaley, 1999). In addition, the outcome of delivering healthcare information, particularly medical disclosures that result in bad news, has serious implications for the physician–patient interaction and is directly related to important communication variables such as patient satisfaction and compliance (Thompson, 1994). Moreover, recent research indicates that delivering bad news requires complex communicative strategies that tend to differ from other kinds of medical interactions (Gillotti et al., 2002). Patients, however, increasingly desire to know more about the state of their health and related diagnoses, which indicates that the ability to deliver health information in an appropriate way is now a necessity (Gillotti & Applegate, 1999). Patients want to know the truth about their diagnoses, particularly in acute situations such as cancer (Sparks, 2003a, 2003b).

Defining bad news

Bad news has been defined in the medical literature as a multi-step process that creates situations where there is either a feeling of no hope, a threat to a person's mental or physical well-being, a risk of upsetting an established lifestyle, or a message is given which conveys to an individual fewer choices in his or her life (Barnett, 2004; Bor, Miller, Goldman, & Scher, 1993). In other words, bad news in the healthcare context refers to any information that creates a negative view of a person's health (Buckman, 1996). Although most of the medical literature on breaking bad news has focused on conveying diagnoses of objectively serious conditions, especially cancer (Hoy, 1985), bad news can range from a wart, to psoriasis, to pink eye, to infertility.

Regardless of the type of bad news, there are many reasons why physicians have difficulty breaking it. A common concern is how the news will affect the patient, and this is often used to justify withholding bad news. For example, physicians often conceal information from patients because they are afraid that bad news might cause their condition to deteriorate (Mueller, 2002). The

American Medical Association's first code of medical ethics advised physicians to be leery of breaking bad news to ill patients (Vanderkieft, 2001).

Demographic effects on bad news delivery

An important component of breaking bad news is that communication from physicians can vary in its subjective and objective severity. When providers deliver bad news, a number of different demographic characteristics potentially influence how the news is delivered. Patients' and providers' sex, age, ethnicity, and education level may modify the message strategy that providers use to deliver bad news.

For example, the sex of provider–patient dyads can alter providers' delivery of bad news. When female providers encounter female patients, they are more likely to communicate about preventive care, such as breast and pelvic exams (Franks & Bertakis, 2003). Same-sex provider–patient dyads experience fewer communication barriers. As such, providers consistently engage in the comforting strategy (Gjerberg, 2002). In addition, the age of providers and patients modifies provider–patient interactions (Eva, 2002). Older providers play a parenting role and tend to comfort patients habitually (Thom, 2001). Regardless of who is older or younger in the provider–patient dyad, research demonstrates that age impacts patients' perceptions of communication satisfaction (Eva, 2002). Finally, the ethnicity of the patient also changes the providers' delivery of bad news. When providers deliver bad news to Caucasian and African American patients, they are direct (Ishikawa, Roter, Yamazaki, & Takayama, 2005; Johnson, Roter, Powe, & Cooper, 2004). Providers who deliver bad news to Latinos and Asians are consistently comforting (Sleath, Rubin, & Huston, 2003; Sung, 1999).

Providers also alter their communication strategies for breaking bad news based on patients' education levels. Patients who are less educated often have a lower socioeconomic status. Due to a common misperception on the part of some providers that more educated patients know more about medical issues in general, patients with higher education tend to receive less information and comfort when receiving bad news from providers (Alshidi, Bener, Brebner, & Dunn, 2001; Duran-Tauleria & Rona, 1999; Gergen, 1996; Mitchell, Stewart, Pattenmore, & Asher, 1989).

Patients' perception of bad news is likely impacted not only by demographic characteristics but also by their individual thoughts and experiences. Patients do not uniformly consider a majority of diagnoses as bad news. An individual's reactions to bad news will vary depending on a host of personal factors, including age, familial obligations, and culture (Davis, 1991). For instance, while the vast majority of patients in English-speaking countries want to know about their diagnosis and treatment, the proportion of individuals who want and receive relatively full disclosure in other countries is much lower (Davis, 1991).

Effective doctor–patient communication can alter patients' behavior both prior to (preventive) and after a diagnosis is received while patients are undergoing treatment (Dearing et al., 1996; Greenfield, Kaplan, & Ware, 1985; Kreps & O'Hair, 1995). Research suggests that many factors influence a patient's satisfaction with the manner in which communication and breaking bad news occurs. For instance, it is well documented that the style of bad news delivery can greatly affect the manner in which the patient reacts to the news (Kreps & O'Hair, 1995; Mast et al., 2005; Mueller, 2002).

Current provider education in breaking bad news

Despite the fact that breaking bad news is frequently cited as one of a physician's most difficult duties, medical schools do not typically offer formal training for this complicated undertaking (Vanderkieft, 2001; Yedidia et al., 2003). This void creates a demand for health communication scholars to assist healthcare providers in competently addressing the discomfort and uncertainty associated with breaking bad news (Cegala & Lenzimeir Broz, 2003). When healthcare providers are given the opportunity to practice breaking bad news through skills training and simulated encounters, they feel more confident and less isolated (Eggly & Tzelepis, 2001; Wakefield, Cooke, & Boggis, 2003). Effective training allows providers to become aware of their personal attitudes and emotional reactions when breaking bad news. In addition, it helps skill physicians in crisis intervention and communication techniques (Ungar, Alperin, Amiel, Beharier, & Reis, 2002).

Physicians note the importance of the physical and social settings of bad news interactions. Physicians agree that the news should be delivered in a comfortable location that offers patients privacy and is relatively quiet. The space should be large enough to comfortably accommodate multiple staff and family members (Buckman, 1996; Maynard, 1991). Second, the timing of the news is important, and arrangements should be made to convey the information at a time that is convenient for the patient. If rushed, the physician may be perceived as uninterested in the patient and the process. However, evidence suggests that physicians may delay breaking bad news despite the fact that the majority of patients want to hear it (Blanchard, Labrecque, Ruckdeschel, & Blanchard, 1988; Hopper & Fischbach, 1989) and that some physicians want to avoid situations in which a prognosis is discussed (Seale, 1991), possibly because of the discomfort associated with such interactions.

Whatever the severity of the diagnosis, it is clear that breaking bad news is a frightening and stressful aspect of the healthcare profession. Medical students should be exposed to various communication strategies to employ when breaking bad news. Providers have a substantial amount of power over patient satisfaction and compliance in such situations. More training programs need to be created and implemented, not only for medical students but also for practicing physicians. By using the communication guidelines set forth, formal and informal providers, educators, and trainers can enable their students and employees to have greater confidence during bad news interactions.

Health Communication and Older Adults

Another rather large health communication issue is the rapid increase in older adults in the United States and the impact this will have on healthcare and health communication. Older adults are the fastest-growing segment of the US population. At the time of the 2000 Census there were an estimated 25 million men and 31 million women aged 55 years or older living in the United States, and there were approximately 35 million people over the age of 65 (US Census Bureau, 2000). Individuals aged 85 and older were the fastest-growing segment of the older adult population (US Census Bureau, 2000). The number of individuals aged 65 and older is projected to increase from 35 million (in 2000) to nearly 80 million in 2050 (Federal Interagency Forum on Aging-Related Statistics, 2000a).

One reason for the large number of older Americans is that the average life span is increasing. At the beginning of the twentieth century, the average life span was around 47 years, but since then life expectancy has increased to an average of 74 years for men and 79 years for women (US Census Bureau, 2000). Infant mortality rates have decreased substantially in the US during the last several decades, and this, coupled with advances in preventive health efforts and healthcare, will likely contribute to further increases in the life span.

Older individuals face a variety of unique health concerns. While the majority of older adults tend to be healthy, the sheer number of people over the age of 65 makes them a large proportion of consumers of the US healthcare system. Many of these individuals are on fixed incomes that may make it difficult to meet all of their healthcare needs. In addition, most healthcare providers in the United States tend to be from younger age cohorts, and many of these individuals have a relatively limited knowledge of aging and health issues. Even worse, some older individuals are negatively stereotyped by healthcare providers and by people in general, and this can often lead to depression and other negative psychological health outcomes for older people. Given the scope and importance of this issue, this section examines many of the unique health concerns and health communication issues related to older adults.

Getting older and experiencing health problems

How do you feel about getting older? If you are like many Americans, you are probably not overly enthusiastic about the idea. In our society, individuals often associate aging with health problems, and this belief is supported by some scientific evidence. People are more likely to develop health problems such as chronic illness and physical/cognitive impairments as they age (Mosqueda & Burnight, 2000). For example, older adults are diagnosed with cancer more than any other segment of the population (Hewitt, Rowland, & Yancik, 2003), and they have higher incident rates of arthritis and hypertension than other age groups. In addition, individuals 85 and older have higher incidents of memory impairment than younger age cohorts (Federal Interagency Forum on Aging-Related Statistics, 2000b). However, while the elderly often do contract more disease and illness than other groups, many of the conditions are not intrinsic to aging (Nussbaum, Pecchioni, Robinson, & Thompson, 2000; Stahl & Feller, 1990). Instead, other factors such as lifestyle choices and genetic predispositions for disease or negative health conditions are more likely to cause health problems for older people than the process of aging itself.

In terms of mental health, it is a common belief that aging is associated with a decreased ability to function mentally. Yet, cognitive decline is not necessarily related to the aging process, but may be more likely to occur due to conditions such as high blood pressure (Eisdorfer & Cohen, 1980; Sparks, in press). Unfortunately, it is a common misperception that the majority of older adults are unhealthy or experience major health problems. To make matters worse, many older individuals believe this stereotype about aging, and they may attribute health problems to age as opposed to other variables. Yet, as we will see, aging is not necessarily related to poor health. And while there are some physical aspects of aging that can certainly lead to health problems, the next section will examine how social factors such as communication problems can actually create more difficulties for older adults than physical problems associated with aging.

Age–related issues affecting older adult health and healthcare

Presbycusis

Have you ever raised the volume of your voice when talking to a grandparent or another older person you know? It is a common belief that older people have difficulty hearing us. However, as we will see, severe hearing problems among older people are relatively rare. Presbycusis is defined as age-related hearing loss, and hearing problems do tend to increase after the age of 45. However, most people do not realize that older adult deafness is relatively rare. For example, only 15 percent of individuals over the age of 75 are considered to be deaf (Darbyshire, 1984; Verbrugge, 1984). Presbycusis is caused by a number of age-related changes to the ear, including deterioration of parts of the outer ear, hair loss in the cochlea in the inner ear, and nerve damage in the auditory systems within the brain (Villaume, Brown, & Darling, 1994). These changes affect the reception of sound waves and transformation of these sound waves to neural signals to the brain. In addition, according to Villaume et al. (1994), common types of background noise in social situations where older individuals communicate (e.g., simultaneous conversations, street noise, television) can significantly increase hearing problems for older people with presbycusis, even when it is only in mild form.

Presbycusis can make it difficult for older adults to process speech content quickly during conversations. However, many individuals with average hearing loss can usually compensate for this loss by using proactive strategies, such as lipreading, relying on information from the context of the conversation or the environment to interpret meaning, or by requests for clarification from their conversational partners. Presbycusis reduces a person's ability to decipher the content of speech by "detecting, discriminating, and recognizing words, phrases, and sentences" (Villaume et al., 1994, p. 85). One of the biggest problems associated with presbycusis is the reduced ability to decipher paralinguistic cues (e.g., fluctuations in the voice that convey meaning). Paralinguistic cues are very important in conveying relational messages, or nonverbal messages that convey social cues such as affection, emotion, and power (Villaume, Darling, Brown, Richardson, & Clark-Lewis, 1993). The inability to hear paralinguistic cues can make it difficult for people to understand many of the complex aspects of everyday language, such as assessing whether someone is sad, tired, or being sarcastic in a conversation. However, it is important to point out that while these aspects of presbycusis do present problems for many older adults, the majority of older adults with average levels of presbycusis can compensate for their hearing loss with relatively little trouble (although conversations may be more time consuming and mentally exhausting for them).

Younger people (including many healthcare providers) are often unfamiliar with the characteristics of presbycusis, and they can become frustrated by the increased amount of time it takes some individuals with hearing loss to process information and create a response. They often perceive older individuals with presbycusis as less competent conversational partners than older people without hearing problems, despite the fact that most people with age-related hearing loss are fully competent and able to adapt to their situation (Villaume et al.,

1994). As a result, people often withdraw from conversations with individuals with presbycusis or do not give the individual an adequate amount of time to compensate for their hearing loss during a conversation. Thus, the perception that an older person cannot hear is often more problematic than the hearing loss itself.

Older adults with hearing loss can quicky lose confidence about their hearing abilities when people treat them differently or avoid conversations with them. This phenomenon is known as the *communicative predicament of aging model* (Nussbaum et al., 2000), and the loss of confidence, coupled with the common stereotype that older adults have poor conversational skills, can cause many problems for seniors with presbycusis when others avoid communicating with them. It can lead to a reduction in the size and quality of an older person's social network, diminishing the amount of social support he or she receives. This, in turn, can lead to feelings of inadequacy, loneliness, and depression. In addition, healthcare providers who perceive an older patient's hearing loss to be worse than it actually is may spend less time with the patient or negatively influence the interaction in other ways.

Cognitive decline, Alzheimer's disease, and dementia

Another popular stereotype of older people is that many become senile or lose their mental abilities as they age. While Alzheimer's disease and other types of dementia affect older individuals more than any other age group, and the number of people with Alzheimer's disease and other types of dementia is increasing, relatively few older adults experience substantial cognitive declines as they age (Gatz, Kasl-Godley, & Karel, 1996; Kemper & Lyons, 1994).

Alzheimer's disease is a degenerative and fatal disease that is estimated to affect nearly 4.5 million Americans, and the number of Alzheimer's disease cases is expected to increase to between 11 and 16 million by 2050 (Hebert, Scherr, Bienias, Bennett, & Evans, 2003). While people can be diagnosed with Alzheimer's disease at younger ages, risk for the disease increases with age, and it is seen most frequently among people over the age of 85. Alzheimer's disease is named after Dr. Alois Alzheimer, a German doctor who lived during the early 1900s and studied changes in the brain tissue of mentally ill patients. In 1906, Alzheimer linked a specific pattern of neurological degeneration with symptoms of dementia, and this later became known as Alzheimer's disease (Kemper & Lyons, 1994).

The disease is characterized in the brain by abnormal clumps (amyloid plaques) and tangled bundles of fibers (neurofibrillary tangles) composed of misplaced proteins (Kemper & Lyons, 1994). The causes of Alzheimer's disease are still unclear, but genetics, diet, exercise, and mental activity throughout the life span are all thought to contribute to risk for the disease.

The symptoms of Alzheimer's disease change as the disease progresses. Early symptoms include short-term memory problems, confusion, and communication impairments, such as failure to take part in family conversations and inability to start and sustain conversations. While these problems are not major threats to an older individual's physical health, they can lead to feelings of frustration and social isolation (Kemper & Lyons, 1994). Later symptoms of the disease may include inability to perform everyday tasks, such as getting dressed and bathing, and changes in mood and behavior, such as increased irritability or aggressiveness. In the late stages of Alzheimer's disease, people typically become dependent on caregivers, they suffer further cognitive decline, and eventually die from the disease. The life expectancy for individuals with Alzheimer's disease ranges from 5 to 20 years, with an average survival rate of 8.5 years from initial diagnosis (Kemper & Lyons, 1994).

Many other types of dementia can be confused with Alzheimer's disease. In addition, healthy older adults often experience short-term memory problems, difficulties remembering names during conversations, slower processing speed when interpreting and recalling information, and mild forms of non-Alzheimer's dementia that may lead people to believe they have Alzheimer's disease (Cohen, 1994; Kemper, 1992; Salthouse, 1992). Unfortunately, when people meet an older individual who exhibits some of these characteristics, they often assume the person is suffering from Alzheimer's disease or are "losing it" mentally, despite the fact that the person is healthy and fully capable of carrying on a conversation.

In terms of the ways in which Alzheimer's disease affects communication, Kemper and Lyons (1994) mention cognitive problems, such as attention deficits, and short- and long-term memory problems, which lead to the disruption of communication within Alzheimer's patients. Specifically, people with Alzheimer's often use vague words or words with nonspecific references during conversations (e.g., words like "stuff" or "things"), and they have difficulty adapting speech to changing situations. In addition, they often have difficulty interpreting complex sentence structures when interacting with others. As a result of these communication problems, "Alzheimer's patients themselves may become socially withdrawn, irritable, and physically agitated as their efforts to communicate or to understand others fail" (Kemper & Lyons, 1994, p. 75).

Communication problems associated with Alzheimer's disease can be challenging and frustrating for people caring for Alzheimer's patients, both health-care professionals and lay caregivers (e.g., a spouse or family member). Nearly 75 percent of care for people with Alzheimer's disease is provided by family and friends at home (Rice et al., 1993). Caring for these individuals is expensive for most lay caregivers (Ernst & Hay, 1994), and the symptoms of the disease make interaction with the person with Alzheimer's disease difficult (Query & Kreps, 1996).

Physical activity/mobility

Physical activity is an important predictor of health status throughout the life span. Most Americans, young and old, do not engage in a sufficient amount of physical activity, despite the fact that insufficient activity has been linked to a host of health problems including obesity, cardiovascular disease, osteoporosis, hypertension, and increased risk of certain types of cancer. Among older adults, increased exercise is associated with reduced risk for these health problems and with many physical and psychological benefits, such as reduced fatigue, anxiety, and depression, and increased mood and emotional well-being. A number of factors associated with aging may limit mobility and subsequently the ability to engage in physical activity among older adults. In addition, decreased mobility among older adults may decrease social contact. This section briefly explores the effects of decreased activity/mobility on physical and psychological health.

According to Burns (2002), after age 65 a large proportion of older women and men report reduced levels of physical activity, and for adults over the age of 75, 34 percent of men and 50 percent of women report no regular physical exercise. There are a number of reasons why older individuals may find it harder to engage in regular physical activity. Nearly 35 percent of individuals over 65 have impaired walking ability (Burns, 2002), 50–60 percent of people 65 and older have arthritis (Center for Disease Control, 1996), and these conditions can limit mobility. While many of these health conditions may not physically prevent older individuals from engaging in adequate levels of some form of physical activity to keep them healthy, they may experience feelings of discomfort, frustration, and fear that greater physical exertion might lead to larger health problems (e.g., a heart attack). Providers frequently perceive that older patients may be at greater risk for cardiac events due to heavy exertion, and this may make them reluctant to recommend more physical exercise, even among older individuals who may not be at significant risk and may actually benefit from increased activity (Burns, 2002).

In addition to physical problems that limit physical activity, factors such as living on a fixed income, access to transportation, and a declining social network can present barriers to sufficient exercise. Health clubs and access to walking areas can be limited for older people with restricted financial means or those without a vehicle or nearby public transportation. While a person does not need to join a health club in order to be physically active, there may be social reasons why some older people do not engage in inexpensive physical activities such as shopping or taking walks around the neighborhood. Older individuals living alone or those with fewer friends may find it hard to locate companions who are willing to participate in physical activities with them. Some senior centers and other community-based facilities often host activities that may help older individuals get more exercise (e.g., aerobics classes, trips to museums), although these types of services may be far from where many older people live or nonexistent in more rural areas of the country. As the older population increases, greater awareness of the physical activity needs of older adults is needed so that communities can provide resources for seniors.

Polypharmacy

Older patients are also more likely than younger patients to experience multiple illnesses (Nussbaum, Ragan, & Whaley, 2004), a situation that can lead to the need to take multiple medications to treat these conditions. Unfortunately, this often leads to *polypharmacy*, or the problems that arise from the prescription of an excessive number of medications and the interactions between them. Polypharmacy is common among older patients, particularly those individuals who are coping with multiple health conditions. Older adults account for almost a third of all prescribed medications and about 40 percent of all over-the-counter medications (Colley & Lucas, 1993; Ghandi, Burstin, Cook et al., 2000).

For example, an older patient who already has hypertension and arthritis may be diagnosed with cancer and require chemotherapy. Her oncologist needs to know what medications she is taking for hypertension and arthritis to assess which types of chemotherapy will not interact with these medications. Because drug interactions can produce a variety of unpleasant and sometimes life-threatening complications (such as fatigue, hallucinations, dizziness, and falls), physicians and other providers need to have a complete list of medications an older patient is taking in order to avoid problems (Colley & Lucas, 1993). However, many older patients do not know all of the medications they are taking, and this situation is complicated by multiple classes of medications, different brand names, and generic versions of medications. In addition, many patients are unaware of how prescription medications interact with over-the-counter medications, vitamins, and herbal supplements, which can also cause drug interaction effects. Our kidneys and liver are important organs for removing toxins from the blood stream, and as we age these organs often work more slowly. This can cause problems for older adults taking multiple medications when medications take hours or days apart to interact with one another.

Other problems can occur when older individuals do not adhere to some or all of the medications (e.g., not taking the proper dosage, irregular use of medications) for reasons such as being unclear about the directions or taking or not taking the drug depending upon how they feel, or if they are not aware of or do not understand the various interaction effects that can occur among their medications (Hanlon, Schmader, Koronkowski et al., 1997). Older people sometimes take medications on an irregular basis, take only half the prescribed amount, or they simply do not refill prescriptions in an effort to help lower the cost of medications. To help prevent polypharmacy, providers often urge older patients to bring their medication bottles or a list of medications with them to healthcare visits, and this helps to circumvent memory problems about which medications a patient is taking. Providers also need to inform older patients about interaction effects prescribed medications can have with over-the-counter drugs, vitamins, alcohol, and other substances an older person might be taking.

Provider–older patient interaction

People aged 65 and older spend a significant portion of their time interacting with physicians, and they are more likely to spend time in hospital than younger patients (Thompson, Robinson, & Beisecker, 2004). The number of physician visits by older Americans is expected to increase in the next 20 years as people live longer and medical technologies and new medications allow them to manage health problems for longer periods of time than in previous decades (Thompson et al., 2004). Interactions with physicians have important consequences for the quality of life of older patients (Beisecker & Thompson, 1995). Most older individuals report being satisfied with their healthcare providers. However, studies of provider–older patient interaction have demonstrated that many communication problems do occur between providers and older patients and that these can have negative implications for healthcare and quality of life for older individuals (Adelman & Greene, 2000; Greene & Adelman, 2001, 2002). These communication issues are discussed in greater detail below.

Adelman, Greene, and Charon (1991) found physicians to be more condescending and indifferent towards older patients compared to younger patients. Physicians are often less likely to share decision-making with older patients (Greene, Adelman, Charon, & Hoffman, 1989), although again this depends upon the training the provider has received in working with older patients. Physicians often initiate more of the topics in conversations with older patients, although patients also initiate a relatively high percentage of topics (Thompson et al., 2004).

In many cases of problematic interaction between providers and older patients, the patient may not have his or needs met. One study found that 27 percent of older diabetic patients' current problems were not addressed during the medical encounter with their physician (Rost & Frankel, 1993). As with other age groups, many physicians avoid addressing older patients' psychosocial concerns. Researchers have found that physicians often focus on medical issues when communicating with older patients and tend to spend relatively little time discussing psychosocial concerns. This is because many of these issues, such as relationship problems and financial difficulties, are uncomfortable topics for many physicians to discuss since they often elicit strong emotions such as embarrassment and fear. Physicians are often reluctant to address psychosocial concerns with older patients. Psychosocially oriented communication during medical encounters may facilitate an exchange of social support between provider and patient, and it could also play an important role in enabling accurate diagnosis of health problems and the prescription of more appropriate treatments. Most studies of providers and older patients have focused on physician–patient relationships, and less is known about older patient interactions with nurses, clinical staff, and other types of providers.

Older patients often have more paternalistic attitudes towards providers, especially physicians, and they may be less likely than younger patients to be assertive with their doctor, initiate a topic change during a medical encounter, or challenge their doctor's decisions. Older patients are often reluctant to express complaints, confusion, disappointment, or misunderstandings to physicians, and they ask fewer questions than younger patients when talking to physicians (Adelman et al., 1991). Older patients are often reluctant to communicate their concerns in medical encounters (Adelman et al., 1991), but researchers have argued that if given time to present their concerns and raise issues, older patients may engage in more information-seeking behaviors.

Compliance with medical regimes can be a significant problem for older patients, especially when they have multiple chronic conditions and must follow a number of medication treatments (Coe, 1997; Haug & Ory, 1987). However, lack of compliance does not appear to be due to reluctance to follow instructions on the part of older patients. When providers spend more time explaining medications, interaction effects, and other important aspects of treatment to older adults, this appears to increase compliance with medical regimes (Beisecker & Thompson, 1995).

Stereotypes of older patients

Like other individuals in our society (including older adults themselves), many physicians have negative stereotypes of older people, and this can affect their communication and treatment decisions. Older people are often viewed by providers as being too open about negative topics such as bereavement or health problems. Unfortunately, like all stereotypes, stereotypes of older people are often based on misconceptions about older adults and the aging process (Hummert, Shaner, & Garstka, 1995). Providers with negative stereotypes of older patients may attempt to limit their time with them or communicate in ways that are based upon negative stereotypes, such as engaging in patronizing behaviors (e.g., talking to the elderly patient as if he or she is a child). In addition, providers who are less knowledgeable about geriatric medicine may attribute some health problems to age as opposed to illness, and this may influence their medical decision-making. While physicians receive some geriatric medical training in medical school, only a relatively small number specialize in geriatric medicine. Other types of providers who see older patients may be even less knowledgeable about the aging process and older adult health issues.

Communication accommodation theory (CAT) is a useful framework for understanding the relationship between stereotypes of older people and provider–older patient interaction. As we saw in chapter 2, CAT proposes that when speakers from different social groups interact, they adjust or modify their verbal and nonverbal communication in order to accommodate each other (Gallois, Ogay, & Giles, 2004; Giles, Coupland, & Coupland, 1991; Giles, Mulac, Bradac, & Johnson, 1987).

Recall that as we make evaluations based upon whether a person is part of one of our in-groups or a member of some out-group, we have a number of choices about how to adapt our communication to that person, including convergence, divergence, overaccommodation, and underaccommodation. One common type of communication behavior that providers engage in with older patients is *overaccommodation*. For example, it is common for younger healthcare providers to raise the volume of their voice or speak more slowly when talking with older people, especially if they perceive the older person to be hard of hearing or cognitively deficient. Moreover, *underaccommodation* can occur when people from different social groups feel that they do not have anything in common to talk about. Providers may stick to "safe" topics, such as talk about the weather, if they perceive they do not have much in common with the older patient. Underaccommodation may deprive an older patient of more meaningful types of talk. In general, overaccommodating behaviors are often perceived as patronizing and underaccommodating behaviors lead to dissatisfying conversations. While healthcare providers often need to *diverge* from patients when interacting with other providers or for other professional reasons, during interactions with elderly patients providers should attempt to *converge* with the older patient's communication style and avoid overaccommodating or underaccommodating communication.

Discourse management is an important communication skill to learn for providers who work with older patients. Discourse management focuses on the receiver's conversational needs and the receptor's ability to attune to those needs, such as topic selection, backchanneling (e.g., noises like "humm" and "uh huh" that people make during conversation), or turn-taking behaviors (Gallois et al., 2004; Shepard, Giles, & Le Poire, 2001). Discourse management can be very important during communication to show conversation partners that they are being listened to and that the receptor understands what they are trying to communicate. Behaviors like backchanneling let the speaker know that the listener is still there and paying attention. It is important for healthcare providers communicating with older patients to employ discourse management to ensure that patients feel able to discuss their needs and concerns.

Similar to other age groups, successful communication between physicians and older patients has been linked to higher satisfaction with care, better disclosure of patient problems, improved compliance with physician treatment recommendations, and decreased use of emergency services (Stuart, 2002; Wasson et al., 1984). In addition, Weiss and Blustein (1996) found that older patients in long-term relationships with physicians were less likely to be hospitalized and used fewer costly services than individuals who had shorter relationships with physicians.

Companions and provider–older patient interaction

The presence of a companion (typically a spouse or an adult child) can have a significant impact on communication between older patients and healthcare providers (Adelman, Parks, & Albrecht, 1987). Beisecker (1989) found that about half of the older people in her study brought a companion to the medical interview. When a companion is present, older patients tend to raise fewer topics with physicians, tend to be less assertive, and engage in fewer joint decisions with physicians.

Companions often play a variety of roles in interaction during medical visits, including helping older individuals to remember information, providing emotional support and companionship, aiding in decisions, and serving as an advocate or interpreter for the patient. Beisecker and Thompson (1995) identify three distinct roles for companions of older patients during medical visits. According to these researchers, companions who take on the _watchdog_ role give information on behalf of the patient, or elaborate upon information provided by the patient, encouraging the provision of precise, complete, and accurate information to the doctor. Those who play the _significant other_ role provide feedback to both the patient and the physician about the interview. Finally, the _surrogate patient_ role is characterized by the companion taking a more active role in the medical encounter than the actual patient, such as answering questions for the patient or raising concerns. In these cases providers may communicate with the companion more than with the patient.

Managed care influences on provider–older patient interaction

Issues related to managed care organizations, health insurance, and Medicare often impact provider–older patient relationships. At age 65, older Americans are eligible for Medicare, and Medicare benefits make it possible for older individuals who are managing ongoing health problems to receive affordable healthcare. Services that are reimbursed by Medicare are often subject to restrictions, such as limited access to certain providers, procedures, and medications. Older adults often receive only minimal reimbursement through Medicare for medications they need for managing ongoing health conditions, and many older people must reduce expenses in other areas of their life in order to fill prescriptions. Many of these same individuals are not able to afford (or obtain) supplementary health insurance to make up the difference between the price of medications and what Medicare will reimburse. Unfortunately, this means that older people with limited financial means may have to give up food or other necessities in order to have medications, or they may decide not to take the medications altogether (which can worsen their health condition).

While managed care helps to make healthcare more affordable, its focus on cost-cutting can negatively affect provider–older patient interactions. According to Crystal (2002), pressure from managed care organization administrators to keep physician visit lengths brief can significantly affect the ability of providers to effectively influence elderly patients' health behaviors. Moreover, the managed care administrative practice of frequently changing the providers who are allowed to participate in managed care networks in an effort to reduce costs can undermine older patients' trust, deny access to physicians and other providers with whom older patients have a history, and lead to greater dissatisfaction with overall healthcare (Crystal, 2002). In addition, both providers and older patients may become frustrated by the limitations of managed care plans (Stuart, 2002).

Institutionalized older adults

Approximately 25 percent of adults aged 65 and older die in nursing homes and other longer-term care facilities each year in the United States (Gabrel, 2000; Happ et al., 2002), although only about 4–5 percent of people over the age of 65 reside in a nursing home at any one point in time (Magaziner, Zimmerman, Fox, & Burns, 1998; Nussbaum et al., 2004). With the increase in the older adult population, particularly in individuals aged 85 and older, it is estimated that the number of seniors requiring long-term institutional care will double by 2040 (Magaziner et al., 1998; Schneider & Guralnik, 1990).

Given the rapid growth of the older adult population, there is a great deal of concern among healthcare professionals about the ability of current long-term care facilities to meet the needs of the increasing number of older Americans who will require such services. Moving an elderly loved one to a nursing home is typically a stressful event for family members, and it can be traumatic for older adults who are being relocated to a nursing home, particularly since few older individuals participate in the decision to relocate and many are in poor physical health at the time of relocation (Nussbaum et al., 2004). Once an elderly person is relocated to a nursing home, many face a variety of undesirable conditions.

Currently, many nursing homes and other long-term care facilities for older adults frequently consist of staff members who have limited knowledge of aging issues or who are unprepared to provide comprehensive end-of-life care (Happ et al., 2002). When nursing home residents need treatment for more severe health problems, they are typically hospitalized outside of the nursing home. Unfortunately, nursing home residents often experience poor continuity of care between the nursing home and hospitalization. This lack of continuity of care often stems from the absence of coordination between hospital staff and nursing home staff, and it can lead to unnecessary suffering for older residents. One quarter of nursing home residents with daily pain report receiving no pain treatment (Won, Lapane, Gambassi, et al., 1999), and many experience unwanted interventions and have little control over end-of-life care decision-making (Happ et al., 2002).

There are many reasons for the poor quality of care within many nursing homes. Nursing home personnel are often poorly paid, they receive inadequate training, there is a high rate of staff turnover, and they must cope with very challenging and stressful work conditions. Approximately 40–50 percent of all older residents in long-term care institutions are diagnosed with some form of dementia, with the highest percentage of individuals with dementia over the age of 85 (Magaziner et al., 1998), and this can lead to numerous problems for nursing home staff when interacting with residents and attempting to meet their needs. Between 45 and 58 percent of nursing home residents require assistance to bathe, about 25 percent suffer from urinary incontinence, and a large proportion of individuals spend the majority of their time in bed or in a wheelchair due to physical disabilities (Morgan et al., 1995). Working with residents who have these conditions requires a great deal of patience and understanding, and it can be difficult for many staff members to consistently provide quality care when they feel overloaded, tired, or emotionally drained from working with residents each day.

As regards staff communication with residents within nursing homes and meeting residents' social needs, several researchers have found nursing homes to be poor communication environments (Grainger, 2004; Nussbaum, 1983). Nussbaum (1983) found that residents in nursing homes often experience "interactive starvation" due to limited (and poor-quality) interaction with other residents and staff members. Grainger (2004) found that older adults in nursing homes often suffer from an absence of talk due to environmental barriers to communication within these facilities, such as loud televisions in sitting areas and placement of chairs that inhibit conversations among residents. In addition, residents are rarely given any incentive to talk to other residents because of activities that do not encourage interaction. Nursing home staff members often complain that their busy schedules do not leave much time for conversing with residents. In addition, the heavy use of medications in many nursing homes can impair the communicative abilities of older residents who would otherwise be able to communicate effectively (Nussbaum et al., 2004).

When communication does occur between staff members and residents, it is often task-oriented talk (Grainger, 2004). Task-oriented talk may consist of brief interactions between staff and residents centered around day-to-day physical care tasks that workers must accomplish, such as feeding residents, bathing, changing bedding, and providing medication. Grainger (2004) contends that the majority of talk between workers and residents is to ensure efficient execution of tasks as opposed to more meaningful conversations (e.g., such as talk about life experiences and feelings). Too much talk that is task-oriented can be dehumanizing to residents, especially if staff members treat interactions as tasks to be accomplished as opposed to real conversations.

Task-oriented talk is also related to busy work schedules, which often leave little time for quality interaction with residents, but Grainger maintains that the preponderance of task-oriented talk is also linked to lack of education and/or inadequate training about such issues among nursing home staff. Finally, Grainger argues that much of the communication between nursing home staff and residents consists of dependency-inducing talk. Researchers have found that nursing home staff members frequently engage in patronizing talk, or "baby talk," with older residents (Caporael, 1981; Caporael & Culbertson, 1986). Baby talk with seniors is a form of speech that is almost indistinguishable from speech addressed to young children, and it includes less complex sentence structures, shorter utterances, and more questions (Grainger, 2004). Nursing home residents often engage in interaction with staff members who use baby talk because many are starved of any type of conversation in what is typically an interaction-deficient environment. Caporael and others (e.g., Ryan, Hummert, & Boich, 1995) have argued that baby talk actually induces dependency by undermining an older person's confidence in his or her own abilities to communicate and to perform ordinary tasks over time. In other words, through repeated statements like "Let me move that for you, sweety," older individuals actually learn to become dependent on nursing home staff members, believing that they could not perform the task on their own.

The decision to move an older loved one to a nursing home often leads to an increased financial burden for family members (Nussbaum et al., 2004). Long-term institutional care is quite expensive, and unfortunately the nursing homes that provide the best quality of care are also typically the most expensive. In addition, moving a parent or an aging spouse to a nursing home is a stressful event for family members who often do not have the ability to care for them, and yet they simultaneously do not want to make things worse for their loved ones. Given the number of older individuals who are expected to require long-term care over the next several decades, more education about long-term care and current nursing home problems for family members is needed, as well as more counseling and support.

Summary

Health literacy, breaking bad news to patients, and older adult health communication are among the many important issues associated with health communication research. These contexts of communication will likely continue to be dynamic areas for health communication research in the coming years given our changing perceptions of healthcare and significant demographic changes in the population. Of course, there are many other important areas of health communication that scholars are currently studying. The study of health communication will continue to evolve as new contexts and issues are discovered that influence our health and well-being.

References

Adelman, R. D., & Greene, M. G. (2000). Communication between older patients and their physicians. *Clinics in Geriatric Medicine, 16*(1), 1–24.

Adelman, R. D., Greene, M. G., & Charon, R. (1991). Issues in physician–elderly patient interaction. *Ageing and Society, 2*, 127–148.

Adelman, M. B., Parks, M. R., & Albrecht, T. L. (1987). Beyond close relationships: Support in weak ties. In T. L. Albrecht & M. B. Adelman (Eds.), *Communicating social support* (pp. 126–147). Newbury Park, CA: Sage.

Albrecht, T., Burleson, B., & Goldsmith, D. (1994). Supportive communication. In M. Knapp & G. Miller (Eds.), *Handbook of interpersonal communication* (pp. 419–459). Thousand Oaks, CA: Sage.

Alshidi, A. M., Bener, A., Brebner, J., & Dunn, E. V. (2001). Asthma diagnosis and management in adults: Is the risk of underdiagnosis and undertreatment related to patients' education levels? *Journal of Asthma, 38*, 121–126.

Anderson, J., & Geist-Martin, P. (2003). Narratives and healing: Exploring one family's stories of cancer survivorship. *Health Communication, 15*(2), 133–144.

Anstey, K. J., & Smith, G. A. (1999). Interrelationships among biological markers of aging, health, activity, acculturation, and cognitive performance in older adults. *Psychology and Aging, 14*, 615–618.

Anstey, K. J., Hofer, S. M., & Luszcz, M. A. (2003). Cross-sectional and longitudinal patterns of dedifferentiation in late-life cognitive and sensory function: The effects of age, ability, attrition, and occasion of measurement. *Journal of Experimental Psychology: General, 32*(3), 470–487.

Anstey, K. J., Lord, S. R., & Williams, P. (1997). Strength in the lower limbs, visual contrast sensitivity, and simple reaction time predict cognition in older women. *Psychology and Aging, 12,* 137–144.

Anstey, K. J., Stankov, L., & Lord, S. R. (1993). Primary aging, secondary aging, and intelligence. *Psychology and Aging, 8,* 562–570.

Arenberg, D., & Robertson-Tchabo, E. (1977). Learning and aging. In J. Birren & K. Schaie (Eds.), *Handbook of the psychology of aging* (pp. 721–749). New York: Van Nostrand Reinhold.

Baile, W. F., Buckman, R., Lenzi, R., Glober, G., Beale, E., & Kudelka, A. P. (2000). SPIKES – A six-step protocol for delivering bad news: Application to the patient with cancer. *Oncologist, 5,* 302–311.

Banks, A. T., Zimmerman, H. J., Ishak, K. G., & Harter, J. G. (1995). Diclofenac-associated hepatotoxicity: Analysis of 180 cases reported to the Food and Drug Administration as adverse reactions. *Hepatology, 22*(3), 820–827.

Barnett, M. (2004). A GP guide to breaking bad news. *The Practitioner, 2,* 392–404.

Beisecker, A. E., & Thompson, T. L. (1995). The elderly patient–physician interaction. In J. F. Nussbaum & J. Coupland (Eds.), *The handbook of communication and aging research* (pp. 397–416). Mahwah, NJ: Lawrence Erlbaum.

Berg, S. (1996). Aging, behavior, and terminal decline. In J. E. Birren & K. W. Schaie (Eds.), *Handbook of the psychology of aging* (4th ed., pp. 323–337). San Diego, CA: Academic Press.

Berkman, L., & Syme, S. (1979). Social networks, host resistance, and mortality. *American Journal of Epidemiology, 109,* 186–204.

Birren, J. E., & Cunningham, W. (1985). Research on the psychology of aging: Principles, concepts, and theory. In J. E. Birren & W. Schaie (Eds.), *Handbook of the psychology of aging* (2nd ed., pp. 3–34). New York: Van Nostrand Reinhold.

Birren, J. E., Woods, A., & Williams, M. (1980). Behavioral slowing with age: Causes, organization, and consequences. In L. Poon (Ed.), *Aging in the 1980's* (pp. 293–308). Washington, DC: American Psychological Association.

Blanchard, C. G., Labrecque, M. S., Ruckdeschel, J. C., & Blanchard, E. B. (1988). Information and decision-making preferences of hospitalized adult cancer patients. *Social Science Medicine, 27,* 1139–1145.

Blanchard-Fields, F., & Abeles, R. (1996). Social cognition and aging. In J. E. Birren & K. W. Schaie (Eds.), *Handbook of the psychology of aging* (4th ed., pp. 150–161). San Diego, CA: Academic Press.

Booth-Butterfield, M. (2003). Embedded health behaviors from adolescence to adulthood: The impact of tobacco. *Health Communication, 15*(2), 171–185.

Bor, R., Miller, R., Goldman, E., & Scher, I. (1993). The meaning of bad news in HIV disease: Counseling about dreaded issues revisited. *Counsel Psychological Quarterly, 6,* 69–80.

Botwinick, J. (1973). *Aging and behavior.* New York: Springer.

Botwinick, J. (1977). Intellectual abilities. In J. Birren & K. Schaie (Eds.), *Handbook of the psychology of aging* (pp. 580–605). New York: Van Nostrand Reinhold.

Botwinick, J. (1978). *Aging and behavior* (2nd ed.). New York: Springer.

Botwinick, J., & Storandt, M. (1974). *Memory-related functions and age.* Springfield, IL: Thomas.

Buckman, R. (1996). Talking to patients about cancer. *British Medical Journal, 31,* 699–700.

Burns, E. A. (2002). Commentary: Challenges to using exercise interventions in older adults. In K. W. Schaie, H. Leventhal, & S. L. Willis (Eds.), *Effective health behavior in older adults* (pp. 179–189). New York: Springer.

Busse, E. (1969). Theories of aging. In E. Busse & E. Pfeiffer (Eds.), *Behavior and adaptation in later life* (pp. 11–32). Boston: Little, Brown.

Byock, I. (2000). Completing the continuum of cancer care: Integrating life-prolongation and palliation. *CA: A Cancer Journal for Clinicians, 50,* 123–132.

Caporael, L. R. (1981). The paralanguage of caregiving: Baby talk to the institutionalized aged. *Journal of Personality and Social Psychology, 40,* 876–884.

Caporael, L. R., & Culbertson, G. H. (1986). Verbal response modes of baby talk and other speech at institutions for the aged. *Language and Communication, 6,* 99–112.

Carstensen, L. L. (1992). Social and emotional patterns in adulthood: Support for socioemotional selectivity theory. *Psychology and Aging, 7,* 331–338.

Cegala, D. J., & Lenzimeir Broz, S. (2003). Provider and patient communication skills training. In T. L. Thompson, A. M. Dorsey, K. I. Miller, & R. Parrott (Eds.), *Handbook of health communication* (pp. 95–119). Mahwah, NJ: Lawrence Erlbaum.

Center for Disease Control (CDC). (1996). *Physical activity and health: A report of the Surgeon General.* Hyattsville, MD: US Public Health Service.

Chase, W., & Simon, H. (1973). The mind's eye in chess. In W. G. Chase (Ed.), *Visual information processing* (pp. 215–281). New York: Academic Press.

Coe, R. M. (1987). Communication and medical care outcomes: Analysis of conversations between doctors and elderly patients. In R. A. Ward & S. S. Tobin (Eds.), *Health in aging* (pp. 180–193). New York: Springer.

Cohen, G. (1979). Language comprehension in old age. *Cognitive Psychology, 11,* 423–429.

Cohen, G. (1994). Age-related problems in the use of proper names in communication. In M. L. Hummert, J. M. Wiemann, & J. F. Nussbaum (Eds.), *Interpersonal communication in older adulthood: Interdisciplinary theory and research* (pp. 40–57). Thousand Oaks, CA: Sage.

Colley, C. E., & Lucas, L. M. (1993). Polypharmacy: The cure becomes the disease. *Journal of General Internal Medicine, 8,* 278–283.

Corso, J. (1971). Sensory processes and age effects in normal adults. *Journal of Gerontology, 26,* 90–105.

Coupland, N., Coupland, J., Giles, H., & Henwood, K. (1988). Accommodating the elderly: Invoking and extending the theory. *Language in Society, 17,* 1–41.

Craik, F. (1977). Age differences in human memory. In J. Birren & K. W. Schaie (Eds.), *Handbook of the psychology of aging* (pp. 384–420). New York: Van Nostrand Reinhold.

Craik, F., & Rabinowitz, J. (1985). The effects of presentation rate and encoding task on age-related memory deficits. *Journal of Gerontology, 40,* 309–315.

Crystal, S. (2002). Commentary: Health care organizational structure, prevention, and health behavior among the elderly. In K. W. Schaie, H. Leventhal, & S. L. Willis (Eds.), *Effective health behavior in older adults* (pp. 287–299). New York: Springer.

Cutrona, C., & Russell, D. (1990). Type of social support and specific stress: Toward a theory of optimal matching. In B. Sarason, I. Sarason, & G. Pierce (Eds.), *Social support: An interactional view* (pp. 319–366). New York: John Wiley.

Darbyshire, J. (1984). The hearing loss epidemic: A challenge to gerontology. *Research on Aging, 6*, 384–394.

Davis, H. (1991). Breaking bad news. *Practitioner, 235*, 522–526.

Davis, T. C., Williams, M. V., Marin, E., Parker, R. M., & Glass, J. (2002). Health literacy and communication. *CA: A Cancer Journal for Clinicians, 52*, 134–149.

Dearing, J. W., Rogers, E. M., Meyer, G., Casey, M. K., Rao, N., Campo, S., & Henderson, G. M. (1996). Social marketing and diffusion-based strategies for communicating health with unique populations: HIV prevention in San Francisco. *Journal of Health Communication, 1*, 343–363.

Duran-Tauleria, E., & Rona, R. J. (1999). Geographical and socioeconomic variation in the prevalence of asthma symptoms in English and Scottish children. *Thorax, 54*, 476–481.

Edwards, B. K., Howe, H. L., Ries, L. A. G., Thun, M. J., Rosenberg, H. M., Yancik, R., Wingo, P. A., Jemal, A., & Feigal, E. G. (2002). Annual report to the nation on the status of cancer, 1973–1999, featuring implications of age and aging on the US cancer burden. *Cancer, 94*(10), 2766–2792.

Egbert, N., Kreps, G. L., Sparks, L., & du Pré, A. (in press). Finding meaning in the journey: Methods of spiritual coping for aging cancer patients. In L. Sparks, H. D. O'Hair, & G. L. Kreps (Eds.), *Cancer communication and aging*. Cresskill, NJ: Hampton Press.

Eggly, S., & Tzelepis, A. (2001). Relational control in difficult physician–patient encounters: Negotiating treatment for pain. *Journal of Health Communication, 6*, 323–333.

Eisdorfer, C., & Cohen, D. (1980). The issue of biological and psychological deficits. In E. Borgatta & N. McCluskey (Eds.), *Aging and society: Current research and policy perspectives* (pp. 49–70). Beverly Hills, CA: Sage.

Elias, M. F., & Elias, P. K. (1977). Motivation and activity. In J. Birren & K. W. Schaie (Eds.), *Handbook of the psychology of aging* (pp. 357–383). New York: Van Nostrand Reinhold.

Ernst, R. L., & Hay, J. W. (1994). The US economic and social costs of Alzheimer's disease revisited. *American Journal of Public Health, 84*, 1261–1264.

Eva, K. W. (2002). The aging physician: Changes in cognitive processing and their impact on medical practice. *Academic Medicine, 77*, S1–S6.

Federal Interagency Forum on Aging-Related Statistics. (2000a). Older Americans 2000: Key indicators of well-being [On-line]. Retrieved August 25, 2004, from www.agingstats.gov/chartbook2000/default.htm.

Federal Interagency Forum on Aging-Related Statistics. (2000b). Older Americans 2000: Key indicators of well-being [On-line]. Retrieved August 25, 2004, from www.agingstats.gov/chartbook2000/healthstatus.html.

Festinger, L. (1954). A theory of social comparison processes. *Human Relations*, 7(1), 152–163.

Franks, P., & Bertakis, K. D. (2003). Physician gender, patient gender, and primary care. *Journal of Women's Health*, *12*, 73–80.

Gabrel, C. S. (2000). *Characteristics of elderly nursing home residents and discharges: Data from the 1997 National Nursing Home Survey*. Washington, DC: US Department of Health and Human Services, Centers for Disease Control and Prevention.

Gallois, C., Franklyn-Stokes, A., Giles, H., & Coupland, N. (1988). Communication accommodation theory and intercultural encounters: Intergroup and interpersonal considerations. In Y. Y. Kim & W. B. Gudykunst (Eds.), *Theories in intercultural communication* (pp. 157–185). Newbury Park, CA: Sage.

Gallois, C., Ogay, T., & Giles, H. (2004). Communication accommodation theory: A look back and a look ahead. In W. Gudykunst (Ed.), *Theorizing about intercultural communication* (pp. 121–148). Thousand Oaks, CA: Sage.

Gatz, M., Kasl-Godley, J. E., & Karel, M. J. (1996). Aging and mental disorders. In J. E. Birren & K. W. Schaie (Eds.), *Handbook of psychology and aging* (4th ed., pp. 365–382). San Diego, CA: Academic Press.

Gergen, P. (1996). Social class and asthma, distinguishing between the disease and the diagnosis. *International Journal of Epidemiology*, *25*, 388–393.

Ghandi, T. K., Burstin, H. R., Cook, E. F., et al. (2000). Drug complications in outpatients. *Journal of General Internal Medicine*, *15*, 149–154.

Giles, H. (1973). Communication effectiveness as a function of accented speech. *Speech Monographs*, 40, 330–331.

Giles, H., Coupland, N., & Coupland, J. (1991). Accommodation theory: Communication, context, and consequence. In H. Giles, J. Coupland, & N. Coupland (Eds.), *Contexts of accommodation: Developments in applied sociolinguistics* (pp. 1–68). Cambridge: Cambridge University Press.

Giles, H., Mulac, A., Bradac, J. J., & Johnson, P. (1987). Speech accommodation theory: The first decade and beyond. In M. L. McLaughlin (Ed.), *Communication yearbook 10* (pp. 13–48). Beverly Hills, CA: Sage.

Gillotti, C. M., & Applegate, J. L. (1999). Explaining illness as bad news: Individual differences in explaining illness-related information. In B. B. Whaley (Ed.), *Explaining illness: Research, theory, and strategies* (pp. 101–120). Mahwah, NJ: Lawrence Erlbaum.

Gillotti, C. M., Thompson, T., & McNeilis, K. (2002). Communicative competence in the delivery of bad news. *Social Science and Medicine*, *54*, 1011–1023.

Gjerberg, E. (2002).Gender differences in doctors' preference – and gender differences in final specialization. *Social Science Medicine*, *54*, 591–605.

Grainger, K. (2004). Communication and the institutionalized elderly. In J. F. Nussbaum & J. Coupland (Eds.), *Handbook of communication and aging research* (2nd ed., pp. 479–497). Mahwah, NJ: Lawrence Erlbaum.

Greene, M. G., & Adelman, R. D. (2001). Building the physician–older patient relationship. In M. L. Hummert & J. F. Nussbaum (Eds.), *Aging, communication, and health: Linking research and practice for successful aging* (pp. 101–120). Mahwah, NJ: Lawrence Erlbaum.

Greene, M., & Adelman, R. (2002, January). Physician–older adult patient communication about cancer. In G. L. Kreps (Chair), Consumer–Provider Communication Symposium, Bethesda, MD.

Greene, M. G., Adelman, R., Charon, R., & Hoffman, S. (1989). Concordance between physicians and their older and younger patients in the primary care medical encounter. *Gerontologist, 29*, 808–813.

Greenfield, S., Kaplan, S., & Ware, J. E. (1985). Expanding patient involvement in care: Effects on patient outcomes. *Annals of Internal Medicine, 102*, 520–528.

Hanley-Dunn, P., & McIntosh, J. (1984). Meaningfulness and recall of names by young and old adults. *Journal of Gerontology, 39*, 583–585.

Hanlon, J. T., Schmader, K. E., Koronkowski, M. J., et al. (1997). Adverse drug events in high-risk older patients. *Journal of the American Geriatric Society, 145*, 945–948.

Happ, M., Capezuti, E., Strumpf, N., Wagner, L., Cunningham, S., Evans, L., & Maislin, G. (2002). Advance care planning and end-of-life care for hospitalized nursing home residents. *Journal of the American Geriatrics Society, 50*, 829–835.

Harwood, J., & Sparks, L. (2003). Social identity and health: An intergroup communication approach to cancer. *Health Communication, 15*, 145–170.

Harzold, E., & Sparks, L. (2007). Adult child perceptions of communication and humor when the parent is diagnosed with cancer: A suggestive perspective from communication theory. *Qualitative Research Reports in Communication, 7*, 1–13.

Haug, M. R., & Ory, M. G. (1987). Issues in elderly patient–provider relations. *Research on Aging, 9*, 3–44.

Hebert, L. E., Scherr, P. A., Bienias, J. L., Bennett, D. A., & Evans, D. A. (2003). Alzheimer's disease in the US population: Prevalence estimates using the 2000 Census. *Archives of Neurology, 60*, 1119–1122.

Hewitt, M., Rowland, J., & Yancik, R. (2003). Cancer survivors in the United States: Age, health, and disability. *Journals of Gerontology, Series A, 58*(1), 82–92.

Hiatt, R. A., & Rimer, B. K. (1999). A new strategy for cancer control research. *Cancer Epidemiology, Biomarkers, and Prevention, 8*, 957–964.

Hopper, S. V., & Fischbach, R. L. (1989). Patient–physician communication when blindness threatens. *Patient Education Counsel, 14*, 69–79.

Horn, J. L., & Donaldson, G. (1980). Cognitive development in adulthood. In O. G. Brim, Jr., & J. Kagen (Eds.), *Constancy and change in human development* (pp. 445–529). Cambridge, MA: Harvard University Press.

Hoy, A. M. (1985). Breaking bad news to patients. *British Journal of Hospital Medicine, 34*, 96–99.

Hummert, M. L., Shaner, J. L., & Garstka, T. A. (1995). Cognitive processes affecting communication with older adults: The case for stereotypes, attitudes, and beliefs about communication. In J. F. Nussbaum & J. Coupland (Eds.), *Handbook of communication and aging research* (pp. 105–131). Mahwah, NJ: Lawrence Erlbaum.

Hummert, M. L., Shaner, J. L., Garstka, T. A., & Henry, C. (1998). Communication with older adults: The influence of age stereotypes, context, and communicator age. *Human Communication Research, 25*(1), 124–142.

Hutchinson, J., & Beasley, D. (1981). Speech and language functioning among the aging. In H. Oyer & E. Oyer (Eds.), *Aging and communication* (pp. 155–174). Baltimore: University Park Press.

Ishikawa, H., Roter, D. L., Yamazaki, Y., & Takayama, T. (2005). Physician–elderly patient–companion communication and the roles of companions in geriatric encounters. *Social Science Medicine, 60,* 2307–2320.

Jackson, L. D., & Duffy, B. K. (Eds.). (1998). Health communication research. Westport, CT: Greenwood.

Jarvik, L., & Bank, L. (1983). Aging twins: Longitudinal psychometric data. In K. Schaie (Ed.), *Longitudinal studies of adult psychological development* (pp. 40–63). New York: Guilford.

Johnson, R. L., Roter, D., Powe, N. R., & Cooper, L. A. (2004). Patient race/ ethnicity and quality of patient–physician communication during medical visits. *Journal of General Internal Medicine, 19,* 101–110.

Kahneman, D., & Tversky, A. (1979). "Prospect theory": An analysis of decision under risk. *Econometrica, 47,* 263–291.

Kemper, S. (1992). Language and aging. In F. M. Craik & T. Salthouse (Eds.), *Handbook of aging and cognition* (pp. 213–270). Hillsdale, NJ: Lawrence Erlbaum.

Kemper, S., & Lyons, K. (1994). The effects of Alzheimer's dementia on language and communication. In M. L. Hummert, J. M. Weimann, & J. F. Nussbaum (Eds.), *Interpersonal communication in older adulthood: Interdisciplinary theory and research* (pp. 58–82). Thousand Oaks, CA: Sage.

Kleemeier, R. (1962). Intellectual changes in the senium. *Proceedings of the Social Statistics Section of the American Statistics Association, 1,* 290–295.

Kline, D. W., & Scialfa, C. T. (1996). Visual and auditory aging. In J. E. Birren & K. W. Schaie (Eds.), *Handbook of the psychology of aging* (4th ed., pp. 181–203). San Diego, CA: Academic Press.

Kreps, G. L. (1988a). Relational communication in health care. *Southern Speech Communication Journal, 53,* 344–359.

Kreps, G. L. (1988b). The pervasive role of information in health and health care: Implications for health communication policy. In J. Anderson (Ed.), *Communication yearbook* (Vol. 11, pp. 238–276). Newbury Park, CA: Sage.

Kreps, G. L. (2003). Impact of communication on cancer risk, incidence, morbidity, and quality of life [Special issue]. *Health Communication, 15*(2), 163–170.

Kreps, G. L., & Chapelsky Massimilla, D. (in press). Cancer communications research and health outcomes: Review and challenge. *Communication Studies.*

Kreps, G. L., & O'Hair, D. (Eds.). (1995). *Communication and health outcomes.* Cresskill, NJ: Hampton Press.

Kreps, G. L., & Viswanath, K. (2001). Communication interventions and cancer control: A review of the National Cancer Institute's health communication intervention research initiative. *Family and Community Health, 24*(3), ix–xiv.

Kundrat, A., & Nussbaum, J. F. (2003). The impact of invisible illness on identity and contextual age across the life span. *Health Communication, 15*(3).

Lapinski, M. K., & Levine, T. R. (2000). Culture and manipulation theory: The effects of self-construal and locus of benefit on information manipulation. *Communication Studies, 51*(1), 55–73.

Larson, E. B., & Bruce, R. A. (1997). Exercise. In C. K. Cassel, H. J. Cohen, E. B. Larson, D. E. Meier, N. M. Resnick, L. Z. Rubenstein, & L. B. Sorenson (Eds.), *Geriatric medicine* (3rd ed., pp. 815–821). New York: Springer.

Lewis, J., Ng, K., Hung, K. E., Bilker, W. B., Berlin, J. A., Brensinger, C., & Rustgi, A. K. (2003). Detection of proximal adenomatous polyps with screening sigmoidoscopy: A systematic review and meta-analysis of screening colonoscopy. *Archives of Internal Medicine*, *163*(4), 413–421.

Li, S.-C. (2002). Connecting the many levels and facets of cognitive aging. *Trends in Cognitive Neuroscience*, *11*, 38–43.

Li, S.-C., & Lindenberger, U. (1999). Cross-level unification: A computational exploration of the link between deterioration of neurotransmitter systems and dedifferentiation of cognitive abilities in old age. In L.-G. Nilsson & H. Markowitsch (Eds.), *Cognitive neuroscience and memory* (pp. 103–146). Toronto: Hogrefe & Huber.

McFarland, R. (1968). The sensory and perceptual processes in aging. In K. Schaie (Ed.), *Theory and methods in research on aging* (pp. 9–52). Morgantown, WV: West Virginia University Press.

MacKay, D. G., & Abrams, L. (1996). Language, memory, and aging: Distributed deficits and the structure of new-versus-old connections. In J. E. Birren & K. W. Schaie (Eds.), *Handbook of the psychology of aging* (4th ed., pp. 251–265). San Diego, CA: Academic Press.

Magaziner, J., Zimmerman, S. I., Fox, K. M., & Burns, B. J. (1998). Dementia in United States nursing homes: Descriptive epidemiology and implications for long-term residential care. *Aging and Mental Health*, *2*, 28–35.

Maibach, E. W., Kreps, G. L., & Bonaguro, E. W. (1996). Developing strategic communication campaigns for HIV/AIDS prevention. In S. Ratzan (Ed.), *AIDS: Effective communication for the 90s* (pp. 15–35). Washington, DC: Taylor & Francis.

Mast, M. S., Kindlimann, A., & Langewitz, W. (2005). Recipients' perspective on breaking bad news: How you put it really makes a difference. *Patient Education and Counseling*, *58*, 244–251.

Maynard, D. W. (1991). Bearing bad news in clinical settings. In B. Dervin & M. J. Voigt (Eds.), *Progress in communication sciences* (Vol. 10, pp. 143–172). Norwood, NJ: Ablex.

Merriman, B., Ades, T., & Seffrin, J. R. (2002). Health literacy in the information age: Communicating cancer information to patients and families. *CA: A Cancer Journal for Clinicians*, *52*, 130–133.

Meyerowitz, B. E., & Chaiken, S. (1987). The effect of message framing on breast self-examination attitudes, intentions, and behaviors. *Journal of Personality and Social Psychology*, *52*(3), 500–511.

Mitchell, E. A., Stewart, A. W., Pattenmore, P. K., & Asher, M. I. (1989). Socioeconomic status in childhood asthma. *International Journal of Epidemiology*, *18*, 888–890.

Mitchell, M. M. (2000). Motivated, but not able? The effects of positive and negative mood on persuasive message processing. *Communication Monographs*, *67*, 215–225.

Mitchell, M. M., Brown, K. M., Morris Villagran, M., & Villagran, P. D. (2001). The effects of anger, sadness and happiness on persuasive message processing: A test of the negative state relief model. *Communication Monographs*, *68*, 347–359.

Monge, R. (1969). Learning in adult years set or rigidity. *Human Development*, *12*, 131–140.

Morgan, L. A., et al. (Eds.). (1995). *Small board-and-care homes: Residential care in transition.* Baltimore and London: Johns Hopkins University Press.

Mosqueda, L., & Burnight, K. (2000). Multidimensional assessment in the ambulatory clinic. In D. Osterweil, K. Brummel-Smith, & J. C. Beck (Eds.), *Comprehensive geriatric assessment* (pp. 187–202). New York: McGraw-Hill.

Mueller, P. S. (2002). Breaking bad news to patients. *Postgraduate Medicine, 112,* 3–18.

National Center for Health Statistics. (2000). *Health, United States, 2000.* Hyattsville, MD: US Department of Health and Human Services.

Ng, S., Liu, J., Weatherall, A., & Loong, C. (1997). Younger adults' communication experiences and contact with elders and peers. *Human Communication Research, 24*(1), 82–107.

Nussbaum, J. F. (1983). Relational closeness of elderly interaction: Implications for life satisfaction. *Western Journal of Speech, 47,* 229–243.

Nussbaum, J. F., Baringer, D., & Kundrat, A. (2003). Health, communication, and aging: Cancer and the older adult [Special issue]. *Health Communication, 15*(2), 185–194.

Nussbaum, J. F., Pecchioni, L., Robinson, J. D., & Thompson, T. (2000). *Communication and aging* (2nd ed.). Mahwah, NJ: Lawrence Erlbaum.

Nussbaum, J. F., Ragan, R., & Whaley, B. (2004). Children, older adults, and women: Impact on provider–patient interaction. In T. L. Thompson, A. M. Dorsey, K. I. Miller, & R. Parrott (Eds.), *Handbook of health communication* (pp. 183–204). Mahwah, NJ: Lawrence Erlbaum.

Nussbaum, J. F., Robinson, J. D., & Grew, D. (1983, May). *Nursing staff–resident communication within the long-term health care facility.* Paper presented at the International Communication Association, Dallas, TX.

Nussbaum, J. F., Robinson, J. D., & Grew, D. (1985). Communicative behavior of the long-term health care employee: Implications for the elderly resident. *Communication Research Reports, 2,* 16–22.

O'Hair, H. D., Kreps, G. L., & Sparks, L. (in press). Conceptualizing cancer care and communication. In H. D. O'Hair, G. L. Kreps, & L. Sparks (Eds.), *Handbook of communication and cancer care.* Cresskill, NJ: Hampton Press.

O'Hair, H. D., Villagran, M. M., Wittenberg, E., Brown, K., Ferguson, M., Hall, H. T., & Doty, T. (2003). Cancer survivorship and agency model (CSAM): Implications for patient choice, decision-making, and influence [Special issue]. *Health Communication, 15*(2), 195–202.

Okun, M. (1976). Adult age and cautiousness in decision. *Human Development, 19,* 220–233.

Ong, L., Visser, M., Kruyver, I., Bensing, J. M., Brink-Muinen, A., Stouthard, J., Lammes, F., & de Haes, J. (1998). The Roter Interaction Analysis System (RIAS) in oncological consultations: Psychometric properties. *Psycho-oncology, 7,* 387–401.

Parks, M., & Floyd, K. (1996). Making friends in cyberspace. *Journal of Communication, 46*(1), 80–97.

Pecchioni, L., & Sparks, L. (2002). *Health information sources of individuals with cancer and their family members.* A paper presented to the Health Communication Division of the Eastern Communication Association, New York.

Pecchioni, L., & Sparks, L. (in press). Health information sources of individuals with cancer and their family members. *Health Communication*.

Pecchioni, L., Krieger, J. C., Sparks, L., Pitts, M., & Ota, H. (in press). Investigating cancer and ageing from a cultural perspective. In L. Sparks, H. D. O'Hair, & G. L. Kreps (Eds.), *Cancer communication and aging*. Cresskill, NJ: Hampton Press.

Pecchioni, L., Ota, H., & Sparks, L. (2004). Cultural issues in communication and aging. In J. F. Nussbaum & J. Coupland (Eds.), *Handbook of communication and aging research* (2nd ed., pp. 167–207). Mahwah, NJ: Lawrence Erlbaum.

Ptacek, J. T., & Eberhardt, T. L. (1996). Breaking bad news: A review of literature. *JAMA, 276*, 496–502.

Ptacek, J. T., & Ellison, N. M. (2000). Health care providers' perspectives on breaking bad news to patients. *Critical Care Nursing Quarterly, 23*, 51–59.

Query, J. L., Jr., & Kreps, G. L. (1996). Testing a relational model for health communication competence among caregivers for individuals with Alzheimer's disease. *Journal of Health Psychology, 3*, 335–351.

Query, J., & Wright, K. (2003). Assessing communication competence in an online study: Towards informing subsequent interventions among older adults with cancer, their lay caregivers and peers [Special issue]. *Health Communication, 15*(2), 203–218.

Ragan, S., Wittenberg, E., & Hall, H. T. (2003). The communication of palliative care for the elderly cancer patient [Special issue]. *Health Communication, 15*(2), 219–228.

Rice, D. P., et al. (1993). The economic burden of Alzheimer's disease. *Health Affairs, 12*, 164–176.

Robinson, J. D., & Turner, J. (2003). Interpersonal and hyperpersonal social support: Cancer and the elderly adult [Special issue]. *Health Communication, 15*(2), 229–238.

Rost, K., & Frankel, R. (1993). The introduction of the older patient's problems in the medical visit. *Journal of Health and Aging, 5*, 387–401.

Rothman, A. J., Salovey, P., Antone, C., Keough, K., & Martin, C. D. (1993). The influence of message framing on intentions to perform health behaviors. *Journal of Experimental Social Psychology, 29*(5), 408.

Rowan, K., Sparks, L., Pecchioni, L., & Villagran, M. (2003). The CAUSE model: A research supported aid for physicians communicating about cancer risk. *Health Communication, 15*(2), 239–252.

Rubin, A. M., & Rubin, R. B. (1981). Age, context and television use. *Journal of Broadcasting, 25*, 1–13.

Rubin, A. M., & Rubin, R. B. (1986). Contextual age as a life-position index. *International Journal of Aging and Human Development, 23*, 27–45.

Rubin, H. J., & Rubin, I. S. (1995). *Qualitative interviewing: The art of hearing data.* Thousand Oaks, CA: Sage.

Ryan, E. B., Hummert, M. L., & Boich, L. (1995). Communication predicaments of aging: Patronizing behavior towards older adults. *Journal of Language and Social Psychology, 14*, 144–166.

Salthouse, T. A. (1992). *Mechanisms of age–cognition relations in adulthood.* Hillsdale, NJ: Lawrence Erlbaum.

Schaie, K. (1975). Age changes in adult intelligence. In D. Woodruff & J. Birren (Eds.), *Aging* (pp. 111–124). New York: Van Nostrand.

Schaie, K. (1983). The Seattle longitudinal study: A 21-year exploration of psychometric intelligence in adulthood. In K. Schaie (Ed.), *Longitudinal studies of adult psychological development* (pp. 64–135). New York: Guilford.

Schaie, K. (1996). Intellectual development in adulthood. In J. E. Birren & K. W. Schaie (Eds.), *Handbook of the psychology of aging* (4th ed., pp. 266–286). San Diego, CA: Academic Press.

Schneider, E. L., & Guralnik, J. M. (1990). The aging of America: Impact on health care costs. *Journal of the American Medical Association, 263*, 2335–2340.

Seale, C. (1991). Communication and awareness about death: A study of a random sample of dying people. *Social Science Medicine, 32*, 943–952.

Shepard, C. A., Giles, H., & Le Poire, B. A. (2001). Communication accommodation theory. In W. P. Robinson & H. Giles (Eds.), *The new handbook of language and social psychology* (2nd ed.). Chichester: John Wiley.

Sleath, B., Rubin, R. H., & Huston, S. A. (2003). Hispanic ethnicity, physician–patient communication, and antidepressant adherence. *Comprehensive Psychiatry, 44*, 198–204.

Smith, B. (1996). Memory. In J. E. Birren & K. W. Schaie (Eds.), *Handbook of the psychology of aging* (4th ed., pp. 236–250). San Diego, CA: Academic Press.

Smith, B., Thompson, L., & Michalewski, H. (1980). Average evoked potential research in adult aging: Status and prospects. In L. Poon (Ed.), *Aging in the 1980's* (pp. 135–151). Washington, DC: American Psychological Association.

Sparks, L. (Ed.). (2003a). Cancer communication and aging [Special issue]. *Health Communication, 15*(2).

Sparks, L. (2003b). An introduction to cancer communication and aging: Theoretical and research insights. *Health Communication, 15*, 123–132.

Sparks, L. (2007). Cancer care and the aging patient: Complexities of age-related communication barriers. In H. D. O'Hair, G. L. Kreps, & L. Sparks (Eds.), *Handbook of communication and cancer care* (pp. 233–249). Cresskill, NJ: Hampton Press.

Sparks, L. (in press). The SMILE health care communication model (SMILE-HCCM): An interpersonal theory-based approach to message framing in health care interventions. In S. S. Travis & R. Talley (Eds.), *Caregiving across the professions*. Oxford: Oxford University Press. Project supported by a grant from Johnson and Johnson and the Rosalynn Carter Institute for Human Development.

Sparks, L., & Harwood, J. (in press). Cancer, aging, and social identity: Development of an integrated model of social identity theory and health communication. In L. Sparks, H. D. O'Hair, & G. L. Kreps, (Eds.), *Cancer communication and aging*. Cresskill, NJ: Hampton Press.

Sparks, L., & McPherson, J. (in press). Cross-cultural differences in choices of health information by older cancer patients and their family caregivers. In K. Wright & S. D. Moore (Eds.), *Applications in health communication* (pp. 179–205). Cresskill, NJ: Hampton Press.

Sparks, L., & Mittapalli, K. (2004). To know or not to know: The case of communication by and with older adult Russians diagnosed with cancer. *Journal of Cross Cultural Gerontology, 19*, 383–403.

Sparks, L., & Turner, M. M. (in press). Cognitive and emotional processing of cancer messages and information seeking with older adults. In L. Sparks, H. D. O'Hair, & G. L. Kreps (Eds.), *Cancer communication and aging*. Cresskill, NJ: Hampton Press.

Sparks, L., O'Hair, H. D., & Kreps, G. L. (in press). Conceptualizing cancer communication and aging: New directions for research. In L. Sparks, H. D. O'Hair, & G. L. Kreps (Eds.), *Cancer communication and aging*. Cresskill, NJ: Hampton Press.

Sparks, L., Villagran, M. M., Parker-Raley, J., & Cunningham, C. B. (in press). A patient-centered approach to breaking bad news: Communication guidelines for healthcare professionals. *Journal of Applied Communication Research*.

Sparks-Bethea, L., & Balazs, A. (1997). Improving intergenerational healthcare communication. *Journal of Health Communication, 2*, 129–137.

Sparks-Bethea, L., Travis, S. S., & Pecchioni, L. L. (2000). Family caregivers' use of humor in conveying information about caring for dependent older adults. *Health Communication, 12*, 361–376. Project supported by a grant from the Nursing Research Program, Clinical Applications Research, Glaxo-Wellcome, Inc.

Stahl, S. M., & Feller, J. R. (1990). Old equals sick: An ontogenetic fallacy. In S. M. Stahl (Ed.), *The legacy of longevity: Health and health care in later life* (pp. 21–34). Newbury Park, CA: Sage.

Street, R. L. (1982). Evaluation of non-content speech accommodation. *Language and Communication, 2*, 13–31.

Street, R. L. (1991). Information-giving in medical consultations: The influence of patients' communicative styles and personal characteristics. *Social Science and Medicine, 32*(5), 541–548.

Stuart, B. (2002). How provider payment policies affect the health-care-seeking behavior of the elderly. In K. W. Schaie, H. Leventhal, & S. L. Willis (Eds.), *Effective health behavior in older adults* (pp. 191–228). New York: Springer.

Sung, C. L. (1999). Asian patients' distrust of western medical care: One perspective. *Mount Sinai Journal of Medicine, 66*, 259–320.

Takeda, S., & Matsuzawa, T. (1985). Age-related brain atrophy: A study with computer tomography. *Journal of Gerontology, 40*, 159–163.

Thom, D. H. (2001). Physician behaviors that predict patient trust. *Journal of Family Practice, 50*, 323–328.

Thompson, T. L. (1994). Interpersonal communication and health care. In M. L. Knapp & G. R. Miller (Eds.), *Handbook of interpersonal communication* (pp. 696–725). Newbury Park, CA: Sage.

Thompson, T. L., Robinson, J. D., & Beisecker, A. E. (2004). The older patient–physician interaction. In J. F. Nussbaum & J. Coupland (Eds.), *Handbook of communication and aging research* (2nd ed., pp. 451–477). Mahwah, NJ: Lawrence Erlbaum.

Travis, S. S., & Sparks-Bethea, L. (2001). Medication administration by family members of dependent elders in shared care arrangements. *Journal of Clinical Geropsychology, 7*(3), 231–243. Project supported by a grant from the Nursing Research Program, Clinical Applications Research, Glaxo-Wellcome, Inc.

Travis, S., Sparks-Bethea, L., & Winn, P. (2000). Medication hassles reported by family caregivers of dependent elders. *Journals of Gerontology: Medical Sciences, 55A*, 7, M412–M417. Project supported by a grant from the Nursing Research Program, Clinical Applications Research, Glaxo-Wellcome, Inc.

Turner, J. W., Grube, J., & Meyers, J. (2001). Developing an optimal match within online communities: An exploration of CMC support communities and traditional support. *Journal of Communication, 51*(2), 231–251.

Ungar, L., Alperin, M., Amiel, G. E., Beharier, Z., & Reis, S. (2002). Breaking bad news: Structured training for family medicine residents. *Patient Education and Counseling, 48*, 63–68.

US Census Bureau. (2000). Keeping up with older adults: Older adults 2000 [On-line]. Retrieved August 25, 2004, from www.census.gov/population/pop-profile/2000/chap18.pdf.

Vanderkieft, G. K. (2001). Breaking bad news. *American Family Physician, 64*, 1975–1978.

Verbrugge, L. (1984). A health profile of older women with comparisons to older men. *Research on Aging, 6*, 291–322.

Villaume, W. A., Brown, M. H., & Darling, R. (1994). Presbycusis, communication, and older adults. In M. L. Hummert, J. M. Wiemann, & J. F. Nussbaum (Eds.), *Interpersonal communication in older adulthood.* Thousand Oaks, CA: Sage.

Villaume, W. A., Darling, R., Brown, M. H., Richardson, D., & Clark-Lewis, S. (1993). The multidimensionality of presbycusis: Hearing losses on the content and relational dimensions of speech. *Journal of the International Listening Association, 7*, 111–128.

Waitzkin, H. (1985). Information giving in medical care. *Journal of Health and Social Behavior, 26*, 81–101.

Wakefield, A., Cooke, S., & Boggis, C. (2003). Learning together: Use of simulated patients with nursing and medical students for breaking bad news. *International Journal of Palliative Nursing, 9*, 32–38.

Walther, J. B., & Boyd, S. (in press). Attraction to computer-mediated social support. In C. A. Lin & D. Atkin (Eds.), *Communication technology and society: Audience adoption and uses of the new media.* New York: Hampton Press.

Wanzer, M., Sparks, L., & Frymier, A. B. (forthcoming). The function of communication within the lives of older adults: An exploration of the relationships among humor, coping efficacy, age, and life satisfaction.

Wasson, J. H., Sauvigne, A. E., Mogielmicki, R. P., Frey, W. G., Sox, C. H., Gaudette, C., & Rockwell, A. (1984). Continuity of outpatient medical care in elderly men: A randomized trial. *Journal of the American Medical Association, 252*, 2413–2417.

Watson, B., & Gallois, C. (1998). Nurturing communication by health professionals toward patients: A communication accommodation approach. *Health Communication, 10*, 343–355.

Weiss, L., & Blustein, J. (1996). Faithful patients: The effect of long-term physician–patient relationships on the costs and use of health care by older Americans. *American Journal of Public Health, 86*, 1742–1747.

Wellman, B., & Gulia, M. (1999). Net surfers don't ride alone: Virtual communities as communities. In M. A. Smith & P. Kollock (Eds.), *Communities in cyberspace* (pp. 167–194). London: Routledge.

Whaley, B. B. (Ed.). (1999). *Explaining illness: Research, theory, and strategies*. Mahwah, NJ: Lawrence Erlbaum.

Willeford, J. A. (1971). The geriatric patient. In D. Rose (Ed.), *Audiological assessment* (pp. 281–319). Englewood Cliffs, NJ: Prentice-Hall.

Williams, A., & Nussbaum, J. F. (2001). *Intergenerational communication across the life span*. Mahwah, NJ: Lawrence Erlbaum.

Williams, A., Harwood, J., Ota, H., Giles, H., Pierson, H., Gallois, C., Ng, S., Lim, T., Ryan, E., Cai, D., Somera, L., & Maher, J. (1997). Young people's beliefs about intergenerational communication: An initial cross-cultural comparison. *Communication Research, 24*(4), 370–393.

Willis, S. L. (1996). Everyday problem solving. In J. E. Birren & K. W. Schaie (Eds.), *Handbook of the psychology of aging* (4th ed., pp. 287–307). San Diego, CA: Academic Press.

Wohlwill, J. F. (1970). The age variable in psychological research. *Psychological Review, 77*, 49–64.

Won, A., Lapane, K., Gambassi, G., et al. (1999). Correlates and management of nonmalignant pain in the nursing home. *Journal of the American Geriatric Society, 47*, 936–942.

Yedidia, M. J., Gillespie, C. C., Kachur, E., Schwartz, M. D., Ockene, J. O., Chepatis, A. E., Snyder, C. S., Lazare, A., & Lipkin, M. (2003). Effect of communications training on medical student performance. *JAMA, 290*, 1157–1165.

Index

DATE DUE

OCT 0 1 2012			